GROWING UP: ISSUES AFFECTING AMERICA'S YOUTH

ISSN 1939-084X

GROWING UP: ISSUES AFFECTING AMERICA'S YOUTH

Melissa J. Doak

INFORMATION PLUS® REFERENCE SERIES
Formerly Published by Information Plus, Wylie, Texas

GALE
CENGAGE Learning

Detroit • New York • San Francisco • New Haven, Conn • Waterville, Maine • London

Growing Up: Issues Affecting America's Youth

Melissa J. Doak
Paula Kepos, Series Editor

Project Editors: Kathleen J. Edgar, Elizabeth Manar

Rights Acquisition and Management: Aja Perales, Kelly Quin

Composition: Evi Abou-El-Seoud, Mary Beth Trimper

Manufacturing: Cynde Lentz

For product information and technology assistance, contact us at
Gale Customer Support, 1-800-877-4253.
For permission to use material from this text or product,
submit all requests online at **www.cengage.com/permissions.**
Further permissions questions can be e-mailed to
permissionrequest@cengage.com

Cover photograph: Image copyright 2009. Used under license from Jupiterimages.

Gale
27500 Drake Rd.
Farmington Hills, MI 48331-3535

ISBN-13: 978-0-7876-5103-9 (set)   ISBN-10: 0-7876-5103-6 (set)
ISBN-13: 978-1-4144-3377-6   ISBN-10: 1-4144-3377-8

ISSN 1939-084X

This title is also available as an e-book.
ISBN-13: 978-1-4144-5765-9 (set)
ISBN-10: 1-4144-5765-0 (set)
Contact your Gale sales representative for ordering information.

Printed in the United States of America
1 2 3 4 5 6 7 13 12 11 10 09

TABLE OF CONTENTS

PREFACE

Growing Up: Issues Affecting America's Youth is part of the *Information Plus Reference Series*. The purpose of each volume of the series is to present the latest facts on a topic of pressing concern in modern American life. These topics include the most controversial and studied social issues in the twenty-first century: abortion, capital punishment, care of senior citizens, crime, the environment, health care, immigration, minorities, national security, social welfare, women, and many more. Even though this series is written especially for high school and undergraduate students, it is an excellent resource for anyone in need of factual information on current affairs.

By presenting the facts, it is the intention of Gale, Cengage Learning to provide its readers with everything they need to reach an informed opinion on current issues. To that end, there is a particular emphasis in this series on the presentation of scientific studies, surveys, and statistics. These data are generally presented in the form of tables, charts, and other graphics placed within the text of each book. Every graphic is directly referred to and carefully explained in the text. The source of each graphic is presented within the graphic itself. The data used in these graphics are drawn from the most reputable and reliable sources, such as from the various branches of the U.S. government and from major independent polling organizations. Every effort was made to secure the most recent information available. Readers should bear in mind that many major studies take years to conduct and that additional years often pass before the data from these studies are made available to the public. Therefore, in many cases the most recent information available in 2009 is dated from 2006 or 2007. Older statistics are sometimes presented as well, if they are of particular interest and no more-recent information exists.

Even though statistics are a major focus of the *Information Plus Reference Series*, they are by no means its only content. Each book also presents the widely held positions and important ideas that shape how the book's subject is discussed in the United States. These positions are explained in detail and, where possible, in the words of their proponents. Some of the other material to be found in these books includes historical background, descriptions of major events related to the subject, relevant laws and court cases, and examples of how these issues play out in American life. Some books also feature primary documents or have pro and con debate sections that provide the words and opinions of prominent Americans on both sides of a controversial topic. All material is presented in an even-handed and unbiased manner; readers will never be encouraged to accept one view of an issue over another.

HOW TO USE THIS BOOK

Childhood and adolescence are perhaps the most critical period in any person's life. The education one receives during this time; the environment one is raised in; and the way one is treated by family, friends, and society, go a long way toward determining how the rest of an individual's life will turn out. This volume addresses various factors that affect youth, including family income, who cares for children, health and safety issues, educational matters, and teen sexuality and pregnancy. Also, crime, violence, and victimization are addressed, including gang violence, school violence, and crime prevention and punishment.

Growing Up: Issues Affecting America's Youth consists of ten chapters and three appendixes. Each chapter is devoted to a particular aspect of youth in the United States. For a summary of the information covered in each chapter, please see the synopses provided in the Table of Contents at the front of the book. Chapters generally begin with an overview of the basic facts and background information on the chapter's topic, then proceed to examine subtopics of particular interest. For example, Chapter 6, Getting an

Education, begins by discussing the No Child Left Behind Act. Topics such as accountability, proficiency testing, flexibility, parental options, the voucher controversy, and charter schools are covered. Next it briefly highlights the cost of public education. The chapter then delves into the different levels of education. The first level discussed is preprimary school and the Head Start program that operates within it. The second level is elementary and secondary school. Topics covered in this section are compulsory attendance, enrollment, private schools, dropout rates, and special populations, such as students with disabilities, homeless children, and homeschooled children. The third level is higher education, which examines college entrance examinations, projected enrollment rates, and the cost of a college education. The chapter concludes by discussing educational attainment and people's earnings based on their level of education. Readers can find their way through a chapter by looking for the section and subsection headings, which are clearly set off from the text. Or they can refer to the book's extensive Index, if they already know what they are looking for.

Statistical Information

The tables and figures featured throughout *Growing Up: Issues Affecting America's Youth* will be of particular use to readers in learning about this topic. These tables and figures represent an extensive collection of the most recent and valuable statistics on growing up in the United States, as well as related issues—for example, graphics cover the number of children without health insurance, the percentage of students who consume alcohol, the rate of teens having abortions, the number of youth in gangs, and the presence of violence at school. Gale, Cengage Learning believes that making this information available to readers is the most important way to fulfill the goal of this book: to help readers understand the issues and controversies surrounding youth in the United States and reach their own conclusions.

Each table or figure has a unique identifier appearing above it for ease of identification and reference. Titles for the tables and figures explain their purpose. At the end of each table or figure, the original source of the data is provided.

To help readers understand these often complicated statistics, all tables and figures are explained in the text. References in the text direct readers to the relevant statistics. Furthermore, the contents of all tables and figures are fully indexed. Please see the opening section of the Index at the back of this volume for a description of how to find tables and figures within it.

Appendixes

Besides the main body text and images, *Growing Up: Issues Affecting America's Youth* has three appendixes. The first is the Important Names and Addresses directory. Here, readers will find contact information for a number of organizations that study children, adolescents, and families. The second appendix is the Resources section, which can also assist readers in conducting their own research. In this section, the author and editors of *Growing Up: Issues Affecting America's Youth* describe some of the sources that were most useful during the compilation of this book. The final appendix is the Index.

ADVISORY BOARD CONTRIBUTIONS

The staff of Information Plus would like to extend its heartfelt appreciation to the Information Plus Advisory Board. This dedicated group of media professionals provides feedback on the series on an ongoing basis. Their comments allow the editorial staff who work on the project to make the series better and more user-friendly. The staff's top priority is to produce the highest-quality and most useful books possible, and the Advisory Board's contributions to this process are invaluable.

The members of the Information Plus Advisory Board are:

- Kathleen R. Bonn, Librarian, Newbury Park High School, Newbury Park, California
- Madelyn Garner, Librarian, San Jacinto College, North Campus, Houston, Texas
- Anne Oxenrider, Media Specialist, Dundee High School, Dundee, Michigan
- Charles R. Rodgers, Director of Libraries, Pasco-Hernando Community College, Dade City, Florida
- James N. Zitzelsberger, Library Media Department Chairman, Oshkosh West High School, Oshkosh, Wisconsin

COMMENTS AND SUGGESTIONS

The editors of the *Information Plus Reference Series* welcome your feedback on *Growing Up: Issues Affecting America's Youth*. Please direct all correspondence to:

Editors
Information Plus Reference Series
27500 Drake Rd.
Farmington Hills, MI 48331-3535

CHAPTER 1
CHILDREN AND FAMILIES IN THE UNITED STATES

DEFINING CHILDHOOD AND ADULTHOOD

Exactly when childhood ends and adulthood begins differs among cultures and over periods of time within cultures. People in some societies believe adulthood begins with the onset of puberty, arguing that people who are old enough to have children are also old enough to assume adult responsibilities. This stage of life is often solemnized with special celebrations. In the Jewish tradition, for example, the bar mitzvah ceremony for 13-year-old boys and the bat mitzvah ceremony for 13-year-old girls commemorates the attainment of adult responsibility for observing Jewish law.

Modern American society identifies an interim period of life between childhood and adulthood known as adolescence, during which teens reach a series of milestones as they accept increasing amounts of adult responsibility. At age 16 most Americans can be licensed to drive. At 18 most young people leave the public education system and are eligible to vote. At that time they can join the military without parental permission and are tried as adults for all crimes in all states (although some states try younger people as adults, and in serious offenses such as murder, rape, or armed robbery, juveniles are sometimes tried as adults). There are contradictions in the rights and privileges conferred, however. In many states, teens under the age of 18 can marry but cannot see X-rated movies.

In general, American society recognizes 21 as the age of full adulthood. At 21, young men and women are considered legally independent of their parents and are completely responsible for their own decisions. At that time, they are allowed to buy alcoholic beverages.

According to the Federal Interagency Forum on Child and Family Statistics, in *America's Children in Brief: Key National Indicators of Well-Being, 2008* (2008, http://www.childstats.gov/pdf/ac2008/ac_08.pdf), in 2007, 73.9 million children younger than the age of 18 lived in the United States, 1.5 million more than in 2000. This number is expected to increase to 80 million by 2020. However, because the coun-

try's entire population will increase, the percentage of children in the population is projected to remain fairly steady, decreasing slightly from 25% in 2007 to 24% by 2020.

BIRTH AND FERTILITY RATES

Fertility is measured in a number of ways. One such measure, called the crude birthrate, is the number of live births per 1,000 women in the population, regardless of their age, in any given year. In 2005 the crude birthrate was 14 live births per 1,000 women. (See Table 1.1.) The crude birthrate for Hispanic women (of any race) was considerably higher (23.1) than for Asian or Pacific Islander women (16.5), non-Hispanic African-American women (15.7), Native American or Alaskan Native women (14.2), and non-Hispanic white women (11.5).

Another way to measure the number of births is the fertility rate, the number of live births per 1,000 women in the population between the ages of 15 and 44 years in any given year. These are the years generally considered to be a woman's reproductive age range. During the first 10 years of the baby boom that immediately followed World War II (1939–1945), fertility rates were well over 100 births per 1,000 women. (See Table 1.1.) In contrast, the fertility rate for American women in 2005 was 66.7 births per 1,000 women, just over half the 1960 fertility rate of 118 births per 1,000 women. However, some groups in American society have much higher fertility rates than the average. In 2005 the fertility rate for Hispanic women was 99.4 births per 1,000 women; non-Hispanic African-American women, 67.2; Asian or Pacific Islander women, 66.6; Native American or Alaskan Native mothers, 59.9; and non-Hispanic white women, 58.3.

Birth Trends

According to Frederick W. Hollmann, Tammany J. Mulder, and Jeffrey E. Kallan of the U.S. Census Bureau, in *Methodology and Assumptions for the Population Projections of the United States: 1999 to 2100* (January

TABLE 1.1

Crude birth rates, fertility rates, and birth rates by age of mother, according to race and Hispanic origin, selected years 1950–2005

[Data are based on birth certificates]

Race, Hispanic origin, and year	Crude birth rate[a]	Fertility rate[b]	10–14 years	15–19 years Total	15–17 years	18–19 years	20–24 years	25–29 years	30–34 years	35–39 years	40–44 years	45–54 years[c]
All races					Live births per 1,000 women							
1950	24.1	106.2	1.0	81.6	40.7	132.7	196.6	166.1	103.7	52.9	15.1	1.2
1960	23.7	118.0	0.8	89.1	43.9	166.7	258.1	197.4	112.7	56.2	15.5	0.9
1970	18.4	87.9	1.2	68.3	38.8	114.7	167.8	145.1	73.3	31.7	8.1	0.5
1980	15.9	68.4	1.1	53.0	32.5	82.1	115.1	112.9	61.9	19.8	3.9	0.2
1985	15.8	66.3	1.2	51.0	31.0	79.6	108.3	111.0	69.1	24.0	4.0	0.2
1990	16.7	70.9	1.4	59.9	37.5	88.6	116.5	120.2	80.8	31.7	5.5	0.2
1995	14.6	64.6	1.3	56.0	35.5	87.7	107.5	108.8	81.1	34.0	6.6	0.3
2000	14.4	65.9	0.9	47.7	26.9	78.1	109.7	113.5	91.2	39.7	8.0	0.5
2003	14.1	66.1	0.6	41.6	22.4	70.7	102.6	115.6	95.1	43.8	8.7	0.5
2004	14.0	66.3	0.7	41.1	22.1	70.0	101.7	115.5	95.3	45.4	8.9	0.5
2005	14.0	66.7	0.7	40.5	21.4	69.9	102.2	115.5	95.8	46.3	9.1	0.6
Race of child:[d] White												
1950	23.0	102.3	0.4	70.0	31.3	120.5	190.4	165.1	102.6	51.4	14.5	1.0
1960	22.7	113.2	0.4	79.4	35.5	154.6	252.8	194.9	109.6	54.0	14.7	0.8
1970	17.4	84.1	0.5	57.4	29.2	101.5	163.4	145.9	71.9	30.0	7.5	0.4
1980	14.9	64.7	0.6	44.7	25.2	72.1	109.5	112.4	60.4	18.5	3.4	0.2
Race of mother:[e] White												
1980	15.1	65.6	0.6	45.4	25.5	73.2	111.1	113.8	61.2	18.8	3.5	0.2
1985	15.0	64.1	0.6	43.3	24.4	70.4	104.1	112.3	69.9	23.3	3.7	0.2
1990	15.8	68.3	0.7	50.8	29.5	78.0	109.8	120.7	81.7	31.5	5.2	0.2
1995	14.1	63.6	0.8	49.5	29.6	80.2	104.7	111.7	83.3	34.2	6.4	0.3
2000	13.9	65.3	0.6	43.2	23.3	72.3	106.6	116.7	94.6	40.2	7.9	0.4
2003	13.6	66.1	0.5	38.3	19.8	66.2	100.6	119.5	99.3	44.8	8.7	0.5
2004	13.5	66.1	0.5	37.7	19.5	65.0	99.2	118.6	99.1	46.4	8.9	0.5
2005	13.4	66.3	0.5	37.0	18.9	64.7	99.2	118.3	99.3	47.3	9.0	0.6
Race of child:[d] Black or African American												
1960	31.9	153.5	4.3	156.1	—	—	295.4	218.6	137.1	73.9	21.9	1.1
1970	25.3	115.4	5.2	140.7	101.4	204.9	202.7	136.3	79.6	41.9	12.5	1.0
1980	22.1	88.1	4.3	100.0	73.6	138.8	146.3	109.1	62.9	24.5	5.8	0.3
Race of mother:[e] Black or African American												
1980	21.3	84.9	4.3	97.8	72.5	135.1	140.0	103.9	59.9	23.5	5.6	0.3
1985	20.4	78.8	4.5	95.4	69.3	132.4	135.0	100.2	57.9	23.9	4.6	0.3
1990	22.4	86.8	4.9	112.8	82.3	152.9	160.2	115.5	68.7	28.1	5.5	0.3
1995	17.8	71.0	4.1	94.4	68.5	135.0	133.7	95.6	63.0	28.4	6.0	0.3
2000	17.0	70.0	2.3	77.4	49.0	118.8	141.3	100.3	65.4	31.5	7.2	0.4
2003	15.7	66.3	1.6	63.8	38.2	103.7	126.1	100.4	66.5	33.2	7.7	0.5
2004	16.0	67.6	1.6	63.3	37.2	104.4	127.7	103.6	67.9	34.0	7.9	0.5
2005	16.2	69.0	1.7	62.0	35.5	104.9	129.9	105.9	70.3	35.3	8.5	0.5
American Indian or Alaska Native mothers[e]												
1980	20.7	82.7	1.9	82.2	51.5	129.5	143.7	106.6	61.8	28.1	8.2	*
1985	19.8	78.6	1.7	79.2	47.7	124.1	139.1	109.6	62.6	27.4	6.0	*
1990	18.9	76.2	1.6	81.1	48.5	129.3	148.7	110.3	61.5	27.5	5.9	*
1995	15.3	63.0	1.6	72.9	44.6	122.2	123.1	91.6	56.5	24.3	5.5	*
2000	14.0	58.7	1.1	58.3	34.1	97.1	117.2	91.8	55.5	24.6	5.7	0.3
2003	13.8	58.4	1.0	53.1	30.6	87.3	110.0	93.5	57.4	25.4	5.5	0.4
2004	14.0	58.9	0.9	52.5	30.0	87.0	109.7	92.8	58.0	26.8	6.0	0.2
2005	14.2	59.9	0.9	52.7	30.5	87.6	109.2	93.8	60.1	27.0	6.0	0.3

13, 2000, http://www.census.gov/population/www/documentation/twps0038.pdf), fertility rates among racial and ethnic groups are expected to differ markedly in the twenty-first century. Total fertility rate refers to the average number of children a woman will give birth to in her lifetime. The total fertility rate of white women is expected to rise slightly through the century but not to reach the population replacement rate (the fertility rate needed to keep the population stable, which is 2,100 births per 1,000 women). The total fertility rate for non-Hispanic African-American women will remain steady at about the population replacement rate. Native American and Asian or Pacific Islander total fertility rates are expected to decrease slightly but remain well above the population replacement rate through the twenty-first century. The Hispanic total fertility rate is also expected to decrease from a high of 2,920.5 births per 1,000 women over their lifetime in 1999 to 2,333.8 births per 1,000 women in 2100—a rate still well above the

TABLE 1.1

Crude birth rates, fertility rates, and birth rates by age of mother, according to race and Hispanic origin, selected years 1950–2005 [CONTINUED]

[Data are based on birth certificates]

Race, Hispanic origin, and year	Crude birth rate[a]	Fertility rate[b]	10–14 years	Age of mother 15–19 years Total	15–17 years	18–19 years	20–24 years	25–29 years	30–34 years	35–39 years	40–44 years	45–54 years[c]
Asian or Pacific Islander mothers[e]				Live births per 1,000 women								
1980	19.9	73.2	0.3	26.2	12.0	46.2	93.3	127.4	96.0	38.3	8.5	0.7
1985	18.7	68.4	0.4	23.8	12.5	40.8	83.6	123.0	93.6	42.7	8.7	1.2
1990	19.0	69.6	0.7	26.4	16.0	40.2	79.2	126.3	106.5	49.6	10.7	1.1
1995	16.7	62.6	0.7	25.5	15.6	40.1	64.2	103.7	102.3	50.1	11.8	0.8
2000	17.1	65.8	0.3	20.5	11.6	32.6	60.3	108.4	116.5	59.0	12.6	0.8
2003	16.8	66.3	0.2	17.4	8.8	29.8	59.6	108.5	114.6	59.9	13.5	0.9
2004	16.8	67.1	0.2	17.3	8.9	29.6	59.8	108.6	116.9	62.1	13.6	1.0
2005	16.5	66.6	0.2	17.0	8.2	30.1	61.1	107.9	115.0	61.8	13.8	1.0
Hispanic or Latina mothers[e, f]												
1980	23.5	95.4	1.7	82.2	52.1	126.9	156.4	132.1	83.2	39.9	10.6	0.7
1990	26.7	107.7	2.4	100.3	65.9	147.7	181.0	153.0	98.3	45.3	10.9	0.7
1995	24.1	98.8	2.6	99.3	68.3	145.4	171.9	140.4	90.5	43.7	10.7	0.6
2000	23.1	95.9	1.7	87.3	55.5	132.6	161.3	139.9	97.1	46.6	11.5	0.6
2003	22.9	96.9	1.3	82.3	49.7	132.0	163.4	144.4	102.0	50.8	12.2	0.7
2004	22.9	97.8	1.3	82.6	49.7	133.5	165.3	145.6	104.1	52.9	12.4	0.7
2005	23.1	99.4	1.3	81.7	48.5	134.6	170.0	149.2	106.8	54.2	13.0	0.8
White, not Hispanic or Latina mothers[e, f]												
1980	14.2	62.4	0.4	41.2	22.4	67.7	105.5	110.6	59.9	17.7	3.0	0.1
1990	14.4	62.8	0.5	42.5	23.2	66.6	97.5	115.3	79.4	30.0	4.7	0.2
1995	12.5	57.5	0.4	39.3	22.0	66.2	90.2	105.1	81.5	32.8	5.9	0.3
2000	12.2	58.5	0.3	32.6	15.8	57.5	91.2	109.4	93.2	38.8	7.3	0.4
2003	11.8	58.5	0.2	27.4	12.4	50.0	83.5	110.8	97.6	43.2	8.1	0.5
2004	11.6	58.4	0.2	26.7	12.0	48.7	81.9	110.0	97.1	44.8	8.2	0.5
2005	11.5	58.3	0.2	25.9	11.5	48.0	81.4	109.1	96.9	45.6	8.3	0.5
Black or African American, not Hispanic or Latina mothers[e, f]												
1980	22.9	90.7	4.6	105.1	77.2	146.5	152.2	111.7	65.2	25.8	5.8	0.3
1990	23.0	89.0	5.0	116.2	84.9	157.5	165.1	118.4	70.2	28.7	5.6	0.3
1995	18.2	72.8	4.2	97.2	70.4	139.2	137.8	98.5	64.4	28.8	6.1	0.3
2000	17.3	71.4	2.4	79.2	50.1	121.9	145.4	102.8	66.5	31.8	7.2	0.4
2003	15.9	67.1	1.6	64.7	38.7	105.3	128.1	102.1	67.4	33.4	7.7	0.5
2004	15.8	67.0	1.6	63.1	37.1	103.9	126.9	103.0	67.4	33.7	7.8	0.5
2005	15.7	67.2	1.7	60.9	34.9	103.0	126.8	103.0	68.4	34.3	8.2	0.5

—Data not available.
*Rates based on fewer than 20 births are considered unreliable and are not shown.
[a]Live births per 1,000 population.
[b]Total number of live births regardless of age of mother per 1,000 women 15–44 years of age.
[c]Prior to 1997, data are for live births to mothers 45–49 years of age per 1,000 women 45–49 years of age. Starting with 1997 data, rates are for live births to mothers 45–54 years of age per 1,000 women 45–49 years of age.
[d]Live births are tabulated by race of child.
[e]Live births are tabulated by race and/or Hispanic origin of mother.
[f]Prior to 1993, data from states lacking an Hispanic-origin item on the birth certificate were excluded. Rates in 1985 were not calculated because estimates for the Hispanic and non-Hispanic populations were not available.
Notes: Data are based on births adjusted for underregistration for 1950 and on registered births for all other years. Starting with 1970 data, births to persons who were not residents of the 50 states and the District of Columbia are excluded. Starting with *Health, United States, 2003*, rates for 1991–1999 were revised using intercensal population estimates based on the 2000 census. Rates for 2000 were computed using the 2000 census counts and starting in 2001 rates were computed using 2000-based postcensal estimates. The race groups, white, black, American Indian or Alaska Native, and Asian or Pacific Islander, include persons of Hispanic and non-Hispanic origin. Persons of Hispanic origin may be of any race. Starting with 2003 data, some states reported multiple-race data. The multiple-race data for these states were bridged to the single-race categories of the 1977 Office of Management and Budget standards for comparability withother states. Interpretation of trend data should take into consideration expansion of reporting areas and immigration. Data for additional years are available.

SOURCE: "Table 4. Crude Birth Rates, Fertility Rates, and Birth Rates by Age, Race and Hispanic Origin of Mother: United States, Selected Years 1950–2005," in *Health, United States, 2007. With Chartbook on Trends in the Health of Americans*, Centers for Disease Control and Prevention, National Center for Health Statistics, 2007, http://www.cdc.gov/nchs/data/hus/hus07.pdf (accessed September 15, 2008)

population replacement rate and well above the rates of other ethnic and racial groups. As a result, the proportion of American children who are non-Hispanic white is expected to decrease from 57% in 2007 to 52.9% in 2020, and the proportion of children who are Hispanic is expected to increase from 20.9% in 2007 to 23.6% in 2020, whereas other race and ethnic groups will proportionally stay about the same. (See Table 1.2.)

TABLE 1.2

Children under age 18 by race and Hispanic origin, 1980–2007 and projected 2008–20

Race and Hispanic origin[a]	1980	1981	1982	1983	1984	1985	1986	1987	1988	1989	1990	1991	1992	1993	1994	1995	1996	1997	1998	1999
White, non-Hispanic[b]	74	73	73	72	72	72	71	70	70	69	69	68	68	67	66	66	65	64	64	63
Black, non-Hispanic[b]	15	15	15	15	15	15	15	15	15	15	15	15	15	15	15	15	15	15	15	15
American Indian or Alaskan Native[b]	1	1	1	1	1	1	1	1	1	1	1	1	1	1	1	1	1	1	1	1
Asian or Pacific Islander[b]	2	2	2	2	2	3	3	3	3	3	3	3	3	3	3	4	4	4	4	4
Hispanic[d]	9	9	10	10	10	10	11	11	12	12	12	13	13	13	14	14	15	15	16	17

Race and Hispanic origin[a]	2000	2001	2002	2003	2004	2005	2006	2007	2008	2009	2010	2011	2012	2013	2014	2015	2016	2017	2018	2019	2020
White	76.8	76.7	76.6	76.6	76.5	76.4	76.2	76.2	75.8	75.6	75.5	75.4	75.2	75.1	74.9	74.8	74.6	74.5	74.4	74.2	74.1
White, non-Hispanic[b]	61.2	60.6	60.1	59.5	58.9	58.2	57.6	57.0	57.0	56.6	56.2	55.8	55.4	55.1	54.7	54.4	54.1	53.8	53.5	53.2	52.9
Black	15.6	15.6	15.6	15.5	15.5	15.5	15.4	15.4	15.4	15.4	15.3	15.3	15.3	15.3	15.3	15.3	15.4	15.4	15.4	15.4	15.4
Asian	3.6	3.7	3.7	3.8	3.9	4.0	4.0	4.1	4.1	4.2	4.3	4.3	4.4	4.4	4.5	4.5	4.6	4.6	4.7	4.7	4.7
All other races[c]	4.0	4.0	4.1	4.1	4.2	4.2	4.3	4.3	4.7	4.8	4.9	5.0	5.1	5.2	5.3	5.4	5.4	5.5	5.6	5.7	5.7
Hispanic[d]	17.2	17.6	18.1	18.6	19.2	19.7	20.3	20.9	20.7	21.0	21.3	21.6	21.9	22.1	22.3	22.6	22.8	23.0	23.2	23.4	23.6

[a]For race and Hispanic-origin data in this table: In 1980 and 1990, following the 1977 OMB standards for collecting and presenting data on race, the decennial census asked respondents to choose one race from the following: White, Black, American Indian or Alaskan Native, or Asian or Pacific Islander. The Census Bureau also offered an "other" category. Beginning in 2000, following the 1997 OMB standards for collecting and presenting data on race, the decennial census asked respondents to choose one or more races from the following: white, black, Asian, American Indian or Alaska Native, and Native Hawaiian or other Pacific Islander. In addition, "some other race" category was included with OMB approval. Those who chose more than one race were classified as "two or more races." Except for the "all other races" category, all race groups discussed in this table from 2000 onward refer to people who indicated *only one* racial identity within the racial categories presented. (Those who were "two or more races" were included in the "all other races" category, along with American Indians or Alaska Natives and Native Hawaiians or other Pacific Islanders.) People who responded to the question on race by indicating *only one* race are referred to as the race-alone population. The use of the race-alone population in this table does not imply that it is the preferred method of presenting or analyzing data. Data from 2000 onward are not directly comparable with data from earlier years. Data on race and Hispanic origin are collected seperately; Hispanics may be any race.

[b]Excludes persons in this race group who are of Hispanic origin.

[c]Includes American Indian, Eskimo and Aleut, Native Hawaiian and other Pacific Islander, and all multiple race (Two-or-more races).

[d]Persons of Hispanic origin may be of any race.

SOURCE: "POP3. Racial and Ethnic Composition: Percentage of U.S. Children Ages 0–17 by Race and Hispanic Origin, Selected Years 1980–2007 and Projected 2008–2020," in *America's Children in Brief: Key National Indicators of Well-Being, 2008*, Federal Interagency Forum on Child and Family Statistics, July 2008, http://www.childstats.gov/americaschildren/tables.asp (accessed September 15, 2008)

TABLE 1.3

Projected population of the United States, by race and Hispanic origin, 2010–50

[Resident population as of July 1. Numbers in thousands.]

Sex, race, and Hispanic origin*	2010	2015	2020	2025	2030	2035	2040	2045	2050
Population total	**310,233**	**325,540**	**341,387**	**357,452**	**373,504**	**389,531**	**405,655**	**422,059**	**439,010**
White alone, not Hispanic	200,853	203,208	205,255	206,662	207,217	206,958	206,065	204,772	203,347
Black alone	37,985	39,916	41,847	43,703	45,461	47,144	48,780	50,380	51,949
AIAN alone	2,392	2,548	2,697	2,830	2,946	3,053	3,157	3,260	3,358
Asian alone	14,083	16,141	18,308	20,591	22,991	25,489	28,064	30,704	33,418
NHPI alone	452	497	541	585	628	672	716	760	803
Two or more races	4,743	5,519	6,374	7,309	8,329	9,442	10,650	11,950	13,342
Hispanic	49,726	57,711	66,365	75,772	85,931	96,774	108,223	120,231	132,792

*Hispanics may be of any race.
Abbreviations: Black = Black or African American; AIAN = American Indian and Alaska Native; NHPI = Native Hawaiian and Other Pacific Islander
Note: The original race data from Census 2000 are modified to eliminate the "some other race" category.

SOURCE: Adapted from "Table 4. Projections of the Population by Sex, Race, and Hispanic Origin for the United States: 2010 to 2050," in *U.S. Population Projections*, U.S. Census Bureau, Population Division, August 14, 2008, http://www.census.gov/population/www/projections/summarytables.html (accessed September 15, 2008)

After 2020 Hispanic births are expected to add more people each year to the U.S. population than all other non-white racial and ethnic groups combined. The non-Hispanic white population is projected to rise from 200.9 million in 2010 to 203.1 million in 2050, an increase of 2.2 million, whereas the Hispanic population will increase by 83.1 million (due to high birthrates and continued immigration), from 49.7 million to 132.8 million. (See Table 1.3.) In 2010 non-Hispanic whites will make up 64.7% (200.9 million out of 310.2 million) of the population, whereas Hispanics will make up 16% (49.7 million out of 310.2 million). By contrast, in 2050 non-Hispanic whites are expected to make up 46.3% (203.3 million out of 439 million) of the population, whereas Hispanics will make up 30.2% (132.8 million out of 439 million).

As a result, the youth segment of the U.S. population is becoming more racially diverse. Between 1980 and 2007 the non-Hispanic white share of the under-18 population dropped from 74% to 57%. (See Table 1.2.) During this same period the non-Hispanic African-American share of this population remained stable, increasing only slightly from 15% to 15.4%. In contrast, the Asian or Pacific Islander share of the under-18 population increased from 2% in 1980 to 4.1% in 2007. The Hispanic share of the under-18 population showed the highest increase, from 9% in 1980 to 20.9% in 2007. In other words, in 2007 more than one out of every five children in the United States was of Hispanic origin.

Evidence also suggests that racial and ethnic lines became less rigid in the United States in the last two decades of the twentieth century, as people from different ethnic and racial backgrounds parented children together. In *Age: 2000* (October 2001, http://www.census.gov/prod/2001pubs/c2kbr01-12 .pdf), Julie Meyer of the Census Bureau notes that people who reported in the 2000 census that they came from more than one ethnic or racial background had a significantly younger

median age than all single-race groups, at 22.7 years. Nearly four out of ten (41.9%) people with a mixed ethnic or racial background were under the age of 18.

The number of children under the age of 18 with a biracial background continued to increase between 2000 and 2007, from 1.8 million in 2000 to 2.2 million in 2007. (See Table 1.4.) The median age of people of two or more races was young, at 20.6 in 2007. These findings may indicate that distinctions between racial and ethnic groups in the United States will continue to blur in the twenty-first century.

THE CHANGING FAMILY
Family and Household Size

The composition of households in American society changed markedly in the twentieth century. Frank Hobbs and Nicole Stoops of the Census Bureau indicate in *Demographic Trends in the 20th Century* (November 2002, http://www.census.gov/prod/2002pubs/censr-4.pdf) that in 1950 families accounted for 89.4% of all households; by 2000 this number had decreased to 68.1%. The proportion of married-couple households that included at least one child under the age of 18 had also decreased. In *America's Children in Brief*, the Federal Interagency Forum on Child and Family Statistics states that in 1980, 77% of all family groups with children were married-couple households; this percentage had dropped to 67.8% by 2007.

The American family shrank in size during the twentieth century. In 1900 most households consisted of five or more people. According to the Census Bureau, in *Families and Living Arrangements* (July 2008, http://www.census.gov/ population/www/socdemo/hh-fam.html), by 1950 two-person families became the most common family type and remained so to the end of the century. The proportion of one- and two-person households increased from 1960 to 2007, whereas the

TABLE 1.4

Two or more races population by sex and age, 2000–07

	Population estimates								April 1, 2000	
Sex and age	July 1, 2007	July 1, 2006	July 1, 2005	July 1, 2004	July 1, 2003	July 1, 2002	July 1, 2001	July 1, 2000	Estimates base	Census
Both sexes	**4,856,136**	**4,711,932**	**4,571,079**	**4,435,854**	**4,302,374**	**4,177,961**	**4,053,393**	**3,928,008**	**3,897,722**	**3,897,680**
Under 18 years	2,193,316	2,137,582	2,081,963	2,028,097	1,975,006	1,924,786	1,875,189	1,825,314	1,813,533	1,813,503
Under 5 years	690,757	668,430	649,218	641,200	635,577	629,893	622,839	614,660	613,159	613,147
5 to 13 years	1,090,988	1,070,047	1,048,638	1,018,796	988,101	956,072	924,783	892,874	885,026	885,012
14 to 17 years	411,571	399,105	384,107	368,101	351,328	338,821	327,567	317,780	315,348	315,344
18 to 64 years	2,414,950	2,337,096	2,261,537	2,189,397	2,117,019	2,050,991	1,983,215	1,914,862	1,898,095	1,898,085
18 to 24 years	595,702	577,053	559,768	541,865	520,448	498,852	475,557	450,114	443,508	443,537
25 to 44 years	1,111,446	1,077,788	1,045,922	1,019,275	994,964	976,950	959,454	942,341	938,067	938,039
45 to 64 years	707,802	682,255	655,847	628,257	601,607	575,189	548,204	522,407	516,520	516,509
65 years and over	247,870	237,254	227,579	218,360	210,349	202,184	194,989	187,832	186,094	186,092
16 years and over	2,864,950	2,768,042	2,671,699	2,582,779	2,496,731	2,417,625	2,337,155	2,256,835	2,237,493	2,237,479
18 years and over	2,662,820	2,574,350	2,489,116	2,407,757	2,327,368	2,253,175	2,178,204	2,102,694	2,084,189	2,084,177
15 to 44 years	2,013,099	1,950,273	1,888,203	1,829,457	1,773,591	1,725,973	1,677,039	1,627,344	1,614,505	1,614,503
Median age (years)	20.6	20.5	20.4	20.3	20.2	20.1	20.0	19.9	19.8	19.8

Note: The April 1, 2000 population estimates base reflects changes to the Census 2000 population from the Count Question Resolution program. Median age is calculated based on single year of age.

SOURCE: "Table 4. Annual Estimates of the Two or More Races Population by Sex and Age for the United States: April 1, 2000 to July 1, 2007," U.S. Census Bureau, Population Division, May 1, 2008, http://www.census.gov/popest/national/asrh/NC-EST2007-asrh.html (accessed September 21, 2008)

TABLE 1.5

Households by size, selected years, 1960–2007

[Numbers in thousands]

Year	All households	One person	Two persons	Three persons	Four persons	Five persons	Six persons	Seven or more persons	Persons per household
2007	116,011	31,132	38,580	18,808	16,172	7,202	2,702	1,415	2.56
2000	104,705	26,724	34,666	17,172	15,309	6,981	2,445	1,428	2.62
1990	93,347	22,999	30,114	16,128	14,456	6,213	2,143	1,295	2.63
1980	80,776	18,296	25,327	14,130	12,666	6,059	2,519	1,778	2.76
1970	63,401	10,851	18,333	10,949	9,991	6,548	3,534	3,195	3.14
1960	52,799	6,917	14,678	9,979	9,293	6,072	3,010	2,851	3.33

SOURCE: Adapted from "HH-4. Households by Size: 1960 to Present," in *Families and Living Arrangements*, U.S. Census Bureau, July 2008, http://www.census.gov/population/www/socdemo/hh-fam.html#wp (accessed September 15, 2008)

proportion of households with three or more people steadily decreased. In addition, average household size declined from 3.14 people in 1970 to 2.56 in 2007. (See Table 1.5.) This is true partly because the population is getting older, which means that a smaller proportion of households consists of parents and their children.

Fewer "Traditional" Families

One of the more significant social changes to occur in the last decades of the twentieth century was a shift away from the traditional family structure—a married couple with their own child or children living in the home. The Census Bureau divides households into two major categories: family households (defined as groups of two or more people living together related by birth, marriage, or adoption) and nonfamily households (consisting of a person living alone or an individual living with others to whom he or she is not related). As a percentage of all households, family households declined during the period 1970 to 2003. According to

the Census Bureau, in 1970, 51.5 million (81%) out of 63.4 million total households were family households. (See Table 1.6.) By 2007 only 78.4 million (68%) out of 116 million households were family households.

The rise in nonfamily households is the result of many factors, some of the most prominent being:

- People are postponing marriage until later in life and are thus living alone or with nonrelatives for a longer period

- A rising divorce rate translates into more people living alone or with nonrelatives

- A rise in the number of people who cohabit before or instead of marriage results in higher numbers of nonfamily households

- The oldest members of the U.S. population are living longer and often live in nonfamily households as widows/widowers or in institutional settings

TABLE 1.6

Households by type, selected years 1940–2007

[Numbers in thousands]

Year	Total households	Family households					Nonfamily households		
				Other family				
		Total	Married couples	Male householder	Female householder	Total	Male householder	Female householder
2007	116,011	78,425	58,945	5,063	14,416	37,587	17,338	20,249
2000	104,705	72,025	55,311	4,028	12,687	32,680	14,641	18,039
1990	93,347	66,090	52,317	2,884	10,890	27,257	11,606	15,651
1980	80,776	59,550	49,112	1,733	8,705	21,226	8,807	12,419
1970	63,401	51,456	44,728	1,228	5,500	11,945	4,063	7,882
1960	52,799	44,905	39,254	1,228	4,422	7,895	2,716	5,179
1950	43,554	38,838	34,075	1,169	3,594	4,716	1,668	3,048
1940	34,949	31,491	26,571	1,510	3,410	3,458	1,599	1,859

SOURCE: Adapted from "HH-1. Households, by Type: 1940 to Present," in *Families and Living Arrangements*, U.S. Census Bureau, July 2008, http://www.census.gov/population/www/socdemo/hh-fam.html#wp (accessed September 15, 2008)

Even though family households were a smaller proportion of all households in 2007 than in 1950, they were still the majority of households. The Census Bureau breaks family households into three categories: married couples with their own children, married couples without children, and other family households. This last category includes single-parent households and households made up of relatives (such as siblings) who live together or grandparents who live with grandchildren without members of the middle generation being present. Of the three categories, the "other family household" grew the most between 1970 and 2007, increasing from 11.9 million (19%) out of 63.4 million of all households in 1970 to 37.6 million (32%) out of 116 million in 2007. (See Table 1.6.) Married couples headed 44.7 million (71%) out of 63.4 million of households in 1970 but only 58.9 million (51%) out of 116 million in 2007.

One- and Two-Parent Families

Among all families with children, married two-parent families accounted for 25.9 million (87%) out of 29.6 million families in 1970 and 26.8 million (67%) out of 39.9 million families in 2007. (See Table 1.7.) Overall, most households with children are still headed by married couples. However, the decline in the percentage of children being raised in two-parent households has been the subject of much study and attention.

In 2007, 11.7 million (29%) families with children out of a total of 39.9 million were maintained by a single parent, compared to 3.8 million (13%) out of 29.6 million in 1970. (See Table 1.7.) In 2007 mothers maintained over 9.9 million families with children, whereas fathers maintained only 1.7 million; mothers headed families alone nearly six times as often as fathers did. In 1970 this figure was close to nine times as often; in 1970 there were very few single-father families. Between 2000 and 2007 the number of families headed by a single father actually shrank, whereas the number headed by a single mother continued to rise.

The proportion of families headed by a single parent increased from 1980 to 2007 in all racial and ethnic groups. (See Table 1.7.) African-American children were the least likely of all racial and ethnic groups to live in two-parent households throughout this period.

The rise in single-parent families is the result of several factors, all pointing to a change in American lifestyles and values. Among these changes is an escalating divorce rate. The Census Bureau explains in the 2007 American Community Survey (ACS; http://factfinder.census.gov/) that in 2007, 25.3 million individuals in the United States were divorced and had not remarried. This number was nearly four times the 6.5 million divorced individuals in 1975, as reported in the Census Bureau's *Current Population Reports, 1975* (June 1975, http://www.census.gov/population/socdemo/marr-div/p20-297/p20-297.pdf).

The rise in the number of single-parent family households can also be attributed to the dramatic rise in the number of births to unmarried women. In "Births: Final Data for 2005" (*National Vital Statistics Reports*, vol. 56, no. 6, December 5, 2007), Joyce A. Martin et al. of the Centers for Disease Control and Prevention report that 36.9% of births in 2005 were to unmarried women. (See Table 1.8.) Nonmarital birthrates differed significantly by race and ethnicity. Hispanic women had the highest birthrate among unmarried mothers in 2005, at 100.3 births per 1,000 women of childbearing age. The birthrate for unmarried African-American women that year was 67.8 births per 1,000 women, and for unmarried, non-Hispanic white women it was 30.1 births per 1,000 women. The rate of births to unmarried women was highest among women in their 20s; the birthrate for unmarried women aged 20 to 24 years was 74.9 births per 1,000 women, and the rate for women aged 25 to 29 was 71.1 births per 1,000 women. Unmarried teen birthrates had fallen steadily since the 1990s and hit the lowest ever recorded rate for 15- to 19-year-olds in 2005.

TABLE 1.7

All parent/child situations, by type, race, and Hispanic origin of householder or reference person, selected years 1970–2007

[Numbers in thousands. Family groups with children[a] include all parent-child situations (two-parent and one-parent): those that maintain their own household (family households with children); those that live in the home of a relative (related subfamilies); and those that live in the home of a nonrelative (unrelated subfamilies). Data based on the Current Population Survey (CPS).]

| | | All family groups | | | | | |
| | | Two-parent | | | One parent | Maintained by | |
Years	Total with children under 18[b]	Total	Married	Unmarried	Total	Mother	Father
All races							
2007[e]	39,983	28,276	26,802	1,474	11,707	9,965	1,742
2000	37,496	25,771	25,771	(N/A)	11,725	9,681	2,044
1990	34,670	24,921	24,921	(N/A)	9,749	8,398	1,351
1980	32,150	25,231	25,231	(N/A)	6,920	6,230	690
1970	29,626	25,823	25,823	(N/A)	3,803	3,410	393
White							
2007[c, e]	31,358	23,646	22,519	1,127	7,712	6,359	1,353
2000	30,079	22,241	22,241	(N/A)	7,838	6,216	1,622
1990	28,294	21,905	21,905	(N/A)	6,389	5,310	1,079
1980	27,294	22,628	22,628	(N/A)	4,664	4,122	542
1970	26,115	23,477	23,477	(N/A)	2,638	2,330	307
Black							
2007[c, e]	5,760	2,404	2,182	222	3,356	3,067	289
2007[d, e]	5,957	2,511	2,277	234	3,446	3,149	297
2000	5,530	2,135	2,135	(N/A)	3,395	3,060	335
1990	5,087	2,006	2,006	(N/A)	3,081	2,860	221
1980	4,074	1,961	1,961	(N/A)	2,114	1,984	129
1970	3,219	2,071	2,071	(N/A)	1,148	1,063	85
Hispanic origin[b]							
2007[e]	7,192	4,984	4,628	356	2,208	1,987	221
2000	5,503	3,625	3,625	(N/A)	1,878	1,565	313
1990	3,429	2,289	2,289	(N/A)	1,140	1,003	138
1980	2,194	1,626	1,626	(N/A)	568	526	42
1970	(NA)	(NA)	(NA)	(N/A)	(NA)	(NA)	(NA)

NA—Not available
[a]Family groups prior to 2007 were restricted to married couple and single-parent families and their "own" children. In 2007, unmarried two-parent families were added to the table. Unmarried two-parent family groups are opposite sex partners who have at least one joint child under 18.
[b]Persons of Hispanic origin may be of any race.
[c]Householder whose race was reported as only one race.
[d]Householder whose race was reported as only a single race or in combination with one or more other races.
[e]Estimates produced using PELNMOM and PELNDAD, the new parent pointer variables introduced in 2007.

SOURCE: Adapted from "FM-2. All Parent/Child Situations, by Type, Race, and Hispanic Origin of Householder or Reference Person: 1970 to Present," in *Families and Living Arrangements*, U.S. Census Bureau, July 2008, http://www.census.gov/population/www/socdemo/hh-fam.html (accessed September 15, 2008)

LIVING ARRANGEMENTS OF CHILDREN
Single-Parent Families

Many children who live in single-parent households face significant challenges that can be exacerbated by racial and ethnic inequalities. According to the Federal Interagency Forum on Child and Family Statistics, in *America's Children in Brief*, the poverty rate for African-American children was 33% and for Hispanic children was 27%, but for non-Hispanic white children it was only 10%. Children who lived in minority families with a single parent were especially likely to have greatly reduced economic, educational, and social opportunities. Single parents were more likely to have a low income and less education and were more likely to be unemployed and to be renting a home or apartment or living in public housing. In 2004, 10% of children living with married parents lived below the poverty level, whereas 36.5% of children living with an unmar-

ried mother were. (See Table 1.9.) Children living with an unmarried father also had an elevated poverty rate of 16.6%.

Table 1.10 shows the dramatic differences in the proportion of children living with single parents by race and ethnic group. In 2007 children from all backgrounds were much more likely to be living with a single mother (22.6%) than a single father (3.2%), and 67.8% lived with two married parents. Among African-Americans, however, the percent of children who lived with a single mother was much higher (49.8%), whereas only 36.8% lived with married parents.

Nontraditional Families

Many single-parent families, however, are not single adult families; some single parents maintain a household with an unmarried partner. In 1990 the Census Bureau sought to reflect changing lifestyles in the United States

TABLE 1.8

Number, birth rate, and percentage of births to unmarried women, by age, race, and Hispanic origin of mother, 2005

Measure and age of mother	All races[a]	White Total[b]	White Non-Hispanic	Black Total[b]	Black Non-Hispanic	American Indian or Alaska Native[b]	Asian or Pacific Islander[b]	Hispanic[c]
Number								
All ages	1,527,034	1,022,560	577,617	438,614	407,756	28,461	37,399	472,649
Under 15 years	6,590	3,520	1,304	2,833	2,694	136	101	2,365
15–19 years	345,413	232,747	130,155	99,904	93,604	6,996	5,766	108,457
15 years	17,458	10,846	4,469	5,961	5,588	389	262	6,728
16 years	37,936	24,971	11,598	11,486	10,752	858	621	14,070
17 years	65,718	44,533	23,080	18,767	17,515	1,357	1,061	22,638
18 years	97,363	66,126	37,978	27,680	25,855	1,923	1,634	29,846
19 years	126,938	86,271	53,030	36,010	33,894	2,469	2,188	35,175
20–24 years	584,792	393,403	237,500	168,183	157,361	10,885	12,321	165,600
25–29 years	331,820	219,861	118,275	96,528	89,079	5,982	9,449	108,316
30–34 years	161,752	107,832	53,759	45,111	41,219	2,888	5,921	57,506
35–39 years	75,717	51,046	28,030	20,506	18,688	1,236	2,929	24,514
40 years and over	20,950	14,151	8,594	5,549	5,111	338	912	5,891
Rate per 1,000 unmarried women in specified group								
15–44 years[d]	47.5	43.0	30.1	67.8	—	—	24.9	100.3
15–19 years	34.5	29.9	20.9	60.6	—	—	13.1	68.0
15–17 years	19.7	16.8	10.3	35.4	—	—	7.3	42.7
18–19 years	58.4	50.9	37.4	101.6	—	—	22.1	112.4
20–24 years	74.9	66.6	49.1	120.7	—	—	29.7	150.4
25–29 years	71.1	66.3	45.0	93.8	—	—	35.1	153.5
30–34 years	50.0	49.1	31.2	54.0	—	—	36.6	118.1
35–39 years	24.5	23.8	16.0	26.1	—	—	24.7	59.2
40–44 years[e]	6.2	5.8	4.2	7.1	—	—	9.4	14.3
Percent of births to unmarried women								
All ages	36.9	31.7	25.3	69.3	69.9	63.5	16.2	48.0
Under 15 years	98.0	96.6	98.0	99.9	99.9	100.0	97.1	95.9
15–19 years	83.3	78.8	78.9	96.1	96.7	89.6	75.7	79.2
15 years	95.7	93.7	95.0	99.5	99.8	97.0	92.9	92.9
16 years	92.4	89.6	91.5	99.0	99.3	96.0	88.1	88.3
17 years	89.0	85.5	87.1	98.2	98.7	92.9	85.4	84.2
18 years	83.6	79.2	80.2	96.5	97.1	89.8	75.7	78.4
19 years	77.0	71.7	71.8	93.5	94.1	84.8	67.8	72.1
20–24 years	56.2	49.8	46.1	82.6	83.4	71.0	39.9	57.5
25–29 years	29.3	24.4	18.4	61.8	62.3	53.5	14.6	40.6
30–34 years	17.0	14.1	9.2	44.7	44.6	43.6	7.4	30.9
35–39 years	15.7	13.1	9.2	39.7	39.4	41.6	7.5	28.6
40 years and over	18.8	16.1	12.5	39.8	39.5	44.5	10.6	30.2

—Data not available.

[a]Includes races other than white and black and origin not stated.

[b]Race and Hispanic origin are reported separately on the birth certificate. Race categories are consistent with the 1977 Office of Management and Budget (OMB) standards. Data for persons of Hispanic origin are included in the data for each race group according to the mother's reported race. Nineteen states reported multiple-race data for 2005. The multiple-race data for these states were bridged to the single-race categories of the 1977 OMB standards for comparability with other states.

[c]Includes all persons of Hispanic origin of any race.

[d]Birth rates computed by relating total births to unmarried mothers regardless of age of mother to unmarried women aged 15–44 years.

[e]Birth rates compute by relating births to unmarried mothers aged 40 years and over to unmarried women aged 40–44 years.

Notes: For 48 states and the District of Columbia marital status is reported in the birth registration process; for Michigan and New York mother's marital status is inferred. Rates cannot be computed for unmarried non-Hispanic black women or for American Indian women because the necessary population are not available.

SOURCE: Joyce A. Martin et al., "Table 18. Number, Birth Rate, and Percentage of Births to Unmarried Women by Age, Race, and Hispanic Origin of Mother: United States, 2005," in "Births: Final Data for 2005," *National Vital Statistics Reports*, vol. 56, no. 6, December 5, 2007, http://www.cdc.gov/nchs/data/nvsr/nvsr56/nvsr56_06.pdf (accessed September 15, 2008)

by asking for the first time whether unmarried couples maintained households together. Even though in 2000 a slight majority (52%) of U.S. households were headed by married couples, a significant number of unmarried couples also maintained households together. The Census Bureau indicates in the 2007 ACS that in 2007, 6.2 million unmarried couples cohabited in the United States. Most of these couples were opposite-sex couples, but approximately 754,000 of them were same-sex couples.

A significant portion of all coupled households in 2007 contained children under the age of 18. According to the ACS, 4.8 million children lived with a partner and his or her unmarried partner. In *America's Families and Living Arrangements: 2007* (July 2008, http://www.census.gov/population/www/socdemo/hh-fam/cps2007.html), the Census Bureau finds that among opposite-sex unmarried couples, 2.5 million (39%) out of 6.4 million had at least one child with them. Among married couples, 26.8 million

TABLE 1.9

Children by presence and type of parents by poverty status, 2004

[Numbers in thousands]

	Children		Percent of children below poverty level
Living arrangements of children	Number	Percent	Estimate
Total	73,227	100.0	17.7
Living with no parent	2,878	3.9	28.5
Living with an unmarried parent[a]	21,563	29.4	33.7
Living with unmarried mother and father	2,227	3.0	31.4
Living with unmarried mother only	16,973	23.2	36.5
Living with unmarried father only	2,363	3.2	16.6
Parent has an unmarried partner	3,857	5.3	31.8
Biological mother and father	1,814	2.5	32.4
Biological mother, step or adoptive father	324	0.4	26.9
Biological father, step or adoptive mother	87	0.1	28.7
Biological mother, partner	1,271	1.7	36.2
Biological father, partner	308	0.4	19.8
Step or adoptive parent, partner	51	0.1	(B)
Parent has no unmarried partner	17,705	24.2	34.2
Biological mother	15,303	20.9	36.6
Living with other adult relative[b]	3,197	4.4	23.9
Living with opposite sex adult nonrelative[c]	380	0.5	32.1
Biological father	1,972	2.7	15.8
Living with other adult relative[b]	375	0.5	15.5
Living with opposite sex adult nonrelative[c]	66	0.1	(B)
Stepparent or adoptive parent	429	0.6	31.9

B Base less than 75,000.
[a]Unmarried includes married spouse absent, widowed, divorced, separated, and never married.
[b]The category "other adult relative" does not include the child's siblings.
[c]Only includes adult nonrelatives who are not in the category "married spouse present."

SOURCE: Rose M. Kreider, "Table 2. Children by Presence and Type of Parents by Poverty Status: 2004," in *Living Arrangements of Children: 2004*, U.S. Census Bureau, Current Population Reports, February 2008, http://www.census.gov/prod/2008pubs/p70–114.pdf (accessed November 2, 2008)

(44%) out of 60.7 million had children under the age of 18 living with them. Same-sex partnered households also often contained children. According to Tavia Simmons and Martin O'Connell of the Census Bureau, in *Married-Couple and Unmarried-Partner Households: 2000* (February 2003, http://www.census.gov/prod/2003pubs/censr-5.pdf), in 2000, the most recent year for which data are available, nearly a quarter (22.3%) of households headed by male partners had children living in them, and a third (34.3%) of households headed by female partners had children living with them. One out of 20 (5.3%) children lived with a parent and his or her unmarried partner in 2004. (See Table 1.9.)

Grandparents

Grandparents sometimes provide housing for, and sometimes reside in, the homes of their children and grandchildren. According to the Child Trends Databank (2007, http://

www.childtrendsdatabank.org/tables/59_Table_2.htm), in 2006, 5.1% of children under the age of 18 lived in the homes of their grandparents, and 2% lived with their grandparents without a parent present. This percentage remained fairly steady from 1970 to 2006, varying from a low of 1.3% in 1992 to the high of 2.2% in 2005. These caretaking grandparents were responsible for most of the basic needs (food, shelter, and clothing) of one or more of the grandchildren living with them.

Living and caretaking arrangements of grandparents and grandchildren varied by race and ethnicity in 2007. The Census Bureau explains in *America's Families and Living Arrangements* that non-Hispanic white children were less likely to live with their grandparents than Hispanic, Asian-American, and African-American children— only 5.5% of white children lived with their grandparents, whereas 10.4% of Hispanic children, 12.2% of Asian-American children, and 14.1% of African-American children did. However, African-American children were much more likely than other groups to be living with a grandparent with no parent present. Of all children living with their grandparents in 2004, 38% of African-American children, 23% of non-Hispanic white children, 16% of Hispanic children, and 4% of Asian-American children had no parent present in the home. (See Figure 1.1.)

The homes maintained by grandparents without parents present were more likely to experience economic hardship than families with a parent present, reflecting the often limited and fixed resources of senior citizens. In *Children's Living Arrangements and Characteristics: March 2002* (June 2003, http://www.census.gov/prod/2003pubs/p20-547.pdf), Jason Fields of the Census Bureau states that of all grandchildren, 18% lived below the poverty line in 2002, 23% were not covered by health insurance, and 9% received public assistance. Among children who lived with their grandparents with their parents absent, the numbers were much higher: 30% were below the poverty line, 36% were not covered by health insurance, and 17% received public assistance. These numbers suggest that children who live with their grandparents without a parent present are at an economic disadvantage; grandchildren's presence in their grandparents' home without an economic contribution from the middle generation appears to severely tax the economic resources of grandparents.

Foster Care and Adoption

There is currently no comprehensive federal registry system for adoptions, which can be arranged by government agencies, private agencies, or through private arrangements between birth mothers and adoptive parents with the assistance of lawyers. The federally funded National Center for Social Statistics collected information on all finalized adoptions from 1957 to 1975, but with the dissolution of the center, limited statistical information is now available.

TABLE 1.10

Percentage of children under age 18, by presence of married parents in household and race and Hispanic origin, 1980–2007

Race[a] and Hispanic origin, and family structure	1980	1981	1982	1983	1984	1985	1986	1987	1988	1989	1990	1991	1992	1993
Total														
Two parents	—	—	—	—	—	—	—	—	—	—	—	—	—	—
Two married parents	77	76	75	75	75	74	74	73	73	73	73	72	71	71
Mother only	18	18	20	20	20	21	21	21	21	22	22	22	23	23
Father only	2	2	2	2	2	2	3	3	3	3	3	3	3	3
No parent	4	4	3	3	3	3	3	3	3	3	3	3	3	3
White, non-Hispanic														
Two married parents	—	—	—	—	—	—	—	—	—	—	81	80	79	79
Mother only	—	—	—	—	—	—	—	—	—	—	15	15	16	16
Father only	—	—	—	—	—	—	—	—	—	—	3	3	3	3
No parent	—	—	—	—	—	—	—	—	—	—	2	2	1	1
White-alone, non-Hispanic														
Two parents	—	—	—	—	—	—	—	—	—	—	—	—	—	—
Two married parents	—	—	—	—	—	—	—	—	—	—	—	—	—	—
Mother only	—	—	—	—	—	—	—	—	—	—	—	—	—	—
Father only	—	—	—	—	—	—	—	—	—	—	—	—	—	—
No parent	—	—	—	—	—	—	—	—	—	—	—	—	—	—
Black														
Two married parents	42	43	42	41	41	39	41	40	39	38	38	36	36	36
Mother only	44	43	47	51	50	51	51	50	51	51	51	54	54	54
Father only	2	3	2	2	3	3	2	3	3	3	4	4	3	3
No parent	12	11	8	6	6	7	6	7	7	7	8	7	7	7
Black-alone														
Two parents	—	—	—	—	—	—	—	—	—	—	—	—	—	—
Two married parents	—	—	—	—	—	—	—	—	—	—	—	—	—	—
Mother only	—	—	—	—	—	—	—	—	—	—	—	—	—	—
Father only	—	—	—	—	—	—	—	—	—	—	—	—	—	—
No parent	—	—	—	—	—	—	—	—	—	—	—	—	—	—
Hispanic[c]														
Two parents	—	—	—	—	—	—	—	—	—	—	—	—	—	—
Two married parents	75	70	69	68	70	68	66	66	66	67	67	66	65	65
Mother only	20	23	25	27	25	27	28	28	27	28	27	27	28	28
Father only	2	2	2	2	2	2	3	3	3	3	3	3	4	4
No parent	3	4	4	3	3	3	3	4	4	2	3	4	3	4

Race[a] and Hispanic origin, and family structure	1994	1995	1996	1997	1998	1999	2000	2001	2002	2003	2004	2005	2006	2007
Total														
Two parents	—	—	—	—	—	—	—	—	—	—	—	—	—	70.7
Two married parents	69	69	68	68	68	68	69	69	69	68.4	67.8	67.3	67.4	67.8
Mother only	23	23	24	24	23	23	22	22	23	23.0	23.3	23.4	23.3	22.6
Father only	3	4	4	4	4	4	4	4	5	4.6	4.6	4.8	4.7	3.2
No parent	4	4	4	4	4	4	4	4	4	4.1	4.3	4.5	4.6	3.5
White, non-Hispanic														
Two married parents	79	78	77	77	76	77	77	78	77	—	—	—	—	—
Mother only	16	16	16	17	16	16	16	16	16	—	—	—	—	—
Father only	3	3	4	4	5	4	4	4	4	—	—	—	—	—
No parent	3	3	3	3	3	3	3	2	3	—	—	—	—	—
White-alone, non-Hispanic														
Two parents	—	—	—	—	—	—	—	—	—	—	—	—	—	78.6
Two married parents	—	—	—	—	—	—	—	—	—	76.9	76.9	75.9	75.9	76.2
Mother only	—	—	—	—	—	—	—	—	—	15.9	15.9	16.4	16.0	15.3
Father only	—	—	—	—	—	—	—	—	—	4.3	4.3	4.8	4.8	3.6
No parent	—	—	—	—	—	—	—	—	—	2.9	2.9	2.9	3.2	2.5

With the passage of the Adoption and Safe Families Act of 1997, there was a renewed effort to improve the data available about adoption. The U.S. Department of Health and Human Services, through the Adoption and Foster Care Analysis and Reporting System (AFCARS), now tracks adoptions arranged through the foster care system, but this represents only some of the children adopted by American families each year.

In *The AFCARS Report* (September 2006, http://www.acf.hhs.gov/programs/cb/stats_research/afcars/tar/report14.htm), AFCARS states that on September 30, 2006, 510,000 children were living in foster homes with foster parents. Foster parents are trained people supervised by local social service agencies who provide space in their home and care for children who have been neglected, abused, or abandoned, or whose parents have surrendered them to public

TABLE 1.10

Percentage of children under age 18, by presence of married parents in household and race and Hispanic origin, 1980–2007 [CONTINUED]

Race[a] and Hispanic origin, and family structure	1994	1995	1996	1997	1998	1999	2000	2001	2002	2003	2004	2005	2006	2007
Black														
Two married parents	33	33	33	35	36	35	38	38	38	—	—	—	—	—
Mother only	53	52	53	52	51	52	49	48	48	—	—	—	—	—
Father only	4	4	4	5	4	4	4	5	5	—	—	—	—	—
No parent	10	11	9	8	9	10	9	10	8	—	—	—	—	—
Black-alone														
Two parents	—	—	—	—	—	—	—	—	—	—	—	—	—	39.8
Two married parents	—	—	—	—	—	—	—	—	—	36.0	35.0	35.0	34.6	36.8
Mother only	—	—	—	—	—	—	—	—	—	51.0	50.0	50.2	51.2	49.8
Father only	—	—	—	—	—	—	—	—	—	5.0	6.0	5.0	4.8	3.5
No parent	—	—	—	—	—	—	—	—	—	9.0	9.0	9.8	9.4	6.8
Hispanic[c]														
Two parents	—	—	—	—	—	—	—	—	—	—	—	—	—	69.8
Two married parents	63	63	62	64	64	63	65	65	65	64.6	64.6	64.7	65.9	65.5
Mother only	28	28	29	27	27	27	25	25	25	24.5	25.4	25.4	25.0	24.5
Father only	4	4	4	4	4	5	4	5	5	5.5	5.3	4.8	4.1	2.1
No parent	5	4	5	5	5	5	5	6	5	5.3	4.7	5.1	5.0	3.6

—Not available.

[a]For race and Hispanic-origin data in this table: From 1980 to 2002, following the 1977 OMB standards for collecting and presenting data on race, the Current Population Survey (CPS) asked respondents to choose one race from the following: white, black, American Indian or Alaskan Native, or Asian or Pacific Islander. The Census Bureau also offered an "other" category. Beginning in 2003, following the 1997 OMB standards for collecting and presenting data on race, the CPS asked respondents to choose one or more races from the following: white, black, Asian, American Indian or Alaska Native, and Native Hawaiian or other Pacific Islander. All race groups discussed in this table from 2003 onward refer to people who indicated only one racial identity within the racial categories presented. People who responded to the question on race by indicating only one race are referred to as the race-alone population. The use of the race-alone population in this table does not imply that it is the preferred method of presenting or analyzing data. Data from 2003 onward are not directly comparable with data from earlier years. Data on race and Hispanic origin are collected separately. Persons of Hispanic origin may be of any race.
[b]Beginning with March 2001, data are from the expanded CPS sample and use population controls based on Census 2000.
[c]Persons of Hispanic origin may be of any race.
Note: Prior to 2007, CPS data identified only one parent on the child's record. This meant that a second parent could only be identified if they were married to the first parent. In 2007, a second parent identifier was added to CPS. This permits identification of two coresident parents, even if the parents are not married to each other. In this table, "two parents" reflects all children who have both a mother and father identified in the household, including biological, step and adoptive parents. Before 2007, "mother only" and "father only" included some children who lived with a parent who was living with the other parent of the child, but was not married to them. Beginning in 2007, "mother only" and "father only" refer to children for whom only one parent has been identified, whether biological, step or adoptive.

SOURCE: "FAM1.A. Family Structure and Children's Living Arrangements: Percentage of Children Ages 0–17 by Presence of Married Parents in Household, and Race and Hispanic Origin, 1980–2007," in *America's Children in Brief: Key National Indicators of Well-Being, 2008*, Federal Interagency Forum on Child and Family Statistics, July 2008, http://www.childstats.gov/americaschildren/tables.asp (accessed September 15, 2008)

agencies because they are unable to care for them. According to the American Public Welfare Association, foster care is the most common type of substitute care, but children needing substitute care might also live in group homes, emergency shelters, child care facilities, hospitals, correctional institutions, or on their own. It is becoming more difficult to place children in foster care. The number of potential foster care families is down, due in part to the fact that women, the primary providers of foster care, are entering the paid labor force in greater numbers.

AFCARS estimates that in fiscal year 2006, 303,000 children younger than 18 years old entered foster care, with an average age of 8.1 years. A disproportionate share of children entering foster care were African-American—26% of children entering foster care were African-American, but according to the Census Bureau's *National Population Estimates—Characteristics* (April 30, 2008, http://www.census.gov/popest/national/asrh/), only 17% of all Americans under the age of 18 were African-American (alone or in combination) in that year. Non-Hispanic white children were underrepresented among those entering foster care—45% were non-Hispanic white children, compared to 57% of all non-Hispanic white children under the age of 18.

Hispanic and Native American or Alaskan Native children were more proportionally represented—19% entering foster care were Hispanic (compared to 20% of children in the general population), and 2% were Native American or Alaskan Native (compared to 2% of children in the general population). Asian-American children were underrepresented in foster care; only 1% of children in foster care were Asian-American, compared to 5% of all children in the general population.

A child's stay in foster care can vary from just a few days to many years. Fifteen percent of children who left foster care in fiscal year 2006 had been in care less than a month, 34% had been in care from one to 11 months, 23% had been in care from one to two years, and 28% had lived in foster care for two years or longer. (See Table 1.11.)

AFCARS states that more than half (53%) of the children who left foster care in fiscal year 2006 were reunited with their parents. (See Table 1.11.) About one out of 10 (11%) of these children moved to a relative's or guardian's home. Nine percent were emancipated, or "aged out" of the system when they turned 18 years old, and 17% of the children who left foster care were adopted.

FIGURE 1.1

Percent distribution of children living with grandparents by presence of parents and race and Hispanic origin, 2004

[Percent distribution]

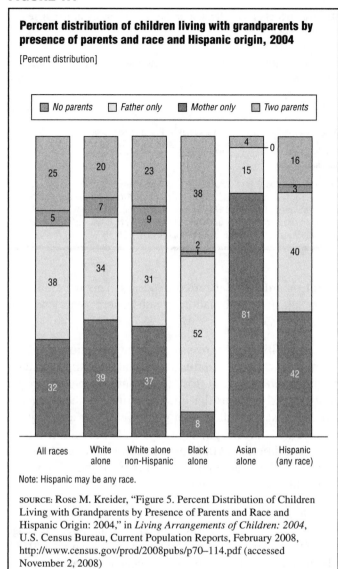

Note: Hispanic may be any race.

SOURCE: Rose M. Kreider, "Figure 5. Percent Distribution of Children Living with Grandparents by Presence of Parents and Race and Hispanic Origin: 2004," in *Living Arrangements of Children: 2004*, U.S. Census Bureau, Current Population Reports, February 2008, http://www.census.gov/prod/2008pubs/p70–114.pdf (accessed November 2, 2008)

TABLE 1.11

Children who exited foster care, fiscal year 2006

How many children exited foster care during fiscal year 2006? 289,000
What were the ages of the children who exited care during fiscal year 2006?

Mean years	9.8	
Median years	9.5	
Less than 1 year	5%	13,948
1 year	7%	19,929
2 years	7%	19,851
3 years	6%	17,770
4 years	6%	15,960
5 years	5%	14,355
6 years	5%	13,276
7 years	4%	12,776
8 years	4%	11,402
9 years	4%	10,584
10 years	3%	10,044
11 years	3%	9,803
12 years	4%	10,201
13 years	4%	11,128
14 years	5%	13,364
15 years	6%	16,355
16 years	6%	18,264
17 years	9%	24,597
18 years	7%	19,230
19 years	1%	3,599
20 years	1%	2,561

What were the outcomes for the children exiting foster care during fiscal year 2006?

Reunification with parent(s) or primary caretaker(s)	53%	154,103
Living with other relative(s)	11%	30,751
Adoption	17%	50,379
Emancipation	9%	26,517
Guardianship	5%	15,010
Transfer to another agency	2%	6,683
Runaway	2%	5,049
Death of child	0%	509

What were the lengths of stay of the children who exited foster care during fiscal year 2006?

Mean months	20.9	
Median months	12.2	
Less than 1 month	15%	42,960
1 to 5 months	16%	47,506
6 to 11 months	18%	52,921
12 to 17 months	14%	39,485
18 to 23 months	9%	26,487
24 to 29 months	7%	19,128
30 to 35 months	5%	13,604
3 to 4 years	9%	26,415
5 years or more	7%	20,492

What was the race/ethnicity of the children who exited care during fiscal year 2006?

AI/AN—non-Hispanic	2%	6,243
Asian—non-Hispanic	1%	2,384
Black—non-Hispanic	27%	77,720
Hawaiian/ PI—non-Hispanic	0%	840
Hispanic	18%	51,711
White—non-Hispanic	46%	130,945
Unknown/unable to determine	2%	6,910
Two or more—non-Hispanic	4%	10,246

Note: AI/AN = American Indian/Alaska Native. PI = Pacific Islander.

SOURCE: Adapted from "How Many Children Exited Foster Care during FY 2006?" in *The AFCARS Report*, no. 14, U.S. Department of Health and Human Services, Administration for Children and Families, January 2008, http://www.acf.hhs.gov/programs/cb/stats_research/afcars/tar/report14.htm (accessed September 15, 2008)

According to AFCARS, adopted children were on average younger (6.6 years) than children still in foster care (9.8 years), reflecting the preference of adoptive parents for younger children. Of those adopted children in fiscal year 2006, 25,994 were male and 25,006 were female. (See Table 1.12.) Foster parents adopted 59% of these children, relatives adopted 26%, and nonrelatives who had not fostered the child previously adopted 15%. Even though traditional families (married couples) made up slightly more than two-thirds (69%) of families who adopted children from foster care, a significant share were nontraditional families—26% of adopters were single women, 3% were single men, and 2% were unmarried couples.

In 1996 the federal government began providing incentives to potential adoptive parents to move children into adoptive homes more quickly. The government provided a $5,000 tax credit for adoptive parents to cover adoption expenses; the credit was $6,000 if the adopted child had

special needs. Children with special needs were defined as those with physical, mental, or emotional problems; children needing to be adopted with siblings; or children who were difficult to place because of age, race, or ethnicity. In

TABLE 1.12

Children adopted from the public foster care system, fiscal year 2006

How many children were adopted with public agency involvement in fiscal year (FY) 2006? 51,000

What is the gender distribution of the children adopted from the public foster care system?

Male	51%	25,994
Female	49%	25,006

How old were the children when they were adopted from the public foster care system?

Mean years	6.6	
Median years	5.4	
Less than 1 year	2%	1,099
1 year	11%	5,567
2 years	13%	6,735
3 years	11%	5,647
4 years	9%	4,666
5 years	8%	3,914
6 years	7%	3,562
7 years	6%	3,063
8 years	5%	2,686
9 years	5%	2,422
10 years	4%	2,138
11 years	4%	2,012
12 years	4%	1,785
13 years	3%	1,618
14 years	3%	1,378
15 years	2%	1,070
16 years	2%	830
17 years	1%	636
18 years	0%	148
19 years	0%	17
20 years	0%	6

What percentage of the children adopted receive an adoption subsidy?

Yes	89%	45,541
No	11%	5,459

What is the racial/ethnic distribution of the children adopted from the public foster care system?

AI/AN—non-Hispanic	1%	693
Asian—non-Hispanic	1%	289
Black—non-Hispanic	27%	13,783
Hawaiian/PI—non-Hispanic	0%	125
Hispanic	19%	9,569
White—non-Hispanic	45%	22,979
Unknown/unable to determine	2%	1,049
Two or more—non-Hispanic	5%	2,512

How many months did it take after termination of parental rights for the children to be adopted?

Mean months	14.5	
Median months	10.4	
Less than 1 month	3%	1,576
1 thru 5 months	22%	11,325
6 thru 11 months	32%	16,379
12 thru 17 months	18%	9,320
18 thru 23 months	10%	4,988
24 thru 29 months	5%	2,638
30 thru 35 months	3%	1,424
3 thru 4 years	5%	2,322
5 years or more	2%	1,028

What is the family structure of the child's adoptive family?

Married couple	69%	35,278
Unmarried couple	2%	857
Single female	26%	13,370
Single male	3%	1,496

TABLE 1.12

Children adopted from the public foster care system, fiscal year 2006 [CONTINUED]

What was the relationship of the adoptive parents to the child prior to the adoption?

Non-relative	15%	7,646
Foster parent	59%	29,997
Step-parent	0%	36
Other relative	26%	13,321

Note: AI/AN = American Indian/Alaska Native. PI = Pacific Islander.
Using U.S. Bureau of the Census standards, children of Hispanic origin may be of any race. Beginning in FY 2000, children could be identified with more than one race designation.

SOURCE: Adapted from "How Many Children Were Adopted with Public Agency Involvement in FY 2006?" in *The AFCARS Report*, no. 14, U.S. Department of Health and Human Services, Administration for Children and Families, January 2008, http://www.acf.hhs.gov/programs/cb/stats_research/afcars/tar/report14.htm (accessed September 15, 2008)

credit regardless of incurred expenses. This tax credit has been adjusted for inflation in subsequent years and was $12,150 in 2009.

In addition, Congress passed the Adoption and Safe Families Act in 1997, providing fiscal incentives to states to move children from foster care into adoptive families more quickly. States that increased the number of adoptions of foster children (in a given year over a base year) received a standard payment of $4,000 per adopted child and an additional $2,000 for the adoption of each special-needs child and an additional $4,000 for the adoption of each child aged nine and older.

Despite these incentives, many children who enter foster care will never have a permanent family, but instead will age out of the system. On September 30, 2006, there were 129,000 children whose parents' rights had been terminated living in foster homes. (See Table 1.13.) These "waiting children" were disproportionately African-American. Whereas 17% of all children under the age of 18 were African-American and 26% of children entering foster care were African-American in 2006, 32% of waiting children were African-American. The majority (54%) of waiting children lived in foster homes with nonrelatives while waiting to be adopted.

Living Arrangements of Young Adults

A young person's transition into adult independence does not necessarily occur at age 18. The marriage age has risen since the 1950s, and, as obtaining a college education has become the norm, young people have delayed finding employment that allows them to support themselves independently of their parents. A growing number of young adults older than the age of 18 continue to live in, or return to, their parents' homes. Some young people live with their parents until their mid-20s, and others are likely to return home at some time after moving out, especially after college or service in the military. Many young adults also share households with others.

2002 the tax credit was increased to $10,000 to cover adoption expenses for children without special needs; adoptive parents of special-needs children, including many children from foster care, received the full amount of the tax

TABLE 1.13

Children waiting to be adopted on September 30, 2006

How many children were waiting to be adopted on September 30, 2006? 129,000
What is the gender distribution of the waiting children?

Male	53%	68,006
Female	47%	60,994

How many months have the waiting children been in continuous foster care?

Mean months	39.4	
Median months	28.9	
Less than 1 month	1%	656
1 through 5 months	4%	4,843
6 through 11 months	9%	11,079
12 through 17 months	14%	17,463
18 through 23 months	14%	17,557
24 through 29 months	12%	15,536
30 through 35 months	9%	11,767
36 through 59 months	20%	25,792
60 or more months	19%	24,307

What is the racial/ethnic distribution of the waiting children?

AI/AN—non-Hispanic	2%	2,223
Asian—non-Hispanic	1%	651
Black—non-Hispanic	32%	41,591
Hawaiian/PI—non-Hispanic	0%	301
Hispanic	20%	25,481
White—non-Hispanic	38%	49,637
Unknown/unable to determine	3%	3,362
Two or more—non-Hispanic	4%	5,754

How old were the waiting children when they were removed from their parents or caretakers?

Mean years	4.9	
Median years	4.2	
Less than 1 year	25%	32,082
1 year	9%	11,270
2 years	8%	9,920
3 years	7%	9,139
4 years	7%	8,836
5 years	7%	8,449
6 years	6%	8,269
7 years	6%	7,645
8 years	5%	6,956
9 years	5%	6,220
10 years	4%	5,552
11 years	4%	4,647
12 years	3%	3,811
13 years	2%	2,850
14 years	1%	1,856
15 years	1%	1,041
16 years	0%	372
17 years	0%	87

Where were the waiting children living on September 30, 2006?

Pre-adoptive home	13%	16,163
Foster family home (relative)	21%	27,619
Foster family home (non-relative)	54%	70,230
Group home	4%	4,834
Institution	6%	8,216
Supervised independent living	0%	109
Runaway	1%	982
Trial home visit	1%	847

Socioeconomic experts attribute this phenomenon to the rising cost of living in the United States. Wages have not increased at the same rate as the cost of living; therefore, the same amount of money buys less than it did in previous years. Furthermore, credit markets tightened during the economic recession that began in 2008, which made it difficult to qualify for a mortgage and may have further delayed young people leaving home. At the same time, foreclosures skyrocketed; young adults who found themselves in foreclosure may have returned to their parents' homes.

How old were the waiting children on September 30, 2006?

Mean years	8.2	
Median years	7.7	
Less than 1 year	4%	5,102
1 year	9%	11,023
2 years	8%	10,420
3 years	7%	9,463
4 years	6%	8,362
5 years	6%	7,840
6 years	6%	7,150
7 years	5%	6,978
8 years	5%	6,688
9 years	5%	6,372
10 years	5%	6,208
11 years	5%	6,267
12 years	5%	6,473
13 years	5%	6,844
14 years	5%	6,907
15 years	6%	7,207
16 years	4%	5,607
17 years	3%	4,089

Note: AI/AN = American Indian/Alaska Native. PI = Pacific Islander.
Using U.S. Bureau of the Census standards, children of Hispanic origin may be of any race. Beginning in fiscal year 2000, children could be identified with more than one race designation.

SOURCE: Adapted from "How Many Children Were Waiting to Be Adopted on September 30, 2006?" in *The AFCARS Report*, no. 14, U.S. Department of Health and Human Services, Administration for Children and Families, January 2008, http://www.acf.hhs.gov/programs/cb/stats_research/afcars/tar/report14.htm (accessed September 15, 2008)

In 2007, 14.4 million young men and 13.9 million young women between the ages of 18 and 24 lived in their parents' homes. (See Table 1.14; this figure includes those who were living in college dormitories who were still counted as residing at their parental residences.) Males in this age group were more likely (54.7%) than females (47.6%) to live with their parents. This was primarily because men tend to marry at a later age than women do. Almost all men and women in this age group who lived with their parents had never been married. Jason Fields of the Census Bureau indicates in *America's Families and Living Arrangements: 2003* (November 2004, http://www.census.gov/prod/2004pubs/p20-553.pdf) that the percentage of both men and women aged 20 to 24 and 25 to 29 that had never married rose dramatically between 1970 and 2003, but that the percentage of men who had never married was consistently higher. The Census Bureau notes in *America's Families and Living Arrangements: 2007* that these percents held constant in 2007.

Young adults who live by themselves for any length of time are unlikely to return home after experiencing independence. By contrast, those who move in with roommates or who cohabit without marrying are more likely to return to the parental home if the living situation does not work out or the relationship fails. Some young people struggle on their own only to return home for respite from financial pressures, loneliness, or because they need emotional support or security.

TABLE 1.14

Young adults living at home, selected years 1960–2007

[Numbers in thousands. Data based on Current Population Survey (CPS).]

	Male			Female		
Age	Total	Child of householder	Percent	Total	Child of householder	Percent
18 to 24 years						
2007	14,409	7,880	54.7	13,976	6,648	47.6
2006	14,100	7,573	53.7	13,841	6,466	46.7
2005	14,060	7,448	53.0	13,933	6,413	46.0
2004	14,165	8,010	56.5	13,611	6,327	46.5
2003	13,811	7,569	54.8	13,592	6,215	45.7
2002	13,696	7,575	55.3	13,602	6,252	46.0
2001	13,412	7,385	55.1	13,361	6,068	45.4
2000	13,291	7,593	57.1	13,242	6,232	47.1
1990	12,450	7,232	58.1	12,860	6,135	47.7
1980 census	14,278	7,755	54.3	14,844	6,336	42.7
1970 census	10,398	5,641	54.3	11,959	4,941	41.3
1960 census	6,842	3,583	52.4	7,876	2,750	34.9
25 to 34 years						
2007	20,002	2,849	14.2	19,828	1,850	9.3
2006	19,824	2,840	14.3	19,653	1,731	8.8
2005	19,656	2,660	13.5	19,632	1,597	8.1
2004	19,553	2,720	13.9	19,587	1,559	8.0
2003	19,543	2,631	13.5	19,659	1,375	7.0
2002	19,220	2,610	13.6	19,428	1,618	8.3
2001	19,308	2,520	13.1	19,527	1,583	8.1
2000	18,563	2,387	12.9	19,222	1,602	8.3
1990	21,462	3,213	15.0	21,779	1,774	8.1
1980 census	18,107	1,894	10.5	18,689	1,300	7.0
1970 census	11,929	1,129	9.5	12,637	829	6.6
1960 census	10,896	1,185	10.9	11,587	853	7.4

Note: In CPS data, unmarried college students living in dormitories are counted as living in their parent(s) home.

SOURCE: Adapted from "Table AD-1. Young Adults Living at Home: 1960 to Present," in *Families and Living Arrangements*, U.S. Census Bureau, July 2008, http://www.census.gov/population/www/socdemo/hh-fam.html (accessed September 15, 2008)

Even if they do not settle into careers immediately, most young adults living at home work for wages. Those young people who lived away from home and then moved back were more likely to pay rent or make some financial contribution to the household than those who never lived on their own, even if they were employed.

HOW LONG DO THEY STAY? Young men are more likely than young women to stay with their parents indefinitely. This may be because young men typically lose less of their autonomy when they return home than young women do. Young women report they have more responsibility to help around the house and more rules to obey than do their young male counterparts.

CHAPTER 2
CHILDREN, TEENS, AND MONEY

FAMILY INCOME

Almost all children are financially dependent on their parents, with their financial condition directly dependent on how much their parents earn. Carmen DeNavas-Walt, Bernadette D. Proctor, and Jessica C. Smith of the U.S. Census Bureau report in *Income, Poverty, and Health Insurance Coverage in the United States: 2007* (August 2008, http://www.census.gov/prod/2008pubs/p60-235.pdf) that real income rose throughout the 1990s and then declined in the early twenty-first century. The median (half were higher and half were lower) household income in 2007 was $50,233, up 1.3% from the previous year. (See Table 2.1.) For married-couple families, the median household income was $72,785, up 1.5% from the previous year.

DeNavas-Walt, Proctor, and Smith find that single-parent families, particularly those headed by single mothers, fared worse than other households in 2007. Families with female heads-of-household and no husband present had a median income of $33,370, up 2% from the previous year, whereas male-headed households with no wife present had a median income of $49,839, 2.9% higher than the year before. (See Table 2.1.)

According to DeNavas-Walt, Proctor, and Smith, the median income varied greatly by race and ethnic group. Asian-American households had the highest median income, at $66,103, followed by non-Hispanic white households at $54,920. (See Table 2.1.) The median income for Hispanic households was $38,679, and the median income for African-American households, at $33,916, was the lowest of any reported race or ethnic group, even though it had risen 3.2% over the previous year, the largest increase of any group.

The Cost of Raising a Child

Since the 1960s the Family Economics Research Group of the U.S. Department of Agriculture (USDA) has provided estimates on the cost of rearing a child to adulthood. The estimates are calculated per child in a household with two children and are categorized by the age of the child using different family income levels. Attorneys and judges use these estimates in determining child-support awards in divorce cases as well as in cases involving the wrongful death of a parent. Public officials use the estimates to determine payments for the support of children in foster care and for subsidies to adoptive families. Financial planners and consumer educators use them in helping people determine their life insurance needs.

INCOME LEVELS. Estimated annual family expenditures for a child vary widely depending on the income level of the household. The estimated amount a family spends on a child also tends to increase as the child ages. The USDA estimates that in 2007 married-couple households that earned less than $45,800 per year spent amounts ranging from $7,830 for very young children to $8,830 for 12- to 14-year-olds. (See Table 2.2.) Estimates for middle-income, married-couple families ranged from $10,930 for 9- to 11-year-olds to $12,030 for 15- to 17-year-olds. Estimates for married-couple families with incomes above $77,100 ranged from $15,980 to $17,500, depending on the age of the child.

Estimated annual expenditures for single-parent families that earned less than $45,800 per year spent slightly less than those of two-parent families, most likely because their average incomes were lower ($19,700 for single-parent families and $28,600 for two-parent families). (See Table 2.3 and Table 2.2.) The USDA estimates that in 2007 these single parents spent an annual average of $6,490 to $8,960, depending on the age of the child. Single-parent families that earned $45,800 or more spent $14,940 to $17,760 per child, slightly more than the middle-income, two-parent families.

Even though the USDA estimates that in 2007 the highest-income households spent about twice the amount on their children than the lowest-income households, this difference varied by the type of expense. For example, the estimated food expenditure for children aged 15 to 17 in the

TABLE 2.1

Median income by type of household and race and Hispanic origin of householder, 2006–07

[Income in 2007 dollars. Households and people as of March of the following year.]

| | 2006 | | 2007 | | Percentage change in real median income (2007 less 2006) |
| | Number (thousands) | Median income (dollars) Estimate | Number (thousands) | Median income (dollars) Estimate | Estimate |
Characteristic					
Households	116,011	49,568	116,783	50,233	1.3
All households					
Type of household					
Family households	78,425	61,593	77,873	62,359	1.2
Married-couple	58,945	71,694	58,370	72,785	1.5
Female householder, no husband present	14,416	32,721	14,404	33,370	2
Male householder, no wife present	5,063	48,414	5,100	49,839	2.9
Nonfamily households	37,587	29,908	38,910	30,176	0.9
Female householder	20,249	24,553	21,038	24,294	−1.1
Male householder	17,338	36,624	17,872	36,767	0.4
Race* and Hispanic origin of householder					
White	94,705	52,111	95,112	52,115	—
White, not Hispanic	82,675	53,910	82,765	54,920	1.9
Black	14,354	32,876	14,551	33,916	3.2
Asian	4,454	66,060	4,494	66,103	0.1
Hispanic (any race)	12,973	38,853	13,339	38,679	−0.4

—Represents or rounds to zero.

*Federal surveys now give respondents the option of reporting more than one race. Therefore, two basic ways of defining a race group are possible. A group such as Asian may be defined as those who reported Asian and no other race (the race-alone or single-race concept) or as those who reported Asian regardless of whether they also reported another race (the race-alone-or-in-combination concept). This table shows data using the first approach (race alone). The use of the single-race population does not imply that it is the preferred method of presenting or analyzing data. The Census Bureau uses a variety of approaches.

About 2.6 percent of people reported more than one race in Census 2000. Data for American Indians and Alaska Natives, Native Hawaiians and other Pacific Islanders, and those reporting two or more races are not shown separately in this table.

SOURCE: Adapted from Carmen DeNavas-Walt, Bernadette D. Proctor, and Jessica C. Smith, "Table 1. Income and Earnings Summary Measures by Selected Characteristics: 2006 and 2007," in *Income, Poverty, and Health Insurance Coverage in the United States: 2007*, U.S. Census Bureau, August 2008, http://www.census.gov/prod/2008pubs/p60–235.pdf (accessed September 21, 2008).

---

highest-income husband-wife families was $2,970, compared to $2,080 in the lowest-income group. (See Table 2.2.) The estimated annual expense for education and child care for children aged 15 to 17 in these high-income families ($2,120) was nearly four times that for a child the same age in the lowest-income families ($580). These variations among income groups by type of expense held true for single-parent households as well. (See Table 2.3.)

AGE OF CHILD. The 2007 estimates of family expenditures on a child generally increased with the child's age, except for housing, education, and child care. (See Table 2.2 and Table 2.3.) Households with young children are more likely to have recently purchased homes at higher prices and with higher interest rates, which helps explain the higher housing estimates for young children. Estimates for education, child care, and related expenses were also highest for preschoolers (under the age of six) in all income groups. Many women with children this age are in the labor force and must pay for child care. Once children enter school, the child care costs decrease. As school-age children grow up, the need for after-school and summer care also decreases. The estimates do not include expenses related to college attendance, which typically do not occur until the child is at least 18.

FUTURE COSTS. The USDA also estimates the total cost of raising a child born in 2007 who will reach the age of seventeen in 2024, incorporating an average annual inflation rate of 3.1% (the average annual inflation rate over the previous twenty years). The total family expenses for raising a child born in 2007 were estimated to be $196,010 for the lowest-income group, $269,040 for the middle-income group, and $393,230 for the highest-income group. (See Table 2.4.)

CHILDREN IN POVERTY

Children are the largest group of poor in the United States. In 1975 they replaced the elderly as the poorest age group. (See Figure 2.1.) DeNavas-Walt, Proctor, and Smith state that in 2007 the poverty rate for all children younger than 18 years of age was 18%, or 13.3 million children, which was up from 17.4%, or 12.8 million children, in 2006. Children under 18 years old made up a quarter (24.8%) of the population of the United States, but they made up over one-third (35.7%) of the people living below the poverty line. (For population estimates for July 1, 2007, by age, see the Census Bureau's *National Population Estimates— Characteristics* [April 30, 2008, http://www.census.gov/popest/national/asrh/NC-EST2007-sa.html].) Children under the age of six are particularly vulnerable to poverty. Accord-

TABLE 2.2

Estimated annual expenditures on a child by husband-wife families, 2007

Age of child	Total	Housing	Food	Transportation	Clothing	Health care	Child care and education	Miscellaneous*
Before-tax income: less than $45,800 (average = $28,600)								
0–2	$7,830	$2,970	$1,070	$930	$340	$600	$1,220	$700
3–5	8,020	2,930	1,190	900	340	570	1,370	720
6–8	8,000	2,830	1,530	1,050	370	650	810	760
9–11	7,950	2,560	1,830	1,140	420	710	490	800
12–14	8,830	2,850	1,930	1,290	700	720	340	1,000
15–17	8,810	2,300	2,080	1,730	620	770	580	730
Total	**$148,320**	**$49,320**	**$28,890**	**$21,120**	**$8,370**	**$12,060**	**$14,430**	**$14,130**
Before-tax income: $45,800 to $77,100 (average = $61,000)								
0–2	$10,960	$4,010	$1,280	$1,390	$410	$780	$2,000	$1,090
3–5	11,280	3,980	1,470	1,360	400	750	2,210	1,110
6–8	11,130	3,880	1,880	1,510	440	850	1,420	1,150
9–11	10,930	3,600	2,210	1,600	480	920	930	1,190
12–14	11,690	3,900	2,230	1,740	820	930	680	1,390
15–17	12,030	3,350	2,480	2,200	730	980	1,170	1,120
Total	**$204,060**	**$68,160**	**$34,650**	**$29,400**	**$9,840**	**$15,630**	**$25,230**	**$21,150**
Before-tax income: more than $77,100 (average = $115,400)								
0–2	$16,290	$6,380	$1,690	$1,950	$530	$900	$3,020	$1,820
3–5	16,670	6,340	1,910	1,910	520	860	3,290	1,840
6–8	16,310	6,240	2,310	2,060	570	990	2,260	1,880
9–11	15,980	5,970	2,680	2,150	620	1,060	1,580	1,920
12–14	16,810	6,260	2,820	2,300	1,030	1,070	1,210	2,120
15–17	17,500	5,710	2,970	2,780	940	1,120	2,120	1,860
Total	**$298,680**	**$110,700**	**$43,140**	**$39,450**	**$12,630**	**$18,000**	**$40,440**	**$34,320**

Notes: Estimates are based on 1990–92 Consumer Expenditure Survey data updated to 2007 dollars using the Consumer Price Index. For each age category, the expense estimates represent average child-rearing expenditures for each age (e.g., the expense for the 3–5 age category, on average, applies to the 3-year-old, the 4-year-old, or the 5-year-old). The figures represent estimated expenses on the younger child in a two-child family. Estimates are about the same for the older child, so to calculate expenses for two children, figures should be summed for the appropriate age categories. To estimate expenses for an only child, multiply the total expense for the appropriate age category by 1.24. To estimate expenses for each child in a family with three or more children, multiply the total expense for each appropriate age category by 0.77. For expenses on all children in a family, these totals should be summed.

*Miscellaneous expenses include personal care items, entertainment, and reading materials.

SOURCE: Mark Lino, "Table ES1. Estimated Annual Expenditures on a Child by Husband-Wife Families, Overall United States, 2007," in *Expenditures on Children by Families, 2007*, U.S. Department of Agriculture, Center for Nutrition Policy and Promotion, March 2008, http://www.cnpp.usda.gov/Publications/CRC/crc2007.pdf (accessed November 2, 2008)

ing to DeNavas-Walt, Proctor, and Smith, in 2007 the poverty rate for families with children under the age of six was 20.8%, which was higher than the overall rate of child poverty. In addition, over half (54%) of children younger than the age of six living with a single mother were in poverty, which was more than five times the rate of poverty for children younger than the age of six living in married-couple families (9.5%).

The child poverty rate declined between 1995 and 2000, but the rate of children living in poverty (100% of the poverty line or below) and in low-income families (100% to 200% of the poverty line) began to rise again in 2000. By 2007, 39.1% of children lived in low-income or poor families. (See Figure 2.2.) In *Basic Facts about Low-Income Children: Birth to Age 18* (October 2008, http://www.nccp.org/publications/pdf/text_845.pdf), Ayana Douglas-Hall and Michelle Chau of the National Center for Children in Poverty note that even though the largest group of low-income children in 2007 were white (38%), Hispanic and African-American children were disproportionately poor. (See Figure 2.3.) The majority of both African-American children (60%) and Hispanic children (61%) lived in low-income or poor families. Preschoolers

were particularly likely to live in low-income families (43%), including poor families (21%). (See Figure 2.4.) Another trend in child poverty emerged in the twenty-first century. The Children's Defense Fund notes in *The State of America's Children 2005* (2005, http://www.childrensdefense.org/site/DocServer/Greenbook_2005.pdf?docID=1741) that the number of children living in extreme poverty (below one-half of the poverty level) increased by 20% between 2000 and 2004, almost twice as fast as the number of children in poverty overall. According to Kathy R. Thornburg, Jacqueline L. Scott, and Hailey Stout of the Center for Family Policy and Research, in "The State of Children and Families: 2008" (February 2008, http://mucenter.missouri.edu/MOchildfam08.pdf), approximately 5.5 million children lived in extreme poverty in 2006.

Government Aid to Children

Many programs exist in the United States to assist families and children living with economic hardship. Some of these programs are federally run, and others are run at the state level. In many cases the programs are mandated at the federal level and administered by the states, which can make tracking them complicated.

TABLE 2.3

Estimated annual expenditures on a child by single-parent families, 2007

Age of child	Total	Housing	Food	Transportation	Clothing	Health care	Child care and education	Miscellaneous*
Before-tax income: less than $45,800 (average = $19,200)								
0–2	$6,490	$2,660	$1,180	$870	$310	$290	$760	$420
3–5	7,380	3,030	1,240	760	330	420	1,040	560
6–8	8,260	3,220	1,570	890	390	500	940	750
9–11	7,620	3,090	1,820	640	390	630	450	600
12–14	8,130	3,090	1,820	740	660	670	570	580
15–17	8,960	3,280	1,980	1,160	770	660	440	670
Total	**$140,520**	**$55,110**	**$28,830**	**$15,180**	**$8,550**	**$9,510**	**$12,600**	**$10,740**
Before-tax income: $45,800 or more (average = $69,600)								
0–2	$14,940	$5,730	$1,820	$2,660	$440	$660	$1,870	$1,760
3–5	16,140	6,090	1,930	2,550	460	880	2,340	1,890
6–8	17,100	6,280	2,320	2,680	530	1,010	2,190	2,090
9–11	16,360	6,160	2,790	2,430	540	1,220	1,280	1,940
12–14	17,320	6,160	2,730	2,530	890	1,280	1,820	1,910
15–17	17,760	6,350	2,890	2,740	1,020	1,270	1,480	2,010
Total	**$298,860**	**$110,310**	**$43,440**	**$46,770**	**$11,640**	**$18,960**	**$32,940**	**$34,800**

Notes: Estimates are based on 1990–92 Consumer Expenditure Survey data updated to 2007 dollars using the Consumer Price Index. For each age category, the expense estimates represent average child-rearing expenditures for each age (e.g., the expense for the 3–5 age category, on average, applies to the 3-year-old, the 4-year-old, or the 5-year-old). The figures represent estimated expenses on the younger child in a single-parent, two-child family. For estimated expenses on the older child, multiply the total expense for the appropriate age category by 0.93. To estimate expenses for two children, the expenses on the younger child and older child after adjusting the expense on the older child downward should be summed for the appropriate age categories. To estimate expenses for an only child, multiply the total expense for the appropriate age category by 1.35. To estimate expenses for each child in a family with three or more children, multiply the total expense for each appropriate age category by 0.72 after adjusting the expenses on the older children downward. For expenses on all children in a family, these totals should be summed.
*Miscellaneous expenses include personal care items, entertainment, and reading materials.

SOURCE: Mark Lino, "Table 7. Estimated Annual Expenditures on a Child by Single-Parent Families, Overall United States, 2007," in *Expenditures on Children by Families, 2007*, U.S. Department of Agriculture, Center for Nutrition Policy and Promotion, March 2008, http://www.cnpp.usda.gov/Publications/CRC \crc2007.pdf (accessed November 2, 2008)

TABLE 2.4

Estimated annual expenditures on children born in 2007, by income group

Year	Age	Income group Lowest	Income group Middle	Income group Highest
2007	<1	$7,830	$10,960	$16,290
2008	1	8,070	11,300	16,790
2009	2	8,320	11,650	17,320
2010	3	8,790	12,360	18,270
2011	4	9,060	12,750	18,840
2012	5	9,340	13,140	19,420
2013	6	9,610	13,370	19,590
2014	7	9,910	13,780	20,200
2015	8	10,210	14,210	20,820
2016	9	10,460	14,390	21,030
2017	10	10,790	14,830	21,690
2018	11	11,120	15,290	22,360
2019	12	12,740	16,860	24,250
2020	13	13,130	17,390	25,000
2021	14	13,540	17,920	25,770
2022	15	13,930	19,020	27,660
2023	16	14,360	19,610	28,520
2024	17	14,800	20,210	29,410
Total		**$196,010**	**$269,040**	**$393,230**

Note: Estimates are for the younger child in husband-wife families with two children.

SOURCE: Mark Lino, "Table 12. Estimated Annual Expenditures on Children Born in 2007, by Income Group, Overall United States," in *Expenditures on Children by Families, 2007*, U.S. Department of Agriculture, Center for Nutrition Policy and Promotion, March 2008, http://www.cnpp.usda.gov/Publications/ CRC/crc2007.pdf (accessed November 2, 2008)

TEMPORARY ASSISTANCE FOR NEEDY FAMILIES. Under the Temporary Assistance for Needy Families (TANF) program, states receive a fixed amount from the federal government to provide "welfare" to residents with few federal constraints on how they manage the funds. The Administration for Children and Families (ACF) of the U.S. Depart-

FIGURE 2.1

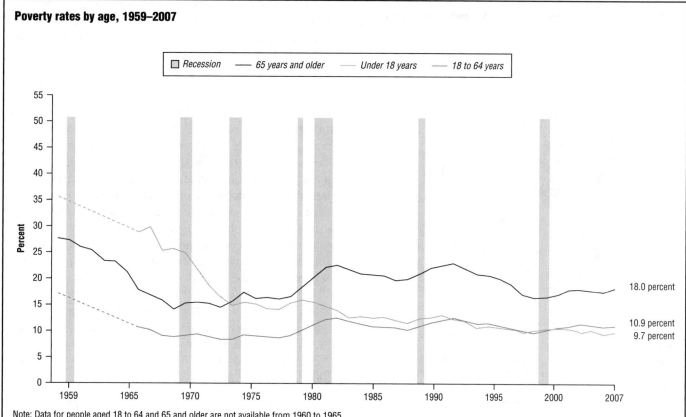

Poverty rates by age, 1959–2007

Legend: ☐ Recession — 65 years and older — Under 18 years — 18 to 64 years

Percent (y-axis: 0 to 55)

Years (x-axis): 1959, 1965, 1970, 1975, 1980, 1985, 1990, 1995, 2000, 2007

18.0 percent
10.9 percent
9.7 percent

Note: Data for people aged 18 to 64 and 65 and older are not available from 1960 to 1965.

SOURCE: Carmen DeNavas-Walt, Bernadette D. Proctor, and Jessica C. Smith, "Figure 4. Poverty Rates by Age: 1959 to 2007," in *Income, Poverty, and Health Insurance Coverage in the United States: 2007*, U.S. Census Bureau, August 2008, http://www.census.gov/prod/2008pubs/p60–235.pdf (accessed November 2, 2008)

FIGURE 2.2

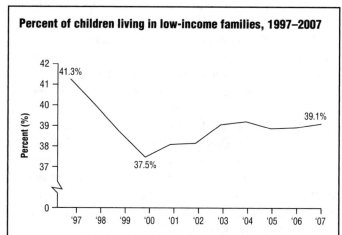

Percent of children living in low-income families, 1997–2007

Percent (%) (y-axis)

41.3%

37.5%

39.1%

Years (x-axis): '97, '98, '99, '00, '01, '02, '03, '04, '05, '06, '07

SOURCE: Ayana Douglas-Hall and Michelle Chau, "Children Living in Low-Income Families, 1997–2007," in *Basic Facts about Low-Income Children: Birth to Age 18*, National Center for Children in Poverty, Columbia University, Mailman School of Public Health, October 2008, http://www.nccp.org/publications/pdf/text_845.pdf (accessed November 2, 2008)

ment of Health and Human Services (January 8, 2009, http://www.acf.hhs.gov/programs/ofs/data/2006/tableA_spending_2006.html) indicates that the total federal funds spent on TANF expenditures for fiscal year (FY) 2006 were $20.5 billion.

Under TANF each state decides what categories of children receive aid. TANF requires that an adult recipient work in exchange for time-limited assistance. In *Temporary Assistance for Needy Families Program (TANF): Seventh Annual Report to Congress* (December 2006, http://www.acf.hhs.gov/programs/ofa/data-reports/annualreport7/TANF_7th_Report_Final_101006.pdf), the ACF notes that in FY 2003, the latest year for which detailed data are available, 22.9% of adult TANF recipients were employed, down from 25.3% the year before.

The size of families receiving public assistance was decreasing in 2003. According to the ACF, the average number of people in a TANF family was 2.5 in 2003, down from an average of 2.8 in 1996. Half of TANF families in 2003 included only one child recipient, whereas only 10% had four or more children. More than one-third (38.6%) of TANF families were child-only cases, including no adult recipients.

The amount of government assistance provided to individuals and families was down sharply in the first years of the twenty-first century. The average monthly benefit per

FIGURE 2.3

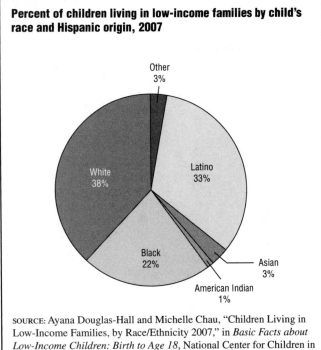

Percent of children living in low-income families by child's race and Hispanic origin, 2007

Other
3%

White
38%

Latino
33%

Black
22%

Asian
3%

American Indian
1%

SOURCE: Ayana Douglas-Hall and Michelle Chau, "Children Living in Low-Income Families, by Race/Ethnicity 2007," in *Basic Facts about Low-Income Children: Birth to Age 18*, National Center for Children in Poverty, Columbia University, Mailman School of Public Health, October 2008, http://www.nccp.org/publications/pdf/text_845.pdf (accessed November 2, 2008)

TANF recipient in 2005 was $157, down from a high of $228 (in 2005 dollars) in 1978 under the old Aid to Families with Dependent Children program. (See Figure 2.5.) Benefits included cash and work-based assistance, child care, and transportation assistance. In addition, the number of families receiving income assistance continued to decline in 2006. (See Figure 2.6.) In response to the economic recession that began in 2008, Congress allocated additional contingency funds of $5 billion to help states that see increases in families needing TANF assistance. Liz Schott of the Center on Budget and Policy Priorities explains in "An Introduction to TANF" (March 19, 2009, http://www.cbpp.org/cms/index.cfm?fa=view&id=936) that when TANF comes up for reauthorization in 2010, Congress will likely examine the extent to which TANF assistance programs responded to increased need during the recession and have questions about how well the program prepares families to overcome employment barriers.

Reductions in welfare rolls and expenditures may actually harm poor children. Olivia Golden (1955–), the assistant secretary for children and families in the U.S. Department of Health and Human Services under President Bill Clinton (1946–), states in "Welfare Reform Mostly Worked" (*Orlando Sentinel*, July 24, 2005) that she believes the welfare-to-work model "mostly worked" in the sense that welfare caseloads had dropped and that most low-income parents began working to support their families. However, this very success brought about additional prob-

lems. She notes, "In less than a decade, welfare has faded as a means of support for impoverished families. Many of these families are working long hours despite low wages, shrinking health-insurance coverage and serious trade-offs between work and decent care for their children. Yet, neither our politics nor our policies have adjusted to our success at bringing more of these parents into the labor force."

THE SUPPLEMENTAL NUTRITION ASSISTANCE PROGRAM. The Supplemental Nutrition Assistance Program, known previously as the food stamp program, which is administered by the USDA, provides low-income households with electronic benefit cards that can be used at most grocery stores, much like debit cards, in place of cash. This assistance is intended to ensure that recipients have access to a nutritious diet. It is available to households that have a gross monthly income of no more than 130% of the poverty line and a net monthly income at or below the poverty line. According to the USDA's Food and Nutrition Service (FNS), in *Characteristics of Food Stamp Households: Fiscal Year 2007—Summary* (September 2008, http://www.fns.usda.gov/oane/menu/Published/snap/FILES/Participation/2007CharacteristicsSummary.pdf), almost nine out of ten (87%) households that received food stamp benefits in 2007 lived in poverty.

The amount of money a family receives on its benefit card is based on the USDA's estimate of how much it costs to provide households with nutritious, low-cost meals, called the thrifty food plan. This estimate changes yearly to reflect inflation. In FY 2007 the FNS indicates that the maximum monthly benefit for a family of four was $506. The average monthly benefit for all households in FY 2007 was $212. Supplemental Nutrition Assistance Program households containing children received an average of $312 in benefits per month, in part because households with children tended to be larger (3.3 people) than households in general (2.2 people). (See Table 2.5.) Because funds provided to nutritional assistance programs are extremely likely to be spent, such funds are considered economic stimulus. On February 17, 2009, President Barack Obama (1961–) signed the American Recovery and Reinvestment Act into law in response to the severe economic recession that began in 2008. The legislation provided an additional $500 million to support participation in the State Nutrition Action Plan and to increase benefits up to 113.6% of the value of the thrifty food plan.

According to Kari Wolkwitz and Joshua Leftin, in *Characteristics of Food Stamp Households: Fiscal Year 2007* (September 2008, http://www.fns.usda.gov/oane/menu/Published/snap/FILES/Participation/2007Characteristics.pdf), the majority of households that received supplemental nutrition assistance in FY 2007 contained children—51.3%, or 5.9 million households. One-third (32.1%) of all Supplemental Nutrition Assistance Program households were single-parent households, most of them headed by single mothers.

FIGURE 2.4

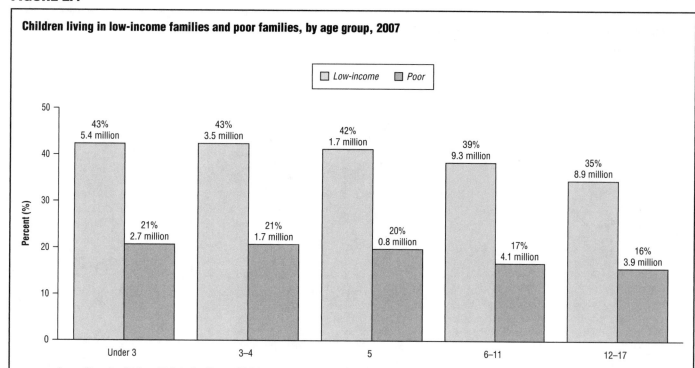

Children living in low-income families and poor families, by age group, 2007

SOURCE: Ayana Douglas-Hall and Michelle Chau, "Children Living in Low-Income Families and Poor Families, by Age Group, 2007," in *Basic Facts about Low-Income Children: Birth to Age 18*, National Center for Children in Poverty, Columbia University, Mailman School of Public Health, October 2008, http://www.nccp.org/publications/pdf/text_845.pdf (accessed November 2, 2008)

THE SPECIAL SUPPLEMENTAL NUTRITION PROGRAM FOR WOMEN, INFANTS, AND CHILDREN. The Special Supplemental Nutrition Program for Women, Infants, and Children (WIC) provides food assistance and nutritional screening for low-income pregnant and postpartum women and their infants and children under the age of five. This program can help women and young children with household incomes that are too high to receive food stamps. In "Frequently Asked Questions about WIC" (October 2008, http://www.fns.usda.gov/wic/FAQs/FAQ.HTM), the FNS explains that income eligibility guidelines for the period July 1, 2007, to June 30, 2008, required applicants to have an income at or below 185% of the poverty level and be nutritionally "at risk," meaning that to be eligible an individual must have medically or diet-based risks. The income eligibility guidelines state that a family of one (in other words, a single, pregnant woman) could earn up to $1,604 per month and still qualify for WIC. A family of four could earn $3,269 per month and participate in WIC. The FNS states in *WIC Participant and Program Characteristics, 2006 Summary* (December 2007, http://www.fns.usda.gov/oane/menu/Published/WIC/FILES/PC2006Summary.pdf) that two-thirds (67.4%) of WIC participants in 2006 had household incomes below the poverty line.

According to the FNS, in April 2006 nearly 8.8 million women and children participated in WIC, an increase of 2.2% since April 2004. Twenty-six percent of WIC participants were infants, 49% were children aged one to four years old, and 25% were pregnant, postpartum, or breast-

feeding women. Recipients receive food items or vouchers for purchases of certain items in retail stores. The WIC program is federally funded but administered by state and local health agencies. In "WIC Program Participation and Costs" (December 30, 2008, http://www.fns.usda.gov/pd/wisummary.htm), the FNS states that in FY 2008 the WIC program's estimated food cost was $4.5 billion and its estimated administrative costs were $1.6 billion, for a total cost of $6.2 billion.

SCHOOL NUTRITION PROGRAMS. School nutrition programs offer food assistance to school-age children. The programs provide millions of children with nutritious food each day. Children whose families earn no more than 185% of the poverty level are eligible for reduced-price school meals; children whose families earn no more than 130% of the poverty level are eligible for free school meals. The FNS reports in "Federal Cost of School Food Programs" (December 30, 2008, http://www.fns.usda.gov/pd/cncosts.htm) that in FY 2007 the U.S. government spent $10.9 billion on school nutrition programs, including the National School Lunch Program, the School Breakfast Program, and the Special Milk Program. In that year 30.5 million children took part in the school lunch program. (See Table 2.6.)

CHILD SUPPORT

Children living in single-parent families are far more likely to be poor than children living in two-parent households, and the number of children living with only one

FIGURE 2.5

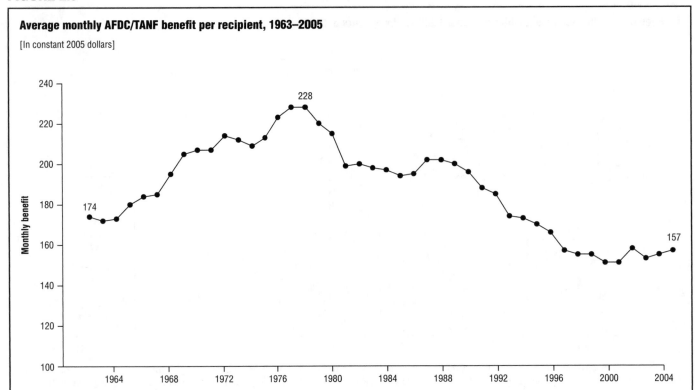

Average monthly AFDC/TANF benefit per recipient, 1963–2005

[In constant 2005 dollars]

Notes: Comparison of trends in the average monthly AFDC/TANF benefit per recipient in current and constant 2005 dollars with the weighted average maximum benefit in current and constant 2005 dollars since 1988 indicates that the primary cause of the decline in the average monthly benefit has been the erosion of the real value of the maximum benefit due to inflation. The current value of the maximum benefits has not shown much increase in most states.

SOURCE: Gil Crouse, Sarah Douglas, and Susan Hauan, "Figure TANF2. Average Monthly AFDC/TANF Benefit per Recipient in Constant 2005 Dollars," in *Indicators of Welfare Dependence, Annual Report to Congress, 2007*, U.S. Department of Health and Human Services, 2007, http://aspe.hhs.gov/hsp/indicators07/apa.pdf (accessed November 2, 2008).

parent—usually the mother—is increasing. According to Timothy S. Grall of the Census Bureau, in *Custodial Mothers and Fathers and Their Child Support: 2005* (August 2007, http://www.census.gov/prod/2007pubs/p60-234.pdf), in the spring of 2006, 13.6 million parents had custody of 21.2 million children under the age of 21 whose other parent lived elsewhere. Mothers accounted for 83.8% of all custodial parents; 16.2% of custodial parents were fathers. These proportions have not changed significantly since 1994.

Grall indicates that 7.8 million (57.3%) of the 13.6 million custodial parents in 2006 had a child support agreement with the other parent. Most of these agreements required child support payments from the noncustodial parent. In 2005, 77.2% of custodial parents due support received at least some payments. (See Figure 2.7.) Almost half (46.9%) received all the payments they were due, up from only a little more than a third (36.9%) in 1993. Grall also notes that noncustodial parents who had either joint custody agreements or visitation rights to their children were more likely to pay child support (84.6% and 77.6%, respectively) than parents who did not have any visitation rights at all (61.5%).

Differences existed in the child support arrangements for custodial mothers and custodial fathers. In 2005 cus-

todial mothers were much more likely than custodial fathers to be awarded child support (61.4% and 36.4%, respectively). (See Table 2.7.) On average, custodial mothers were due $5,660 in child support in 2005, and received $3,660. Custodial fathers were due, on average, $4,895 and actually received $3,491. As noted earlier, fewer than half of all custodial parents actually received the full child support due them; only 47.3% of custodial mothers and 46.2% of custodial fathers received the total amount due.

Grall explains that receipt of child support payments made a significant difference in the household incomes of single-parent families. In 2005 the average family income of custodial parents who received at least some of the child support due them was $29,500, and the child support represented 10.7% of the total household income. Child support represented 18.8% of the total household income for those parents who received all of the child support due them. In contrast, custodial parents who had child support agreements but received none of the child support due had an average income of only $26,000.

Government Assistance in Obtaining Child Support

As demonstrated earlier, inadequate financial support from noncustodial parents contributes to the high inci-

FIGURE 2.6

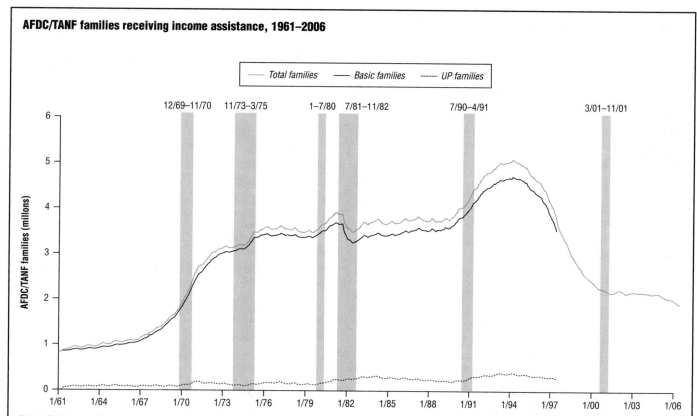

AFDC/TANF families receiving income assistance, 1961–2006

Notes: "Basic families" are single-parent families and "UP families" are two-parent cases receiving benefits under AFDC Unemployed Parent programs that operated in certain states before FY 1991 and in all states after October 1, 1990. The AFDC Basic and UP programs were replaced by TANF as of July 1, 1997 under the Personal Responsibility and Work Opportunity Reconciliation Act of 1996. Shaded areas indicate NBER designated periods of recession from peak to trough. The decrease in number of families receiving assistance during the 1981–82 recession stems from changes ineligibility requirements and other policy changes mandated by OBRA 1981. Beginning in 2000, "Total families" includes TANF and SSP families. Last data point plotted is June 2006.

SOURCE: Gil Crouse, Sarah Douglas, and Susan Hauan, "Figure TANF1. AFDC/TANF Families Receiving Income Assistance," in *Indicators of Welfare Dependence, Annual Report to Congress, 2007*, U.S. Department of Health and Human Services, 2007, http://aspe.hhs.gov/hsp/indicators07/apa.pdf (accessed November 2, 2008)

dence of poverty among children living in single-parent families. When custodial parents are not paid the child support due them, their families suffer financially and often must turn to public welfare. Therefore, government agencies have an interest in recovering child support from delinquent parents.

In 1975 Congress established the Child Support Enforcement (CSE) Program, a collaborative effort among local, state, and federal agencies, to ensure that children received financial support from both parents. Under the Child Support Recovery Act of 1992, noncustodial parents delinquent on child support due in another state can be prosecuted. CSE services are automatically provided to families receiving assistance under TANF; any support collected usually reimburses the state and federal governments for TANF payments made to the family. Child support services are also available for a small application fee to families not receiving TANF.

Provisions in the Personal Responsibility and Work Opportunity Reconciliation Act of 1996 strengthened and improved child support collection activities. The law estab-

lished a National Directory of New Hires to track parents across state lines, made the process for establishing paternity faster and easier, and enacted tough new penalties for delinquent parents, including expanded wage garnishment and suspension or revocation of driver's licenses. The law also required single-mother TANF applicants to disclose the paternity of their children and to assign any child support payments to the state. According to the ACF, in *Child Support Enforcement FY 2006 Preliminary Report* (March 2007, http://www.acf.hhs.gov/programs/cse/pubs/2007/preliminary_report/), these efforts have paid off; in FY 2006 CSE handled 15.8 million cases and collected nearly $24 billion.

TEENS AND MONEY

Teen Employment

The Bureau of Labor Statistics (BLS) reports in the press release "The Employment Situation: November 2008" (December 5, 2008, http://www.bls.gov/news.release/pdf/empsit.pdf) that in November 2008, 6.5 million (38.3%) people aged 16 to 19 were employed or looking for work.

TABLE 2.5

Income, monthly food stamp benefits, and household size by household composition, fiscal year 2007

Households with:	Average values				
	Gross monthly countable income (dollars)	Net monthly countable income (dollars)[a]	Monthly FSP benefit (dollars)	Household size (persons)	Monthly FSP benefit per person (dollars)
Total	691	330	212	2.2	97
Children	826	415	312	3.3	99
Single-adult household	736	361	303	3.1	100
Male adult	688	343	274	2.8	101
Female adult	739	362	305	3.1	100
Multiple-adult household	1,154	645	362	4.4	85
Married head household	1,214	677	365	4.5	83
Other multiple-adult household	1,046	590	355	4.1	88
Children only	551	168	244	2.1	123
Elderly individuals	735	367	90	1.3	71
Living alone	676	310	72	1.0	72
Not living alone	975	569	163	2.4	68
Disabled nonelderly individuals[b]	859	456	148	2.0	75
Living alone	695	297	76	1.0	76
Not living alone	1,080	655	244	3.3	74
Other households[c]	222	68	150	1.1	139
Single-person household	188	52	142	1.0	142
Multi-person household	588	247	227	2.1	108
Single-person households	504	202	100	1.0	100

[a]Because net income is not used in their benefit determination, 29,916 households participating in the Minnesota Family Investment Program (MFIP) and 321,492 households participating in an SSI Combined Application Project (SSI-CAP) in Kentucky, Louisiana, Mississippi, New York, North Carolina, Pennsylvania, South Carolina, Texas or Virginia are excluded from this column.
[b]Due to changes in the FSPQC data, the definition of disabled changed in 2003. Beginning with the 2003 report, we are only able to identify households that contain a disabled person. In previous reports, we had additional information that helped to identify which household member was disabled.
[c]Households not containing children, elderly individuals, or disabled individuals.

SOURCE: Kari Wolkwitz and Joshua Leftin, "Table 3.4. Average Values of Selected Characteristics by Household Composition, Fiscal Year 2007," in *Characteristics of Food Stamp Households: Fiscal Year 2007*, Mathematica Policy Research, Inc., September 2008, http://www.mathematica-mpr.com/publications/pdfs/characteristics2007.pdf (accessed November 2, 2008)

The unemployment rate in this age group was 20.4%, up from 16.4% from the year before. Job loss continued to be heavy in early 2009 due to the global financial crisis. In the press release "The Employment Situation: February 2009" (March 6, 2009, http://www.bls.gov/news.release/pdf/empsit.pdf), the BLS indicates that by February 2009 the rate of unemployment among teenagers had increased to 21.6%; the overall rate for all workers was 8.1%. Employment rates among young people are highest during the summer months, when many full-time students are out of school. For example, in the press release "Employment and Unemployment among Youth—Summer 2008" (August 28, 2008, http://www.bls.gov/news.release/pdf/youth.pdf), the BLS states that the employment of youth between the ages of 16 and 24 increased by 1.9 million between April and July 2008.

Most teens are employed as hourly workers, and they make low wages compared to other age groups. The BLS reports in *Characteristics of Minimum Wage Workers: 2007* (May 7, 2008, http://www.bls.gov/cps/minwage2007tbls.htm) that in 2007, 6.9% of 16- to 19-year-olds earned the federal minimum hourly wage ($5.15 before July 24, 2007, and $5.85 thereafter), compared to only 1.5% of workers aged 25 years and older.

HOW DOES WORKING AFFECT ACADEMIC ACHIEVEMENT? In "Employment during High School and Student Achievement" (*Journal of Educational Research*, vol. 95, no. 1, 2001), Kimberly J. Quirk, Timothy Z. Keith, and Jeffrey T. Quirk present the results of a longitudinal study examining the effects of high school student employment on academic achievement. The researchers conclude that "working displayed a moderate, significant, and negative effect on high school grades." However, smaller amounts of work (12 hours or less per week) seemed to slightly improve grades. Quirk, Keith, and Quirk also find that the lower a student's grades were, the more likely he or she was to get a job. Nancy F. Weller et al. note in "School-Year Employment among High School Students: Effects on Academic, Social, and Physical Functioning" (*Adolescence*, vol. 38, no. 151, 2003) that students who worked longer hours had lower grade-point averages. The researchers state that "in light of our findings and those of other studies, we believe that parents and professionals involved with youth should supervise the number of weekly hours that adolescents work while attending school."

TABLE 2.6

National School Lunch Program, total participation, 2003–07

State/territory	FY 2003	FY 2004	FY 2005	FY 2006	FY 2007 Preliminary
Alabama	549,241	558,455	565,932	574,060	577,931
Alaska	52,962	52,069	52,091	53,363	53,233
Arizona	517,837	545,033	579,435	607,905	633,312
Arkansas	317,843	322,753	335,891	345,909	347,752
California	2,732,303	2,798,852	2,866,247	2,896,209	2,988,383
Colorado	327,775	335,266	336,565	347,945	364,749
Connecticut	283,625	291,886	301,773	307,389	316,382
Delaware	75,377	78,045	81,032	83,648	85,672
District of Columbia	47,961	46,536	46,976	45,229	41,501
Florida	1,397,558	1,463,971	1,523,765	1,523,315	1,536,860
Georgia	1,129,503	1,170,116	1,205,372	1,252,790	1,272,122
Guam	17,408	15,951	17,055	20,190	19,052
Hawaii	131,954	123,721	121,189	112,822	101,584
Idaho	148,798	152,570	155,700	161,257	165,308
Illinois	1,097,467	1,079,949	1,104,595	1,104,942	1,121,027
Indiana	663,592	679,283	700,890	723,568	744,055
Iowa	380,864	385,111	385,011	390,385	392,976
Kansas	317,481	323,008	326,805	336,461	344,187
Kentucky	511,470	528,271	534,807	542,971	548,586
Louisiana	626,152	629,519	615,879	571,269	583,224
Maine	103,840	106,064	107,685	109,152	108,738
Maryland	435,790	426,182	438,302	444,058	439,590
Massachusetts	541,767	548,522	558,107	559,612	561,853
Michigan	842,678	858,209	869,217	884,793	896,908
Minnesota	577,644	583,455	590,260	597,113	607,542
Mississippi	395,089	399,474	398,951	404,503	405,056
Missouri	603,434	610,807	624,385	634,351	639,003
Montana	77,464	78,651	79,664	83,073	83,844
Nebraska	222,865	225,506	228,691	232,823	237,410
Nevada	136,856	145,963	172,292	181,940	193,461
New Hampshire	109,815	111,863	113,074	112,654	113,628
New Jersey	604,595	616,759	629,815	638,688	654,779
New Mexico	201,272	208,483	211,792	213,111	221,055
New York	1,788,136	1,803,687	1,823,454	1,820,880	1,821,469
North Carolina	863,716	886,274	915,560	945,601	962,768
North Dakota	77,230	77,924	78,418	78,388	78,909
Ohio	1,028,227	1,046,400	1,060,938	1,085,362	1,100,214
Oklahoma	382,577	389,245	402,917	413,003	421,624
Oregon	275,713	284,467	291,326	301,199	304,241
Pennsylvania	1,057,774	1,086,661	1,121,383	1,136,502	1,141,571
Puerto Rico	392,900	379,940	369,889	362,119	384,531
Rhode Island	82,161	83,188	84,080	83,806	85,009
South Carolina	466,847	473,208	482,820	491,154	496,534
South Dakota	103,592	103,809	103,986	105,036	106,222
Tennessee	635,613	648,215	660,282	685,621	584,437
Texas	2,671,975	2,776,775	2,892,593	3,007,594	3,079,947
Utah	283,627	289,402	297,669	304,678	312,438
Vermont	54,356	54,808	55,363	55,431	55,451
Virginia	687,945	705,401	730,970	745,038	749,911
Virgin Islands	15,450	14,286	13,474	11,064	10,552
Washington	495,468	505,999	513,488	522,978	526,724
West Virginia	204,626	201,002	202,574	207,594	208,846
Wisconsin	561,150	569,642	583,338	591,223	598,369
Wyoming	49,485	49,449	51,187	52,305	53,564
Dept. of Defense	33,489	31,534	31,237	28,866	28,824
Total	28,392,337	28,961,618	29,646,190	30,132,941	30,512,921

Participation data are nine-month averages; summer months (June-August) are excluded.
Participation is based on average daily meals divided by an attendance factor of 0.927.
Department of Defense activity represents children of armed forces personnel attending schools overseas.
Data are subject to revision.
FY = Fiscal Year.

SOURCE: "National School Lunch Program: Total Participation," U.S. Department of Agriculture, Food and Nutrition Service, October 29, 2008, http://www
.fns.usda.gov/pd/01slfypart.htm (accessed November 2, 2008)

The BLS finds in "The Relationship of Youth Employment to Future Educational Attainment and Labor Market Experience" (*Report on the Youth Labor Force*, November 2000) a correlation between teen employment and future college education. Adults who had worked one to 20 hours per week as 16- and 17-year-olds were more likely than other adults to have completed at least some college education by age 30. In contrast, less than half of adults who had not worked at all or who had worked more than 20 hours per week had completed some college education.

FIGURE 2.7

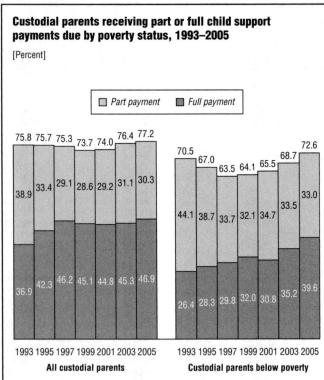

Custodial parents receiving part or full child support payments due by poverty status, 1993–2005

[Percent]

□ *Part payment* ■ *Full payment*

All custodial parents

Year	Part	Full	Total
1993	38.9	36.9	75.8
1995	33.4	42.3	75.7
1997	29.1	46.2	75.3
1999	28.6	45.1	73.7
2001	29.2	44.8	74.0
2003	31.1	45.3	76.4
2005	30.3	46.9	77.2

Custodial parents below poverty

Year	Part	Full	Total
1993	44.1	26.4	70.5
1995	38.7	28.3	67.0
1997	33.7	29.8	63.5
1999	32.1	32.0	64.1
2001	34.7	30.8	65.5
2003	33.5	35.2	68.7
2005	33.0	39.6	72.6

SOURCE: Timothy S. Grall, "Figure 4. Custodial Parents Receiving Part or Full Child Support Payments Due by Poverty Status: 1993–2005," in *Custodial Mothers and Fathers and Their Child Support: 2005*, U.S. Census Bureau, August 2007, http://www.census.gov/prod/2007pubs/p60–234.pdf (accessed November 2, 2008)

These findings suggest that working a limited number of hours during the junior and senior years of high school has a positive effect on educational attainment.

Teens as Consumers

By the last decades of the twentieth century, teens had a big influence on the economy—from affecting major family purchases to buying groceries. In *Spending Power of the Teen Consumer* (September 2006, http://www.marketresearch.com), the Mintel International Group indicates that teens had an estimated spending power of $153 billion in 2006. However, the spending power of teens had declined 12% from 2003 to 2006, probably reflecting the economic downturn of the early twenty-first century. The report also examines teens' spending habits. Even though teens were attracted to the youthful image of retailers such as Abercrombie & Fitch, they actually spent their money in more affordable stores such as Old Navy and Target.

TABLE 2.7

Comparison of custodial parents and those with child support awarded, due, and received, selected years 1993–2005

[Numbers in thousands as of spring of the following year. Parents living with own children under 21 years of age whose other parent is not living in the home. Amounts in 2005 dollars.]

Item	1993 Number	1995 Number	1997 Number	1999 Number	2001 Number	2003 Number	2005 Number
All custodial parents							
Total							
Awarded child support	7,800	7,967	7,876	7,945	7,916	8,376	7,802
Percent	57.0	58.1	56.5	58.7	59.1	60.0	57.3
Due child support	6,688	6,958	7,018	6,791	6,924	7,256	6,809
Average child support due	$4,764	$5,173	$5,031	$5,570	$5,562	$5,416	$5,584
Average child support received	$3,101	$3,409	$3,352	$3,269	$3,485	$3,713	$3,643
Received any child support	5,070	5,269	5,282	5,005	5,119	5,548	5,259
Percent	75.8	75.7	75.3	73.7	73.9	76.5	77.2
Received full amount of child support	2,466	2,945	3,240	3,066	3,093	3,290	3,192
Percent	36.9	42.3	46.2	45.1	44.7	45.3	46.9
Not awarded child support	5,889	5,747	6,074	5,584	5,466	5,576	5,803
Custodial mothers	**11,505**	**11,607**	**11,872**	**11,499**	**11,291**	**11,587**	**11,406**
Total							
Awarded child support	6,878	7,123	7,080	7,150	7110	7,436	7,002
Percent	59.8	61.4	59.6	62.2	63.0	64.2	61.4
Due child support	5,913	6,224	6,342	6,133	6,212	6,516	6,131
Average child support due	$4,827	$5,261	$5,054	$5,625	$6,385	$5,176	$5,660
Average child support received	$3,166	$3,451	$3,373	$3,361	$3,708	$3,579	$3,660
Received any child support	4,501	4,742	4,802	4,578	4,639	5,018	4,754
Percent	76.1	76.2	75.7	74.6	74.7	77.0	77.5
Received full amount of child support	2,178	2,674	2,945	2,818	2,815	2,948	2,900
Percent	36.8	43.0	46.4	45.9	45.3	45.2	47.3
Not awarded child support	4,627	4,484	4,792	4,349	4,181	4,151	4,404
Custodial fathers	**2,184**	**2,108**	**2,077**	**2,030**	**2,092**	**2,364**	**2,199**
Total							
Awarded child support	922	844	796	795	807	940	800
Percent	42.2	40.0	38.3	39.2	38.6	39.8	36.4
Due child support	775	733	676	658	712	740	678
Average child support due	$4,290	$4,423	$4,808	$5,055	$4,655	$4,471	$4,895
Average child support received	$2,689	$3,059	$3,169	$2,415	$3,177	$2,797	$3,491
Received any child support	569	527	479	427	480	530	505
Percent	73.4	71.9	70.9	64.9	67.4	71.6	74.5
Received full amount of child support	288	270	295	248	278	342	292
Percent	37.2	36.8	43.6	37.7	39.0	39.0	46.2
Not awarded child support	1,262	1,263	1,281	1,235	1,285	1,424	1,399

SOURCE: Timothy S. Grall, "Table 1. Comparison of Custodial Parent Population and Those with Child Support Awarded, Due, and Received: 1993–2005," in *Custodial Mothers and Fathers and Their Child Support: 2005*, U.S. Census Bureau, August 2007, http://www.census.gov/prod/2007pubs/p60–234.pdf (accessed November 2, 2008)

CHAPTER 3

CARING FOR CHILDREN

SOCIETAL CHANGES AND WORKING MOTHERS

In the early twenty-first century, women with young children were much more likely to work outside the home than they had been three decades previously. Jane Lawler Dye of the U.S. Census Bureau reports in *Fertility of American Women: June 2004* (December 2005, http://www.census.gov/prod/2005pubs/p20-555.pdf) that in 1976, 31% of women aged 15 to 44 with a child under 12 months old worked. By 1998, this number had risen to 59% of all women with a child under 12 months old; from 2000 through 2004 the number stabilized at 55% of all women who had given birth in the past year. The Bureau of Labor Statistics (BLS) indicates in the press release "Employment Characteristics of Families in 2007" (May 30, 2008, http://www.bls.gov/news.release/pdf/famee.pdf) that in 2007 this percentage had increased slightly to 55.1%. In 2007, 63.3% of mothers with children under the age of six and 77.2% of mothers with school-age children were in the labor force. (See Table 3.1.)

Many factors contributed to the greater proportion of mothers in the workforce. Legislation passed in the late 1970s made it more possible for women to return to work after the birth of a child. In 1976 tax code changes allowed families a tax credit on child care costs, making it more financially feasible for women to return to work. In 1978 the Pregnancy Discrimination Act was passed, making it illegal for employers to discriminate in hiring, firing, promoting, or determining pay levels based on pregnancy or childbirth. In 1993 the Family and Medical Leave Act was passed, requiring employers to give eligible employees up to 12 weeks of unpaid leave for childbearing or family care each year.

Societal changes also contributed to the greater number of women with young children participating in the labor force. In *Maternity Leave and Employment Patterns, 1961–1995* (November 2001, http://www.census.gov/prod/2001pubs/p70-79.pdf), Kirsten Smith, Barbara Downs, and Martin O'Connell of the Census Bureau review the changing demographic profile of first-time mothers between the

1960s and 1990s to explain, in part, this increase. The researchers emphasize that during this period the incidence of first-time motherhood at age 30 and older tripled and that first-time mothers in the 1990s tended to be better educated than their 1960 counterparts. These older, well-educated mothers often viewed their jobs as long-term careers and believed time lost could adversely affect their ability to hold a position and earn promotions and could decrease contributions to retirement funds. This trend continued into the twenty-first century. Joyce A. Martin et al. of the Centers for Disease Control and Prevention (CDC) note in "Births: Final Data for 2005" (*National Vital Statistics Reports*, vol. 56, no. 6, December 5, 2007) that the mean age of first-time mothers reached 25.2 years in 2003, up from 22.7 years in 1980 and an all-time high for American women; this age remained unchanged in 2005. However, by the end of 2006, Martin et al. indicate in "Births: Final Data for 2006" (*National Vital Statistics Reports*, vol. 57, no. 7, January 7, 2009) that the age had dropped to 25—the first decline in some 40 years.

Furthermore, the increasing number of single mothers meant that more women had to work to support their families. In 1970, 3.4 million women maintained single-parent households; by 2007 this number had tripled to 9.9 million. (See Table 1.7 in Chapter 1.) Changes in government programs that provided assistance to poor families also resulted in increasing numbers of single mothers entering the workforce. In 1996 the federal government placed a two-year time limit on receiving public assistance benefits while not working, requiring poor parents to work even if they had to place young children in day care. In 2007, 72.8% of mothers in single-parent households worked. (See Table 3.2.) Nearly two-thirds (64.1%) of single mothers with children under three years old were in the labor force, with a 13.4% unemployment rate. (See Table 3.3.)

Married women have also entered the workforce in larger numbers. A decline in men's real wages plus a

TABLE 3.1

Employment status of population, by sex, marital status, and presence and age of own children under age 18, 2007

[Numbers in thousands]

Characteristic	2007		
	Total	Men	Women
With own children under 18 years			
Civilian noninstitutional population	66,801	29,684	37,117
Civilian labor force	54,370	28,002	26,368
Participation rate	81.4	94.3	71.0
Employed	52,373	27,216	25,157
Employment-population ratio	78.4	91.7	67.8
Full-time workers[a]	45,336	26,282	19,053
Part-time workers[b]	7,037	933	6,104
Unemployed	1,998	786	1,211
Unemployment rate	3.7	2.8	4.6
Married, spouse present			
Civilian noninstitutional population	53,432	27,205	26,227
Civilian labor force	43,824	25,784	18,041
Participation rate	82.0	94.8	68.8
Employed	42,625	25,134	17,492
Employment-population ratio	79.8	92.4	66.7
Full-time workers[a]	37,120	24,332	12,788
Part-time workers[b]	5,505	802	4,704
Unemployed	1,199	650	549
Unemployment rate	2.7	2.5	3.0
Other marital status[c]			
Civilian noninstitutional population	13,369	2,479	10,890
Civilian labor force	10,546	2,219	8,328
Participation rate	78.9	89.5	76.5
Employed	9,747	2,082	7,665
Employment-population ratio	72.9	84.0	70.4
Full-time workers[a]	8,216	1,950	6,266
Part-time workers[b]	1,531	132	1,400
Unemployed	799	137	662
Unemployment rate	7.6	6.2	8.0
With own children 6 to 17 years, none younger			
Civilian noninstitutional population	36,983	16,384	20,599
Civilian labor force	31,179	15,269	15,910
Participation rate	84.3	93.2	77.2
Employed	30,176	14,866	15,310
Employment-population ratio	81.6	90.7	74.3
Full-time workers[a]	26,288	14,378	11,910
Part-time workers[b]	3,888	488	3,400
Unemployed	1,003	403	600
Unemployment rate	3.2	2.6	3.8
With own children under 6 years			
Civilian noninstitutional population	29,818	13,299	16,518
Civilian labor force	23,192	12,733	10,458
Participation rate	77.8	95.7	63.3
Employed	22,197	12,350	9,847
Employment-population ratio	74.4	92.9	59.6
Full-time workers[a]	19,048	11,904	7,143
Part-time workers[b]	3,149	446	2,704
Unemployed	995	383	611
Unemployment rate	4.3	3.0	5.8

TABLE 3.1

Employment status of population, by sex, marital status, and presence and age of own children under age 18, 2007 [CONTINUED]

[Numbers in thousands]

Characteristic	2007		
	Total	Men	Women
With no own children under 18 years			
Civilian noninstitutional population	165,066	82,489	82,577
Civilian labor force	98,754	54,134	44,620
Participation rate	59.8	65.6	54.0
Employed	93,674	51,039	42,635
Employment-population ratio	56.7	61.9	51.6
Full-time workers[a]	75,755	43,752	32,003
Part-time workers[b]	17,919	7,286	10,632
Unemployed	5,080	3,095	1,984
Unemployment rate	5.1	5.7	4.4

[a]Usually work 35 hours or more a week at all jobs.
[b]Usually work less than 35 hours a week at all jobs.
[c]Includes never married, divorced, separated, and widowed persons.
Notes: 2006 estimates for total and for men differ from those published in the "Employment Characteristics of Families in 2006" news release (USDL 07–0673) due to a change in the weights for the estimates of married men. Own children include sons, daughters, step-children, and adopted children. Not included are nieces, nephews, grandchildren, and other related and unrelated children. Data may not sum to totals due to rounding. Updated population controls are introduced annually with the release of January data.

SOURCE: Adapted from "Table 5. Employment Status of the Population by Sex, Marital Status, and Presence and Age of Own Children under 18, 2006–07 Annual Averages," in *Employment Characteristics of Families in 2007*, U.S. Department of Labor, Bureau of Labor Statistics, May 30, 2008, http://www.bls.gov/news.release/pdf/famee.pdf (accessed November 2, 2008)

not in the paid labor force. Table 3.1 shows that 68.8% of married women with children under the age of 18 were in the labor force in 2007, and Table 3.3 shows that 57.4% of married women with children under the age of three were in the labor force in that year. According to Table 3.2, in 62.2% of married-couple families with children under 18 years old, both parents were employed. Many families have come to depend on women's economic contributions to the household.

WHO CARES FOR CHILDREN IN THE UNITED STATES?
School-Age Children

Married parents who both work and single parents who work need reliable child care. The Federal Interagency Forum on Child and Family Statistics reports in *America's Children in Brief: Key National Indicators of Well-Being, 2008* (2008, http://www.childstats.gov/pdf/ac2008/ac_08.pdf) that about half of children in kindergarten through eighth grade were cared for by someone other than their parents in 2005. (See Figure 3.1.) Of those who were cared for by someone other than parents, younger children were more likely to receive home- or center-based care for before- or after-school hours; children in grades four and up were less likely to receive these types of care and more likely to care for themselves. Only 2.6% of children in kindergarten through third grade cared for themselves regularly, whereas 22.2% of older children did. (See Table 3.4.)

rising cost of living has led some two-parent families to decide to maintain two incomes to meet financial obligations and pay for their children's future college expenses. According to the Census Bureau, in *The 2009 Statistical Abstract* (2008, http://www.census.gov/compendia/statab/tables/09s0678.pdf), the median income in 2006 for married couples with one or more children under the age of 18 in which both the husband and wife worked was $86,338, which was significantly higher than the $57,452 median income for married-couple families in which the wife was

TABLE 3.2

Employment status of parents, by age of youngest child and family type, 2007

[Numbers in thousands]

Characteristic	Number 2007	Percent distribution 2007
With own children under 18 years		
Total	35,856	100.0
Parent(s) employed	32,538	90.7
No parent employed	3,318	9.3
Married-couple families	25,125	100.0
Parent(s) employed	24,459	97.3
Mother employed	16,855	67.1
Both parents employed	15,627	62.2
Mother employed, not father	1,228	4.9
Father employed, not mother	7,604	30.3
Neither parent employed	666	2.7
Families maintained by women*	8,554	100.0
Mother employed	6,224	72.8
Mother not employed	2,330	27.2
Families maintained by men*	2,177	100.0
Father employed	1,855	85.2
Father not employed	322	14.8
With own children 6 to 17 years, none younger		
Total	20,361	100.0
Parent(s) employed	18,619	91.4
No parent employed	1,742	8.6
Married-couple families	13,823	100.0
Parent(s) employed	13,435	97.2
Mother employed	10,126	73.3
Both parents employed	9,341	67.6
Mother employed, not father	785	5.7
Father employed, not mother	3,309	23.9
Neither parent employed	388	2.8
Families maintained by women*	5,224	100.0
Mother employed	4,070	77.9
Mother not employed	1,155	22.1
Families maintained by men*	1,314	100.0
Father employed	1,115	84.9
Father not employed	199	15.1
With own children under 6 years		
Total	15,495	100.0
Parent(s) employed	13,918	89.8
No parent employed	1,576	10.2
Married-couple families	11,302	100.0
Parent(s) employed	11,024	97.5
Mother employed	6,729	59.5
Both parents employed	6,287	55.6
Mother employed, not father	442	3.9
Father employed, not mother	4,295	38.0
Neither parent employed	278	2.5
Families maintained by women*	3,329	100.0
Mother employed	2,154	64.7
Mother not employed	1,175	35.3
Families maintained by men*	863	100.0
Father employed	740	85.7
Father not employed	123	14.3

*No spouse present.
Note: Own children include sons, daughters, step-children, and adopted children. Not included are nieces, nephews, grandchildren, and other related and unrelated children. Data may not sum to totals due to rounding. Updated population controls are introduced annually with the release of January data.

SOURCE: Adapted from "Table 4. Families with Own Children: Employment Status of Parents by Age of Youngest Child and Family Type, 2006–07 Annual Averages," in *Employment Characteristics of Families in 2007*, U.S. Department of Labor, Bureau of Labor Statistics, May 30, 2008, http://www.bls.gov/news.release/pdf/famee.pdf (accessed November 2, 2008)

SELF-CARE—LATCHKEY KIDS. The term *latchkey kids* is used to describe children left alone or unsupervised either during the day or before or after school. These are children five to 14 years of age whose parents report "child cares for self" as either the primary or secondary child care arrangement. In 2005 approximately 5.6 million school-age children cared for themselves regularly without adult supervision. (See Table 3.5.) Self-care was higher among children who lived with their fathers without their mother present than it was among children who lived with their mothers, with or without their fathers present, in all age groups. Most of these children were 12 and older, but 1.5 million children 11 years of age and younger regularly took care of themselves. In *Who's Minding the Kids? Child Care Arrangements: Winter 2002* (October 2005, http://www.census.gov/prod/2005pubs/p70-101.pdf), Julia Overturf Johnson of the Census Bureau finds that the percentage of children in self-care held steady between 1997 and 2002 in both families with married parents and in families living with an unemployed single parent; however, the percentage of children of a single, employed parent in self-care actually declined from 24% in 1997 to 18% in 2002.

TWENTY-FIRST-CENTURY COMMUNITY LEARNING CENTERS. More than half of all families use after-school programs, and in many families, parents rely on after-school care to provide a safe and nurturing place for their children while they are working. In response to concerns about the availability of quality after-school programs, the U.S. Department of Education initiated Twenty-First-Century Community Learning Centers (21st CCLC), which was authorized under Title X, Part I, of the Elementary and Secondary Education Act and reauthorized under Title IV, Part B, of the No Child Left Behind Act. This initiative gives grants to low-performance elementary and middle schools in rural and urban areas to provide after-school opportunities for their students, both educational and recreational. In 1997 the 21st CCLC had a budget of only $1 million; by fiscal year 2008 the program's budget had increased tenfold, to $1.1 billion. According to the Department of Education, in "21st CCLC Profile and Performance Information Collection System" (2008, http://ppics.learningpt.org/ppics/publicGrantSearch.asp), by 2008 the 21st CCLC supported 4,183 after-school programs across the country.

Deborah Lowe Vandell, Elizabeth R. Reisner, and Kim M. Pierce note in *Outcomes Linked to High-Quality Afterschool Programs: Longitudinal Findings from the Study of Promising Afterschool Programs* (October 2007, http://www.policystudies.com/studies/youth/Promising%20Programs%20Final%20Report%20FINAL%2010-23-07.pdf) that participation in high-quality afterschool programs in 2007 was associated with improved outcomes among disadvantaged students. The study included a group of 3,000 low-income, ethnically diverse elementary and middle school students. These students improved their

TABLE 3.3

Employment status of mothers with own children under three years old, by single year of age of youngest child and marital status, 2007

[Numbers in thousands]

Characteristic	Civilian noninstitutional population	Civilian labor force							
		Total	Percent of population	Employed				Unemployed	
				Total	Percent of population	Full-time workers[a]	Part-time workers[b]	Number	Percent of labor force
2007									
Total mothers									
With own children under 3 years old	9,659	5,721	59.2	5,354	55.4	3,783	1,571	367	6.4
2 years	2,812	1,808	64.3	1,694	60.2	1,225	469	114	6.3
1 year	3,501	2,068	59.1	1,938	55.4	1,350	589	130	6.3
Under 1 year	3,346	1,845	55.1	1,721	51.4	1,208	513	123	6.7
Married, spouse present									
With own children under 3 years old	7,018	4,027	57.4	3,888	55.4	2,730	1,157	140	3.5
2 years	2,076	1,281	61.7	1,230	59.2	881	349	51	4.0
1 year	2,536	1,433	56.5	1,388	54.7	954	434	46	3.2
Under 1 year	2,406	1,313	54.6	1,270	52.8	896	374	43	3.3
Other marital status[c]									
With own children under 3 years old	2,641	1,694	64.1	1,466	55.5	1,052	414	227	13.4
2 years	736	528	71.6	464	63.1	344	120	63	12.0
1 year	965	635	65.8	551	57.1	396	155	84	13.2
Under 1 year	940	531	56.5	451	48.0	312	139	80	15.1

[a]Usually work 35 hours or more a week at all jobs.
[b]Usually work less than 35 hours a week at all jobs.
[c]Includes never married, divorced, separated, and widowed persons.
Notes: Own children include sons, daughters, step-children, and adopted children. Not included are nieces, nephews, grandchildren, and other related and unrelated children. Data may not sum to totals due to rounding. Updated population controls are introduced annually with the release of January data.

SOURCE: Adapted from "Table 6. Employment Status of Mothers with Own Children Under 3 Years Old by Single Year of Age of Youngest Child and Marital Status, 2006–07 Annual Averages," in *Employment Characteristics of Families in 2007*, U.S. Department of Labor, Bureau of Labor Statistics, May 30, 2008, http://www.bls.gov/news.release/pdf/famee.pdf (accessed November 2, 2008)

FIGURE 3.1

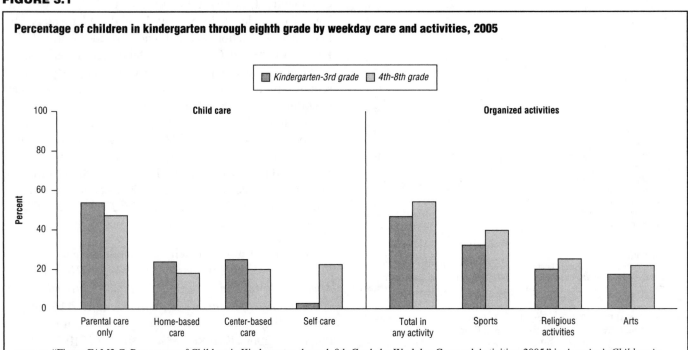

Percentage of children in kindergarten through eighth grade by weekday care and activities, 2005

SOURCE: "Figure FAM3.C. Percentage of Children in Kindergarten through 8th-Grade by Weekday Care and Activities, 2005," in *America's Children in Brief: Key National Indicators of Well-Being, 2008*, Federal Interagency Forum on Child and Family Statistics, 2008, http://www.childstats.gov/americaschildren/fam_fig.asp#famfigure3c (accessed November 2, 2008)

TABLE 3.4

Percentage of children in kindergarten through eighth grade by weekday care and before- and after-school activities, by grade level, poverty, race, and Hispanic origin, 2005

Grade level, care arrangement, and activity		Poverty status			Race and Hispanic origin[a]			
	Total	Below 100% poverty	100–199% poverty	200% poverty and above	White, non-Hispanic	Black, non-Hispanic	Asian	Hispanic
Kindergarten through 3rd grade								
Care arrangements								
Parental care only	53.1	52.0	54.5	53.0	58.3	34.6	49.9	55.3
Nonparental care[b]	46.9	48.0	45.5	47.0	41.7	65.4	50.1	44.7
Home-based care[c]	23.6	25.2	24.5	22.6	22.0	32.2	26.5	20.4
Center-based care	24.4	25.0	21.6	25.2	20.5	39.8	21.4	23.4
Activities used for supervision	5.2	3.1	5.3	6.0	4.8	5.8	13.4	3.2
Self care	2.6	5.1	3.6	1.3	1.6	4.1	3.6	4.2
Activities								
Any activity[b]	46.2	24.3	34.0	59.5	56.2	30.4	45.8	30.4
Sports	31.8	12.1	19.5	44.3	40.2	16.8	29.3	20.8
Religious activities	19.4	13.5	14.8	23.4	24.0	14.6	11.5	11.9
Arts[d]	17.2	6.0	10.8	24.1	21.8	8.3	27.1	8.2
Scouts	12.9	5.3	8.0	17.8	18.2	4.9	11.1	3.8
Academic activities[e]	4.7	3.8	3.8	5.3	5.1	4.4	7.4	3.5
Community services	4.2	1.9	3.0	5.5	5.3	3.3	2.6	1.7
Clubs	3.2	1.3	2.4	4.3	4.3	1.1	4.2	1.8
4th through 8th grade								
Care arrangements								
Parental care only	46.9	46.7	45.2	47.6	51.2	34.5	44.2	45.0
Nonparental care[b]	53.1	53.3	54.8	52.4	48.8	65.5	55.8	55.0
Home-based care[c]	18.1	15.0	20.0	18.4	16.4	24.1	17.5	18.6
Center-based care	19.0	21.3	21.3	17.4	14.2	28.9	21.9	25.4
Activities used for supervision	9.0	7.8	6.9	10.2	8.9	10.5	11.9	7.5
Self care	22.2	23.5	23.8	21.2	21.1	27.1	21.0	19.6
Activities								
Any activity[b]	53.7	30.4	40.5	65.9	63.3	39.7	51.2	35.4
Sports	39.3	18.6	26.1	50.8	47.8	24.2	37.2	26.7
Religious activities	24.9	12.5	20.0	30.7	29.7	20.9	18.3	14.8
Arts[d]	21.5	9.7	12.5	28.5	25.8	13.3	25.5	13.2
Scouts	10.1	4.8	6.4	13.2	13.3	5.6	7.7	5.4
Academic activities[e]	9.7	6.6	7.1	11.6	10.0	12.0	13.0	5.9
Community services	12.7	5.0	10.6	15.9	15.6	8.2	13.1	7.1
Clubs	8.7	3.7	4.6	11.8	11.0	4.9	8.9	4.1

[a]The 1997 OMB Standards for Data on Race and Ethnicity were used, allowing persons to select one or more of five racial groups: White, Black or African American, American Indian or Alaska Native, Asian, and Native Hawaiian or other Pacific Islander. Included in the total but not shown separately are American Indian or Alaska Native and respondents with two or more races. Respondents who reported the child being Asian or Native Hawaiian or other Pacific Islander were combined. Data on race and Hispanic origin are collected separately. Persons of Hispanic origin may be of any race.
[b]Children may have multiple nonparental child care arrangements, in addition to being involved in more than one activity; thus, the total of the four kinds of nonparental arrangements may not sum to the category "nonparental care." Likewise, the seven activities listed may not sum to the category "any activity." Activities include organized programs a child participates in outside of school hours that are not part of a before- or after-school program.
[c]Home-based care includes care that takes place in a relative's or nonrelative's private home.
[d]Arts include activities such as music, dance, and painting.
[e]Academic activities include activities such as tutoring or math lab.

SOURCE: "Table FAM3.C. Child Care: Percentage of Children in Kindergarten through 8th-Grade by Weekday Care and Before-and After-School Activities by Grade Level, Poverty Status, and Race and Hispanic Origin, 2005," in *America's Children in Brief: Key National Indicators of Well-Being, 2008*, Federal Interagency Forum on Child and Family Statistics, 2008, http://www.childstats.gov/americaschildren/tables.asp (accessed November 2, 2008)

standardized test scores and work habits and reduced problem behaviors. They also posted gains in teacher-reported social skills.

Children Younger Than Five (Preschoolers)

In 2005, 50.7% of children under the age of two and 73.7% of children aged three to six were in nonparental care at least some of the time. (See Table 3.6.) Among the youngest children, home-based care by a relative was most common (22%), followed by care in a center-based program (19.6%) and home-based care by a nonrelative (15.6%). Among older preschoolers, center-based programs were by far the most common; 57.1% of three- to six-year-olds were

enrolled in these programs, whereas 22.7% were cared for in a home by a relative, and only 11.7% were cared for in a home by a nonrelative. These numbers reflect the fact that as their children grow from infancy to school age, working mothers often change child care arrangements to meet the needs of their children, their families, and their employers. Making child care arrangements for infants and toddlers is often more difficult than for older children, because fewer organized child care facilities admit infants and very young children, primarily due to the cost involved in hiring enough workers and adapting facilities to care adequately for babies. In addition, many parents prefer, if possible, to keep their infants in a home environment as long as possible. Also,

TABLE 3.5

Prevalence of self-care among grade school-aged children, by selected characteristics, 2005

[Numbers in thousands, except for percents]

	Child 5 to 8 years			Child 9 to 11 years			Child 12 to 14 years		
		In self-care			In self-care			In self-care	
Characteristics	Total	Number	Percent	Total	Number	Percent	Total	Number	Percent
Total	**14,889**	**284**	**1.9**	**12,097**	**1,196**	**9.9**	**12,584**	**4,135**	**32.9**
Living with father only	527	16	3.0	522	60	11.5	683	254	37.2
Living with mother	14,362	269	1.9	11,575	1,135	9.8	11,901	3,881	32.6
Marital status of mother									
Married	10,590	172	1.6	8,363	754	9.0	8,435	2,698	32.0
Widowed, separated, divorced	1,844	57	3.1	1,959	270	13.8	2,306	862	37.4
Never married	1,928	40	2.1	1,253	111	8.9	1,160	320	27.6
Race and Hispanic origin of mother									
White alone	11,182	209	1.9	9,037	958	10.6	9,256	3,138	33.9
Non-Hispanic	8,624	161	1.9	7,052	829	11.8	7,398	2,694	36.4
Black alone	2,082	37	1.8	1,843	130	7.1	1,867	518	27.7
Asian alone	563	10	1.8	392	17	4.3	395	87	22.0
Hispanic (of any race)	2,774	53	1.9	2,100	132	6.3	2,004	482	24.1
Age of mother									
15–24 years	664	5	0.8	80	14	17.5	37	9	24.3
25–34 years	6,238	105	1.7	3,528	320	9.1	2,145	587	27.4
35+ years	7,460	159	2.1	7,967	802	10.1	9,719	3,286	33.8
Education level of mother									
Less than high school	1,662	18	1.1	1,369	70	5.1	1,314	254	19.3
High school graduate	3,766	97	2.6	2,995	263	8.8	3,350	1,058	31.6
Some college	5,200	83	1.6	4,442	525	11.8	4,605	1,516	32.9
Bachelor's degree or higher	3,734	70	1.9	2,769	278	10.0	2,632	1,053	40.0
Employment status of mother									
Employed	9,285	208	2.2	7,931	889	11.2	8,459	3,149	37.2
Not employed									
In school and not in labor force	363	9	2.5	274	19	6.9	197	48	24.4
Looking for work	783	4	0.5	553	69	12.5	458	112	24.5
Not in labor force	3,932	48	1.2	2,816	159	5.6	2,786	572	20.5
Family poverty level									
Below poverty level	2,543	62	2.4	2,070	175	8.5	1,963	450	22.9
At or above poverty level	11,498	199	1.7	9,229	948	10.3	9,767	3,387	34.7
100–199 percent of poverty level	3,493	59	1.7	2,629	190	7.2	2,606	671	25.7
200+ percent of poverty level	8,006	139	1.7	6,600	759	11.5	7,160	2,716	37.9
Missing	320	9	2.8	275	13	4.7	171	44	25.7

SOURCE: "Table 4. Children in Self-Care, by Age of Child, Employment Status of Mother, and Selected Characteristics for Children Living with Mother: Spring 2005," in *Who's Minding the Kids? Child Care Arrangements: Spring 2005*, U.S. Census Bureau, February 2008, http://www.census.gov/population/www/socdemo/child/ppl-2005.html (accessed November 2, 2008)

many mothers view center-based programs, which often have an educational focus, as most appropriate for older preschoolers.

FACTORS THAT AFFECT CHILD CARE
Preschool Child Care

RACIAL AND ETHNIC DIFFERENCES. In 2005 African-American mothers of preschoolers relied more heavily on relatives to provide child care than did other mothers. More than one out of four (27.7%) African-American preschoolers were cared for by relatives in that year, compared to 21% of non-Hispanic white preschoolers, 21.2% of Hispanic preschoolers, and 21.3% of Asian-American preschoolers. (See Table 3.6.) Non-Hispanic white preschoolers (54.8%), African-American preschoolers (54.1%), and Asian-American preschoolers (46%) were all more likely to be cared for by nonrelatives or in center-based programs than were Hispanic preschoolers (35.6%).

POVERTY MAKES A DIFFERENCE. In 2005, 85.3% of preschoolers whose mothers worked full time (35 hours or more each week) and 69.7% of preschoolers whose mothers worked part time were regularly in nonparental care. (See Table 3.6.) However, the type of care varied by the income levels of these families. A substantial number of children from low-income families are cared-for in unregulated home-based settings. Gina Adams, Kathryn Tout, and Martha Zaslow note in *Early Care and Education for Children in Low-Income Families* (January 12, 2006, http://www.urban.org/UploadedPDF/411482_early_care.pdf) that "several observational studies have found unregulated home-based care of lower quality than regulated home-based settings in which low-income children participate. Studies question specific aspects of quality, such as prolonged exposure to television, missed opportunities for learning, and health and safety issues." In "Snapshots of America's Families III: Children in Low-Income Families Are Less Likely to Be in Center-Based Child Care" (January 27, 2004, http://

TABLE 3.6

Percentage of preschool children by type of care arrangement and child and family characteristics, 1995, 2001, and 2005

	Parental care only			Type of nonparental care arrangement											
				Total in nonparental care[b]			Care in a home[a]						Center-based program[c]		
							By a relative			By a nonrelative					
Characteristic	1995	2001	2005	1995	2001	2005	1995	2001	2005	1995	2001	2005	1995	2001	2005
Total	39.9	38.8	39.2	60.1	61.2	60.8	21.1	23.1	22.3	18.0	16.3	13.9	30.5	33.4	36.1
Age															
Ages 0–2	50.5	48.0	49.3	49.5	52.0	50.7	22.5	23.3	22.0	18.9	18.0	15.6	11.9	16.5	19.6
Ages 3–6, not yet in kindergarten	25.9	26.3	23.6	74.1	73.7	73.7	19.4	22.7	22.7	16.9	14.0	11.7	55.0	56.3	57.1
Race and Hispanic origin[d]															
White, non-Hispanic	38.3	38.4	37.2	61.7	61.6	62.8	17.9	20.3	21.0	21.3	18.7	17.0	32.9	35.1	37.8
Black, non-Hispanic	34.2	26.1	30.1	65.8	73.9	69.9	31.4	34.6	27.7	11.6	12.9	10.2	33.0	40.2	43.9
Asian	41.8	43.2	43.5	58.2	56.8	56.5	26.6	22.9	21.3	9.1	8.7	9.0	29.6	34.1	37.0
Hispanic	53.7	52.0	50.5	46.3	48.0	49.5	23.4	22.9	21.2	11.8	11.8	10.4	17.0	20.7	25.2
Poverty status															
Below 100% poverty	50.4	45.3	49.2	49.6	54.7	50.8	23.2	27.4	23.3	10.0	10.6	8.0	23.5	26.9	28.3
100–199% poverty	47.7	46.3	47.2	52.3	53.7	52.8	23.0	22.5	23.5	13.3	12.6	9.3	23.7	27.8	29.4
200% poverty and above	29.9	32.7	31.6	70.1	67.3	68.4	19.1	21.4	21.4	25.1	20.5	18.3	37.9	38.7	42.2
Family type															
Two parents[e]	42.0	42.7	42.9	58.0	57.3	57.1	17.2	19.0	18.8	19.2	16.2	14.1	29.9	32.3	34.4
Two parents, married	—	42.2	41.8	—	57.8	58.2	—	18.4	18.6	—	16.6	14.2	—	33.1	35.8
Two parents, unmarried	—	47.3	53.0	—	52.7	47.0	—	24.4	20.4	—	12.4	13.0	—	25.0	21.7
One parent	33.0	26.5	24.9	67.0	73.5	75.1	33.3	36.6	36.0	15.2	17.3	13.4	32.4	36.1	42.3
No parents	45.3	17.9	33.1	54.8	82.1	66.9	17.4	38.5	28.3	10.8	9.2	10.0	30.5	47.9	43.6
Mother's highest level of education[f]															
Less than high school	61.7	55.5	63.7	38.3	44.5	36.3	19.8	21.7	16.1	6.6	8.3	5.5	15.7	20.8	18.9
High school diploma or equivalent	43.7	42.3	44.4	56.3	57.7	55.6	23.4	26.2	24.1	15.0	13.3	9.9	26.0	28.1	30.7
Some college, including vocational/technical/associate's degree	34.1	36.7	36.5	65.9	63.3	63.5	23.6	25.3	25.8	19.3	15.4	14.5	33.5	35.3	35.2
Bachelor's degree or higher	27.7	31.3	30.5	72.3	68.7	69.5	15.2	16.9	19.1	28.4	23.6	19.2	42.7	42.1	45.8
Mother's employment status[f]															
35 hours or more per week	11.9	14.8	14.7	88.1	85.2	85.3	33.4	34.0	31.8	31.7	26.2	23.3	38.9	42.1	47.6
Less than 35 hours per week	24.9	29.0	30.3	75.1	71.0	69.7	30.1	31.6	30.5	25.6	19.9	18.0	35.0	35.6	37.8
Looking for work	57.6	57.3	53.3	42.4	42.7	46.7	16.3	16.7	20.7	3.7	9.6	7.5	24.7	24.5	23.3
Not in the labor force	67.7	67.6	66.1	32.3	32.4	33.9	7.2	7.0	7.8	5.5	4.8	3.6	22.0	24.1	25.8

—Not available.
[a]Relative and nonrelative care can take place in either the child's own home or another home.
[b]Some children participate in more than one type of nonparental care arrangement. Thus, details do not sum to the total percentage of children in nonparental care.
[c]Center-based programs include day care centers, prekindergartens, nursery schools, Head Start programs, and other early childhood education programs.
[d]In 1995 and 2001, the 1977 OMB Standards for Data on Race and Ethnicity were used to classify persons into one of the following four racial groups: white, black, American Indian or Alaskan Native, or Asian or Pacific Islander. For data from 2005, the revised 1997 OMB standards were used. Persons could select one or more of five racial groups: white, black or African American, American Indian or Alaska Native, Asian, and Native Hawaiian or other Pacific Islander. Included in the total but not shown separately are American Indian or Alaska Native and respondents with two or more races. For continuity purposes, in 2005, respondents who reported the child being Asian or Native Hawaiian or other Pacific Islander were combined. Data on race and Hispanic origin are collected separately. Persons of Hispanic origin may be of any race.
[e]Refers to adults' relationship to child and does not indicate marital status.
[f]Children without a mother in the home are excluded from estimates of mother's highest level of education and mother's employment status.

SOURCE: Adapted from "Table FAM.3.A. Child Care: Percentage of Children Ages 0–6, Not Yet in Kindergarten by Type of Care Arrangement and Child and Family Characteristics, 1995, 2001, and 2005," in *America's Children in Brief: Key National Indicators of Well-Being, 2008*, Federal Interagency Forum on Child and Family Statistics, 2008, http://www.childstats.gov/americaschildren/tables.asp (accessed November 2, 2008)

www.urban.org/UploadedPDF/310923_snapshots3_no16 .pdf), Jeffrey Capizzano and Gina Adams find that preschoolers from lower-income families (families with an income less than 200% of the poverty line) were less likely to be in center-based care (24.9%) than children from higher-income families (31.2%). The Federal Interagency Forum on Child and Family Statistics indicates in *America's Children in Brief* that data support this conclusion. In 2005, 42.2% of preschoolers from families whose incomes were above 200% of the poverty line were in center-based care, compared to 29.4% of children from families with incomes 100% to 199% of the poverty line and 28.3% of children from families with incomes below the poverty line. (See Table 3.6.)

Capizzano and Adams suggest the lower percentage of low-income children in center care reflects the lower cost of home-based care. At the same time, they argue there is evidence that quality, center-based care plays a big role in helping preschoolers make a successful transition to school and that low-income children are in large part missing this opportunity. In *Key Facts: Essential Information about Child Care, Early Education, and School-Age Care* (2003), Karen Blank, Karen Schulman, and Danielle Ewan also stress the importance of providing low-income families with child care assistance to help their children succeed.

FORMAL CHILD CARE FACILITIES

Even though no comprehensive data exist on the types or quality of child care facilities in the United States, the National Association for Regulatory Administration estimates in *The 2005 Child Care Licensing Study Executive Summary* (2006, http://www.nara.affiniscape.com/associations/4734/files/Executive%20Summary.pdf) that in 2005 there were 335,520 licensed child care facilities in the United States, including 105,444 licensed child care centers and 213,966 licensed family child care homes. More than nine million children are taken care of in these licensed facilities, and over 70% of these children are in center-based programs. Many more unlicensed child care facilities exist, but because they are not regulated, no reliable statistics are collected.

In 2005, 50.7% of all children aged two and under and 73.7% of all children aged three to six spent time in non-parental care each week. (See Table 3.6.) Their care providers are major influences in their lives. Many working parents discover that quality and affordable care is very difficult to find. In some communities, child care is hard to find at any cost. Shortages of child care for infants, sick children, children with special needs, and for school children before and after school pose problems for many parents.

Regulations and Quality of Care

Federal assistance to low-income families to pay for child care eroded in the late twentieth century at the same time that the government imposed requirements that more low-income parents work. The 1996 welfare reform law, the Personal Responsibility and Work Opportunity Reconciliation Act, eliminated the guarantee that families on welfare would receive subsidized child care and replaced it with the Child Care and Development Block Grant to states. Even though the legislation gave states wide discretion in the use of these funds, it also imposed penalties if states failed to meet criteria for getting low-income parents into the workforce.

This legislation pushed the issue of regulation of child care facilities to the forefront. In 1989 the National Institute of Child Health and Human Development (NICHD) initiated the Study of Early Child Care. This comprehensive ongoing longitudinal study was designed to answer many questions about the relationship between child care experiences and children's developmental outcomes. The 1999 phase of the study examined whether the amount of time children spent in child care affected their interactions with their mothers. The results showed that the number of hours

infants and toddlers spent in child care was modestly linked to the sensitivity of the mother to her child, as well as to the engagement of the child with the mother in play activities. Children in consistent quality day care showed less problem behavior, whereas those who switched day care arrangements showed more problem behaviors. Children in quality care centers had higher cognitive and language development than those in lower-quality centers.

The second phase of the study, *The NICHD Study of Early Child Care and Youth Development: Findings for Children up to Age 4 1/2 Years* (January 2006, http://www.nichd.nih.gov/publications/pubs/upload/seccyd_051206.pdf), found that the quality of child care had an impact on children's social and intellectual development. The study defined a better quality of care as care that met ideal adult-to-child ratios, maintained ideal group sizes, and had well-trained child care providers. It also focused on the quality of children's actual day-to-day experiences in child care, observing children's social interactions and their activities with toys.

The study found that children who were in higher-quality child care had better cognitive function and language development in the first three years of life, as well as greater school readiness by age four and a half. Children in higher-quality care were also more sensitive to other children, more cooperative, and less aggressive and disobedient than were children in lower-quality care. Lastly, the study found that children who were cared for in child care centers rather than in home-based care had better cognitive and language development, but also showed somewhat more behavior problems both in the child care setting and once they began kindergarten.

Child Care during Nonstandard Hours

Many parents choose to have one parent work non-standard hours to allow both parents to provide child care at different times of the day. According to the BLS, in the press release "Workers on Flexible and Shift Schedules in May 2004" (July 1, 2005, http://www.bls.gov/news.release/pdf/flex.pdf), in 2004, the most recent year for which statistics are available, 27 million workers, or 27.5% of all full-time wage and salary workers, worked flexible hours and were able to vary their work hours to fit their schedules. That number was more than twice as many workers as in May 1985, but down from a high of 28.6% in May 2001. Flexible schedules were most common among management (44.7%) and professionals (31.5%), and were more common among non-Hispanic white (28.7%) and Asian-American (27.4%) workers than among African-American (19.7%) and Hispanic workers (18.4%). By contrast, the percentage of those who worked an evening or overnight shift had fallen from 18% in 1991 to 14.8% in 2004. When asked why they worked a non-daytime schedule, 8.2% of shift workers answered they did so for better family or child care arrangements.

THE COST OF CHILD CARE

In 2008 the National Association of Child Care Resource and Referral Agencies (NACCRRA) published *Parents and the High Price of Child Care: Update 2008* (http://issuu.com/naccrra/docs/price_report_2008), which surveyed child care costs across the country. The survey shows that the average yearly cost for child care in a child care center for a four-year-old ranged from $4,475 in Arkansas to $10,787 in Massachusetts. For an infant, annual costs jumped to $5,231 in Alabama and $14,591 in Massachusetts. Child care in urban care centers was so expensive that it could cost more than public college tuition.

Low-Income Families

NACCRRA notes in *Parents and the High Price of Child Care* that in 2008 a low-income family with two parents working full time, 52 weeks per year, at $5.85 per hour (the minimum wage after July 2007), earned $24,336 per year before taxes. These families spent an exorbitant proportion of their income on child care. For example, in New York, where the average annual cost of infant care was $13,437, the median income for single-parent families was $23,487. This family would spend 57.2% of its annual income on preschool care. Even in Nevada, where the cost of infant care averaged a relatively low $8,391, a single-parent family earning the median income of $26,170 would spend 32.1% of its annual income on child care.

In *Who's Minding the Kids? Child Care Arrangements: Spring 2005 Detailed Tables* (February 28, 2008, http://www.census.gov/population/www/socdemo/child/ppl-2005.html), the Census Bureau estimates that in 2005 the average married-couple family with a working mother with a preschool child spent 7.8% of its income on child care, whereas single mothers spent 13.5% of their family income on child care. Families in poverty in which the mother was employed paid an average of $82 per week in child care costs, 26.6% of the family income, compared to families not in poverty, who paid, on average, $132 per week, or 8.3% of the family income. Many poor and low-income families were forced to enroll their children in low-cost, and often poor-quality, child care centers. As a result, these children spent much of their day in unstimulating and possibly unsafe environments.

Government Assistance with Child Care

BLOCK GRANTS. In some cases, low-income and poor parents can receive government assistance in paying for child care. Recognizing that child care assistance helps contribute to a productive workforce, every state has a child care assistance program that subsidizes some child care using federal block grant money and state funds for those on welfare and for low-income working families. In some cases, parents receive a voucher that they can use to pay for a portion of child care costs; in other states, payments are made directly to the child care provider of the parents' choice. However, according to NACCRRA, in *Breaking the Piggy Bank: Parents and the High Price of Child Care* (February 2006, http://www.naccrra.org/docs/policy/Breaking%20the%20Piggy%20Bank_FINAL(printer).pdf), in 2005 17 states had waiting lists for child care assistance and Tennessee was no longer accepting applications even for its waiting list. Also, the income cut-off to even be eligible for assistance was extremely low. In other words, child care assistance is available to only a small percentage of those families who need it.

HEAD START. Perhaps the best-known and most successful government-funded child care program is Head Start, a federal program begun in 1965 under the Administration for Children and Families (ACF) of the U.S. Department of Health and Human Services. The free program provides early education, health care, social services, and free meals to preschool children in families whose incomes are below the poverty line or who receive public assistance. In "Head Start Program Fact Sheet" (February 2008, http://www.acf.hhs.gov/programs/ohs/about/fy2008.html), the ACF states that Head Start operates in every state, and in fiscal year 2007 it served 908,412 children. The Children's Defense Fund reports in "Head Start Basics: 2005" (April 2005, http://www.childrensdefense.org/site/DocServer/headstartbasics2005.pdf?docID=616) that the program has been shown to provide many benefits, including a greater likelihood that children will do well in school and graduate from high school.

TAX CREDITS. The Federal Dependent Care Tax Credit helps families by allowing them to claim an income tax credit for part of their child care expenses for children under the age of 13 that enabled parents to work outside the home. The credit is on a sliding scale, ranging from 20% to 35% of qualified expenses; therefore, lower-income families receive slightly larger credits. According to the Internal Revenue Service, in "Child and Dependent Care Credit" (2008, http://www.irs.gov/publications/p17/ch32.html#d0e71607), in 2008 parents could claim up to $3,000 in qualified expenses for one child or $6,000 for two or more children.

FAMILY LEAVE. In 1993 Congress enacted the Family and Medical Leave Act (FMLA), requiring employers with 50 or more employees to give unpaid time off—12 weeks in any 12-month period—to employees to care for newborn or newly adopted children, sick family members, or for personal illness. The employee must be returned to the same position—or one equivalent in pay, benefits, and other terms of employment—and must receive uninterrupted health benefits. The U.S. Department of Labor reports that before this legislation, fewer than a quarter of all workers received family leave benefits and that most of those who did worked in establishments of more than 100 employees.

Jane Waldfogel states in "Family and Medical Leave: Evidence from the 2000 Surveys" (*Monthly Labor Review,*

September 2001) that in 2000, 17.9% of FMLA leave takers took their leave to care for a newborn, newly adopted, or newly placed foster child; 9.8% used it to care for a sick child; and 7.8% used it as maternity or disability time. Of all employees covered by the FMLA with children 18 months and younger, 45.1% of men and 75.8% of women had taken an FMLA leave in the previous 18 months.

CHAPTER 4
HEALTH AND SAFETY

FACTORS AFFECTING CHILDREN'S HEALTH

A variety of factors affect children's health. These range from prenatal influences; access to and quality of health care; poverty, homelessness, and hunger; childhood diseases; and diet and exercise. This chapter discusses these factors and looks at the leading causes of death among infants, children, and adolescents.

Birth Defects

In "Birth Defects: Frequently Asked Questions" (December 12, 2006, http://www.cdc.gov/ncbddd/bd/faq1 .htm), the Centers for Disease Control and Prevention (CDC) indicates that birth defects affect one out of every 33 babies born. Birth defects are the leading cause of infant deaths. In addition, these babies have a greater chance of illness and disability than do babies without birth defects. Two major birth defects, neural tube defects and fetal alcohol syndrome, are in large part preventable.

NEURAL TUBE DEFECTS. Major defects of the brain and spine are called neural tube defects. Each year, as many as 3,000 infants are born in the United States with neural tube defects caused by the incomplete closing of the spine and skull. Another estimated 1,500 pregnancies are either still-born or terminated because of these defects. The occurrence of these defects can be greatly reduced by adequate folic acid consumption before and during early pregnancy.

FETAL ALCOHOL SYNDROME. Alcohol consumption by pregnant women can cause fetal alcohol syndrome (FAS), a birth defect characterized by a low birth weight, facial abnormalities such as small eye openings, growth retardation, and central nervous system deficits, including learning and developmental disabilities. The condition is a lifelong, disabling condition that puts these affected children at risk for secondary conditions, such as mental health problems, criminal behavior, alcohol and drug abuse, and inappropriate sexual behavior. Not all children affected by

prenatal alcohol use are born with the full syndrome, but they may have selected abnormalities.

According to the CDC, in "Tracking Fetal Alcohol Syndrome" (December 5, 2006, http://www.cdc.gov/ncbddd/ fas/fassurv.htm), estimates of the prevalence of FAS vary from 0.2 to 1.5 per 1,000 births in different areas of the United States. Other alcohol-related birth defects are thought to occur three times as often as FAS. In "Alcohol Consumption among Women Who Are Pregnant or Who Might Become Pregnant—United States, 2002" (*Morbidity and Mortality Weekly Report*, vol. 53, no. 50, December 2004), the CDC finds that in 2002, 10.1% of pregnant women drank alcohol, putting their babies at risk for FAS. As many as one out of 50 (1.9%) pregnant women frequently drank alcohol. According to James Tsai et al., in "Patterns and Average Volume of Alcohol Use among Women of Child-bearing Age" (*Maternal and Child Health Journal*, vol. 11, no. 5, September 2007), 2% of pregnant women and 13% of nonpregnant women of childbearing age are estimated to engage in binge drinking, and 21.5% reported drinking at least 45 drinks per month.

Health Care

IMMUNIZATIONS. In *America's Children in Brief: Key National Indicators of Well-Being, 2008* (2008, http:// www.childstats.gov/americaschildren/index.asp), the Federal Interagency Forum on Child and Family Statistics explains that the proportion of preschool-age children immunized against communicable and potentially dangerous child-hood diseases—including diphtheria, tetanus, and pertussis (whooping cough), known collectively as DTP, polio, and measles—dropped during the 1980s but rose significantly during the 1990s. By 2006, 85.2% of all children had received four doses of DTP, 92.8% had received three doses of poliovirus vaccine, 93.4% had received *haemophilus influenzae* type b vaccine, 93.3% had received three doses of hepatitis B vaccine, 92.3% had received measles

TABLE 4.1

Percentage of children vaccinated for selected diseases, by poverty status[a], race[b], and Hispanic origin[c], 1996 and 2006

Characteristic	Total 1996	Total 2006	Below poverty 1996	Below poverty 2006	At or above 1996	At or above 2006
Total						
Combined series (4:3:1:3:3:1)[d]	—	76.9	—	73.4	—	78.3
Combined series (4:3:1:3:3)[e]	67.7	80.5	61.4	76.3	69.9	82.2
Combined series (4:3:1:3)[f]	76.4	82.1	68.9	77.8	79.2	83.9
Combined series (4:3:1)[g]	78.4	83.1	71.6	79.0	80.8	84.8
DTP (4 doses or more)[h]	81.1	85.2	73.9	80.8	83.6	86.9
Polio (3 doses or more)[i]	91.0	92.8	87.7	91.9	92.0	93.1
MMR (1 dose or more)[j]	90.6	92.3	87.2	90.9	91.9	93.0
Hib (3 doses or more)k	91.4	93.4	86.9	91.1	93.1	94.2
Hepatitis B (3 doses or more)l	81.8	93.3	78.0	92.7	83.2	93.5
Varicella (1 dose or more)[m]	12.2	89.2	5.4	88.3	15.3	90.0
PCV (3 doses or more)[n]	—	86.9	—	84.1	—	88.0
White, non-Hispanic						
Combined series (4:3:1:3:3:1)[d]	—	77.8	—	69.0	—	78.9
Combined series (4:3:1:3:3)[e]	68.9	82.2	59.3	74.1	70.5	83.1
Combined series (4:3:1:3)[f]	78.5	83.9	68.0	75.2	80.4	84.9
Combined series (4:3:1)[g]	80.1	84.7	70.3	76.7	81.9	85.7
DTP (4 doses or more)[h]	82.7	86.6	72.4	78.0	84.7	87.6
Polio (3 doses or more)[i]	91.9	93.3	88.2	90.1	92.5	93.6
MMR (1 dose or more)[j]	91.4	92.8	85.1	87.7	92.5	93.5
Hib (3 doses or more)k	92.8	94.1	87.4	87.9	93.7	94.8
Hepatitis B (3 doses or more)l	82.1	93.8	76.4	91.7	83.3	94.0
Varicella (1 dose or more)[m]	14.5	88.7	6.4	83.2	16.3	89.4
PCV (3 doses or more)[n]	—	87.2	—	79.5	—	88.4
Black, non-Hispanic						
Combined series (4:3:1:3:3:1)[d]	—	73.8	—	71.7	—	76.8
Combined series (4:3:1:3:3)[e]	66.8	76.7	61.3	74.0	71.9	80.4
Combined series (4:3:1:3)[f]	74.2	78.4	69.3	75.8	79.1	81.9
Combined series (4:3:1)[g]	76.6	78.9	72.5	76.5	80.9	82.4
DTP (4 doses or more)[h]	79.0	81.2	74.3	78.8	83.3	84.8
Polio (3 doses or more)[i]	90.1	90.4	86.8	90.4	92.6	91.4
MMR (1 dose or more)[j]	89.7	90.9	88.3	90.8	90.8	91.6
Hib (3 doses or more)[k]	89.4	91.0	85.9	89.9	92.8	93.4
Hepatitis B (3 doses or more)l	81.9	91.5	77.8	91.6	85.0	92.5
Varicella (1 dose or more)[m]	8.6	89.1	—	89.2	12.9	89.8
PCV (3 doses or more)[n]	—	82.9	—	82.2	—	84.5

vaccines, and 89.2% had received varicella (chickenpox) vaccine. (See Table 4.1.) More than four out of five of these children received the vaccinations in combined series. Children living below the poverty line and African-American children were slightly less likely than the general child population to be immunized.

In 1994 the U.S. Department of Health and Human Services (HHS) implemented the Vaccines for Children (VFC) program, which provides free or low-cost vaccines to children at participating private and public health care provider sites. Eligible children, including children on Medicaid, children without insurance or whose insurance does not cover vaccinations, and Native American or Alaskan Native children can receive the vaccinations through their primary care physician. Children not covered under the program but whose parents cannot afford vaccinations can receive free vaccines at public clinics under local programs. The HHS states in *Budget in Brief, Fiscal Year 2009* (2008, http://www.hhs.gov/budget/09budget/2009BudgetInBrief.pdf) that the VFC program and Section 317 (the supporting vaccine infrastructure) had a budget of $3.2 billion for fiscal year 2009. Vaccines provided through the program represented about 40% of all childhood vaccines purchased in the country.

The World Health Organization (WHO) and the United Nations Children's Fund report in *Global Immunization Vision and Strategy, 2006–2015* (October 2005, http://www.who.int/vaccines-documents/DocsPDF05/GIVS_Final_EN.pdf) that developed nations, including the United States, generally have among the highest immunization rates in the world. The global immunization rate for DTP in 2003 was 78%, up from only 20% in 1980. Immunization rates for the developed world for the same time period were 10 to 20 percentage points higher than the global average, reflecting the low immunization rates in many developing nations. The WHO notes in "Global Immunization Data" (January 2008, http://www.who.int/immunization/newsroom/Global_Immunization_Data.pdf) that in 2006 immunization coverage exceeded 90% in Europe and the Americas, 92% in the western Pacific, and 86% in the eastern Mediterranean.

PHYSICIAN VISITS. Children's health depends on access to and usage of medical care. Based on household interviews of a sample of the civilian noninstitutionalized population, the National Center for Health Statistics (NCHS) finds that in 2006, 57.2% of children under the age of 18 visited the doctor between one and three times, 24.6% saw the doctor between four and nine times, and 7.3% saw the

TABLE 4.1

Percentage of children vaccinated for selected diseases, by poverty status[a], race[b], and Hispanic origin[c], 1996 and 2006 [CONTINUED]

Characteristic	Total		Below poverty		At or above	
	1996	2006	1996	2006	1996	2006
Hispanic[c]						
Combined series (4:3:1:3:3:1)[d]	—	77.0	—	76.4	—	78.3
Combined series (4:3:1:3:3)[e]	63.7	79.7	62.4	78.3	64.1	81.6
Combined series (4:3:1:3)[f]	71.1	81.3	68.2	80.1	72.7	83.2
Combined series (4:3:1)[g]	74.1	82.0	70.9	80.9	74.6	83.9
DTP (4 doses or more)[h]	77.2	84.5	74.0	82.7	77.5	86.3
Polio (3 doses or more)[i]	89.4	93.3	88.0	93.0	89.8	93.4
MMR (1 dose or more)[j]	88.2	92.0	87.4	92.8	89.0	91.9
Hib (3 doses or more)[k]	88.5	93.9	87.1	93.5	90.3	93.9
Hepatitis B (3 doses or more)[l]	80.8	93.6	79.9	93.2	81.1	93.9
Varicella (1 dose or more)[m]	7.6	89.6	6.3	90.5	11.2	90.5
PCV (3 doses or more)[n]	—	88.9	—	87.7	—	89.8

—Not available.

[a]Based on family income and household size using US Bureau of Census poverty thresholds for the year of data collection.

[b]From 1996 to 2000, the 1977 OMB Standards for Data on Race and Ethnicity were used. Beginning in 2002, the 1997 OMB Standards for Data on Race and Ethnicity were used.

[c]Persons of Hispanic origin may be of any race.

[d]The 4:3:1:3:3:1 series consists of 4 doses (or more) of diphtheria, tetanus toxoids and pertussis (DTP) vaccines, diphtheria and tetanus toxoids (DT), or diphtheria, tetanus toxoids and any acellular pertussis (DTaP) vaccines; 3 doses (or more) of poliovirus vaccines; 1 dose (or more) of any measles-containing vaccine; 3 doses (or more) of Haemophilus influenzae type b (Hib) vaccines; 3 doses (or more) of hepatitis B vaccines; and 1 dose (or more) of varicella vaccine. The collection of coverage rate estimates for this series began in 2002.

[e]The 4:3:1:3:3 series consists of 4 doses (or more) of diphtheria, tetanus toxoids and pertussis (DTP) vaccines, diphtheria and tetanus toxoids (DT), or diphtheria, tetanus toxoids and any acellular pertussis (DTaP) vaccines; 3 doses (or more) of poliovirus vaccines; 1 dose (or more) of any measles-containing vaccine; 3 doses (or more) of Haemophilus influenzae type b (Hib) vaccines; and 3 doses (or more) of hepatitis B vaccines.

[f]The 4:3:1:3 series consists of 4 doses (or more) of diphtheria, tetanus toxoids and pertussis (DTP) vaccines, diphtheria and tetanus toxoids (DT), or diphtheria, tetanus toxoids and any acellular pertussis (DTaP) vaccines; 3 doses (or more) of poliovirus vaccines; 1 dose (or more) of any measles-containing vaccine; and 3 doses (or more) of Haemophilus influenzae type b (Hib) vaccines.

[g]The 4:3:1 series consists of 4 doses (or more) of diphtheria, tetanus toxoids and pertussis (DTP) vaccines, diphtheria and tetanus toxoids (DT), or diphtheria, tetanus toxoids and any acellular pertussis (DTaP) vaccines, 3 doses (or more) of poliovirus vaccines; and 1 dose (or more) of any measles-containing vaccine.

[h]Diphtheria, tetanus toxoids, and pertussis vaccine (4 doses or more of any diphtheria, tetanus toxoids, and pertussis vaccines, including diphtheria and tetanus toxoids and any acellular pertussis vaccine).

[i]Poliovirus vaccine (3 doses or more).

[j]Measles-mumps-rubella (MMR) vaccine (1 dose or more) was used beginning in 2005. The previous coverage years reported measles-containing vaccines.

[k]*Haemophilus influenzae* type b (Hib) vaccine (3 doses or more).

[l]Hepatitis B vaccine (3 doses or more).

[m]Varicella vaccine (1 dose or more) is recommended at any visit at or after age 12 months for susceptible children (i.e., those who lack a reliable history of chickenpox).

[n]The heptavalent pneumococcal conjugate vaccine (PCV) is recommended for all children ages 2–23 months and for certain children ages 24–59 months. The series consists of doses at ages 2, 4 and 6 months, and a booster dose at ages 12–15 months.

SOURCE: Adapted from "Table HC3. Childhood Immunization: Percentage of Children Ages 19–35 Months Vaccinated for Selected Diseases by Poverty Status, and Race and Hispanic Origin, 1996–2006," in *America's Children in Brief: Key National Indicators of Well-Being, 2008*, Federal Interagency Forum on Child and Family Statistics, 2008, http://www.childstats.gov/americaschildren/tables.asp (accessed November 2, 2008)

doctor 10 or more times. (See Table 4.2.) However, 10.9% of children did not see a doctor at all. Poor children have less access to health care than nonpoor children.

HEALTH INSURANCE. One reason some children do not have access to medical care is their lack of health insurance. According to the U.S. Census Bureau, 11% (8.1 million) of American children had no health insurance coverage in 2007. (See Figure 4.1.) Factors affecting children's access to coverage included their age, race, and ethnicity, and their family's economic status. Children between the ages of 12 and 17 were more likely to be uninsured (12%) than six- to 11-year-olds (10.3%) and children under the age of six (10.5%). Poor children were proportionately more likely to be uninsured than all children (17.6% versus 11%), and those of Hispanic origin were the least likely racial or ethnic group to receive health insurance coverage—one out of five (20%) Hispanic children were uninsured, compared to 12.2% of African-American children, 11.7% of Asian-American children, and 7.3% of non-Hispanic white children.

Child health insurance coverage increased slightly among all age groups, races, and ethnicities from 2000 to 2004, but then declined from 2004 to 2006. Overall, the percent of children covered by private health insurance declined from 70.2% in 2000 to 64.7% in 2006. (See Table 4.3.) In the press release "HHS Issues New Report Showing More American Children Received Health Insurance in Early 2002" (December 31, 2002, http://www.hhs.gov/news/press/2002pres/20021231.html), the NCHS states that Tommy G. Thompson, the HHS secretary, attributed ongoing increases to a push to provide more government coverage, particularly under the State Children's Health Insurance Program. This trend, however, leveled off in 2005 and 2006.

According to Carmen DeNavas-Walt, Bernadette D. Proctor, and Cheryl Hill Lee of the Census Bureau, in *Income, Poverty, and Health Insurance Coverage in the United States: 2005* (August 2006, http://www.census.gov/prod/2006pubs/p60-231.pdf), in 2005 government programs, such as Medicare, Medicaid, and military insurance, covered a greater proportion of African-American and Hispanic children than other children. Almost half (44.9%) of African-American children and 39.3% of Hispanic

TABLE 4.2

Health care visits to doctor's offices, emergency departments, and home visits over a 12-month period, by selected characteristics, 1997, 2005, and 2006

[Data are based on household interviews of a sample of the civilian noninstitutionalized population]

Characteristic	Number of health care visits[a]											
	None			1–3 visits			4–9 visits			10 or more visits		
	1997	2005	2006	1997	2005	2006	1997	2005	2006	1997	2005	2006
	Percent distribution											
18 years and over, age-adjusted[b, c]	16.5	15.6	17.2	46.2	46.2	46.9	23.6	24.6	23.1	13.7	13.7	12.8
18 years and over, crude[b]	16.5	15.5	17.2	46.5	46.2	46.8	23.5	24.6	23.1	13.5	13.7	12.9
Age												
Under 18 years	11.8	10.2	10.9	54.1	56.3	57.2	25.2	26.1	24.6	8.9	7.4	7.3
Under 6 years	5.0	5.1	4.9	44.9	47.9	50.6	37.0	37.5	34.8	13.0	9.5	9.7
6–17 years	15.3	12.7	13.8	58.7	60.4	60.5	19.3	20.6	19.6	6.8	6.4	6.1
18–44 years	21.7	23.1	25.3	46.7	46.0	45.8	19.0	18.8	17.8	12.6	12.1	11.0
18–24 years	22.0	24.3	25.3	46.8	44.7	47.2	20.0	19.2	17.4	11.2	11.8	10.2
25–44 years	21.6	22.6	25.4	46.7	46.5	45.3	18.7	18.7	17.9	13.0	12.2	11.4
45–64 years	16.9	14.1	16.4	42.9	43.1	44.3	24.7	26.4	23.6	15.5	16.4	15.7
45–54 years	17.9	15.9	18.5	43.9	45.1	46.1	23.4	23.9	21.8	14.8	15.1	13.6
55–64 years	15.3	11.5	13.5	41.3	40.5	41.9	26.7	29.8	26.1	16.7	18.2	18.5
65 years and over	8.9	5.7	6.0	34.7	31.1	33.2	32.5	36.7	36.2	23.8	26.5	24.6
65–74 years	9.8	6.0	6.7	36.9	34.8	34.6	31.6	35.1	36.6	21.6	24.1	22.1
75 years and over	7.7	5.3	5.3	31.8	26.9	31.5	33.8	38.5	35.7	26.6	29.2	27.6
Sex[c]												
Male	21.3	20.4	22.8	47.1	46.9	46.8	20.6	21.9	20.0	11.0	10.8	10.4
Female	11.8	10.8	11.8	45.4	45.5	46.8	26.5	27.3	26.2	16.3	16.4	15.2
Race[c, d]												
White only	16.0	15.2	17.2	46.1	46.0	46.2	23.9	24.9	23.4	14.0	14.0	13.2
Black or African American only	16.8	16.0	16.0	46.1	47.5	49.2	23.2	23.6	23.3	13.9	12.9	11.5
American Indian or Alaska Native only	17.1	20.5	13.5	38.0	36.6	44.2	24.2	29.4	27.6	20.7	13.4	14.7
Asian only	22.8	21.6	21.9	49.1	49.5	51.3	19.7	20.5	18.1	8.3	8.5	8.7
Native Hawaiian or other Pacific Islander only	—	*	*	—	*	*	—	*	*	—	*	*
2 or more races	—	15.6	16.3	—	37.9	44.8	—	26.7	21.3	—	19.9	17.6
Hispanic origin and race[c, d]												
Hispanic or Latino	24.9	24.0	27.1	42.3	42.4	43.0	20.3	21.7	19.6	12.5	11.9	10.3
Mexican	28.9	26.7	31.1	40.8	41.7	40.8	18.5	20.5	18.3	11.8	11.1	9.8
Not Hispanic or Latino	15.4	13.9	15.4	46.7	46.8	47.6	24.0	25.2	23.7	13.9	14.0	13.2
White only	14.7	13.1	15.0	46.6	46.7	46.9	24.4	25.7	24.2	14.3	14.6	13.9
Black or African American only	16.9	16.0	15.7	46.1	47.5	49.5	23.1	23.6	23.4	13.8	12.9	11.4
Respondent-assessed health status[c]												
Fair or poor	7.8	9.2	12.2	23.3	21.9	21.2	29.0	27.1	28.1	39.9	41.9	38.6
Good to excellent	17.2	16.2	17.8	48.4	48.5	49.3	23.3	24.4	22.8	11.1	10.9	10.1
Percent of poverty level[c, e]												
Below 100%	20.6	20.8	21.0	37.8	37.5	39.5	22.7	24.3	22.3	18.9	17.4	17.2
100%–less than 200%	20.1	20.4	21.6	43.3	42.3	43.5	21.7	22.8	21.5	14.9	14.5	13.3
200% or more	14.5	13.3	15.2	48.7	48.7	49.3	24.2	25.2	23.7	12.6	12.8	11.9
Hispanic origin and race and percent of poverty level[c, d, e]												
Hispanic or Latino												
Below 100%	30.2	28.1	32.8	34.8	37.4	35.3	19.9	19.8	19.2	15.0	14.7	12.7
100%–less than 200%	28.7	27.8	29.9	39.7	39.0	42.0	20.4	22.2	19.3	11.2	11.1	8.8
200% or more	18.9	19.4	22.2	48.8	47.1	47.4	20.4	22.7	20.4	11.9	10.8	10.1
Not Hispanic or Latino												
White only												
Below 100%	17.0	16.6	16.3	38.3	36.4	38.7	23.9	27.4	24.2	20.9	19.7	20.8
100%–less than 200%	17.3	17.6	18.8	44.1	42.2	43.7	22.2	23.2	22.2	16.3	17.0	15.4
200% or more	13.8	11.8	14.0	48.2	48.7	48.6	24.9	26.0	24.6	13.1	13.6	12.7
Black or African American only												
Below 100%	17.4	17.9	18.1	38.5	40.2	45.0	23.4	24.5	21.9	20.7	17.4	15.0
100%–less than 200%	18.8	16.2	17.9	43.7	47.1	45.5	22.9	24.0	24.2	14.5	12.7	12.5
200% or more	15.6	15.2	13.5	51.7	50.4	53.6	22.7	23.4	23.5	10.0	11.0	9.3

children had government insurance, compared to only 18% of non-Hispanic white children and 15.9% of Asian-American children.

To remain in the Medicaid program, families must have their eligibility reassessed at least every six months. If the family income or other circumstances change even

TABLE 4.2

Health care visits to doctor's offices, emergency departments, and home visits over a 12-month period, by selected characteristics, 1997, 2005, and 2006 [CONTINUED]

[Data are based on household interviews of a sample of the civilian noninstitutionalized population]

	Number of health care visits[a]											
	None			1–3 visits			4–9 visits			10 or more visits		
Characteristic	1997	2005	2006	1997	2005	2006	1997	2005	2006	1997	2005	2006
	Percent distribution											
Health insurance status at the time of interview[f, g]												
Under 65 years												
Insured	14.3	12.5	14.3	49.0	49.9	50.4	23.6	24.5	23.1	13.1	13.1	12.3
Private	14.7	12.9	14.7	50.6	51.8	52.6	23.1	24.1	22.4	11.6	11.3	10.3
Medicaid	9.8	10.0	11.3	35.5	38.3	37.4	26.5	25.8	25.5	28.2	25.9	25.8
Uninsured	33.7	37.6	39.2	42.8	42.1	42.2	15.3	14.4	12.5	8.2	5.9	6.1
Health insurance status prior to interview[f, g]												
Under 65 years												
Insured continuously all 12 months	14.1	12.4	14.3	49.2	50.1	50.8	23.6	24.5	23.1	13.0	12.9	11.9
Uninsured for any period up to 12 months.	18.9	18.9	19.1	46.0	45.1	46.3	20.8	22.1	20.9	14.4	13.8	13.7
Uninsured more than 12 months	39.0	43.6	45.6	41.4	40.1	40.2	13.2	12.1	9.6	6.4	4.2	4.5
Percent of poverty level and health insurance status prior to interview[e, f, g]												
Under 65 years												
Below 100%												
Insured continuously all 12 months	13.8	12.7	12.6	39.7	40.7	43.1	25.2	25.7	24.2	21.4	21.0	20.1
Uninsured for any period up to 12 months	19.7	19.0	17.8	37.6	37.6	39.3	21.9	23.2	23.4	20.9	20.2	19.5
Uninsured more than 12 months	41.2	46.2	50.1	39.9	35.3	35.3	12.2	14.2	9.9	6.6	4.4	4.8
100–less than 200%												
Insured continuously all 12 months	16.0	14.9	16.3	46.4	46.1	45.9	21.9	23.6	23.0	15.8	15.4	14.8
Uninsured for any period up to 12 months	18.8	19.3	20.6	45.1	44.9	49.8	21.0	21.7	18.7	15.0	14.1	10.9
Uninsured more than 12 months	38.7	43.6	44.3	41.0	39.4	42.1	14.0	12.5	10.2	6.3	4.5	3.4
200% or more												
Insured continuously all 12 months	13.7	11.8	14.1	51.0	51.8	52.6	23.6	24.6	22.9	11.7	11.7	10.4
Uninsured for any period up to 12 months	17.8	18.6	18.6	50.3	48.1	48.0	20.4	22.1	20.7	11.5	11.2	12.7
Uninsured more than 12 months	36.6	41.1	42.8	43.8	44.8	42.4	13.2	10.2	9.3	6.4	3.9	*5.5
Geographic region[c]												
Northeast	13.2	11.4	12.1	45.9	47.1	47.6	26.0	26.5	25.1	14.9	15.0	15.2
Midwest	15.9	13.8	15.2	47.7	47.4	48.4	22.8	24.7	23.6	13.6	14.0	12.7
South	17.2	16.1	18.3	46.1	46.0	45.6	23.3	24.6	23.5	13.5	13.3	12.6
West	19.1	20.1	21.7	44.8	44.4	46.7	22.8	22.8	20.2	13.3	12.6	11.3

slightly, the family can lose its eligibility for the Medicaid program, disrupting health care coverage.

From the late 1980s through the mid-1990s the numbers of uninsured American children rose as coverage rates for employer-sponsored health insurance declined, even though the proportion of children covered by Medicaid also rose. In 1997, as part of the Balanced Budget Act, Congress created the State Children's Health Insurance Program (SCHIP) to expand health insurance to children whose families earned too much money to be eligible for Medicaid but not enough money to pay for private insurance. SCHIP provides funding to states to insure children, offering three alternatives: states may use SCHIP funds to establish separate coverage programs, expand their Medicaid coverage, or use a combination of both. By September 1999 all 50 states had SCHIP plans in place. By September 4, 2003, the program had been expanded to enroll even more children at higher income levels. According to the Centers for Medicare and Medicaid Services, in "FY 2008 Number of Children Ever Enrolled Year—SCHIP by Program Type" (January 20, 2009, http://www.cms.hhs.gov/NationalSCHIPPolicy/downloads/FY2008StateTotalTable012309FINAL.pdf), in fiscal year 2008, 7.4 million children were enrolled in SCHIP, up from 7.1 million the year before.

Homelessness

Under the McKinney-Vento Homeless Assistance Act, the U.S. Department of Education is required to file a report on homeless children served by the act. The Department of Education obtains the data from school districts, which use

TABLE 4.2

Health care visits to doctor's offices, emergency departments, and home visits over a 12-month period, by selected characteristics, 1997, 2005, and 2006 [CONTINUED]

[Data are based on household interviews of a sample of the civilian noninstitutionalized population]

	Number of health care visits[a]											
	None			1–3 visits			4–9 visits			10 or more visits		
Characteristic	1997	2005	2006	1997	2005	2006	1997	2005	2006	1997	2005	2006
	Percent distribution											
Location of residence[c]												
Within MSA[h]	16.2	15.6	16.8	46.4	46.5	47.5	23.7	24.5	23.1	13.7	13.4	12.6
Outside MSA[h]	17.3	15.4	19.2	45.4	44.7	43.7	23.3	25.2	23.3	13.9	14.7	13.8

*Estimates are considered unreliable. Data preceded by an asterisk have a relative standard error (RSE) of 20%–30%. Data not shown have an RSE greater than 30%.
—Data not available.
[a]This table presents a summary measure of health care visits to doctor offices, emergency departments, and home visits during a 12-month period.
[b]Includes all other races not shown separately and unknown health insurance status.
[c]Estimates are age-adjusted to the year 2000 standard population using six age groups: Under 18 years, 18–44 years, 45–54 years, 55–64 years, 65–74 years, and 75 years and over.
[d]The race groups, white, black, American Indian or Alaska Native, Asian, Native Hawaiian or other Pacific Islander, and 2 or more races, include persons of Hispanic and non-Hispanic origin. Persons of Hispanic origin may be of any race. Starting with 1999 data, race-specific estimates are tabulated according to the 1997 Revisions to the Standards for the Classification of Federal Data on Race and Ethnicity and are not strictly comparable with estimates for earlier years. The five single-race categories plus multiple-race categories shown in the table conform to the 1997 Standards. Starting with 1999 data, race-specific estimates are for persons who reported only one racial group; the category 2 or more races includes persons who reported more than one racial group. Prior to 1999, data were tabulated according to the 1977 Standards with four racial groups and the Asian only category included Native Hawaiian or other Pacific Islander. Estimates for single-race categories prior to 1999 included persons who reported one race or, if they reported more than one race, identified one race as best representing their race. Starting with 2003 data, race responses of other race and unspecified multiple race were treated as missing, and then race was imputed if these were the only race responses. Almost all persons with a race response of other race were of Hispanic origin.
[e]Percent of poverty level is based on family income and family size and composition using U.S. Census Bureau poverty thresholds. Missing family income data were imputed for 25%–29% of persons in 1997–1998 and 32%–35% in 1999–2006.
[f]Estimates for persons under 65 years of age are age-adjusted to the year 2000 standard population using four age groups: Under 18 years, 18–44 years, 45–54 years, and 55–64 years of age.
[g]Health insurance categories are mutually exclusive. Persons who reported both Medicaid and private coverage are classified as having private coverage. Starting in 1997, Medicaid includes state-sponsored health plans and State Children's Health Insurance Program (SCHIP). In addition to private and Medicaid, the insured category also includes military plans, other government-sponsored health plans, and Medicare, not shown separately. Persons not covered by private insurance, Medicaid, SCHIP, public assistance (through 1996), state-sponsored or other government-sponsored health plans (starting in 1997), Medicare, or military plans are considered to have no health insurance coverage. Persons with only Indian Health Service coverage are considered to have no health insurance coverage.
[h]MSA is metropolitan statistical area. Starting with 2006 data, MSA status is determined using 2000 census data and the 2000 standards for defining MSAs.
Notes: In 1997, the National Health Interview Survey questionnaire was redesigned.

SOURCE: "Table 82. Health Care Visits to Doctor Offices, Emergency Departments, and Home Visits within the Past 12 Months, by Selected Characteristics: United States, 1997, 2005, and 2006," in *Health, United States, 2007. With Chartbook on Trends in the Health of Americans*, Centers for Disease Control and Prevention, National Center for Health Statistics, 2007, http://www.cdc.gov/nchs/data/hus/hus07.pdf (accessed September 15, 2008)

different methods of estimation. In *Report to the President and Congress on the Implementation of the Education for Homeless Children and Youth Program under the McKinney-Vento Homeless Assistance Act* (2006, http://www.ed.gov/programs/homeless/rpt2006.doc), the Department of Education states that 602,568 children who experienced homelessness at some point during the year were enrolled in school during the 2003–04 school year. Of these children, half (50.3%) lived doubled-up with relatives or friends, a quarter (25.3%) lived in shelters, 9.9% lived in hotels or motels, and 2.6% were unsheltered—in other words, sleeping outside, in vehicles, or in abandoned buildings. This number is almost certainly much lower than the number of children who actually experienced homelessness during this period, as the homeless status of children does not always come to the attention of school officials and many homeless children are not enrolled in school.

The U.S. Conference of Mayors find in *Hunger and Homelessness Survey: A Status Report on Hunger and Homelessness in America's Cities, a 23-City Survey* (December 2007, http://www.usmayors.org/HHSurvey2007/hhsurvey07 .pdf) that 23% of homeless people were in families with children, 76% were single men or women, and 1% were

unaccompanied youth—usually runaways. According to the Conference of Mayors, between 1994 and 2007 the proportion of families among the homeless generally declined, as did the proportion of unaccompanied youth among the homeless population. Data from this survey show city-by-city estimates of children as a percent of homeless family members. In *Mayors Examine Causes of Hunger, Homelessness: The U.S. Conference of Mayors Release 2008 Hunger and Homelessness Survey Results* (December 12, 2008, http://www.usmayors.org/pressreleases/documents/hungerhomelessness_121208.pdf), the Conference of Mayors announces that the homeless rate among cities, in general, grew about 12% from 2007 to 2008, and 16 cities cited an increase in homeless families.

Nearly nine out of 10 (87%) mayors surveyed in the 2007 report said the lack of affordable housing was a principal cause of homelessness among families with children, and 57% cited poverty. Another major cause of family homelessness was domestic violence: 39% of mayors cited such violence as a principal cause of homelessness among families with children. In contrast, 65% of mayors said mental illness and 61% said substance abuse were the principal causes of homelessness among single people and

FIGURE 4.1

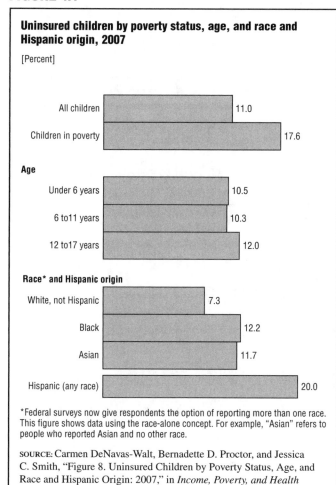

Uninsured children by poverty status, age, and race and Hispanic origin, 2007

[Percent]

All children — 11.0
Children in poverty — 17.6

Age

Under 6 years — 10.5
6 to 11 years — 10.3
12 to 17 years — 12.0

Race* and Hispanic origin

White, not Hispanic — 7.3
Black — 12.2
Asian — 11.7
Hispanic (any race) — 20.0

*Federal surveys now give respondents the option of reporting more than one race. This figure shows data using the race-alone concept. For example, "Asian" refers to people who reported Asian and no other race.

SOURCE: Carmen DeNavas-Walt, Bernadette D. Proctor, and Jessica C. Smith, "Figure 8. Uninsured Children by Poverty Status, Age, and Race and Hispanic Origin: 2007," in *Income, Poverty, and Health Insurance Coverage in the United States: 2007*, U.S. Census Bureau, August 2008, http://www.census.gov/prod/2008pubs/p60–235.pdf (accessed September 21, 2008)

unaccompanied youth. In *Mayors Examine Causes of Hunger, Homelessness: The U.S. Conference of Mayors Release 2008 Hunger and Homelessness Survey Results* "twelve cities (63 percent) reported an increase in homelessness because of the foreclosure crisis."

The poverty and lack of stability that homelessness brings have a very negative impact on children. An example of the poor educational achievement of homeless youths is shown in *Homeless Census and Homeless Youth/Foster Teen Study* (2002, http://www.appliedsurveyresearch.org/www/products/MC_Homeless02_report.pdf), a study of unaccompanied homeless youths conducted in Monterey County, California. According to the survey's findings, 21% of 16-year-olds, 22% of 17-year-olds, 33% of 18-year-olds, 51% of 19-year-olds, 59% of 20-year-olds, and 70% of 21-year-olds were below grade level. Only 13% of the homeless youths in the study had a high school diploma or general equivalency diploma. The remaining 87% were performing below grade level.

Homelessness also has a negative impact on children's health. Catherine Karr of the National Health Care for the Homeless Council argues in *Homeless Children: What Every Health Care Provider Should Know* (December 29, 2003, http://www.nhchc.org/Children/index.htm) that these children suffer from frequent health problems. They are seen in emergency rooms and are hospitalized more often than other poor children. The often crowded and unsanitary conditions they live in lead to a higher rate of infectious diseases, such as upper respiratory infections, diarrhea, and scabies. Homeless children live in less structured and often unsafe environments, leaving them more vulnerable to accidents and injury. They tend not to have access to nutritious food, and are often malnourished or obese. Homeless children tend to lag behind their housed peers developmentally, and school-age homeless children often have academic problems. The greater likelihood that homeless children come from families plagued by mental illness, drug use, and domestic violence negatively affects their own mental health. Homelessness results in serious negative consequences for the children's health.

Hunger

Food insecurity is defined as the lack of access to enough food to meet basic needs. Mark Nord, Margaret Andrews, and Steven Carlson of the U.S. Department of Agriculture report in *Household Food Security in the United States, 2006* (November 2007, http://www.ers.usda.gov/Publications/ERR49/ERR49.pdf) that in 2006, 89.1% of U.S. households were food secure, which remained essentially unchanged from the year before. However, the remaining 10.9% (12.6 million) of U.S. households experienced food insecurity at some time during the year. Most of these households used a variety of coping strategies to obtain adequate food, such as eating less varied diets, participating in food assistance programs, or getting food from community food pantries or soup kitchens. Regardless, 4% (4.6 million) of all households experienced very low food security—in other words, some household members reduced or otherwise altered their normal food intake because of a lack of money.

Nord, Andrews, and Carlson find that a higher percentage of children than adults were food insecure—17.2% of children were food insecure, and 15.6% of households with children were insecure. Households experiencing food insecurity tend to go through a sequence of steps as food insecurity increases: first, families begin to worry about having enough food, then they begin to decrease other necessities, then they reduce the quality and quantity of all household members' diets, then they decrease the frequency of meals and quantity of adult members' food, and finally they decrease the frequency of meals and the quantity of children's food. Even though children are usually protected from being hungry, an estimated one out of every 200 children (0.6%) experienced very low food security on one or more days during the year. Households with incomes below the poverty line,

TABLE 4.3

Percentage of children under age 18 covered by health insurance, by type of insurance, age, race, and Hispanic origin, 1987–2006

Characteristic	1987	1988	1989	1990	1991	1992	1993	1994	1995	1996	1997	1998	1999	2000	2001	2002	2003	2004	2005	2006
Any health insurance																				
Total	**87.1**	**86.9**	**86.7**	**87.0**	**87.3**	**87.3**	**86.3**	**85.8**	**86.2**	**85.3**	**85.3**	**85.0**	**87.5**	**88.4**	**88.7**	**88.8**	**89.0**	**89.5**	**89.1**	**88.3**
Age																				
Ages 0–5	87.6	87.4	87.2	88.5	88.7	89.3	88.5	86.2	86.7	86.4	86.0	84.9	87.6	88.8	89.6	89.5	89.9	90.7	89.6	88.7
Ages 6–11	87.3	87.1	87.1	87.0	87.7	87.6	87.0	86.5	86.5	85.6	86.3	85.6	87.9	88.7	89.1	89.4	89.3	89.8	90.1	88.9
Ages 12–17	86.4	86.3	85.8	85.2	85.4	84.8	83.1	84.8	85.5	84.1	83.6	84.4	87.0	87.7	87.4	87.5	87.8	88.2	87.8	87.4
Race and Hispanic origin[a]																				
White, non-Hispanic	90.3	90.3	90.3	90.0	90.4	90.2	89.4	89.4	89.5	89.6	89.5	89.6	92.5	92.8	93.0	—	—	—	—	—
White-alone, non-Hispanic	—	—	—	—	—	—	—	—	—	—	—	—	—	—	—	92.6	92.9	93.0	93.0	92.7
Black	83.1	84.0	83.5	85.4	84.7	86.3	84.4	83.4	84.7	81.4	81.5	81.0	84.2	86.3	86.8	—	—	—	—	—
Black-alone[b]	—	—	—	—	—	—	—	—	—	—	—	—	—	—	—	86.5	86.1	88.2	88.2	85.9
Hispanic[b]	71.5	70.9	69.8	71.6	73.4	74.5	74.3	71.5	73.2	71.4	71.6	70.5	74.1	75.1	76.2	77.8	79.3	79.7	78.5	77.9
Private health insurance																				
Total	**73.6**	**73.5**	**73.6**	**71.1**	**69.7**	**68.7**	**67.4**	**65.6**	**66.1**	**66.5**	**67.3**	**67.9**	**70.0**	**70.2**	**68.8**	**67.9**	**66.3**	**66.4**	**65.8**	**64.7**
Age																				
Ages 0–5	71.7	71.0	70.6	68.2	66.1	64.6	63.4	59.7	60.4	62.4	63.6	64.3	66.4	66.5	64.9	63.9	62.3	62.3	61.4	60.5
Ages 6–11	74.3	74.1	74.9	72.5	71.2	70.8	70.0	67.3	67.2	67.1	68.4	68.5	70.2	70.4	69.0	68.5	66.6	67.3	66.6	65.4
Ages 12–17	75.1	75.5	75.7	73.0	72.1	70.9	69.0	70.3	71.0	70.2	69.8	70.9	73.2	73.5	72.4	71.2	69.7	69.5	69.2	67.9
Race and Hispanic origin[a]																				
White, non-Hispanic	83.2	83.2	83.1	80.8	79.9	79.5	77.8	77.1	78.0	77.9	78.0	79.3	81.6	81.4	80.2	—	—	—	—	—
White-alone, non-Hispanic	—	—	—	—	—	—	—	—	—	—	—	—	—	—	—	79.6	78.6	77.9	78.1	76.9
Black	49.2	49.9	51.5	48.5	45.4	46.1	45.5	43.0	43.9	45.4	48.2	47.6	52.2	53.9	53.1	—	—	—	—	—
Black-alone[b]	—	—	—	—	—	—	—	—	—	—	—	—	—	—	—	50.8	48.0	49.3	48.7	49.0
Hispanic[b]	47.9	48.3	48.2	44.9	42.8	41.9	41.8	37.7	38.3	39.9	41.8	43.2	46.3	45.2	43.9	43.5	42.4	43.8	42.0	40.9
Public health insurance[c]																				
Total	**19.0**	**19.2**	**19.2**	**21.9**	**23.9**	**25.2**	**26.8**	**26.3**	**26.4**	**24.9**	**23.4**	**22.8**	**23.2**	**24.4**	**25.9**	**26.8**	**29.1**	**29.9**	**29.7**	**29.8**
Age																				
Ages –5	22.1	22.9	23.7	27.6	30.0	32.8	35.1	33.3	32.6	30.8	28.6	26.8	27.3	29.2	31.3	32.1	34.4	35.5	34.7	34.7
Ages 6–11	18.6	18.2	18.0	20.0	22.3	22.9	24.8	25.2	25.6	24.7	23.1	23.0	23.4	24.5	26.4	26.8	28.8	29.5	29.8	29.5
Ages 12–17	16.1	16.2	15.3	17.5	18.6	19.1	19.8	19.9	20.5	19.2	18.6	18.6	19.2	19.8	20.3	21.9	24.4	25.0	24.7	25.5

TABLE 4.3

Percentage of children under age 18 covered by health insurance, by type of insurance, age, race, and Hispanic origin, 1987–2006 [CONTINUED]

Characteristic	1987	1988	1989	1990	1991	1992	1993	1994	1995	1996	1997	1998	1999	2000	2001	2002	2003	2004	2005	2006
Race and Hispanic origin[a]																				
White, non-Hispanic	12.1	12.5	12.7	14.7	16.1	16.7	18.5	18.1	17.5	17.6	17.0	15.8	16.3	17.2	18.7	—	—	—	—	—
White-alone, non-Hispanic	—	—	—	—	—	—	—	—	—	—	—	—	—	—	—	18.5	20.5	21.2	21.2	22.0
Black	42.1	41.9	41.0	45.5	47.5	49.3	49.5	48.5	48.8	44.8	39.6	41.6	39.8	41.9	41.6	—	—	—	—	—
Black-alone	—	—	—	—	—	—	—	—	—	—	—	—	—	—	—	44.2	46.5	48.4	48.0	44.0
Hispanic[b]	28.2	27.4	27.0	31.9	36.5	38.3	40.8	38.4	39.0	35.3	33.9	31.5	32.9	34.6	37.0	39.6	42.0	42.2	41.4	42.3

—Not available.

Notes: Children are considered to be covered by health insurance if they had public or private coverage at any time during the year. Some children are covered by both types of insurance; hence, the sum of public and private is greater than the total. The data from 1996 to 2004 have been revised since initially published.

[a]For race and Hispanic-origin data in this table: From 1987 to 2002, following the 1977 OMB standards for collecting and presenting data on race, the Current Population Survey (CPS) asked respondents to choose one race from the following: white, black, American Indian or Alaskan Native, or Asian or Pacific Islander. The Census Bureau also offered an "other" category. Beginning in 2003, following the 1997 OMB standards for collecting and presenting data on race, the CPS asked respondents to choose one or more races from the following: white, black, Asian, American Indian or Alaska Native, and Native Hawaiian or other Pacific Islander. All race groups discussed in this table from 2002 onward refer to people who indicated only one racial identity within the racial categories presented. People who responded to the question on race by indicating only one race are referred to as the race-alone population. The use of the race-alone population in this table does not imply that it is the preferred method of presenting or analyzing data. Data from 2002 onward are not directly comparable with data from earlier years. Data on race and Hispanic origin are collected separately. Persons of Hispanic origin may be of any race.
[b]Persons of Hispanic origin may be of any race.
[c]Public health insurance for children consists mostly of Medicaid, but also includes Medicare, the State Children's Health Insurance Programs (SCHIP), and the Civilian Health and Medical Care Program of the Uniformed Services (CHAMPUS/Tricare).

SOURCE: Adapted from "Table HC1. Health Insurance Coverage: Percentage of Children Ages 0–17 Covered by Health Insurance by Selected Characteristics, 1987–2006," in *America's Children in Brief: Key National Indicators of Well-Being, 2008*, Federal Interagency Forum on Child and Family Statistics, 2008, http://www.childstats.gov/americaschildren/tables.asp (accessed November 2, 2008)

households with children headed by a single woman, and African-American and Hispanic households were the most likely to experience food insecurity.

EMERGENCY FOOD ASSISTANCE. Feeding America (formerly America's Second Harvest), the nation's largest charitable hunger-relief organization, reports in *Hunger Study, 2006* (2006, http://www.hungerinamerica.org/key_findings/) that in 2005, 25.3 million Americans sought emergency food assistance. In *Hunger and Homelessness Survey*, the Conference of Mayors states that 80% of mayors reported that requests for emergency food assistance had increased in 2007, and that the total number of emergency food assistance requests increased by 12% during that year. The Conference of Mayors note, "Overall, it appears that the need for emergency food assistance programs is continuing to increase and that cities are facing many challenges in responding to the demand for assistance." The most frequent reasons for hunger cited by city officials were poverty (90% of mayors), high housing costs (57% of mayors), and unemployment (52% of mayors). Other causes included high medical, utility, and transportation costs, substance abuse, and a lack of education. In the 2008 report *Mayors Examine Causes of Hunger, Homelessness*, the Conference of Mayors observes that requests for emergency food assistance had continued to increase in most cities. The organization states that "an estimated 59 percent of requests for food assistance were coming from families—many for the first-time."

Exposure to Toxins

Another threat to children's health is exposure to environmental toxins. Two toxins that children are most frequently exposed to are lead and second-hand smoke.

LEAD POISONING. Because they have smaller bodies and are growing, children suffer the effects of lead exposure more acutely than adults do. Lead poisoning causes nervous system disorders, reduction in intelligence, fatigue, inhibited infant growth, and hearing loss. Toxic levels of lead in a parent can also affect unborn children.

In "Toys and Childhood Lead Exposure" (August 31, 2007, http://www.cdc.gov/nceh/lead/faq/toys.htm), the CDC indicates that children are primarily exposed to lead in paint and plastics. Leaded paint was banned in the United States in 1978, although children may be exposed to leaded paint in older homes. Even though leaded paint is not used on toys manufactured in the United States, it is still widely used on toys manufactured in other countries. Therefore, children may be exposed to lead when playing with imported toys. In addition, the use of lead in plastic, which makes it more flexible and able to return to its original shape, has not been banned. The CDC explains that "when the plastic is exposed to substances such as sunlight, air, and detergents the chemical bond between the lead and plastics breaks down and forms a dust."

David Barboza reports in "Why Lead in Toy Paint? It's Cheaper" (*New York Times*, September 11, 2007) that in 2007 nearly two dozen toys were recalled because they contained toxic levels of lead paint. Dozens of children's jewelry products, most of them made in China, had also been recalled in 2006 and 2007. In September 2007 Mattel, the world's largest toy maker, announced its third recall in six weeks, asking people to return certain toys made in China that contained high levels of lead paint. Lead paint is sometimes used in manufacturing products for children because it is less expensive than nonleaded paint. Ashland University randomly tested plastic toys and children's jewelry and found high lead levels in many of them, most of which had not been recalled. According to the article "China Bans Lead Paint in Toys Exported to U.S." (Associated Press, September 11, 2007), China signed an agreement on September 11, 2007, to prohibit the use of lead paint on toys for export to the United States. However, Barboza states that "enforcement of the regulations in China is lax."

In "CDC Surveillance Data, 1997–2006" (November 29, 2007, http://www.cdc.gov/nceh/lead/surv/stats.htm), the CDC states that in 2006, 39,526 children in the United States aged five and under had confirmed blood lead levels greater than the CDC's recommended level of 10 micrograms per deciliter of blood. This was 1.2% of all children tested. According to the Commission for Environmental Cooperation, in *Children's Health and the Environment in North America: A First Report on Available Indicators and Measures* (January 2006, http://www.cec.org/files/PDF/POLLUTANTS/CEH-Indicators-fin_en.pdf), this number had dropped substantially since the early 1970s, due largely to the phasing out of lead in gasoline between 1973 and 1995. Even though children from all social and economic levels can be affected by lead poisoning, children in families with low incomes who live in older, deteriorated housing are at higher risk. Paint produced before 1978 frequently contained lead, so federal legislation now requires owners to disclose any information they may have about lead-based paint before renting or selling a home built earlier than 1978. Lead is also found in lead plumbing and is emitted by factory smokestacks.

SECONDHAND SMOKE AND CHILDREN. Environmental tobacco smoke is a major hazard for children, whose respiratory, immune, and other systems are not as well developed as those of adults. According to the CDC, in "Disparities in Secondhand Smoke Exposure—United States, 1988–1994 and 1999–2004" (*Morbidity and Mortality Weekly Report*, vol. 57, no. 27, July 11, 2008), secondhand or passive smoke (smoke produced by other people's cigarettes) increases the number of attacks and severity of symptoms in children with asthma and can even cause asthma in preschool-age children. It also causes lower respiratory tract infections, middle-ear disease, and a reduction in lung function in children, and it increases the risk of sudden infant death syndrome. The CDC finds the percentage of children aged four to 11 who were regularly exposed to secondhand smoke in their homes decreased from 38.2% in the 1988–94 period to 23.8% in the 1999–2004 period, a reduction of 37.7%. The percentage of children aged 12 to 19 exposed to secondhand smoke decreased from 35.4% in the 1988–94 period to 19.5% in the 1999–2004 period, for an even larger decline of 44.9%.

DISEASES OF CHILDHOOD
Overweight and Obese Children

The number of overweight and obese Americans has reached epidemic proportions and has become a national concern. The percentage of overweight children and adolescents has grown significantly since the 1970s. Between 1976 and 1980, 6.7% of boys and 6.4% of girls aged six to 11 years were overweight. (See Table 4.4.) For boys, this percentage hit a high of 19.9%, or one in five boys, in the 2003–04 period, before dropping to a still high of 16.2% in 2005–06. Girls also hit a high of 17.6% in 2003–04, before it dropped to 14.1% in 2005–06.

An upward trend was also seen in the rates of overweight adolescents; 4.5% of boys and 5.4% of girls aged 12 to 17 were overweight in the period from 1976 to 1980, but 18.1% of adolescent boys and 17.5% of adolescent girls were overweight in the 2005–06 period—and these figures had not dropped from the previous two-year period. (See Table 4.4.) The proportion of overweight children overall between the ages of six and 17 tripled (from 5.7% to 16.5%) between 1976 and 2006.

The percentages of overweight children (in the 85th percentile or above for body mass index) and obese children (in the 95th percentile or above for body mass index) vary by race and ethnicity. In 2007 African-American adolescents were more likely to be overweight (19%) or obese (18.3%) than non-Hispanic white adolescents (14.3% were overweight and 10.8% were obese) or Hispanic adolescents (18.1% were overweight and 16.6% were obese).

(See Table 4.5.) Younger students were more likely than older students to be either overweight or obese.

Medical professionals are concerned about this trend, because overweight children have an increased risk for premature death in adulthood as well as for many chronic diseases, including coronary heart disease, hypertension, diabetes mellitus (type 2), gallbladder disease, respiratory disease, some cancers, and arthritis. Type 2 diabetes, previously considered an adult disease, has increased dramatically in children and adolescents. Being overweight or obese can also lead to poor self-esteem and depression in children.

Weight problems in children are thought to be caused by a lack of physical activity, unhealthy eating habits, or a combination of these factors, with genetics and lifestyle playing important roles in determining a child's weight. Watching television and playing computer and video games contribute to the inactive lifestyles of some children. According to Danice K. Eaton et al. of the CDC, in "Youth Risk Behavior Surveillance—United States, 2007" (*Morbidity and Mortality Weekly Report*, vol. 57, no. SS-4, June 6, 2008), a quarter (24.9%) of high school students spent three or more hours per school day on the computer and more than a third (35.4%) spent three or more hours per school day watching television, often not getting a sufficient amount of physical exercise as a consequence.

Physical activity patterns established during youth may extend into adulthood and may affect the risk of illnesses such as coronary heart disease, diabetes, and cancer. Mental health experts correlate increased physical activity with improved mental health and overall improvement in life satisfaction. Eaton et al. report that only 43.7% of high school boys and 25.6% of high school girls met recommended levels of physical activity. (See Table 4.6.) White students were somewhat more likely to meet recommended levels of physical activity (37%) than African-American (31.1%) or Hispanic (30.2%) students. Only about half (53.6%) of high school students attended physical education classes, 56.3% played on a sports team, and only

TABLE 4.4

Percentage of children 6–17 who are overweight, by gender and age group, selected years 1976–2006

	Total						Male						Female					
Age group	1976–1980	1988–1994	1999–2000	2001–2002	2003–2004	2005–2006	1976–1980	1988–1994	1999–2000	2001–2002	2003–2004	2005–2006	1976–1980	1988–1994	1999–2000	2001–2002	2003–2004	2005–2006
Ages 6–17																		
Total	5.7	11.2	15.0	16.5	18.0	16.5	5.5	11.8	15.7	18.0	19.1	17.2	5.8	10.6	14.3	15.1	16.8	15.9
Ages 6–11																		
Total	6.5	11.3	15.1	16.3	18.8	15.1	6.7	11.6	15.7	17.5	19.9	16.2	6.4	11.0	14.3	14.9	17.6	14.1
Ages 12–17																		
Total	5.0	11.1	14.9	16.8	17.2	17.8	4.5	12.0	15.6	18.4	18.3	18.1	5.4	10.2	14.2	15.2	16.0	17.5

Note: Overweight is defined as body mass index (BMI) at or above the 95th percentile of the 2000 Centers for Disease Control and Prevention sex specific BMI-for-age growth charts.

SOURCE: "Table HEALTH5. Overweight: Percentage of Children Ages 6–17 Who Are Overweight by Gender and Age Group, 1976–1980, 1988–1994, and 1999–2000, 2001–2002, 2003–2004, and 2005–2006," in *America's Children in Brief: Key National Indicators of Well-Being, 2008*, Federal Interagency Forum on Child and Family Statistics, 2008, http://www.childstats.gov/americaschildren/tables.asp (accessed November 2, 2008)

TABLE 4.5

Percentage of high school students who were obese and who were overweight, by sex, race/ethnicity, and grade, 2007

	Obese			Overweight		
	Female	Male	Total	Female	Male	Total
Category	%	%	%	%	%	%
Race/ethnicity						
White*	6.8	14.6	10.8	12.8	15.7	14.3
Black*	17.8	18.9	18.3	21.4	16.6	19.0
Hispanic	12.7	20.3	16.6	17.9	18.3	18.1
Grade						
9	10.7	16.6	13.8	18.3	17.0	17.6
10	9.8	16.4	13.2	14.2	17.7	16.0
11	8.1	17.3	12.7	14.2	15.9	15.1
12	9.3	14.7	12.0	13.1	14.9	14.0
Total	**9.6**					

*Non-Hispanic.

Notes: Students who were ≥95th percentile for body mass index (BMI), by age and sex, based on reference data. Previous Youth Risk Behavior Survey reports used the term "overweight" to describe youth with a BMI ≥95th percentile for age and sex and "at risk for overweight" for those with a BMI ≥85th percentile and <95th percentile. However, this report uses the terms "obese" and "overweight" in accordance with the 2007 recommendations from the Expert Committee on the Assessment, Prevention, and Treatment of Child and Adolescent Overweight and Obesity convened by the American Medical Association (AMA) and cofunded by AMA in collaboration with the Health Resources and Services Administration and CDC.
Students who were ≥85th percentile but <95th percentile for body mass index, by age and sex, based on reference data.

SOURCE: Danice K. Eaton, "Table 82. Percentage of High School Students Who Were Obese and Who Were Overweight, by Sex, Race/Ethnicity, and Grade— United States, Youth Risk Behavior Survey, 2007," in "Youth Risk Behavior Surveillance—United States, 2007," *Morbidity and Mortality Weekly Report*, vol. 57, no. SS-4, June 6, 2008, http://www.cdc.gov/HealthyYouth/yrbs/pdf/yrbss07_mmwr.pdf (accessed November 5, 2008)

TABLE 4.6

High school participation in physical activity, by demographic characteristics, 2007

	Met recommended levels of physical activity			Did not participate in 60 or more minutes of physical activity on any day		
	Female	Male	Total	Female	Male	Total
Category	%	%	%	%	%	%
Race/ethnicity						
White*	27.9	46.1	37.0	28.2	16.7	22.4
Black*	21.0	41.3	31.1	42.1	21.8	32.0
Hispanic	21.9	38.6	30.2	35.2	18.8	27.1
Grade						
9	31.5	44.4	38.1	26.1	17.1	21.5
10	24.4	45.1	34.8	31.7	16.3	24.0
11	24.6	45.2	34.8	34.3	18.0	26.2
12	20.6	38.7	29.5	36.2	21.5	28.9
Total	**25.6**	**43.7**	**34.7**	**31.8**	**18.0**	**24.9**

Notes: Were physically active doing any kind of physical activity that increased their heart rate and made them breathe hard some of the time for a total of at least 60 minutes/day on 5 or more days during the 7 days before the survey.
Did not participate in 60 or more minutes of any kind of physical activity that increased their heart rate and made them breathe hard some of the time on at least 1 day during the 7 days before the survey.
*Non-Hispanic.

SOURCE: Danice K. Eaton, "Table 52. Percentage of High School Students Who Met Recommended Levels of Physical Activity and Who Did Not Participate in 60 or More Minutes of Physical Activity on Any Day, by Sex, Race/Ethnicity, and Grade—United States, Youth Risk Behavior Survey, 2007," in "Youth Risk Behavior Surveillance—United States, 2007," *Morbidity and Mortality Weekly Report*, vol. 57, no. SS-4, June 6, 2008, http://www.cdc.gov/HealthyYouth/yrbs/pdf/yrbss07_mmwr.pdf (accessed November 5, 2008)

30.3% attended physical education classes daily. (See Table 4.7.) Rigorous activity among high school students also generally declined with age.

Asthma

Another serious disease affecting children is asthma, a chronic respiratory disease that causes attacks of difficulty breathing. In *The State of Childhood Asthma, United States, 1980–2005* (December 12, 2006, http://www.cdc.gov/nchs/data/ad/ad381.pdf), Lara J. Akinbami of the CDC indicates that millions of children in the United States have asthma. In 2005, 8.9% (6.5 million) of children were currently suffering from asthma, and 12.7% (9 million) of children had suffered with it at some point in their lifetime. Childhood asthma

TABLE 4.7

Percentage of high school students who attended physical education classes and who played on at least one sports team, 2007

Category	Attended PE classes[a]			Attended PE classes daily[b]			Played on at least one sports team		
	Female	Male	Total	Female	Male	Total	Female	Male	Total
	%	%	%	%	%	%	%	%	%
Race/ethnicity									
White[c]	46.8	54.0	50.4	25.6	32.2	28.9	54.8	63.0	58.9
Black[c]	50.6	61.0	55.9	27.8	35.8	31.9	44.7	65.1	54.9
Hispanic	57.3	64.7	61.0	35.5	36.4	36.0	41.8	58.1	50.0
Grade									
9	65.1	68.3	66.8	40.4	39.7	40.1	54.7	63.4	59.2
10	51.2	62.3	56.8	26.1	35.7	30.9	50.8	64.7	57.8
11	38.8	51.4	45.1	19.8	27.9	23.9	52.5	63.0	57.7
12	38.5	44.6	41.5	20.2	27.5	23.8	41.9	56.2	49.0
Total	**49.4**	**57.7**	**53.6**	**27.3**	**33.2**	**30.3**	**50.4**	**62.1**	**56.3**

[a]On 1 or more days in an average week when they were in school.
[b]5 days in an average week when they were in school.
[c]Non-Hispanic.
Notes: Run by their school or community groups during the 12 months before the survey. PE is physical education. During the 30 days before the survey, among the 79.6% of students nationwide who exercised or played sports.

SOURCE: Adapted from Danice K. Eaton, "Table 78. Percentage of High School Students Who Attended Physical Education (PE) Classes, by Sex, Race/Ethnicity, and Grade—United States, Youth Risk Behavior Survey, 2007," and "Table 80. Percentage of High School Students Who Played on at Least One Sports Team and Who Saw a Doctor or Nurse for an Injury That Happened While Exercising or Playing Sports, by Sex, Race/Ethnicity, and Grade—United States, Youth Risk Behavior Survey, 2007," in "Youth Risk Behavior Surveillance—United States, 2007," *Morbidity and Mortality Weekly Report*, vol. 57, no. SS-4, June 6, 2008, http://www.cdc.gov/HealthyYouth/yrbs/pdf/yrbss07_mmwr.pdf (accessed November 5, 2008)

caused 27 hospitalizations per 10,000 children in 2004, and caused 12.8 million missed days of school in 2003. The American Lung Association estimates that up to a million asthmatic children are exposed to secondhand smoke, worsening their condition.

According to Akinbami, African-American children suffer from asthma at a rate 60% higher than that of non-Hispanic white children, and Puerto Rican children suffer from asthma at a rate 140% higher than non-Hispanic white children. In addition, she finds that African-American children's asthma is apparently much less well controlled than that of non-Hispanic white children. African-American children have a 250% higher hospitalization rate, a 260% higher emergency department visit rate, and a 500% higher death rate from asthma. Akinbami speculates that this is due to the lower level and quality of health care received by African-American children.

HIV/AIDS

Acquired immune deficiency syndrome (AIDS) was identified as a new disease in 1981, and, according to the CDC, in *HIV/AIDS Surveillance Report: Cases of HIV Infection and AIDS in the United States and Dependent Areas, 2006* (2008, http://www.cdc.gov/hiv/topics/surveillance/resources/reports/2006report/pdf/2006SurveillanceReport.pdf), an estimated one million cases had been diagnosed in the United States through 2006. AIDS is caused by the human immunodeficiency virus (HIV), which weakens the victim's immune system, making it vulnerable to other opportunistic infections. Young children with AIDS usually have the virus

transmitted to them either by an infected parent or through contaminated transfusions of blood or blood products. Adolescents who are sexually active or experimenting with drugs are also vulnerable to HIV infection, which can be spread through sexual intercourse without the use of a condom or through shared hypodermic needles.

In adults the most common opportunistic infections of AIDS are Kaposi's sarcoma (a rare skin cancer) and *pneumocystis carinii* pneumonia. In infants and children, a failure to thrive and unusually severe bacterial infections characterize the disease. Except for *pneumocystis carinii* pneumonia, children with symptomatic HIV infection seldom develop opportunistic infections as adults do. More often, they are plagued by recurrent bacterial infections, persistent oral thrush (a common fungal infection of the mouth or throat), and chronic and recurrent diarrhea. They may also suffer from enlarged lymph nodes, chronic pneumonia, developmental delays, and neurological abnormalities.

HOW MANY ARE INFECTED? According to the CDC, in *HIV/AIDS Surveillance Report*, by the end of 2006 there were a cumulative total of 9,144 AIDS cases in children under the age of 13 since record-keeping began in 1981. (See Table 4.8.) African-American children made up the overwhelming majority of these cases (5,654 cases), followed by Hispanic children (1,748 cases), non-Hispanic white children (1,599 cases), Asians or Pacific Islanders (54 cases), and Native Americans or Alaskan Natives (31 cases). By the end of 2006, 5,165 children aged 14 and under had died from the disease.

TABLE 4.8

Diagnoses of AIDS in children younger than 13, by year of diagnosis, race and Hispanic origin, and transmission category, 2002–06

	Year of diagnosis					
	2002	2003	2004	2005	2006	Cumulative[a]
Race/ethnicity						
White, not Hispanic	14	12	7	4	4	1,599
Black, not Hispanic	70	46	33	38	30	5,654
Hispanic	18	10	9	8	3	1,748
Asian/Pacific Islander	1	0	1	1	1	54
American Indian/Alaska Native	1	0	1	0	0	31
Transmission category						
Hemophilia/coagulation disorder	0	0	0	0	0	226
Mother with documented HIV infection or 1 of the						
following risk factors	104	70	53	52	37	8,508
Injection drug use	12	8	5	3	4	3,220
Sex with injection drug user	4	6	3	2	1	1,397
Sex with bisexual male	2	0	3	1	1	209
Sex with person with hemophilia	0	0	0	0	0	35
Sex with HIV-infected transfusion recipient	0	0	0	0	0	22
Sex with HIV-infected person, risk factor not specified	36	20	20	25	13	1,530
Receipt of blood transfusion, blood components, or tissue	2	1	0	0	0	144
Has HIV infection, risk factor not specified	47	34	21	21	17	1,951
Receipt of blood transfusion, blood components, or tissue	2	0	0	0	0	374
Other/risk factor not reported or identified	0	0	0	0	0	36
Total[b]	**106**	**70**	**53**	**53**	**38**	**9,144**

Notes: These numbers do not represent reported case counts. Rather, these numbers are point estimates, which result from adjustments of reported case counts. The reported case counts have been adjusted for reporting delays and for redistribution of cases in persons initially reported without an identified risk factor, but not for incomplete reporting.
[a]From the beginning of the epidemic through 2006.
[b]Includes children of unknown race or multiple races. Cumulative total includes 58 children of unknown race or multiple races. Because column totals were calculated independently of the values for the subpopulations, the values in each column may not sum to the column total.

SOURCE: "Table 4. Estimated Numbers of AIDS Cases in Children <13 Years of Age, by Year of Diagnosis and Selected Characteristics, 2002–2006 and Cumulative—50 States and the District of Columbia," in *HIV/AIDS Surveillance Report: Cases of HIV Infection and AIDS in the United States and Dependent Areas, 2006*, vol. 18, Centers for Disease Control and Prevention, 2008, http://www.cdc.gov/hiv/topics/surveillance/resources/reports/2006report/pdf/2006SurveillanceReport.pdf (accessed November 5, 2008)

MEANS OF TRANSMITTAL. Most babies of HIV-infected mothers do not develop HIV. HIV-positive mothers can reduce the risk of transmission by taking antiretroviral drugs during the last two trimesters of pregnancy and during labor; giving birth by caesarean section; giving the infant a short course of antiretroviral drugs after birth; and not breast feeding. With these interventions, the transmission rate can be reduced to as low as 2%.

Even though interventions are effective in preventing HIV transmission from pregnant mothers to babies, the overwhelming majority of children with AIDS contracted it from mothers either infected with HIV or at risk for AIDS (8,508 of 9,144 cases, or 93%). (See Table 4.8.) Another way HIV/AIDS has been transmitted to children was through blood transfusions contaminated with the virus, although this means of transmission has been all but eliminated in the twenty-first century.

ADOLESCENTS WITH AIDS. The number of AIDS cases among adolescents is comparatively low. In *HIV/AIDS Surveillance Report*, the CDC states that by the end of 2006, 6,704 adolescents aged 13 to 19 had been diagnosed with AIDS since the beginning of the epidemic in the early 1980s. However, because of the long incubation period between the time of infection and the onset of symptoms, it is highly probable that many people who develop AIDS

in their early twenties became infected with HIV during their adolescence; 36,225 young adults, 20- to 24-year-olds, had been diagnosed since the beginning of the epidemic by the end of 2006.

MENTAL HEALTH ISSUES IN YOUNG PEOPLE
Marital Conflict and Divorce

Marital conflict hurts children whether it results in the breakup of marriages or not. Nearly all the studies on children of divorce have focused on the period after the parents separated. However, recent studies suggest that the negative effects children experience may not come so much from divorce itself as from marital discord between parents before divorce. In fact, some research suggests that many problems reported with troubled teens not only began during the marriage but may have contributed to the breakup of the marriage. According to the article "Children of Divorce" (*Journal of the American Board of Family Practice*, vol. 14, no. 3, 2001), children raised in discord and marital instability often experience a variety of social, emotional, and psychological problems. Amy L. Baker reports in "The Long-Term Effects of Parental Alienation on Adult Children: A Qualitative Research Study" (*American Journal of Family Therapy*, vol. 33, no. 4, July–September 2005) that negative effects, such as low self-esteem, depression, drug and/or alcohol abuse, lack of trust, alienation from own children, and an elevated risk of divorce, persist among these children into adulthood.

Divorce can cause stressful situations for children in several ways. One or both parents may have to move to a new home, removing the children from family and friends who could have given them support. Custody issues can generate hostility between parents. If one or both parents remarry, children are faced with yet another adjustment in their living arrangements.

Eating Disorders

Even though young people who are overweight increase their risk for certain diseases in adulthood, an overemphasis on thinness during childhood may contribute to eating disorders such as anorexia nervosa (a disorder characterized by voluntary starvation) and bulimia nervosa (a disorder in which a person eats large amounts of food then forces vomiting or uses laxatives to prevent weight gain). Girls are both more likely to have a distorted view of their weight and more likely to have eating disorders than boys.

Eaton et al. report that in 2007 students as a whole had a fairly accurate view of their weight: 15.8% of students were overweight (having a body mass index between the 85th and 95th percentile for their age and sex) and 13% were obese (having a body mass index equal to or greater than the 95th percentile for their age and sex). (See Table 4.5.) Approximately 29.3% said they were slightly or very overweight. (See Table 4.9.) However, girls were much more likely than boys to have a skewed perception of their body size. Even though 32.7% of male students were obese or overweight, 24.2% perceived themselves as overweight and 30.4% were trying to lose weight. Among female students, 24.7% of students

were obese or overweight, 34.5% described themselves as overweight, and fully 60.3% were trying to lose weight.

Most students used healthy ways to lose weight, such as diet and exercise. However, a significant proportion used unhealthy methods such as extended periods of not eating, taking diet pills or laxatives, or inducing vomiting. Over half (53.2%) of female students and a quarter (28.3%) of male students ate less food, fewer calories, or low-fat foods to control their weight. (See Table 4.10.) Another two-thirds (67%) of female students and over half (55%) of male students exercised to control their weight. However, 16.3% of female students and 7.3% of male students had not eaten for 24 hours or more to lose weight; 7.5% of female students and 4.2% of male students had taken diet pills, powders, or liquids to control their weight; and 6.4% of female students and 2.2% of male students had vomited or taken laxatives to control their weight. (See Table 4.11.) A greater proportion of female students than male students used both healthy and unhealthy behaviors for weight control. In addition, Hispanic and non-Hispanic white students were in general more likely than African-American students to use unhealthy methods of weight control and the use of these methods increased somewhat with age.

Hyperactivity

Attention deficit hyperactivity disorder (ADHD) is one of the most common psychiatric disorders to appear in childhood. No one knows what causes ADHD, although research has focused on biological causes and the role of genetics. Symptoms include restlessness, inability to concentrate, aggressiveness, and impulsivity; and the lack of treatment can lead to problems in school, at work, and in making friends. Methylphenidate, a stimulant, is frequently

TABLE 4.9

Percentage of high school students who thought they had a problem with weight and were trying to lose weight, by sex, race/ethnicity, and grade, 2007

Category	Described themselves as overweight			Were trying to lose weight		
	Female	Male	Total	Female	Male	Total
	%	%	%	%	%	%
Race/ethnicity						
White*	34.0	23.6	28.8	62.3	29.0	45.6
Black*	30.1	19.1	24.6	49.5	24.9	37.1
Hispanic	39.3	28.3	33.8	62.1	38.5	50.2
Grade						
9	33.6	24.3	28.8	58.6	31.0	44.4
10	33.8	24.8	29.2	60.2	31.6	45.8
11	36.2	25.8	31.0	61.3	30.1	45.8
12	34.9	21.6	28.3	61.6	28.7	45.3
Total	**34.5**	**24.2**	**29.3**	**60.3**	**30.4**	**45.2**

*Non-Hispanic.

SOURCE: Danice K. Eaton, "Table 84. Percentage of High School Students Who Described Themselves As Slightly or Very Overweight and Who Were Trying to Lose Weight, by Sex, Race/Ethnicity, and Grade—United States, Youth Risk Behavior Survey, 2007," in "Youth Risk Behavior Surveillance—United States, 2007," *Morbidity and Mortality Weekly Report*, vol. 57, no. SS-4, June 6, 2008, http://www.cdc.gov/HealthyYouth/yrbs/pdf/yrbss07_mmwr.pdf (accessed November 5, 2008)

TABLE 4.10

Percentage of high school students who ate less food, fewer calories, or low-fat foods and who exercised, by sex, race, ethnicity, and grade, 2007

	Ate less food, fewer calories, or low-fat foods to lose weight or to keep from gaining weight			Exercised to lose weight or to keep from gaining weight		
	Female	Male	Total	Female	Male	Total
Category	%	%	%	%	%	%
Race/ethnicity						
White*	58.4	28.3	43.3	71.5	53.3	62.4
Black*	34.6	21.0	27.8	50.7	53.7	52.2
Hispanic	52.0	32.3	42.1	66.4	60.1	63.2
Grade						
9	50.5	27.3	38.6	70.6	58.7	64.5
10	53.0	29.1	40.9	67.7	54.2	60.9
11	54.0	29.8	42.0	65.0	54.9	59.9
12	56.4	27.4	42.0	63.7	51.1	57.5
Total	**53.2**	**28.3**	**40.6**	**67.0**	**55.0**	**60.9**

Note: To lose weight or to keep from gaining weight during the 30 days before the survey.
*Non-Hispanic.

SOURCE: Danice K. Eaton, "Table 86. Percentage of High School Students Who Ate Less Food, Fewer Calories, or Low-Fat Foods and Who Exercised, by Sex, Race/Ethnicity, and Grade—United States, Youth Risk Behavior Survey, 2007," in "Youth Risk Behavior Surveillance—United States, 2007," *Morbidity and Mortality Weekly Report*, vol. 57, no. SS-4, June 6, 2008, http://www.cdc.gov/HealthyYouth/yrbs/pdf/yrbss07_mmwr.pdf (accessed November 5, 2008)

TABLE 4.11

Percentage of high school students who engaged in unhealthy behaviors in an effort to lose weight, by sex, race, Hispanic origin, and grade, 2007

	Did not eat for 24 or more hours to lose weight or to keep from gaining weight			Took diet pills, powders or liquids to lose weight or to keep from gaining weight[a]			Vomited or took laxatives to lose weight or to keep from gaining weight		
	Female	Male	Total	Female	Male	Total	Female	Male	Total
Category	%	%	%	%	%	%	%	%	%
Race/ethnicity									
White[b]	16.7	5.7	11.2	8.3	3.7	6.0	6.9	1.3	4.1
Black[b]	13.2	7.4	10.3	3.9	3.6	3.7	3.5	2.5	3.0
Hispanic	17.4	10.7	14.1	7.8	5.1	6.4	7.0	3.7	5.3
Grade									
9	16.8	6.5	11.6	6.1	2.9	4.4	5.5	2.1	3.8
10	19.1	6.5	12.7	6.9	3.8	5.3	7.6	1.8	4.7
11	14.8	8.1	11.5	7.4	5.0	6.2	5.7	2.1	4.0
12	13.6	8.0	10.9	10.2	5.7	8.0	6.6	2.6	4.6
Total	**16.3**	**7.3**	**11.8**	**7.5**	**4.2**	**5.9**	**6.4**	**2.2**	**4.3**

Notes: To lose weight or to keep from gaining weight during the 30 days before the survey.
[a]Without a doctor's advice.
[b]Non-Hispanic.

SOURCE: Adapted from Danice K. Eaton et al., "Table 88. Percentage of High School Students Who Did Not Eat for 24 or More Hours and Who Took Diet Pills, Powders, or Liquids, by Sex, Race/Ethnicity, and Grade—United States, Youth Risk Behavior Survey, 2007," and "Table 90. Percentage of High School Students Who Vomited or Took Laxatives, by Sex, Race/Ethnicity, and Grade—United States, Youth Risk Behavior Survey, 2007," in "Youth Risk Behavior Surveillance—United States, 2007," *Morbidity and Mortality Weekly Report*, vol. 57, no. SS-4, June 6, 2008, http://www.cdc.gov/HealthyYouth/yrbs/pdf/yrbss07_mmwr.pdf (accessed November 5, 2008)

used to treat hyperactive children. In *Summary Health Statistics for U.S. Children: National Health Interview Survey, 2006* (September 2007, http://www.cdc.gov/nchs/data/series/sr_10/sr10_234.pdf), Barbara Bloom and Robin A. Cohen of the CDC explain that boys are more likely to be diagnosed with ADHD than girls; 10.7% of boys aged three to 17 have been diagnosed at some point, compared to 4% of girls.

Drug and Alcohol Use

Few factors negatively influence the health and well-being of young people more than the use of drugs, alcohol, and tobacco. Monitoring the Future, a long-term study on the use of drugs, alcohol, and tobacco conducted by the University of Michigan's Institute for Social Research, annually surveys eighth, 10th, and 12th graders on their use of these substances. According to Lloyd D.

TABLE 4.12

Percentage of high school students who drank alcohol and used marijuana, by sex, race, ethnicity, and grade, 2007

	Lifetime alcohol use[a]			Current alcohol use[b]			Lifetime marijuana use[d]			Current marijuana use[e]		
	Female	Male	Total	Female	Male	Total	Female	Male	Total	Female	Male	Total
Category	%	%	%	%	%	%	%	%	%	%	%	%
Race/ethnicity												
White[c]	76.4	75.8	76.1	47.1	47.4	47.3	34.1	41.8	38.0	17.0	22.7	19.9
Black[c]	70.0	68.4	69.1	34.9	34.1	34.5	35.0	44.5	39.6	17.1	26.0	21.5
Hispanic	79.3	76.5	77.9	47.5	47.7	47.6	35.9	42.0	38.9	16.4	20.5	18.5
Grade												
9	66.1	65.0	65.5	37.2	34.3	35.7	21.7	33.0	27.5	12.5	16.9	14.7
10	74.6	74.9	74.7	42.3	41.4	41.8	34.5	39.2	36.9	16.5	22.0	19.3
11	79.1	79.7	79.4	46.5	51.5	49.0	36.6	48.3	42.4	17.5	25.2	21.4
12	85.2	80.2	82.8	54.2	55.6	54.9	48.3	49.9	49.1	22.6	27.8	25.1
Total	**75.7**	**74.3**	**75.0**	**44.6**	**44.7**	**44.7**	**34.5**	**41.6**	**38.1**	**17.0**	**22.4**	**19.7**

[a]Had at least one drink of alcohol on at least 1 day during their life.
[b]Had at least one drink of alcohol on at least 1 day during the 30 days before the survey.
[c]Non-Hispanic.
[d]Used marijuana one or more times during their life.
[e]Used marijuana one or more times during the 30 days before the survey.

SOURCE: Adapted from Danice K. Eaton, "Table 35. Percentage of High School Students Who Drank Alcohol, by Sex, Race/Ethnicity, and Grade—United States, Youth Risk Behavior Survey, 2007," and "Table 39. Percentage of High School Students Who Used Marijuana, by Sex, Race/Ethnicity, and Grade—United States, Youth Risk Behavior Survey, 2007," in "Youth Risk Behavior Surveillance—United States, 2007," *Morbidity and Mortality Weekly Report*, vol. 57, no. SS-4, June 6, 2008, http://www.cdc.gov/HealthyYouth/yrbs/pdf/yrbss07_mmwr.pdf (accessed November 5, 2008)

Johnston et al. of the Institute for Social Research, in *Monitoring the Future: National Results on Adolescent Drug Use, Overview of Key Findings, 2007* (2008, http://www.monitoringthefuture.org/pubs/monographs/overview2007.pdf), the percentage of high school students who had used an illicit drug during that past year declined between 1997 and 2007, after sharp increases during the early 1990s. Johnston et al. find that in 2007, 35.9% of seniors (who were more likely than eighth or 10th graders to use an illicit drug) had used an illicit drug in the previous 12 months. Concerning the lifetime prevalence rate, 46.8% of 12th graders had tried an illicit drug. Alcohol (72.7% of seniors) and marijuana (41.8% of seniors) were the most commonly used drugs. Eaton et al. find that in 2007, 75% of all high school students had tried alcohol and 44.7% had used it in the past month. (See Table 4.12.) The researchers also note that 38.1% of high school students reported they had tried marijuana, and 19.7% reported they used it at least once in the 30 days before the survey.

TOBACCO. Most states prohibit the sale of cigarettes to anyone under the age of 18, but the laws are often ignored and may carry no penalties for youths who buy cigarettes or smoke in public. In fact, 16% of high school students reported in 2007 that they had bought cigarettes in a store or gas station. (See Table 4.13.) The American Lung Association reports in "Smoking and Teens Fact Sheet" (August 2008, http://www.lungusa.org/site/pp.asp?c=dvLUK9O0E&b=39871) that each day 4,000 children smoke their first cigarette—and almost 1,300 of them will become regular smokers. According to Eaton et al., half (50.3%) of all high school students in 2007 said they had tried cigarettes at some point in their lives. (See Table 4.14.) One out of five (20%) high school

TABLE 4.13

Percentage of high school students who bought cigarettes in a store or gas station, by sex, race, Hispanic origin, and grade, 2007

	Bought cigarettes in a store or gas station		
	Female	Male	Total
Category	%	%	%
Race/ethnicity			
White*	10.9	20.4	15.9
Black*		22.6	19.3
Hispanic	9 9	17.1	13.8
Grade			
9	7.0	11.8	9.7
10	9.4	20.2	15.0
11	13.6	20.9	17.8
12	17.0	34.8	25.6
Total	**11.3**	**20.0**	**16.0**

—Not available.
*Non-Hispanic.
Note: During the 30 days before the survey, among the 16.1% of students nationwide who were aged <18 years and who currently smoked cigarettes.

SOURCE: Adapted from Danice K. Eaton, "Table 31. Percentage of High School Students Who Usually Obtained Their Own Cigarettes by Buying Them in a Store or Gas Station and Who Currently Used Smokeless Tobacco, by Sex, Race/Ethnicity, and Grade—United States, Youth Risk Behavior Survey, 2007," in "Youth Risk Behavior Surveillance—United States, 2007," *Morbidity and Mortality Weekly Report*, vol. 57, no. SS-4, June 6, 2008, http://www.cdc.gov/HealthyYouth/yrbs/pdf/yrbss07_mmwr.pdf (accessed November 5, 2008)

students had smoked at least one cigarette in the month before the survey and 8.1% had smoked at least 20 days in the past month. (See Table 4.15.) Almost twice as many male students smoked heavily than did female students:

TABLE 4.14

Percentage of high school students who ever smoked cigarettes, by sex, race, ethnicity, and grade, 2007

	Lifetime cigarette use[a]			Lifetime daily cigarette use[b]		
	Female	Male	Total	Female	Male	Total
Category	%	%	%	%	%	%
Race/ethnicity						
White[c]	48.3	51.7	50.0	14.9	15.8	15.4
Black[c]	48.8	52.0	50.3	5.0	7.3	6.2
Hispanic	52.1	54.5	53.3	7.1	8.9	8.0
Grade						
9	39.2	46.0	42.7	6.3	10.3	8.3
10	48.7	48.8	48.8	12.4	11.7	12.0
11	51.4	55.4	53.4	14.0	13.4	13.8
12	58.5	60.1	59.3	15.8	18.0	16.8
Total	**48.8**	**51.8**	**50.3**	**11.8**	**13.0**	**12.4**

[a]Ever tried cigarette smoking, even one or two puffs.
[b]Ever smoked at least one cigarette every day for 30 days.
[c]Non-Hispanic.

SOURCE: Danice K. Eaton, "Table 25. Percentage of High School Students Who Ever Smoked Cigarettes, by Sex, Race/Ethnicity, and Grade—United States, Youth Risk Behavior Survey, 2007," in "Youth Risk Behavior Surveillance—United States, 2007," *Morbidity and Mortality Weekly Report*, vol. 57, no. SS-4, June 6, 2008, http://www.cdc.gov/HealthyYouth/yrbs/pdf/yrbss07_mmwr.pdf (accessed November 5, 2008)

TABLE 4.15

Percentage of high school students who currently smoked cigarettes, frequently smoked cigarettes, or smoked more than ten cigarettes per day, by sex, race, ethnicity, and grade, 2007

	Current cigarette use[a]			Current frequent cigarette use[b]			Smoked more than 10 cigarettes/day		
	Female	Male	Total	Female	Male	Total	Female	Male	Total
Category	%	%	%	%	%	%	%	%	%
Race/ethnicity									
White[c]	22.5	23.8	23.2	10.2	10.6	10.4	8.0	15.7	11.9
Black[c]	8.4	14.9	11.6	2.1	5.8	3.9	1.7	8.6	6.1
Hispanic	14.6	18.7	16.7	3.3	5.1	4.2	4.8	8.4	6.8
Grade									
9	12.3	16.2	14.3	3.3	5.4	4.3	6.7	12.6	10.1
10	19.1	20.0	19.6	6.8	7.2	7.0	5.3	12.6	9.0
11	19.6	23.4	21.6	9.7	10.5	10.1	8.1	9.9	9.0
12	25.5	27.4	26.5	11.3	13.1	12.2	7.8	19.2	13.6
Total	**18.7**	**21.3**	**20.0**	**7.4**	**8.7**	**8.1**	**7.1**	**13.8**	**10.7**

[a]Smoked cigarettes on at least 1 day during the 30 days before the survey.
[b]Smoked cigarettes on 20 or more days during the 30 days before the survey.
[c]Non-Hispanic.
Notes: On the days they smoked during the 30 days before the survey, among the 20.0% of students nationwide who currently smoked cigarettes. During the 12 months before the survey, among the 20.0% of students nationwide who currently smoked cigarettes.

SOURCE: Adapted from Danice K. Eaton, "Table 27. Percentage of High School Students Who Currently Smoked Cigarettes, by Sex, Race/Ethnicity, and Grade—United States, Youth Risk Behavior Survey, 2007," and "Table 29. Percentage of High School Students Who Currently Smoked More Than 10 Cigarettes and Who Tried to Quit Smoking Cigarettes, by Sex, Race/Ethnicity, and Grade—United States, Youth Risk Behavior Survey, 2007," in "Youth Risk Behavior Surveillance—United States, 2007," *Morbidity and Mortality Weekly Report*, vol. 57, no. SS-4, June 6, 2008, http://www.cdc.gov/HealthyYouth/yrbs/pdf/yrbss07_mmwr.pdf (accessed November 5, 2008)

13.8% of male adolescents and 7.1% of female adolescents smoked more than 10 cigarettes per day.

Teens say they smoke for a variety of reasons—they "just like it," "it's a social thing," and many young women who are worried about their weight report that they smoke because "it burns calories." Many of them note they have seen their parents smoke. The ALA indicates that youth who have two parents who smoke are more than twice as likely to become smokers than youth whose parents do not smoke. Children in smoking households are at risk not only from secondhand smoke but also from this greater likelihood to take up smoking themselves.

CHILDHOOD DEATHS
Infant Mortality

The NCHS defines the infant mortality rate as the number of deaths of babies younger than one year per 1,000 live births. Neonatal deaths occur within 28 days

TABLE 4.16

Infant mortality rate among selected groups by race and Hispanic origin of mother, selected years 1983–2004

[Data are based on linked birth and death certificates for infants]

Race and Hispanic origin of mother	1983–1985[a, g]	1986–1988[a, g]	1989–1991[a, g]	1995–1997[b, g]	1999–2001[b, g]	2002–2004[b, g]
	Infant [c] deaths per 1,000 live births					
All mothers	10.6	9.8	9.0	7.4	6.9	6.9
White	9.0	8.2	7.4	6.1	5.7	5.7
Black or African American	18.7	17.9	17.1	14.1	13.6	13.5
American Indian or Alaska Native	13.9	13.2	12.6	9.2	9.1	8.6
Asian or Pacific Islander[d]	8.3	7.3	6.6	5.1	4.8	4.8
Chinese	7.4	5.8	5.1	3.3	3.2	—
Japanese	6.0	6.9	5.3	4.9	4.0	—
Filipino	8.2	6.9	6.4	5.7	5.7	—
Hawaiian	11.3	11.1	9.0	7.0	7.8	—
Other Asian or Pacific Islander	8.6	7.6	7.0	5.4	4.9	—
Hispanic or Latino[e, f]	9.2	8.3	7.5	6.1	5.6	5.6
Mexican	8.8	7.9	7.2	5.9	5.4	5.5
Puerto Rican	12.3	11.1	10.4	8.5	8.4	8.1
Cuban	8.0	7.3	6.2	5.3	4.5	4.3
Central and South American	8.2	7.5	6.6	5.3	4.8	4.9
Other and unknown Hispanic or Latino	9.8	9.0	8.2	7.1	6.7	6.8
Not Hispanic or Latino						
White[f]	8.8	8.1	7.3	6.1	5.7	5.7
Black or African American[f]	18.5	17.9	17.2	14.2	13.7	13.7
	Neonatal [c] deaths per 1,000 live births					
All mothers	6.9	6.3	5.7	4.8	4.6	4.6
White	5.9	5.2	4.7	4.0	3.8	3.8
Black or African American	12.2	11.7	11.1	9.4	9.2	9.2
American Indian or Alaska Native	6.7	5.9	5.9	4.4	4.5	4.5
Asian or Pacific Islander[d]	5.2	4.5	3.9	3.3	3.2	3.3
Chinese	4.3	3.3	2.7	2.1	2.1	—
Japanese	3.4	4.4	3.0	2.8	2.6	—
Filipino	5.3	4.5	4.0	3.7	4.0	—
Hawaiian	7.4	7.1	4.8	4.5	4.9	—
Other Asian or Pacific Islander	5.5	4.7	4.2	3.5	3.3	—
Hispanic or Latino[e, f]	6.0	5.3	4.8	4.0	3.8	3.9
Mexican	5.7	5.0	4.5	3.8	3.6	3.7
Puerto Rican	8.3	7.2	7.0	5.7	5.9	5.6
Cuban	5.9	5.3	4.6	3.7	3.1	3.1
Central and South American	5.7	4.9	4.4	3.7	3.3	3.5
Other and unknown Hispanic or Latino	6.1	5.8	5.2	4.6	4.4	4.9
Not Hispanic or Latino						
White[f]	5.7	5.1	4.6	4.0	3.8	3.8
Black or African American[f]	11.8	11.4	11.1	9.4	9.2	9.2

—Data not available.

[a]Rates based on unweighted birth cohort data.

[b]Rates based on a period file using weighted data.

[c]Infant (under 1 year of age), neonatal (under 28 days), and postneonatal (28 days–11 months).

[d]Starting with 2003 data, estimates are not shown for Asian or Pacific Islander subgroups during the transition from single race to multiple race reporting.

[e]Persons of Hispanic origin may be of any race.

[f]Prior to 1995, data shown only for states with an Hispanic-origin item on their birth certificates.

[g]Average annual mortality rate.

Notes: The race groups white, black, American Indian or Alaska Native, and Asian or Pacific Islander include persons of Hispanic and non-Hispanic origin. Starting with 2003 data, some states reported multiple-race data. The multiple-race data for these states were bridged to the single-race categories of the 1977 Office of Management and Budget standards for comparability with other states. National linked files do not exist for 1992–1994. Data for additional years are available.

SOURCE: Adapted from "Table 19. Infant, Neonatal, Postneonatal Mortality Rates, by Detailed Race and Hispanic Origin of Mother: United States, Selected Years 1983–2004," in *Health, United States, 2007. With Chartbook on Trends in the Health of Americans*, Centers for Disease Control and Prevention, National Center for Health Statistics, 2007, http://www.cdc.gov/nchs/data/hus/hus07.pdf (accessed September 15, 2008

after birth and postneonatal deaths occur 28 to 365 days after birth. The U.S. infant mortality rate declined from 165 per 1,000 live births in 1900 to a low of 6.9 per 1,000 live births in between 2002 and 2004. (See Table 4.16.) In *Health, United States, 2007* (2007, http://www.cdc.gov/nchs/data/hus/hus07 .pdf), the CDC notes that several factors—including improved access to health care, advances in neonatal medicine, and educational campaigns—contributed to the overall decline in infant mortality in the twentieth century.

Not all racial and ethnic groups have reached that record-low infant mortality rate. Between 2002 and 2004 the infant mortality rate for non-Hispanic white infants was 5.7 deaths per 1,000 live births, less than half the rate of 13.5 for African-American infants. (See Table 4.16.) Rates for Native American or Alaskan Native, Hispanic, and Asian or Pacific Islander babies were 8.6, 5.6, and 4.8, respectively.

The NCHS lists the 10 leading causes of infant mortality in the United States in 2006. (See Table 4.17.) Birth

TABLE 4.17

Ten leading causes of infant death, by race and Hispanic origin, 2006

[Data are based on a continuous file of records received from the states. Rates are per 100,000 live births. Figures are based on weighted data rounded to the nearest individual, so categories may not add to totals or subtotals. Race and Hispanic origin are reported separately on both the birth and death certificate. Rates for Hispanic origin should be interpreted with caution because of inconsistencies between reporting Hispanic origin on birth and death certificates. Race categories are consistent with the 1977 Office of Management and Budget (OMB) standards. Multiple-race data were reported for deaths by 25 states and the District of Columbia and for births by 23 states. The multiple-race data for these states were bridged to the single-race categories of the 1977 OMB standards for comparability with other states. Data for persons of Hispanic origin are included in the data for each race group, according to the decedent's reported race.]

Rank[a]	Cause of death, race and Hispanic origin	Number	Rate
	All races[b]		
—	All causes	28,609	670.6
1	Congenital malformations, deformations and chromosomal abnormalities	5,827	136.6
2	Disorders related to short gestation and low birth weight, not elsewhere classified	4,841	113.5
3	Sudden infant death syndrome	2,145	50.3
4	Newborn affected by maternal complications of pregnancy	1,694	39.7
5	Newborn affected by complications of placenta, cord and membranes	1,123	26.3
6	Accidents (unintentional injuries)	1,119	26.2
7	Respiratory distress of newborn	801	18.8
8	Bacterial sepsis of newborn	786	18.4
9	Neonatal hemorrhage	598	14.0
10	Diseases of the circulatory system	539	12.6
—	All other causes	9,136	214.2
	Non-Hispanic white		
—	All causes	13,019	563.6
1	Congenital malformations, deformations and chromosomal abnormalities	2,989	129.4
2	Disorders related to short gestation and low birth weight, not elsewhere classified	1,805	78.1
3	Sudden infant death syndrome	1,171	50.7
4	Newborn affected by maternal complications of pregnancy	751	32.5
5	Accidents (unintentional injuries)	547	23.7
6	Newborn affected by complications of placenta, cord and membranes	472	20.4
7	Respiratory distress of newborn	353	15.3
8	Bacterial sepsis of newborn	331	14.3
9	Neonatal hemorrhage	299	12.9
10	Diseases of the circulatory system	239	10.3
—	All other causes	4,062	175.9
	Total black		
—	All causes	8,842	1,335.2
1	Disorders related to short gestation and low birth weight, not elsewhere classified	1,978	298.7
2	Congenital malformations, deformations and chromosomal abnormalities	1,157	174.7
3	Sudden infant death syndrome	656	99.1
4	Newborn affected by maternal complications of pregnancy	595	89.9
5	Newborn affected by complications of placenta, cord and membranes	378	57.1
6	Accidents (unintentional injuries)	351	53.0
7	Bacterial sepsis of newborn	272	41.1
8	Respiratory distress of newborn	267	40.3
9	Necrotizing enterocolitis of newborn	204	30.8
10	Diseases of the circulatory system	175	26.4
—	All other causes	2,809	424.2
	Hispanic[c]		
—	All causes	5,706	549.2
1	Congenital malformations, deformations and chromosomal abnormalities	1,442	138.8
2	Disorders related to short gestation and low birth weight, not elsewhere classified	919	88.4
3	Newborn affected by maternal complications of pregnancy	299	28.8
4	Sudden infant death syndrome	244	23.5
5	Newborn affected by complications of placenta, cord and membranes	227	21.8
6	Accidents (unintentional injuries)	178	17.1
7	Respiratory distress of newborn	159	15.3
8	Bacterial sepsis of newborn	152	14.6
9	Neonatal hemorrhage	113	10.9
10	Diseases of the circulatory system	99	9.5
—	All other causes	1,874	180.4

—Category not applicable.

[a]Rank based on number of deaths.

[b]Includes races other than white and black.

[c]Includes all persons of Hispanic origin of any race. Because of a misclassification error in New Mexico, statistics for Hispanic decedents of all ages were underestimated by about 3.0 percent, and statistics for Hispanic decedents under 1 year of age were underestimated by about 1.0 percent.

Notes: For certain causes of death such as unintentional injuries, homicides, suicides, and sudden infant death syndrome, preliminary and final data may differ because of the truncated nature of the preliminary file. Data are subject to sampling or random variation.

SOURCE: Adapted from Melonie P. Heron et al., "Table 8. Infant Deaths and Infant Mortality Rates for the 10 Leading Causes of Infant Death, by Race and Hispanic Origin: United States, Preliminary 2006," in "Deaths: Preliminary Data for 2006," *National Vital Statistics Report*, vol. 56, no. 16, June 11, 2008, http://www.cdc.gov/nchs/data/nvsr/nvsr56/nvsr56_16.pdf (accessed November 5, 2008)

defects (congenital malformations) were the primary cause of infant mortality (136.6 deaths per 100,000 live births). Premature delivery or low birth weight was the second-leading cause of infant mortality (113.5 per 100,000 live births). Sudden infant death syndrome (50.3), complications of pregnancy (39.7), complications in the placenta or umbilical cord (26.3), accidents (26.2), respiratory distress (18.8), bacterial sepsis (18.4), neonatal hemorrhage (14), and diseases of the circulatory system (12.6) complete the list.

SUDDEN INFANT DEATH SYNDROME. Sudden infant death syndrome (SIDS; sometimes called crib death), the unexplained death of a previously healthy infant, was the third-leading cause of infant mortality in the United States in 2006. Moreover, according to the CDC, in "Safe Sleep for Your Baby: Ten Ways to Reduce the Risk of Sudden Infant Death Syndrome" (August 2003, http://www.nichd.nih.gov/publications/pubs/safe_sleep_gen.cfm), SIDS is the leading cause of death among infants aged one to 12 months. In 1992 the American Academy of Pediatrics recommended that babies sleep on their back to reduce the risk of SIDS and launched its "Back to Sleep" campaign to educate parents. It had been a long-held belief that the best position for babies to sleep was on their stomach. Other risk factors for SIDS include maternal use of drugs or tobacco during pregnancy, low birth weight, and poor prenatal care. For reasons not yet understood, even though the overall rate of SIDS has declined since the beginning of the Back to Sleep campaign, it has declined less among African-Americans and Native Americans than among other groups. The CDC indicates that African-American babies are more than twice as likely to die of SIDS and Native American babies are nearly three times as likely to die of SIDS than white babies.

A number of studies have considered the possible causes of and risk factors for SIDS. For example, the article "SIDS Risk Prevention Research Begins to Define Physical Abnormalities in Brainstem, Points to Possible Diagnostic/Screening Tools" (PR Newswire, October 18, 1999) reports that one study, ongoing since 1985, conducted by Hannah Kinney of Harvard Medical School in Boston, Massachusetts, found a brain defect believed to affect breathing in babies who died of SIDS. Researchers suggest that as carbon dioxide levels rise and oxygen levels fall during sleep, the brains of some babies do not get the signal to regulate breathing or blood pressure accordingly to make up for the change. This condition is particularly dangerous for infants sleeping on their stomachs or on soft bedding. According to the National Institutes of Health, in "SIDS Infants Show Brain Abnormalities," (November 10, 2006, http://www.nih.gov/news/research_matters/november2006/11102006sids.htm), this project found that this type of brain abnormality might be linked to higher levels of serotonin in the brainstem. Duane Alexander stated, "This finding lends credence

to the view that SIDS risk may greatly increase when an underlying predisposition combines with an environmental risk—such as sleeping face down—at a developmentally sensitive time in early life."

Mortality among Older Children

In the second half of the twentieth century, childhood death rates declined dramatically. Most childhood deaths are from injuries and violence. Even though death rates for all ages decreased, the largest declines were among children.

In 2005 three of the leading causes of death of one- to four-year-olds were unintentional injuries, congenital anomalies (birth defects), and malignant neoplasms (cancers). (See Table 4.18.) The remaining deaths were spread across a variety of diseases, including heart disease, pneumonia, influenza, HIV/AIDS, homicide, and suicide.

MOTOR VEHICLE INJURIES. The National Highway Traffic Safety Administration notes in Determine Why There Are Fewer Young Alcohol-Impaired Drivers (September 2001, http://www.nhtsa.dot.gov/people/injury/research/FewerYoungDrivers/) that even though motor vehicle fatalities decreased by 25% between 1982 and 2000 for 15- to 19-year-olds, traffic accidents were still the leading cause of death for this age group. During the 1980s and early 1990s, traffic fatalities linked to teenage drinking fell. This decline was due in large part to stricter enforcement of drinking age laws and driving while intoxicated or driving under the influence laws. Nevertheless, motor vehicle crashes were the leading cause of death among 15- to 20-year-olds in 2003. In the fact sheet "Mortality: Adolescents and Young Adults" (2006, http://nahic.ucsf.edu/downloads/Mortality.pdf), the National Adolescent Health Information Center reports that in 2003, 25.2 of every 100,000 teenagers in this age group were killed in traffic accidents. Many of those killed had been drinking alcohol and were not wearing their seatbelts. Timothy M. Pickrell of the U.S. Department of Transportation reports in "Driver Alcohol Involvement in Fatal Crashes by Age Group and Vehicle Type" (June 2006, http://www-nrd.nhtsa.dot.gov/pdf/nrd-30/NCSA/RNotes/2006/810598.pdf) that 20% of all young drivers aged 15 to 20 who were killed in crashes were intoxicated.

Eaton et al. find that in 2007, in the month before the survey, 18.3% of high school seniors (those most likely to have their driver's licenses) reported they had driven a vehicle after drinking alcohol. (See Table 4.19.) Male seniors (23.6%) were more likely than female seniors (13.1%) to drive after drinking. Another 29.1% of high school students admitted they had ridden with a driver who had been drinking.

SUICIDE. In 2005 suicide was the fifth-leading cause of death among five- to 14-year-olds and the third-leading cause of death in 15- to 24-year-olds. (See Table 4.18.) Debra L. Karch et al. of the CDC report in "Surveillance for Violent

TABLE 4.18

Leading causes of death and numbers of deaths, by age, 1980 and 2005

[Data are based on death certificates]

Age and rank order	1980		2005	
	Cause of death	Deaths	Cause of death	Deaths
Under 1 year				
	All causes	45,526	All causes	28,440
1	Congenital anomalies	9,220	Congenital malformations, deformations and chromosomal abnormalities	5,552
2	Sudden infant death syndrome	5,510	Disorders related to short gestatiion and low birth weight, not elsewhere classified	4,714
3	Respiratory distress syndrome	4,989	Sudden infant death syndrome	2,230
4	Disorders relating to short gestation and unspecified low birthweight	3,648	Newborn affected by maternal complications of pregnancy	1,776
5	Newborn affected by maternal complications of pregnancy	1,572	Newborn affected by complications of placenta, cord and membranes	1,110
6	Intrauterine hypoxia and birth asphyxia	1,497	Unintentional injuries	1,083
7	Unintentional injuries	1,166	Respiratory distress of newborn	860
8	Birth trauma	1,058	Bacterial sepsis of newborn	834
9	Pneumonia and influenza	1,012	Neonatal hemorrhage	665
10	Newborn affected by complications of placenta, cord, and membranes	985	Necrotizing enterocolitis of newborn	546
1–4 years				
	All causes	8,187	All causes	4,756
1	Unintentional injuries	3,313	Unintentional injuries	1,664
2	Congenital anomalies	1,026	Congenital malformations, deformations and chromosomal abnormalities	522
3	Malignant neoplasms	573	Malignant neoplasms	377
4	Diseases of heart	338	Homicide	375
5	Homicide	319	Diseases of heart	151
6	Pneumonia and influenza	267	Influenza and pneumonia	110
7	Meningitis	223	Septicemia	85
8	Meningococcal infection	110	Cerebrovascular dieases	62
9	Certain conditions originating in the perinatal period	84	Certain conditions originating in the perinatal period	58
10	Septicemia	71	Chronic lower respiratory diseases	56
5–14 years				
	All causes	10,689	All causes	6,602
1	Unintentional injuries	5,224	Unintentional injuries	2,415
2	Malignant neoplasms	1,497	Malignant neoplasms	1,000
3	Congenital anomalies	561	Congenital malformations, deformations and chromosomal abnormalities	396
4	Homicide	415	Homicide	341
5	Diseases of heart	330	Suicide	272
6	Pneumonia and influenza	194	Diseases of heart	252
7	Suicide	142	Influenza and pneumonia	106
8	Benign neoplasms	104	Chronic lower respiratory diseases	104
9	Cerebrovascular diseases	95	Cerebrovascular dieases	95
10	Chronic obstructive pulmonary diseases	85	Septicemia	81
15–24 years				
	All causes	49,027	All causes	34,234
1	Unintentional injuries	26,206	Unintentional injuries	15,753
2	Homicide	6,537	Homicide	5,466
3	Suicide	5,239	Suicide	4,212
4	Malignant neoplasms	2,683	Malignant neoplasms	1,717
5	Diseases of heart	1,223	Diseases of heart	1,119
6	Congenital anomalies	600	Congenital malformations, deformations and chromosomal abnormalities	504
7	Cerebrovascular diseases	418	Diabetes mellitus	202
8	Pneumonia and influenza	348	Cerebrovascular dieases	196
9	Chronic obstructive pulmonary diseases	141	Pregnancy, childbirth and puerperuim	183
10	Anemias	133	Influenza and pneumonia	172

—Category not applicable.

SOURCE: Adapted from "Table 32. Leading Causes of Death and Numbers of Deaths, by Age: United States, 1980 and 2005," in *Health, United States, 2007. With Chartbook on Trends in the Health of Americans*, Centers for Disease Control and Prevention, National Center for Health Statistics, 2007, http://www.cdc.gov/nchs/data/hus/hus07.pdf (accessed September 15, 2008)

Deaths—National Violent Death Reporting System, 16 States, 2005" (*Morbidity and Mortality Weekly Report*, vol. 57, no. SS-03, April 11, 2008) that the male suicide rate (18.4 per 100,000) was more than three times higher than the female suicide rate (4.8 per 100,000). According to Melonie Heron of the CDC, in "Deaths: Leading Causes for 2004"

TABLE 4.19

Percentage of high school students who rode with a driver who had been drinking alcohol and who drove when they had been drinking alcohol, by sex, race, ethnicity, and grade, 2007

	Rode with a driver who had been drinking alcohol			Drove when drinking alcohol		
	Female	Male	Total	Female	Male	Total
Category	%	%	%	%	%	%
Race/ethnicity						
White*	28.0	27.8	27.9	9.3	13.9	11.6
Black*	26.9	28.1	27.4	3.9	7.5	5.7
Hispanic	35.1	36.0	35.5	7.7	13.0	10.3
Grade						
9	27.6	27.6	27.6	4.1	6.8	5.5
10	30.4	27.1	28.7	7.3	10.0	8.7
11	26.8	31.4	29.2	9.1	13.7	11.5
12	30.5	32.5	31.5	13.1	23.6	18.3
Total	**28.8**	**29.5**	**29.1**	**8.1**	**12.8**	**10.5**

Note: One or more times during the 30 days before the survey.
*Non-Hispanic.

SOURCE: Danice K. Eaton, "Table 5. Percentage of High School Students Who Rode in a Car or Other Vehicle Driven by Someone Who Had Been Drinking Alcohol and Who Drove a Car or Other Vehicle When They Had Been Drinking Alcohol, by Sex, Race/Ethnicity, and Grade—United States, Youth Risk Behavior Survey, 2007," in "Youth Risk Behavior Surveillance—United States, 2007," *Morbidity and Mortality Weekly Report*, vol. 57, no. SS-4, June 6, 2008, http://www.cdc.gov/HealthyYouth/yrbs/pdf/yrbss07_mmwr.pdf (accessed November 5, 2008)

TABLE 4.20

Percentage of high school students who felt sad or hopeless, who seriously considered attempting suicide, and who made a suicide plan, by sex, race, ethnicity, and grade, 2007

	Felt sad or hopeless			Seriously considered attempting suicide			Made a suicide plan		
	Female	Male	Total	Female	Male	Total	Female	Male	Total
Category	%	%	%	%	%	%	%	%	%
Race/ethnicity									
White*	34.6	17.8	26.2	17.8	10.2	14.0	12.8	8.8	10.8
Black*	34.5	24.0	29.2	18.0	8.5	13.2	12.0	7.1	9.5
Hispanic	42.3	30.4	36.3	21.1	10.7	15.9	15.2	10.4	12.8
Grade									
9	34.8	22.1	28.2	19.0	10.8	14.8	13.4	9.2	11.2
10	37.7	20.3	28.9	22.0	9.3	15.6	16.1	8.9	12.5
11	34.5	19.5	27.1	16.3	10.7	13.5	11.6	9.2	10.4
12	35.9	22.6	29.4	16.7	10.2	13.5	11.7	9.5	10.6
Total	**35.8**	**21.2**	**28.5**	**18.7**	**10.3**	**14.5**	**13.4**	**9.2**	**11.3**

*Non-Hispanic.
Notes: Almost every day for 2 or more weeks in a row so that they stopped doing some usual activities. During the 12 months before the survey.

SOURCE: Adapted from Danice K. Eaton et al., "Table 19. Percentage of High School Students Who Felt Sad or Hopeless, by Sex, Race/Ethnicity, and Grade—United States, Youth Risk Behavior Survey, 2007," and "Table 21. Percentage of High School Students Who Seriously Considered Attempting Suicide, and Who Made a Plan about How They Would Attempt Suicide, by Sex, Race/Ethnicity, and Grade—United States, Youth Risk Behavior Survey, 2007," in "Youth Risk Behavior Surveillance—United States, 2007," *Morbidity and Mortality Weekly Report*, vol. 57, no. SS-4, June 6, 2008, http://www.cdc.gov/HealthyYouth/yrbs/pdf/yrbss07_mmwr.pdf (accessed November 5, 2008)

(*National Vital Statistics Reports*, vol. 56, no. 5, November 20, 2007), in 2004, the latest year for which detailed statistics were available, white males aged 15 to 19 had twice the suicide rate (13.6 per 100,000) of African-American males (7.4 per 100,000) or Hispanic male youth (9.9 per 100,000). Among females aged 15 to 19, the rate for whites (3.7 per 100,000) was considerably higher than that for Hispanics (2.7 per 100,000) or African-Americans (1.9 per 100,000).

Eaton et al. questioned high school students regarding their thoughts about suicide. Almost one out of seven (14.5%) students surveyed in 2007 claimed that they had seriously thought about attempting suicide in the previous 12 months. (See Table 4.20.) Even though the suicide death rate was much higher among males than females, females (18.7%) were more likely to have considered suicide than males (10.3%). Of all students,

TABLE 4.21

Percentage of high school students who attempted suicide and whose suicide attempt resulted in an injury that required medical treatment, by sex, race, ethnicity, and grade, 2007

	Attempted suicide			Suicide attempt treated by a doctor or nurse		
	Female	Male	Total	Female	Male	Total
Category	%	%	%	%	%	%
Race/ethnicity						
White*	7.7	3.4	5.6	2.1	0.9	1.5
Black*	9.9	5.5	7.7	2.1	2.5	2.3
Hispanic	14.0	6.3	10.2	3.9	1.8	2.9
Grade						
9	10.5	5.3	7.9	2.6	1.9	2.3
10	11.2	4.9	8.0	3.1	1.0	2.0
11	7.8	3.7	5.8	1.7	1.4	1.6
12	6.5	4.2	5.4	1.8	1.5	1.7
Total	**9.3**	**4.6**	**6.9**	**2.4**	**1.5**	**2.0**

*Non-Hispanic.
Notes: During the 12 months before the survey. One or more times.

SOURCE: Danice K. Eaton, "Table 23. Percentage of High School Students Who Attempted Suicide and Whose Suicide Attempt Resulted in an Injury, Poisoning, or Overdose That Had to Be Treated by a Doctor or Nurse, by Sex, Race/Ethnicity, and Grade—United States, Youth Risk Behavior Survey, 2007," in "Youth Risk Behavior Surveillance—United States, 2007," *Morbidity and Mortality Weekly Report*, vol. 57, no. SS-4, June 6, 2008, http://www.cdc.gov/HealthyYouth/yrbs/pdf/yrbss07_mmwr.pdf (accessed November 5, 2008)

11.3% (13.4% of females and 9.2% of males) had made a specific plan to attempt suicide. Approximately 6.9% of students (9.3% of females and 4.6% of males) said they had attempted suicide in the previous year, and 2% of high school students (2.4% of females and 1.5% of males) said they had suffered injuries from the attempt that required medical attention. (See Table 4.21.) These numbers reflect the fact that females of all ages tend to choose less fatal methods of attempting suicide, such as overdosing and cutting veins, than males, who tend to choose more deadly methods, such as shooting or hanging.

These rates reflect the fact that a large proportion of students, particularly female students, feel sad or hopeless. In 2007, 35.8% of female students and 21.2% of male students reported these feelings. (See Table 4.20.) The likelihood that a child will commit suicide increases with the presence of certain risk factors. According to the CDC, in "Homicides and Suicides—National Violent Death Reporting System, United States, 2003–2004" (*Morbidity and Mortality Weekly Report*, vol. 55, no. 26, July 7, 2006), among the factors whose presence may indicate heightened risk are depression, mental health problems, relationship conflicts, a history of previous suicide attempts, and alcohol dependence.

In addition, the suicide rate among male homosexual teens is believed to be extremely high. Gary Remafedi of the University of Minnesota notes in "Suicidality in a Venue-Based Sample of Young Men Who Have Sex with Men" (*Journal of Adolescent Health*, vol. 31, no. 4, 2002) that 20% to 42% of teens and young men who have sex with other males attempt suicide. Suicidal gay adolescents are not only coping with stressors but also have few coping resources. In "Gay Adolescents and Suicide: Understanding the Association" (*Adolescence*, vol. 40, no. 159, fall 2005), Robert Li Kitts of Oregon Health and Science University states that "the process of realizing that one is gay and having to accept it is not just an immediate stressor and can actually narrow one's options further by taking away coping resources, such as friends and family.... Gay adolescents who 'come out' (disclose their sexuality) may experience great family discord, rejection, and even failure from the disappointment they elicit.... It would make sense to conclude that homosexuality is an important risk factor for adolescent suicide."

CHAPTER 5
TEEN SEXUALITY AND PREGNANCY

EARLY SEXUAL ACTIVITY

Many teenagers are sexually active. Danice K. Eaton et al. of the Centers for Disease Control and Prevention (CDC) report in "Youth Risk Behavior Surveillance—United States, 2007" (*Morbidity and Mortality Weekly Report*, vol. 57, no. SS-4, June 6, 2008, http://www.cdc.gov/HealthyYouth/yrbs/pdf/yrbss07_mmwr.pdf) that 47.8% of high school students surveyed in grades nine through 12 have had sexual intercourse. (See Table 5.1.) Girls (45.9%) were slightly less likely than boys (49.8%) to have had intercourse. African-American students (66.5%) were more likely than Hispanic (52%) or non-Hispanic white students (43.7%) to be sexually active.

The proportion of students who had intercourse rose with age; 32.8% of ninth graders, 43.8% of 10th graders, 55.5% of 11th graders, and 64.6% of 12th graders had ever had intercourse at the time of the survey. (See Table 5.1.) A number of youth were sexually active before age 13; 7.1% had had intercourse at age 12 or younger. This early sexual activity is of concern, especially among young girls. According to studies such as Sonya S. Brady and Bonnie L. Halpern-Felsher's "Adolescents' Reported Consequences of Having Oral Sex versus Vaginal Sex" (*Pediatrics*, vol. 119, no. 2, February 2007), among sexually active young teens, boys tend to feel good about themselves and experience popularity as a result of sexual activity, whereas girls are more likely to feel used and bad about themselves. In addition, Denise D. Hallfors et al. report in "Which Comes First in Adolescence—Sex and Drugs or Depression?" (*American Journal of Preventive Medicine*, vol. 29, no. 3, 2005) that being sexually active puts adolescents, particularly girls, at risk for depression.

Risk Factors for Early Sexual Activity

In "Early Adolescent Sexual Activity: A Developmental Study" (*Journal of Marriage and the Family*, vol. 61, no. 4, November 1999), Les B. Whitbeck et al. note that "the main predictors of early intercourse were age, associ-ation with delinquent peers, alcohol use, opportunity, and sexually permissive attitudes." Cami K. McBride et al. indicate in "Individual and Familial Influences on the Onset of Sexual Intercourse among Urban African American Adolescents" (*Journal of Consulting and Clinical Psychology*, vol. 71, no. 1, February 2003) that family conflict is also linked to early sexual activity among poor urban African-American adolescents. In "Parental Influences on Adolescent Sexual Behavior in High Poverty Settings" (*Archives of Pediatrics and Adolescent Medicine*, vol. 53, no. 10, 1999), another study of poor African-American children, Daniel Romer et al. find that those who reported high levels of monitoring from parents were less likely to have sex before adolescence (at age 10 or earlier) and had lower rates of sexual initiation in their teen years as well. John S. Santelli et al. report in "Initiation of Sexual Inter-course among Middle School Adolescents: The Influence of Psychosocial Factors" (*Journal of Adolescent Health*, vol. 34, no. 3, March 2004), a study of inner-city seventh graders, that peer norms about refraining from sex were strongly correlated with seventh and eighth graders abstain-ing; on the contrary, drug or alcohol use increased the risk of early sexual activity. Other studies, such as S. Liliana Escobar-Chaves et al.'s "Impact of the Media on Adolescent Sexual Attitudes and Behaviors" (*Pediatrics*, vol. 116, no. 1, July 2005), find a correlation between exposure to sexual themes in mass media and adolescent sexual activity.

Reasons Given for Not Delaying Sex

A number of studies report that both sexes consider social pressure the major factor in engaging in early sexual activity. Peer pressure and a belief that "everyone is doing it" have often been cited as explanations. However, in "Adolescent Girls' Perceptions of the Timing of Their Sexual Initiation: 'Too Young' or 'Just Right'?" (*Journal of Adolescent Health*, vol. 34, no. 5, May 2004), Sian Cotton et al. indicate that most female adolescents (78% of the studied group) felt that they had been "too young" at their first sexual experience.

TABLE 5.1

Percentage of high school students who ever had sexual intercourse and who had sexual intercourse for the first time before age 13 years, by sex, race, ethnicity, and grade, 2007

	Ever had sexual intercourse			Had first sexual intercourse before age 13 years		
	Female	Male	Total	Female	Male	Total
Category	%	%	%	%	%	%
Race/ethnicity						
White*	43.7	43.6	43.7	3.1	5.7	4.4
Black*	60.9	72.6	66.5	6.9	26.2	16.3
Hispanic	45.8	58.2	52.0	4.5	11.9	8.2
Grade						
9	27.4	38.1	32.8	4.9	13.5	9.2
10	41.9	45.6	43.8	4.7	9.1	6.9
11	53.6	57.3	55.5	3.4	9.9	6.6
12	66.2	62.8	64.6	2.4	6.7	4.5
Total	**45.9**	**49.8**	**47.8**	**4.0**	**10.1**	**7.1**

*Non-Hispanic.

SOURCE: Danice K. Eaton, "Table 61. Percentage of High School Students Who Ever Had Sexual Intercourse and Who Had Sexual Intercourse for the First Time before Age 13 Years, by Sex, Race/Ethnicity, and Grade—United States, Youth Risk Behavior Survey, 2007," in "Youth Risk Behavior Surveillance—United States, 2007," *Morbidity and Mortality Weekly Report*, vol. 57, no. SS-4, June 6, 2008, http://www.cdc.gov/HealthyYouth/yrbs/pdf/yrbss07_mmwr.pdf (accessed November 5, 2008)

In addition, some research challenges the theory that social pressure is the strongest influence on teenagers' sexual decisions. The press release "Study Offers Parents New Insights into *When* and *Why* Teens Choose Drinking, Drugs, and Sex" (October 29, 2002, http://www.sadd.org/teenstoday/teenstodaypdfs/study.pdf) discusses the Teens Today survey, which was commissioned by Students against Destructive Decisions and the Liberty Mutual Group. Students in grades six through 11 were asked what factors had most influenced their decisions about sexuality. The most common reasons 11th graders gave for engaging in sexual activity were boredom, curiosity, and to please one's partner. The most commonly mentioned reasons not to have sex were fear of pregnancy, fear of sexually transmitted diseases (STDs), and not being in a relationship or in love.

The Media and Teen Concepts of Sexuality

In *Sex on TV 4* (November 2005, http://www.kff.org/entmedia/upload/Sex-on-TV-4-Full-Report.pdf), the Kaiser Family Foundation and Dale Kunkel et al. of the University of Arizona discuss the results of a study of sexual messages on television. The report finds that the percent of shows with sexual content had increased from 56% in 1998 to 70% in 2005. In addition, in those shows that included sexual content, the number of sexual scenes per hour had risen from 3.2 in 1998 to 5 in 2005—and in the top teen programs, there were on average 6.7 sexual scenes per hour. Of the 20 shows most popular with teenagers, 70% included some sexual content, and 45% included sexual behavior. More than one out of 10 (11%) episodes included scenes in which sexual intercourse was depicted or strongly implied. Only 10% of shows most popular with teens that contained sexual content included a reference to sexual risk or responsibility.

The study's authors note that the portrayal of sex on television does not have wholly negative consequences. In fact, even though references to sexual risk or responsibility are still low, they have increased in recent years. Furthermore, these references can have a big impact. The study's authors state, "New research over the past several years has documented the powerful positive impact television can have on young people—whether it is learning about HIV from an episode of *Girlfriends* or about condom efficacy from an episode of *Friends*. Indeed . . . for many young people, exposure to a higher proportion of shows referencing sexual risks or responsibilities can promote healthier sexual decision-making."

Sexual Activity and Substance Use

Over the years, a number of studies have suggested a link between substance use and sexual activity. Researchers find that both sexual activity and a history of multiple partners correlate with some use of drugs, alcohol, and cigarettes. However, Eaton et al. indicate that among sexually active students, only 22.5% reported in 2007 they had used alcohol or drugs at the time of their last sexual experience. (See Table 5.2.) Males (27.5%) were more likely than females (17.7%) to report this behavior; African-Americans (16.4%) were less likely than Hispanics (21.4%) or non-Hispanic whites (24.8%) to report using alcohol or drugs during sexual activity.

Jie Guo et al. of the University of Washington note in "Developmental Relationships between Adolescent Substance Use and Risky Sexual Behavior in Young Adulthood" (*Journal of Adolescent Health*, vol. 31, no. 4, 2002) that there is a link between adolescent binge drinking and marijuana use and risky sexual behavior. Young people

TABLE 5.2

Percentage of high school students who drank alcohol or used drugs before last sexual intercourse and who were ever taught in school about AIDS or HIV, by sex, race, ethnicity, and grade, 2007

	Drank alcohol or used drugs before last sexual intercourse			Were taught in school about AIDS or HIV infection		
	Female	Male	Total	Female	Male	Total
Category	%	%	%	%	%	%
Race/ethnicity						
White*	19.8	30.5	24.8	91.7	90.5	91.1
Black*	12.9	19.8	16.4	91.8	88.8	90.3
Hispanic	16.5	25.9	21.4	84.8	85.1	85.0
Grade						
9	20.4	22.9	21.8	87.7	86.4	87.1
10	20.0	27.4	23.6	90.3	89.2	89.7
11	14.8	28.3	21.6	92.6	91.0	91.8
12	17.3	29.1	22.6	90.9	89.1	90.0
Total	**17.7**	**27.5**	**22.5**	**90.2**	**88.7**	**89.5**

*Non-Hispanic.
Note: Among the 35.0% of students nationwide who were currently sexually active.

SOURCE: Danice K. Eaton, "Table 67. Percentage of High School Students Who Drank Alcohol or Used Drugs before Last Sexual Intercourse and Who Were Ever Taught in School about Acquired Immunodeficiency Syndrome (AIDS) or Human Immunodeficiency Virus (HIV) Infection, by Sex, Race/Ethnicity, and Grade—United States, Youth Risk Behavior Survey, 2007," in "Youth Risk Behavior Surveillance—United States, 2007," *Morbidity and Mortality Weekly Report*, vol. 57, no. SS-4, June 6, 2008, http://www.cdc.gov/HealthyYouth/yrbs/pdf/yrbss07_mmwr.pdf (accessed November 5, 2008)

who used marijuana or binge drank in high school were more likely at age 21 to have had more sexual partners and to use condoms inconsistently. In "Trends in Sexual Risk Behavior and Unprotected Sex among High School Students, 1991–2006: The Role of Substance Use" (*Journal of School Health*, vol. 78, no. 11, November 2008), John E. Anderson and Trisha E. Mueller of the CDC find that adolescents who use drugs or alcohol are more likely to engage in risky sexual behaviors. The researchers report, "In spite of favorable trends in recent years for both sexual risk and drug use among adolescents, the [Youth Risk Behavior Survey] data show that a high percentage of youth are at risk and that many youth remain at dual risk from substance abuse and sexual behaviors."

Voluntary and Nonvoluntary Experiences

The 1995 and 2002 National Survey of Family Growth asked women whether their first sexual experience was voluntary. In "A Demographic Portrait of Statutory Rape" (2005, http://www.childtrends.org/Files/ConferenceonSexual ExploitationofTeensPresentation.pdf), Kristin Moore and Jennifer Manlove find that 18% of girls whose first sexual experience occurred at age 13 or under said it was nonvoluntary, compared to 10% of 15- and 16-year-olds and 5% of 17- and 19-year-olds. In addition, Elizabeth Terry-Humen, Jennifer Manlove, and Sarah Cottingham report in "Trends and Recent Estimates: Sexual Activity among U.S. Teens" (June 2006, http://www.childtrends.org/Files//Child _Trends-2006_06_01_RB_SexualActivity.pdf) that survey respondents were asked to state which of three statements most closely described how much they wanted their first sexual intercourse experience: "I really didn't want it to happen at the time," "I had mixed feelings—part of me wanted it to happen at the time and part of me didn't," and "I really wanted it to happen at the time." Only 34% of adolescent females said they really wanted it to happen at the time, compared to 62% of adolescent males who felt that way. More than one out of 10 (13%) females, compared to 6% of males, reported that they really did not want their first sexual intercourse to happen at that time.

Additionally, Anita Raj et al. find in "The Relationship between Sexual Abuse and Sexual Risk among High School Students: Findings from the 1997 Massachusetts Youth Risk Behavior Survey" (*Maternal and Child Health Journal*, vol. 4, no. 2, June 2000), that almost one-third (30.2%) of the girls and one-tenth (9.3%) of the boys reported having been sexually abused. Sexually abused females were twice as likely to engage in early sexual intercourse and other risky sexual behaviors as girls who had not been abused. Several studies corroborate evidence of the increased sexual risks taken by sexually abused youth, such as Elizabeth M. Saewyc, Lara Leanne Magee, and Sandra E. Pettingell's "Teenage Pregnancy and Associated Risk Behaviors among Sexually Abused Adolescents" (*Perspectives on Sexual and Reproductive Health*, vol. 36, no. 3, May–June 2004); Regina Jones Johnson, Lynn Rew, and R. Weylin Sternglanz's "The Relationship between Childhood Sexual Abuse and Sexual Health Practices of Homeless Adolescents" (*Adolescence*, vol. 41, no. 162, 2006); and Jonathan G. Tubman et al.'s "Abuse Experiences in a Community Sample of Young Adults: Relations with Psychiatric Disorders, Sexual Risk Behaviors, and Sexually Transmitted Diseases" (*American Journal of Community Psychology*, vol. 34, nos. 1–2, September 2004).

Saewyc, Magee, and Pettingell indicate that teenage pregnancy is also strongly linked to sexual abuse.

According to Child Trends, a nonprofit research organization dedicated to improving the lives of children, early sexual initiation for teenage girls has been linked to several adverse outcomes. The Child Trends publication *Facts at a Glance* (January 1, 1997) indicates that more than half (54%) of females 14 or younger at first sexual intercourse reported experiencing nonvoluntary sex at some point during their teen years. Brent C. Miller, Bruce H. Monson, and Maria C. Norton report in "The Effects of Forced Sexual Intercourse on White Female Adolescents" (*Child Abuse and Neglect*, vol. 19, no. 10, October 1995) that early sexual initiation has also been linked to domestic violence and verbal abuse later in life and to depression and low self-esteem. In "Associations of Dating Violence Victimization with Lifetime Participation, Co-occurrence, and Early Initiation of Risk Behaviors among U.S. High School Students" (*Journal of Interpersonal Violence*, vol. 22, no. 5, May 2007), Danice K. Eaton et al. of the CDC link early sexual intercourse with dating violence victimization among female students. Erin Schelar, Suzanne Ryan, and Jennifer Manlove argue in "Long-Term Consequences for Teens with Older Sexual Partners" (April 2008, http://www.childtrends.org/Files//Child_Trends-2008_05_06_FS_OlderPartners.pdf) that many girls with an early sexual initiation have partners three or more years older; the combination of early sexual initiation with older sexual partners puts girls at a higher risk for contracting STDs. In "Long-Term Health Correlates of Timing of Sexual Debut: Results from a National U.S. Study" (*American Journal of Public Health*, vol. 98, no. 1, January 2008), Theo G. M. Sandfort et al. link early sexual initiation to increased sexual risk behaviors and problems and sexual functioning for both males and females.

CONTRACEPTIVE USE

Too Few Use Contraceptives

Eaton et al. find that in 2007, 61.5% of sexually active teenagers reported that they or their partners used condoms during their last sexual intercourse. (See Table 5.3.) Young African-Americans reported the highest condom use (67.3%) among sexually active youth, Hispanic students reported a rate of 61.4%, and non-Hispanic white students reported the lowest rate of 59.7%. Males (68.5%) were significantly more likely than females (54.9%) to report condom use. However, the use of condoms decreased from the ninth grade (69.3%) to the 12th grade (54.2%), a period during which the frequency of sexual intercourse increased, probably because older adolescents turned to alternative methods of birth control, such as oral contraception.

Among sexually active students nationwide in 2007, 16% reported they or their partners used oral contraceptives, or "the pill." (See Table 5.3.) Even though this form of contraception protects against pregnancy, it does not protect against STDs. Twice as many non-Hispanic white students (20.8%) reported using birth control pills than did Hispanic (9.1%) or African-American students (9.1%). This disparity may be due to the need for a prescription for birth control pills; white students tend to have greater access to medical care than minority students do. Birth control pill use increased between ninth (8.7%) and 12th grade (23.5%).

TABLE 5.3

Percentage of high school students who used a condom during last sexual intercourse and who used birth control pills before last sexual intercourse, by sex, race, ethnicity, and grade, 2007

	Condom use			Birth control pill use		
	Female	Male	Total	Female	Male	Total
Category	%	%	%	%	%	%
Race/ethnicity						
White*	53.9	66.4	59.7	24.0	17.0	20.8
Black*	60.1	74.0	67.3	12.1	6.3	9.1
Hispanic	52.1	69.9	61.4	9.1	9.0	9.1
Grade						
9	61.0	75.8	69.3	9.2	8.3	8.7
10	59.5	73.2	66.1	13.7	9.5	11.6
11	55.1	69.3	62.0	18.9	11.0	15.0
12	49.9	59.6	54.2	25.6	20.8	23.5
Total	**54.9**	**68.5**	**61.5**	**18.7**	**13.1**	**16.0**

*Non-Hispanic.
Notes: Among the 35.0% of students nationwide who were currently sexually active. Birth control pills used to prevent pregnancy.

SOURCE: Danice K. Eaton et al., "Table 65. Percentage of High School Students Who Used a Condom during Last Sexual Intercourse and Who Used Birth Control Pills before Last Sexual Intercourse, by Sex, Race/Ethnicity, and Grade—United States, Youth Risk Behavior Survey, 2007," in "Youth Risk Behavior Surveillance—United States, 2007," *Morbidity and Mortality Weekly Report*, vol. 57, no. SS-4, June 6, 2008, http://www.cdc.gov/HealthyYouth/yrbs/pdf/yrbss07_mmwr.pdf (accessed November 5, 2008)

Drawing on a national survey of male adolescents, Erum Ikramullah and Jennifer Manlove find in "Condom Use and Consistency among Teen Males" (October 2008, http://www.childtrends.org/Files/Child_Trends-2008_10_30_FS_CondomUse.pdf) that even though 71% of male teens reported using a condom the first and most recent time they had sexual intercourse, only half of male teens reported consistent condom use with their most recent sexual partner.

REASONS FOR USE OR NONUSE OF CONDOMS. There are many factors involved in adolescents' decisions to use or not use condoms. The November 2000 SexSmarts (http://www.kff.org/entpartnerships/upload/SexSmarts-Survey-Safer-Sex-Condoms-and-the-Pill-Toplines.pdf), a survey of 519 adolescents aged 12 to 17 by the Henry J. Kaiser Family Foundation and *Seventeen* magazine, highlights teens' fairly casual attitude toward condom use. The survey shows that teens do not completely understand the importance of using condoms consistently to avoid STDs, including HIV and acquired immunodeficiency syndrome (AIDS). Eleven percent agreed with the statement "having sex without a condom every now and then is not that big of a deal," and 9% believed that "if you don't have a lot of partners you don't need to use condoms." One out of four (25%) teenage females agreed with the statement "condoms break so often they are not worth using." In "Gender Roles" (November 2002, http://www.kff.org/entpartnerships/upload/Gender-Rolls-Summary.pdf), a follow-up survey, SexSmarts finds that girls face more negative attitudes than boys do if they carry condoms with them; 70% of boys and 75% of girls agreed with the statement, "If a girl carries a condom people might think she is 'easy'," whereas only 43% of boys and 36% of girls agreed with the statement, "If a boy carries a condom people might think he is 'easy'."

Research indicates that adolescents' attitudes and beliefs about their relationships with their partners influence whether or not they will use condoms. Celia M. Lescano et al. of Brown Medical School find in "Condom Use with 'Casual' and 'Main' Partners: What's in a Name?" (*Journal of Adolescent Health*, vol. 39, no. 3, September 2006) that adolescents were more likely to use a condom with a partner that they perceived as a casual one. However, even when partners were casual ones, teens reported using condoms only about half the time. Therefore, teens were not adequately protecting themselves against STDs even with partners they perceived as more risky. Condom use with partners perceived as main partners was even lower. Lescano et al. state, "Perhaps adolescents overestimate the safety of using condoms 'most of the time' with a casual partner and underestimate the risk of unprotected sex with a 'serious' partner."

Cynthia Grossman et al. find in "Adolescent Sexual Risk: Factors Predicting Condom Use across the Stages of Change" (*AIDS and Behavior*, vol. 12, no. 6, November

2008) that teens who consistently used condoms reported a greater understanding of the importance of using condoms, had better communication about condom use with their partners, and were less likely to perceive themselves as immune to the human immunodeficiency virus (HIV) than their peers who reported inconsistent condom use.

In "Condom Use among High-Risk Adolescents: Anticipation of Partner Disapproval and Less Pleasure Associated with Not Using Condoms" (*Public Health Reports*, vol. 123, no. 5, September–October 2008), Larry K. Brown et al. note that they surveyed 1,410 adolescents and young adults between the ages of 15 and 21 who had unprotected sex in the previous 90 days. The researchers find that nearly two-thirds of adolescents did not use condoms at the time of last intercourse. Teens who did not use condoms were significantly more likely to believe that condoms reduce sexual pleasure. They were also less likely to discuss condom use with their partners, but were more concerned that their partners would not approve of condom use.

According to Tricia Hall et al., in "Attitudes toward Using Condoms and Condom Use: Differences between Sexually Abused and Nonabused African American Female Adolescents" (*Behavioral Medicine*, vol. 34, no. 2, Summer 2008), there is some evidence that teens who have been sexually abused are less likely to use condoms and more likely to have unprotected sex than their nonabused peers.

SEXUALLY TRANSMITTED DISEASES

Adolescents and young adults have a higher risk of acquiring STDs than older adults. Female adolescents may have an increased susceptibility to chlamydia, a bacterial infection that can cause pelvic inflammatory disease and is a contributing factor in the transmission of HIV. In *Child Health USA 2007* (2008, ftp://ftp.hrsa.gov/mchb/chusa_07/c07.pdf), the Maternal and Child Health Bureau states that in 2005 chlamydia was the most common STD among adolescents. It was also more common in adolescents and young adults than in any other age group, with 1,621 cases among every 100,000 teens aged 15 to 19. This group also had the highest rates of gonorrhea infection. As Figure 5.1 shows, non-Hispanic African-American teens had much higher rates of both chlamydia and gonorrhea than non-Hispanic white teens.

Kathleen J. Sikkema et al. emphasize in "HIV Risk Behavior among Ethnically Diverse Adolescents Living in Low-Income Housing Developments" (*Journal of Adolescent Health*, vol. 35, no. 2, August 2004) that half of all new HIV infections in the United States are diagnosed in people under 25 years old. Most of these young people become infected through sexual activity. The researchers find that the risk of HIV infection was highest among older adolescents who did not see a need to practice safer sex because they were with steady partners and among teens who abused drugs and alcohol. Sikkema et al. suggest that their

FIGURE 5.1

Rates of sexually transmitted diseases per 100,000 adolescents and young adults, by age and race/ethnicity, 2005

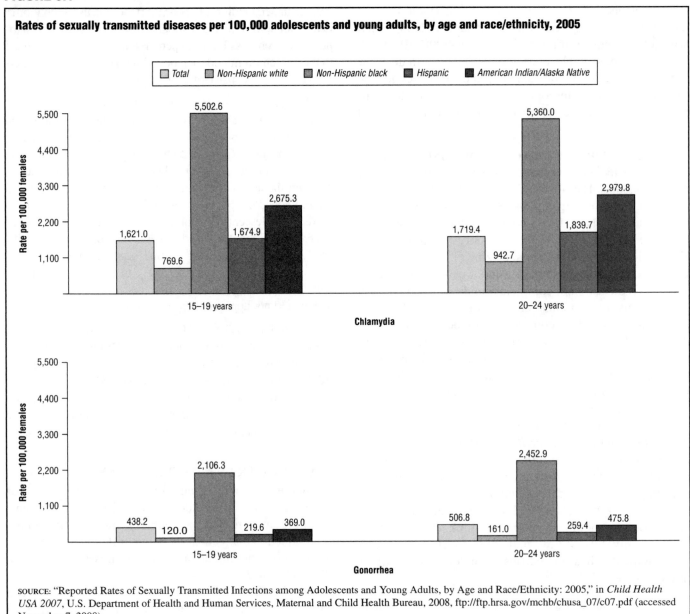

SOURCE: "Reported Rates of Sexually Transmitted Infections among Adolescents and Young Adults, by Age and Race/Ethnicity: 2005," in *Child Health USA 2007*, U.S. Department of Health and Human Services, Maternal and Child Health Bureau, 2008, ftp://ftp.hrsa.gov/mchb/chusa_07/c07.pdf (accessed November 7, 2008)

study results could be used to design prevention programs for those adolescents most at risk.

In "Does Parental Involvement Predict New Sexually Transmitted Diseases in Female Adolescents?" (*Archives of Pediatrics and Adolescent Medicine*, vol. 158, no. 7, July 2004), Julie A. Bettinger et al. test whether parental involvement had any impact on the rates of STDs among low-income African-American adolescent girls. The researchers find that when these high-risk teens perceived their parents as exercising a high degree of supervision over their activities, they had lower rates of both gonorrhea and chlamydia infection. Anne M. Teitelman, Sarah J. Ratcliffe, and Julie A. Cederbaum find in "Parent-Adolescent Communication about Sexual Pressure, Maternal Norms about Relationship Power, and STI/HIV Protective Behaviors of Minority Urban Girls" (*Ameri-*

can Psychiatric Nurses Association Journal, vol. 14, no. 1, 2008) that racial and ethnic minority adolescent females who communicated with their parents about sex were better able to be consistent in condom use.

Human Papilloma Virus Vaccine

One STD, the human papilloma virus (HPV), can cause genital warts and cervical cancer in women. At least half of sexually active people will get HPV; most of the time, it resolves on its own. However, sometimes it lingers and causes cell changes that can lead to cervical cancer. In "What Are the Key Statistics about Cervical Cancer?" (March 26, 2008, http://www.cancer.org/docroot/CRI/content/CRI_2_4_1X_What_are_the_key_statistics_for_cervical_cancer_8.asp), the American Cancer Society estimates that in 2008 about 11,070 women will be diagnosed with cervical cancer, and about 3,870 women will die from it. A large proportion of cervical cancer cases are caused by HPV, perhaps in combination with other factors. Clinical trials for a new vaccine against certain strains of the virus, given in three doses over a six-month period, show that the vaccine is nearly 100% effective. In August 2006 the CDC recommended in "HPV Vaccine Information for Young Women" (http://www.cdc.gov/std/hpv/STDFact-HPV-vaccine.htm) that the new vaccine be given to girls before they become sexually active, around age 12, to prevent the transmission of HPV.

However, such recommendations stirred up controversy, which heated up in February 2007, when Rick Perry (1950–), the governor of Texas, issued an executive order making the state the first to require that girls entering the sixth grade be vaccinated as a condition for enrolling in public school. Liz Austin Peterson reports in "Texas Gov. Orders Anti-cancer Vaccine" (Associated Press, February 2, 2007) that conservative groups feared that such a requirement undermined abstinence education and would condone premarital sex. In "Virginity or Death!" (*Nation*, May 12, 2005), Katha Pollitt explains that others argued for mandatory vaccination because young girls would not abstain from sexual activity due to fear of cervical cancer, HPV cannot be prevented by condom use, and 70% of cases of cervical cancer could be prevented by this vaccine.

TEEN CHILDBEARING TRENDS

Brady E. Hamilton, Joyce A. Martin, and Stephanie J. Ventura of the CDC report in "Births: Preliminary Data for 2006" (*National Vital Statistics Reports*, vol. 56, no. 7, December 5, 2007, http://www.cdc.gov/nchs/data/nvsr/nvsr56/nvsr56_07.pdf) that birthrates for women aged 15 to 19 rose in 2006 for the first time in many years. (See Figure 5.2.) Among girls aged 15 to 17, the birthrate dropped from 38.6 per 1,000 women in 1991 to 21.4 per 1,000 women in 2005, but rose to 22 births per 1,000 women in 2006. Among young women aged 18 to 19 years, the birthrate dropped from 94 per 1,000 in 1991 to 69.9 in 2005, but rose to 73 births per 1,000 in 2006. Most teens who give birth are unmarried. (See Table 5.4.) Childbearing by unmarried women jumped to record high levels that year, to 1.6 million births.

According to Hamilton, Martin, and Ventura, available data by race show that the greatest percentage increase in teen births in 2006 was among African-Americans, whose rate rose 5% to 63.7 births per 1,000. Births to Native American teens increased 4% to 54.7 per 1,000, 3% for non-Hispanic white teenagers to 26.6 births per 1,000, and 2% for Hispanic teens to 83 births per 1,000. The only ethnic group whose birthrate did not see an increase was Asian and Pacific Islanders. In "Births: Final Data for 2006" (*National Vital Statistics Reports*, vol. 57, no. 7, January 7, 2009), Joyce A. Martin et al. of the CDC explain

FIGURE 5.2

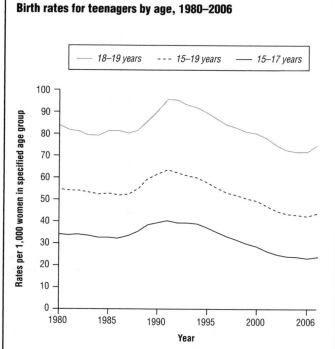

Birth rates for teenagers by age, 1980–2006

SOURCE: Brady E. Hamilton, Joyce A. Martin, and Stephanie J. Ventura, "Figure 1. Birth Rates for Teenagers by Age: United States, Final 1980–2005 and Preliminary 2006," in "Births: Preliminary Data for 2006," *National Vital Statistics Reports*, vol. 56, no. 7, December 5, 2007, http://www.cdc.gov/nchs/data/nvsr/nvsr56/nvsr56_07.pdf (accessed November 7, 2008)

that New Hampshire, Vermont, and Massachusetts had the lowest teen birth rates in 2006, whereas Mississippi, New Mexico, and Texas had the highest rates.

Consequences for Teen Mothers and Their Children

Teenage mothers and their babies face more health risks than older women and their children. Teenagers who become pregnant are more likely than older women to suffer from pregnancy-induced hypertension and eclampsia (a life-threatening condition that sometimes results in convulsions and/or coma). Teenagers are more likely to have their labor induced, and an immature pelvis can cause prolonged or difficult labor, possibly resulting in bladder or bowel damage to the mother, infant brain damage, or even death of the mother and/or the child.

Even though most health risks are similar for children born to teenage and older mothers, teenage mothers may have a higher prevalence of certain risk factors. For example, the CDC notes in *Health, United States, 2007* (2007, http://www.cdc.gov/nchs/data/hus/hus07.pdf) that in 2004 teenagers had very high rates of smoking during pregnancy (10.5% for 15- to 17-year-olds and 16% for 18- to 19-year-olds) and that smokers were nearly twice as likely to have low-birth-weight babies as nonsmokers. In the fact sheet "Preventing Infant Mortality" (January 13, 2006, http://www.hhs.gov/news/fact sheet/infant.html), the U.S. Department of Health and

TABLE 5.4

Births to unmarried women, by age, 2005 and 2006

[Data for 2006 are based on a continuous file of records received from the states. Figures for 2006 are based on weighted data rounded to the nearest individual, so categories may not add to totals]

Age of mother	Number		Percent	
	2006	2005	2006	2005
All ages	1,641,700	1,527,034	38.5	36.9
Under 20 years	372,826	352,003	84.4	83.5
Under 15 years	6,297	6,590	98.3	98.0
15–19 years	366,529	345,413	84.2	83.3
15–17 years	127,718	121,112	91.9	90.9
18–19 years	238,811	224,301	80.5	79.7
20–24 years	625,701	584,792	57.9	56.2
25–29 years	366,056	331,820	31.0	29.3
30–34 years	173,538	161,752	18.3	17.0
35–39 years	81,786	75,717	16.4	15.7
40–54 years	21,792	20,950	19.4	18.8

SOURCE: Brady E. Hamilton, Joyce A. Martin, and Stephanie J. Ventura, "Table 7. Number and Percentage of Births to Unmarried Women, by Age: United States, Final 2005 and Preliminary 2006," in "Births: Preliminary Data for 2006," *National Vital Statistics Reports*, vol. 56, no. 7, December 5, 2007, http://www.cdc.gov/nchs/data/nvsr/nvsr56/nvsr56_07.pdf (accessed November 7, 2008).

Human Services indicates that teenagers in general are at a higher risk of having low-birth-weight babies. Michael Klitsch finds in "Youngest Mothers' Infants Have Greatly Elevated Risk of Dying by Age One" (*Perspectives on Sexual and Reproductive Health*, vol. 35, no. 1, January–February 2003) that babies born to adolescents have a greater risk of dying between one and 12 months after birth.

Few teenage mothers are ready for the emotional, psychological, and financial responsibilities and challenges of parenthood. Becoming a parent at a young age usually cuts short a teenage mother's education, limiting her ability to support herself and her child. According to Sandra L. Hofferth, Lori Reid, and Frank L. Mott, in "The Effects of Early Childbearing on Schooling over Time" (*Family Planning Perspectives*, vol. 33, no. 6, November–December 2001), women who gave birth as teens in the early 1990s had only a 65% probability of graduating from high school, and only a 29% probability of completing some college. David M. Fergusson, Joseph M. Boden, and L. John Horwood report in "Abortion among Young Women and Subsequent Life Outcomes" (*Perspectives on Sexual and Reproductive Health*, vol. 39, no. 1, March 2007) that educational attainment is lower among teen mothers than among teens who had an abortion. Additionally, Susheela Singh et al. note in "Socioeconomic Disadvantage and Adolescent Women's Sexual and Reproductive Behavior: The Case of Five Developed Countries" (*Family Planning Perspectives*, vol. 33, no. 5, November–December 2001) that 40% of American women aged 20 to 24 who gave birth before age 20 had an income of less than 149% of the federal poverty guideline.

The children of teen mothers face consequences as well. In *Playing Catch-up: How Children Born to Teen Mothers Fare* (January 2005, http://www.teenpregnancy.org/works/

pdf/PlayingCatchUp.pdf), Elizabeth Terry-Humen, Jennifer Manlove, and Kristin A. Moore examine data on kindergarteners to determine the relationship between the age a woman has a child and how her child does in several key areas: cognition and knowledge, language and communication skills, approaches to learning, emotional well-being and social skills, and physical well-being and motor development. The researchers find that children born to mothers aged 17 and younger had lower general knowledge scores and language and communication skills, compared to children born to mothers aged 20 and older. Children's approaches to learning, physical well-being, and emotional development, as well as their social skills and emotional well-being, were relatively unaffected by maternal age. In sum, Terry-Humen, Manlove, and Moore state, "Children born to mothers aged 17 and younger began kindergarten with lower levels of school readiness.... The children born to mothers in their 20s clearly outperformed those whose mothers were still teenagers at time of birth, and the most consistent and pronounced differences were observed when comparing children born to mothers aged 17 and younger to those children born to mothers aged 22-29."

Greg Pogarsky, Terence P. Thornberry, and Alan J. Lizotte come to similar conclusions in "Developmental Outcomes for Children of Young Mothers" (*Journal of Marriage and Family*, vol. 68, no. 2, May 2006). The researchers note that boys born to young mothers had elevated risks of drug use, gang membership, unemployment, and early parenthood, whereas girls had elevated risks of becoming young mothers themselves.

Adolescent Fathers

According to the Child Trends Databank, in *Teen Births* (January 2007, http://www.childtrendsdatabank.org/pdf/13 _PDF.pdf), in 2005 15- to 19-year-old males had a birthrate of 16.8 per 1,000, down from a high of 24.7 in 1991. This rate was substantially lower than the 2005 rate for teenage girls of 40.5 per 1,000. The rate was higher for African-American male teens (32.2) than for white male teens (14.2); data for Hispanic male teens were unavailable. The difference between male adolescent and female adolescent birthrates is due in part to the fact that many teen mothers have older partners, as well as to the underreporting of information about fathers on birth certificates. In *Facts at a Glance* (November 2003, http://www.childtrends.org/Files/FAAG2003.pdf), Child Trends reports that 38% of births to mothers aged 18 and younger were to fathers four or more years older than the mother. In some cases teen mothers have been sexually abused by their older partners.

Such studies alert officials who design programs for the prevention of pregnancy and STDs to the need to pay attention not only to preadolescent and adolescent males but also to older males who are partners of teenage girls. Because these men are typically out of the public school system, officials agree that programs must be broader in scope.

TEEN ABORTION

The CDC reports that in 2004, 839,000 abortions were performed; the year before, 848,000 had been performed. (See Table 5.5.) The Guttmacher Institute conducted a survey and estimated that a much higher number of abortions had been performed in 2004—over 1.2 million. The rate of abortions per 100 live births has decreased from a high of 35.9 in 1980 to 23.8 in 2004. Girls under 15 years old had the highest rate of abortions (76.2 per 100 live births) in 2004, followed by teens aged 15 to 19 (36.2 per 100 live births). All other age groups had lower rates of abortion. For all age groups, African-Americans had the highest abortion rate of any race or ethnic group (47.2 per 100 live births), followed by Hispanics (21.1 per 100 live births) and non-Hispanic whites (16.1 per 100 live births).

TABLE 5.5

Legal abortions and legal abortion ratios, by selected patient characteristics, selected years 1973–2004

[Data are based on reporting by state health departments and by hospitals and other medical facilities]

Characteristic	1973	1975	1980	1985	1990	1995	1999[a]	2000[b]	2002[b]	2003[c]	2004[c]
					Number of legal abortions reported in thousands						
Centers for Disease Control and Prevention (CDC)	616	855	1,298	1,329	1,429	1,211	862	857	854	848	839
Guttmacher Institute[d]	745	1,034	1,554	1,589	1,609	1,359	1,315	1,313	1,293	1,287	1,222
					Abortions per 100 live births[e]						
Total CDC	19.6	27.2	35.9	35.4	34.4	31.1	25.6	24.5	24.6	24.1	23.8
Age											
Under 15 years	123.7	119.3	139.7	137.6	81.8	66.4	70.9	70.8	75.3	83.0	76.2
15–19 years	53.9	54.2	71.4	68.8	51.1	39.9	37.5	36.1	36.8	37.4	36.2
20–24 years	29.4	28.9	39.5	38.6	37.8	34.8	31.6	30.0	30.3	30.0	29.1
25–29 years	20.7	19.2	23.7	21.7	21.8	22.0	20.8	19.8	20.0	19.5	19.1
30–34 years	28.0	25.0	23.7	19.9	19.0	16.4	15.2	14.5	14.8	14.4	14.3
35–39 years	45.1	42.2	41.0	33.6	27.3	22.3	19.3	18.1	18.0	17.3	17.0
40 years and over	68.4	66.8	80.7	62.3	50.6	38.5	32.9	30.1	31.0	29.3	28.6
Race											
White[f]	32.6	27.7	33.2	27.7	25.8	20.3	17.7	16.7	16.4	16.5	16.1
Black or African American[g]	42.0	47.6	54.3	47.2	53.7	53.1	52.9	50.3	49.5	49.1	47.2
Hispanic origin[h]											
Hispanic or Latina	—	—	—	—	—	27.1	26.1	22.5	23.3	22.8	21.1
Not Hispanic or Latina	—	—	—	—	—	27.9	25.2	23.3	23.7	23.4	23.6
Marital status											
Married	7.6	9.6	10.5	8.0	8.7	7.6	7.0	6.5	6.5	6.3	6.1
Unmarried	139.8	161.0	147.6	117.4	86.3	64.5	60.4	57.0	57.0	53.8	51.0
Previous live births[i]											
0	43.7	38.4	45.7	45.1	36.0	28.6	24.3	22.6	23.3	22.7	23.0
1	23.5	22.0	20.2	21.6	22.7	22.0	20.6	19.4	19.4	19.0	19.0
2	36.8	36.8	29.5	29.9	31.5	30.6	29.0	27.4	27.9	27.1	26.4
3	46.9	47.7	29.8	18.2	30.1	30.7	29.8	28.5	29.1	28.3	27.4
4 or more[j]	44.7	43.5	24.3	21.5	26.6	23.7	24.2	23.7	23.6	23.4	22.9
					Percent distribution[k]						
Total	100.0	100.0	100.0	100.0	100.0	100.0	100.0	100.0	100.0	100.0	100.0
Period of gestation											
Under 9 weeks	36.1	44.6	51.7	50.3	51.6	54.0	57.6	58.1	60.5	60.5	61.4
9–10 weeks	29.4	28.4	26.2	26.6	25.3	23.1	20.2	19.8	18.4	18.0	17.6
11–12 weeks	17.9	14.9	12.2	12.5	11.7	10.9	10.2	10.2	9.6	9.7	9.3
13–15 weeks	6.9	5.0	5.1	5.9	6.4	6.3	6.2	6.2	6.0	6.2	6.3
16–20 weeks	8.0	6.1	3.9	3.9	4.0	4.3	4.3	4.3	4.1	4.2	4.0
21 weeks and over	1.7	1.0	0.9	0.8	1.0	1.4	1.5	1.4	1.4	1.4	1.4

TABLE 5.5

Legal abortions and legal abortion ratios, by selected patient characteristics, selected years 1973–2004 [CONTINUED]

[Data are based on reporting by state health departments and by hospitals and other medical facilities]

Characteristic	1973	1975	1980	1985	1990	1995	1999[a]	2000[b]	2002[b]	2003[c]	2004[c]
Previous induced abortions											
0	—	81.9	67.6	60.1	57.1	55.1	53.7	54.7	55.3	55.3	55.0
1	—	14.9	23.5	25.7	26.9	26.9	27.1	26.4	25.8	25.7	25.8
2	—	2.5	6.6	9.8	10.1	10.9	11.5	11.3	11.3	11.2	11.3
3 or more	—	0.7	2.3	4.4	5.9	7.1	7.7	7.6	7.6	7.8	7.9

—Data not available.
[a]In 1998 and 1999, Alaska, California, New Hampshire, and Oklahoma did not report abortion data to CDC. For comparison, in 1997, the 48 corresponding reporting areas reported about 900,000 legal abortions.
[b]In 2000, 2001, and 2002, Alaska, California, and New Hampshire did not report abortion data to CDC.
[c]In 2003 and 2004, California, New Hampshire, and West Virginia did not report abortion data to CDC.
[d]No surveys were conducted in 1983, 1986, 1989, 1990, 1993, 1994, 1997, 1998, 2001, 2002, or 2003. Data for these years were estimated by interpolation.
[e]For calculation of ratios by each characteristic, abortions with characteristic unknown were distributed in proportion to abortions with characteristic known.
[f]For 1989 and later years, white race includes women of Hispanic ethnicity.
[g]Before 1989, black race includes races other than white.
[h]Data from 20–22 states, the District of Columbia (DC), and New York City (NYC) were included in 1991–1993. The number of reporting areas increased to 25 states, DC, and NYC in 1994–2004. States were excluded either because they did not collect data on Hispanic origin or due to incomplete reporting of Hispanic data (greater than 15% unknown Hispanic origin).
[i]For 1973–1975, data indicate number of living children.
[j]For 1975, data refer to four previous live births, not four or more. For five or more previous live births, the ratio is 47.3.
[k]For calculation of percent distribution by each characteristic, abortions with characteristic unknown were excluded.
Notes: The number of areas reporting adequate data (less than or equal to 15% missing) for each characteristic varies from year to year. Data for additional years are available.

SOURCE: "Table 16. Legal Abortions and Legal Abortion Ratios, by Selected Patient Characteristics: United States, Selected Years 1973–2004," in *Health, United States, 2007. With Chartbook on Trends in the Health of Americans*, Centers for Disease Control and Prevention, National Center for Health Statistics, 2007, http://www.cdc.gov/nchs/data/hus/hus07.pdf (accessed September 15, 2008). Nongovernmental data from Guttmacher Institute Abortion Provider Survey; L.B. Finer and S.K. Henshaw, "Abortion Incidence and Services in the United States in 2000," *Perspectives on Sexual and Reproductive Health*, vol. 35, no. 1, 2003; L.B. Finer and S.K. Henshaw, *Estimates of U.S. Abortion Incidence, 2001–2003*, The Alan Guttmacher Institute, August 2006; R.K. Jones et al., "Abortion in the United States: Incidence and Access to Services, 2005," *Perspectives on Sexual and Reproductive Health*, vol. 40, no. 1, 2008.

As Table 5.5 shows, the abortion rates for teens have declined dramatically since the late 1980s, as have the pregnancy and birthrates.

States have varying laws on parental involvement in minors' abortion decisions. In "An Overview of Abortion Laws" (January 1, 2009, http://www.guttmacher.org/statecenter/spibs/spib_OAL.pdf), the Guttmacher Institute reports that 16 states and the District of Columbia required no parental involvement in minors' abortions. Thirty-four states required some parental involvement, 22 required parental consent, and 10 required parental notification.

HOMOSEXUALITY

In *Just the Facts about Sexual Orientation and Youth* (2008, http://www.apa.org/pi/lgbc/publications/justthefacts.pdf), a pamphlet for school personnel, the American Psychological Association (APA) stresses that sexual orientation is one aspect of the identity of adolescents—not a mental disorder. According to the APA, sexual orientation is developed across a lifetime and along a continuum; in other words, teens are not necessarily simply homosexual or heterosexual, but may feel varying degrees of attraction to people of both genders. The APA explains that gay, lesbian, and bisexual adolescents face prejudice and discrimination that negatively affect their educational experiences and emotional and physical health. Their legitimate fear of being hurt as a result of disclosing their sexuality often leads to a feeling of isolation. All these factors account for lesbian, gay, and bisexual adolescents' higher

rates of emotional distress, suicide attempts, risky sexual behavior, and substance use. The APA underscores the need for school personnel to be as open and accepting as possible to support these adolescents.

STD AND PREGNANCY PREVENTION PROGRAMS FOR TEENS
Abstinence

In response to the growing concern about out-of-wedlock births and the threat of AIDS, several national youth organizations and religious groups began campaigns in the early and mid-1990s to encourage teens to sign an abstinence pledge—a promise to abstain from sexual activity until marriage. According to the National Institutes of Health, in the news release "Virginity Pledge Helps Teens Delay Sexual Activity" (January 5, 2001, http://www.nichd.nih.gov/news/releases/virginity.cfm), 2.5 million teens had taken the "virginity pledge" by 1995. Debra Hauser of Advocates for Youth indicates in *Five Years of Abstinence-Only-until-Marriage Education: Assessing the Impact* (2004, http://www.advocatesforyouth.org/publications/stateevaluations.pdf) that in 1996 the federal government committed $250 million over the following five years to fund state initiatives to promote abstinence as Title V of the Social Security Act. Even though only 11 states made the results of their evaluations of the effectiveness of these programs public, Hauser states that Advocates for Youth examined these evaluations and found that the programs "showed few short-term benefits and no lasting, positive impact.... No program was able to demonstrate a positive impact on sexual behavior over time."

The administration of U.S. president George W. Bush (1946–) placed a new emphasis on abstinence among teens. According to the White House report *Working toward Independence* (February 2002, http://www.whitehouse.gov/news/releases/2002/02/welfare-reform-announcement-book.pdf), an overview of Bush's suggested plan for welfare reform, "the goal of Federal policy should be to emphasize abstinence as the only certain way to avoid both unintended pregnancies and STDs." In 2007, the U.S. government provided $176 million for abstinence-only programs, but no federal funding for comprehensive sex education programs. Title V, the state abstinence-only education program, provided states with federal funding for abstinence-only sex education programs, but in 2007, 25 of 50 states refused to take the money because they did not want to offer such programs.

Despite the federal funds spent on such programs, Eaton et al. find that in 2007 over one-third (35%) of high school students were sexually active at the time of the survey—35.6% of females and 34.3% of males. Younger students were less likely to be currently sexually active than were older students. Even though 47.8% of all students had ever had sexual intercourse; 64.6% of high school seniors had. (See Table 5.1.)

In this context, abstinence-only education will do little to prevent teen pregnancy or the spread of STDs. As John S. Santelli et al. state in "Abstinence and Abstinence-Only Education: A Review of U.S. Policies and Programs" (*Journal of Adolescent Health*, vol. 38, no. 1, January 2006), "Although abstinence is a healthy behavioral option for teens, abstinence as a sole option for adolescents is scientifically and ethically problematic.... We believe that abstinence-only education programs, as defined by federal funding requirements, are morally problematic, by withholding information and promoting questionable and inaccurate opinions. Abstinence-only programs threaten fundamental human rights to health, information, and life."

In 2007, the Department of Health and Human Services released *Impacts of Four Title V, Section 510 Abstinence Education Programs* (April 2007, http://aspe.hhs.gov/hsp/abstinence07/report.pdf) by Christopher Trenholm et al. The researchers conclude that the youth in the abstinence-only programs were no more likely than youth who were assigned to the control group to have abstained from sex.

Those who reported having sex had similar numbers of sexual partners and had initiated sex at the same mean age. In September 2008, several articles about abstinence-only programs were published in a special issue of the journal *Sexuality Research and Social Policy* (vol. 5, no. 3). Douglas B. Kirby states in "The Impact of Abstinence and Comprehensive Sex and STD/HIV Education Programs on Adolescent Sexual Behavior" that such programs fail to change sexual behavior in teenagers. Other articles concluded that the programs provide inaccurate information about condoms and that they violate human rights principles.

The fate of abstinence-only education was unknown when Barack Obama (1961–) was sworn in as president of the United States in January 2009. Many considered Obama to be in favor of more comprehensive sex education programs. The HHS states in *Budget in Brief, Fiscal Year 2009* (2008, http://www.hhs.gov/budget/09budget/2009BudgetIn Brief.pdf) that in fiscal year 2009, $191 million in grant money was available for abstinence education, up $28 million from the previous year. The White House explains in *A New Era of Responsibility: Renewing America's Promise* (2009, http://www.whitehouse.gov/omb/assets/fy2010 _new_era/A_New_Era_of_Responsibility2.pdf) that President Obama's 2010 budget proposal not only continued funding for abstinence education but also provided funding for "medically-accurate and age-appropriate information to youth who have already become sexually active," signaling a potential change of direction in the new administration.

Sex and STD/HIV Education in Schools

As of November 2008, 35 states and the District of Columbia required schools to provide education on HIV/AIDS and other STDs, although in all cases parents were allowed to remove their children from sex education classes. (See Table 5.6.) Twenty-six states required schools to stress the importance of abstinence in STD and HIV/AIDS education, and 11 states required abstinence to be covered. Seventeen states required schools to teach students about contraception, but none required that it be stressed.

According to Eaton et al., 89.5% of all students had been taught about AIDS or HIV in school, compared to 91.5% in 1997. (See Table 5.2.) As HIV/AIDS is increasingly common among young people, the declining percentages of students who learn about the disease in school is problematic.

TABLE 5.6

Sex and STD/HIV education policy by state, November 2008

State	Sex education			STI/HIV education			Parental role	
		If taught, content required			If taught, content required		Consent required	Opt-out permitted
	Mandated	Abstinence	Contraception	Mandated	Abstinence	Contraception		
Alabama		Stress	Cover	X	Stress	Cover		X[a]
Arizona		Stress			Stress		X[b]	X[b]
Arkansas		Stress			Stress			
California		Cover	Cover	X	Cover	Cover		X
Colorado		Stress	Cover		Stress			X
Connecticut		Cover		X				X
Delaware	X	Cover	Cover	X	Cover	Cover		
Dist. of Columbia	X		Cover	X				X
Florida	X	Cover		X				X
Georgia	X	Cover		X	Cover			X
Hawaii	X	Stress	Cover	X	Stress	Cover		
Idaho								X
Illinois		Stress[c]			Stress[c]	Cover[‡]		X
Indiana		Stress		X	Stress			
Iowa	X			X				X
Kansas	X			X				X
Kentucky	X	Cover		X	Cover			
Louisiana		Stress			Stress	Cover		X
Maine	X	Stress	Cover	X	Stress			X
Maryland	X	Cover	Cover	X	Cover	Cover		X
Massachusetts								X[a]
Michigan		Stress		X	Stress			X
Minnesota	X			X	Cover			X
Mississippi[d]		Stress			Stress			X
Missouri		Stress		X	Stress			X
Montana	X	Cover		X	Cover			X[b]
Nevada	X			X			X	
New Hampshire				X	Cover			X
New Jersey	X			X				X[a]
New Mexico				X	Stress	Cover		
New York				X	Stress	Cover		X[b]
North Carolina	X	Stress		X	Stress			
Ohio				X	Stress			X
Oklahoma		Stress		X	Cover	Cover		X
Oregon	X	Stress	Cover	X	Stress	Cover		X
Pennsylvania				X	Stress			X[†]
Rhode Island	X	Stress	Cover	X	Stress	Cover		X
South Carolina	X	Stress	Cover	X	Stress	Cover		X
South Dakota[e]								
Tennessee	X	Stress		X	Stress			X
Texas		Stress			Stress			X
Utah[f]	X	Stress		X	Stress		X	
Vermont	X	Cover	Cover	X	Cover	Cover		X[a]
Virginia		Cover	Cover		Cover	Cover		X
Washington		Stress	Cover	X	Stress	Cover		X
West Virginia		Stress	Cover	X	Stress	Cover		X
Wisconsin		Stress		X	Stress			X
Total	**20+DC**			**35+DC**			**3**	**36+DC**

[a]Parents' removal of student must be based on religious or moral beliefs.

[b]In AZ, MT, NY and PA, opt-out is only permitted for STI education, including instruction on HIV; in AZ, parental consent is required only for sex education.

[c]IL has a broad set of laws mandating general health education, including abstinence; a more specific second law requires a school district that provides sex education to stress abstinence and to provide statistics on the efficacy of condoms as HIV/STI prevention.

[d]Localities may override state requirements for sex education topics, including abstinence; state prohibits including material that "contradicts the required components."

[e]Abstinence is taught within state-mandated character education.

[f]State prohibits teachers from responding to students' spontaneous questions in ways that conflict with the law's requirements.

SOURCE: Guttmacher Institute, "State Sex and STD/HIV Education Policy," in *State Policies in Brief: Sex and STI/HIV Education*, New York: Guttmacher Institute 2008, http://www.guttmacher.org/statecenter/spibs/spib_SE.pdf (accessed November 7, 2008)

CHAPTER 6
GETTING AN EDUCATION

Despite the controversies surrounding the quality and direction of American education, the United States remains one of the most highly educated nations in the world. According to Thomas D. Snyder, Sally A. Dillow, and Charlene M. Hoffman, in *Digest of Education Statistics, 2007* (March 2008, http://nces.ed.gov/pubs2008/2008022.pdf), in the fall of 2007, 73.7 million Americans were enrolled students in elementary and secondary schools and colleges. (See Table 6.1.) An additional 4.6 million were teachers and faculty at these institutions, and 5.2 million were employed as administrative and support staff.

THE NO CHILD LEFT BEHIND ACT

However, in the 1980s concern grew that American youth were falling behind young people in other industrialized countries in educational achievement. In response, the National Education Goals Panel was created in 1989 to further the achievement of several national goals, including increasing the high school graduation rate and student competency in English, mathematics, science, history, and geography. Even though a task force recommended the panel's reauthorization in 1999, the passage of sweeping educational reform legislation, the No Child Left Behind Act (NCLB), shut down the panel in 2002.

The NCLB made huge changes to the laws defining and regulating the federal government's role in kindergarten through 12th-grade education. The law is based on four basic education reform principles. According to the U.S. Department of Education, in "Four Pillars of NCLB" (July 1, 2004, http://www.ed.gov/nclb/overview/intro/4pillars .html), the four principles are:

- Stronger accountability for results

- Increased flexibility and local control

- Expanded options for parents

- An emphasis on teaching methods that have been proven to work.

Accountability

Under the NCLB, schools are required to demonstrate "adequate yearly progress" toward statewide proficiency goals, including closing the achievement gap between advantaged and disadvantaged students. Those schools that do not demonstrate progress face corrective action and restructuring measures. Progress reports are public, so parents can stay informed about their school and school district. Schools that are making or exceeding adequate yearly progress are eligible for awards.

The accountability outlined under the NCLB is measured through standards testing. States are required to establish strong academic standards and test students annually to see how they are meeting them. The requirement for annual testing was phased in over a six-year period. During the 2002–03 school year, students in grades three to five, six to nine, and 10 to 12 were tested in math and reading. Beginning in the 2005–06 school year, testing expanded to all students in grades three to eight. In the 2007–08 school year, science testing in elementary, middle, and high school was implemented. The NCLB linked federal financing of schools to the results of these mandated tests.

The testing provisions of the NCLB are the subject of much debate. Martin R. West of the Brookings Institution explains in "No Child Left Behind: How to Give It a Passing Grade" (December 2005, http://www.brook.edu/comm/policybriefs/pb149.htm) that advocates see testing as a means of raising expectations and helping guarantee that all children are held to the same high standards. They argue that many young people have passed through school without acquiring the basic reading and math skills needed in society and especially in the information-oriented economy. By contrast, Amanda Paulson indicates in "Next Round Begins for No Child Left Behind" (*Christian Science Monitor*, January 8, 2007) that critics of testing say classroom experiences become limited to the need to teach students with the test in mind—and what is tested is only a

TABLE 6.1

Estimated number of participants in elementary and secondary education and in higher education, fall 2007

[In millions]

Participants	All levels (elementary, secondary, and postsecondary degree-granting)	Elementary and secondary schools			Postsecondary degree-granting institutions		
		Total	Public	Private	Total	Public	Private
1	2	3	4	5	6	7	8
Total	83.5	62.9	55.9	6.8	20.7	15.3	5.4
Enrollment	73.7	55.8	49.6	6.2	18.0	13.5	4.5
Teachers and faculty	4.6	3.7	3.2	0.5	0.9	0.6	0.3
Other professional, administrative, and support staff	5.2	3.4	3.1	0.3	1.8	1.2	0.6

Notes: Includes enrollments in local public school systems and in most private schools (religiously affiliated and nonsectarian). Excludes federal schools. Excludes private preprimary enrollment in schools that do not offer kindergarten or above. Degree-granting institutions grant associate's or higher degrees and participate in Title IV federal financial aid programs. Data for teachers and other staff in public and private elementary and secondary schools and colleges and universities are reported in terms of full-time equivalents. Detail may not sum to totals because of rounding.

SOURCE: Thomas D. Snyder, Sally A. Dillow, and Charlene M. Hoffman, "Table 1. Projected Number of Participants in Educational Institutions, by Level and Control of Institution: Fall 2007," in *Digest of Education Statistics, 2007*, U.S. Department of Education, National Center for Education Statistics, March 2008, http://nces.ed.gov/pubs2008/2008022.pdf (accessed November 7, 2008)

sample of what children should know. Furthermore, critics claim that standards exams tend to test for those things most easily measured and not the critical thinking skills students need to develop. In addition, the tests measure only how students perform on the tests at one point in time, not their progress over time.

Proficiency Testing

The testing requirements of the NCLB will be debated for some time to come as states grapple with the best means of implementing them. Standardized tests have, however, been around for some time. A look at the changes in proficiency test scores over time is one way to gauge the performance of the education system.

In *Condition of Education 2008* (June 2008, http://nces.ed.gov/pubs2008/2008031.pdf), the National Center for Education Statistics (NCES) lists test results for a series of years. The percentage of both fourth and eighth graders who tested at or above proficient (indicating solid academic achievement) in reading rose from about 29% of both groups in 1992 to 33% of fourth graders and 31% of eighth graders in 2007. The percentage of fourth graders at or above proficiency in mathematics rose from 18% in 1992 to 39% in 2007; the percentage of eighth graders at or above proficiency rose from 21% in 1992 to 32% in 2007. Despite improvements, especially in mathematics, fewer than one out of three eighth graders had achieved proficiency in each area by 2007.

The public's opinion of school performance is low. Snyder, Dillow, and Hoffman present data on the "grades" that the public gives to schools nationally. Based on a scale of A=4, B=3, C=2, D=1, and F=0, the average grade given by adults to the nation's schools hit a high of 2.18—slightly better than a C—in 1987. By 2007 the average

grade had dropped to 1.90, lower than it had been in 2002, when the NCLB was passed. When adults with children in the school system were asked to rate their local schools as compared to the nation's schools as a whole, they gave their local schools a higher grade; they rated local schools at 2.54 and national schools at 1.96. Nevertheless, the high rating of local schools was still only about a C+.

Another way to evaluate the educational system in the United States is to compare it to the systems of other industrialized countries. In *Comparative Indicators of Education in the United States and Other G-8 Countries: 2006* (August 2007, http://nces.ed.gov/pubs2007/2007006.pdf), David C. Miller et al. compare the U.S. educational system with the systems in eight other highly industrialized nations: Canada, France, Germany, Italy, Japan, the Russian Federation, Scotland, and the United Kingdom. U.S. students compared poorly to the other countries measured in reading and mathematics proficiency. Fifteen-year-old students in the United States had a mean reading score of 495 and a mean mathematics score of 483, below the scores of every other country measured except the Russian Federation and Italy.

Flexibility

The NCLB gave states and local school districts more control over the federal funding they receive for education. Up to half of all non–Title I federal education funding can be allocated by states to whichever programs they wish. Federal programs were also simplified and consolidated under the law, so receiving funding is easier. However, according to Linda Darling-Hammond, in "Evaluating 'No Child Left Behind'" (*The Nation*, May 2, 2007), critics charge that the law is woefully underfunded—funding allocated under the NCLB is less than 10% of most school districts' budgets.

Parental Options

The NCLB stated that parents of students attending failing schools would be provided with the opportunity and transportation to send their child to an alternative public or charter school. If the parent chose to keep his or her child in a failing school, federal Title I funds would be available for supplemental services such as tutoring and summer school, which would be run by either non-sectarian or faith-based organizations. The creation and use of charter schools were expanded under the NCLB.

Proven Educational Methods

The NCLB attached federal funding to programs that had already been shown to help children learn. The Department of Education reports in "The Budget for Fiscal Year 2009" (2008, http://www.gpoaccess.gov/usbudget/fy09/pdf/budget/education.pdf) that emphasis was placed on the Reading First initiative, nearly tripling funding for reading programs from $393 million in fiscal year 2008 to a proposed $1 billion in fiscal year 2009. Included in this funding was an Early Reading First program, established to support literacy skills among preschool-age children to try to meet President George W. Bush's (1946–) goal of every child being able to read by the third grade. The fiscal year 2009 budget included a proposed $2.8 billion to be used for teacher quality programs, including funding to hire new teachers, increase teacher salaries, and improve teacher training and development.

The Voucher Controversy

Many people believe that problems such as large class sizes, poor teacher training, and lack of computers and supplies in many public schools are unsolvable within the current public school system. One solution proposed in the early 1990s was the school voucher system: The government would provide a certain amount of money each year to parents in the form of a voucher to enroll their children at the school of their choice, either public or private. School vouchers became a highly polarized issue, with strong opinions both for and against the idea.

The National Education Association (NEA), a union of teachers and one of the larger unions in the country, immediately objected to school vouchers, arguing that voucher programs would divert money from the public education system and make the current problems worse. The union also argued that giving money to parents who choose to send their child to a religious or parochial school is unconstitutional. Little evidence exists to support the idea that voucher programs will lead to better educational outcomes. For example, in *An Evaluation of the Effect of D.C.'s Voucher Program on Public School Achievement and Racial Integration after One Year* (January 2006, http://www.manhattan-institute.org/pdf/ewp_10.pdf), Jay P. Greene and Marcus A. Winters indicate that the Washington, D.C., voucher program had no effect on student performance in public schools. Furthermore, Kim K. Metcalf of the Center for Evaluation and Education Policy finds in *Evaluation of the Cleveland Scholarship and Tutoring Program: Exploring Families' Educational Choices* (December 2003, http://ceep.indiana.edu/projects/PDF/200312d_clev_6_phon_rep.pdf) no difference in the academic achievement of voucher-eligible students who used them to attend private school and those who chose to remain in public school.

Supporters of vouchers claim that parents should be able to choose the best educational environment for their children. They also argue that vouchers would give all people, not just the wealthy or middle class, the opportunity for a better education for their children in private schools. Most important, supporters believe that making the educational system a free-market enterprise, in which parents could choose which school their children would attend, would force the public educational system to provide a higher standard of education to compete.

During the legislative process of getting the NCLB through Congress, President Bush agreed to drop the voucher provisions from the legislation, recognizing that debate on the vouchers issue could prevent the bill from being passed. On January 8, 2002, the NCLB became law without specific provisions for a nationwide voucher program. However, in President Bush's final State of the Union address in January 2008, he proposed a new voucher program to be included in a reauthorization of the NCLB. The act was not reauthorized in 2008.

Frustrated at the national level, supporters of vouchers turned to state and local governments. Programs launched in Wisconsin, Florida, and Ohio provided students in some overcrowded or poorly performing schools with vouchers that could be used for private tuition. All these programs were met with court challenges. On June 27, 2002, in *Zelman v. Simmons-Harris* (536 U.S. 639), the U.S. Supreme Court upheld the use of public money for religious school tuition in Cleveland, Ohio, calling the city's voucher plan "a program of true private choice."

Public School Choice—No Child Left Behind and Charter Schools

In lieu of a voucher program, the NCLB offered a public school choice program. Parents of students enrolled in "failing" public schools were allowed to move their children to a better-performing public or charter school. Local school districts were required to provide this choice and provide students with transportation to the alternative school.

Public charter schools are funded by government money and run by a group under an agreement, or charter, with the state that exempts it from many state or local regulations that govern most public schools. In return for these exemptions and funding, the school must meet certain standards. In *A Commitment to Quality: National Charter School Policy Forum Report* (October 2008, http://www.ed.gov/admins/

FIGURE 6.1

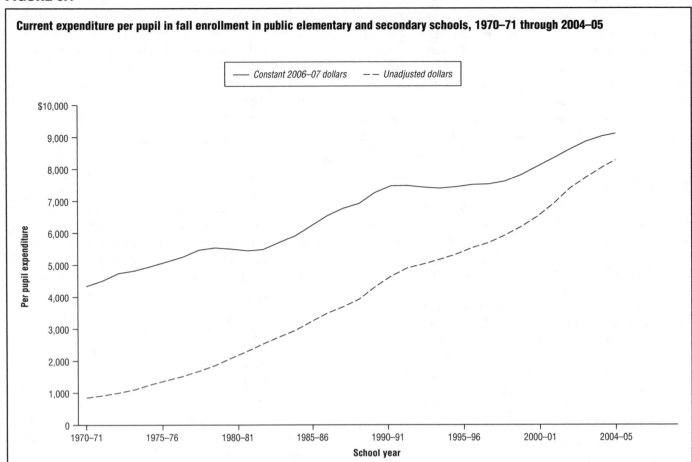

Current expenditure per pupil in fall enrollment in public elementary and secondary schools, 1970–71 through 2004–05

—— Constant 2006–07 dollars   – – Unadjusted dollars

SOURCE: Thomas D. Snyder, Sally A. Dillow, and Charlene M. Hoffman, "Figure 10. Current Expenditure per Pupil in Fall Enrollment in Public Elementary and Secondary Schools: 1970–71 through 2004–05," in *Digest of Education Statistics, 2007*, U.S. Department of Education, National Center for Education Statistics, March 2008, http://nces.ed.gov/pubs2008/2008022.pdf (accessed November 7, 2008).

comm/choice/csforum/report.pdf), the Department of Education notes that by 2008, 40 states and the District of Columbia had 4,300 charter schools, in which more than 1.2 million students were enrolled. Furthermore, the department reports in "The Budget for Fiscal Year 2009" that the fiscal year 2009 budget provided $236 million to help fund new and ongoing charter schools.

Future of the NCLB

During the 2008 U.S. presidential campaign, future president Barack Obama (1961–) promised to reform the NCLB if elected. According to Obama's Web site, www.barackobama.com, he and Vice President Joe Biden "believe teachers should not be forced to spend the academic year preparing students to fill in bubbles on standardized tests." They vowed to "improve the assessments used to track student progress to measure readiness for college."

THE COST OF PUBLIC EDUCATION

The average annual expenditure per student in the public school system in constant 2006–07 dollars more than doubled between 1970 and 2003, from $4,410 per pupil in 1969–70 to $9,910 per pupil during the 2004–05 school year. (See Figure 6.1.) Each year, when the federal budget is determined in Washington, D.C., the battle over the education budget is fierce. Public school officials and teachers stress the importance of investing in the public education system, arguing that more money will provide more teachers, educational materials, and—eventually—a better education to students. They point to school buildings in need of repair and classes that meet in hallways and other cramped areas because of a lack of space. Opponents of increasing public school funding say that more money does not create a better education—better teachers do. To support their argument, they point to the increase in spending per pupil while some measurements of academic achievement remain low.

PREPRIMARY SCHOOL
Preprimary Growth

Participating in early childhood programs such as nursery school, Head Start, prekindergarten, and kindergarten helps prepare children for the academic challenges of first grade. In contrast to the declining elementary and secondary

TABLE 6.2

Enrollment of 3- to 5-year-old children in preprimary programs, by level and control of program and by attendance, selected years 1965–2006

[In thousands]

Year and age	Total population, 3 to 5 years old	Total	Percent enrolled	Enrollment by level and control				Enrollment by attendance		
				Nursery school		Kindergarten				Percent full-day
				Public	Private	Public	Private	Full-day	Part-day	
1	2	3	4	5	6	7	8	9	10	11
Total, 3 to 5 years old										
1965	12,549	3,407	27.1	127	393	2,291	596	—	—	—
1970	10,949	4,104	37.5	332	762	2,498	511	698	3,405	17.0
1975	10,185	4,955	48.7	570	1,174	2,682	528	1,295	3,659	26.1
1980	9,284	4,878	52.5	628	1,353	2,438	459	1,551	3,327	31.8
1985	10,733	5,865	54.6	846	1,631	2,847	541	2,144	3,722	36.6
1990	11,207	6,659	59.4	1,199	2,180	2,772	509	2,577	4,082	38.7
1995*	12,518	7,739	61.8	1,950	2,381	2,800	608	3,689	4,051	47.7
2000*	11,858	7,592	64.0	2,146	2,180	2,701	565	4,008	3,584	52.8
2002*	11,524	7,697	66.8	2,376	2,179	2,621	521	4,191	3,507	54.4
2003*	12,204	7,921	64.9	2,512	2,347	2,539	523	4,429	3,492	55.9
2004*	12,362	7,969	64.5	2,428	2,243	2,812	484	4,507	3,461	56.6
2005*	12,134	7,801	64.3	2,409	2,120	2,804	468	4,548	3,253	58.3
2006*	12,186	8,010	65.7	2,481	2,156	2,960	413	4,723	3,286	59.0

—Not available.

*Data collected using new procedures. May not be comparable with figures prior to 1994.

Note: Data are based on sample surveys of the civilian noninstitutional population. Although cells with fewer than 75,000 children are subject to wide sampling variation, they are included in the table to permit various types of aggregations. Detail may not sum to totals because of rounding.

SOURCE: Adapted from Thomas D. Snyder, Sally A. Dillow, and Charlene M. Hoffman, "Table 41. Enrollment of 3-, 4-, and 5-Year-Old Children in Preprimary Programs, by Level of Program, Control of Program, and Attendance Status: Selected Years, 1965 through 2006," in *Digest of Education Statistics, 2007*, U.S. Department of Education, National Center for Education Statistics, March 2008, http://nces.ed.gov/pubs2008/2008022.pdf (accessed November 7, 2008)

school enrollment between 1970 and 1980, preprimary enrollment showed substantial growth, increasing from 4.1 million in 1970 to 4.9 million in 1980. (See Table 6.2 and Figure 6.2.) Enrollment had grown to eight million by 2006.

Not only did the numbers of children enrolled in early childhood programs increase but also the percentage of all three- to five-year-olds enrolled increased substantially between 1965 and 2006. In 1965, 27.1% of three- to five-year-olds were enrolled in nursery school or kindergarten; by 2006, 65.7% were enrolled. (See Table 6.2.)

Even though programs such as Head Start and other locally funded preschool programs are available to children in low-income families, preprimary school attendance is still generally linked to parental income and educational achievement levels. According to the NCES, in *Condition of Education 2008*, 51% of four-year-olds from households with an income below the poverty level in 2005–06 and 59.6% of four-year-olds from households with an income at or above the poverty level were enrolled in preprimary programs. (See Table 6.3.) Over a quarter (26.3%) of four-year-olds from households with incomes below the poverty threshold were in Head Start programs, compared to just 8.2% of children from households with higher incomes.

Preschool enrollment rates were even more strongly correlated with their parents' educational level. In 2005–06 the enrollment rate of children in center-based care whose parents had not earned a high school diploma was only 43.4%. (See Table 6.3.) The enrollment rate of children whose parents had a high school diploma or equivalent was 51.7%, for those whose parents had some college it was 55.5%, for those whose parents had a bachelor's degree it was 65.7%, and for those whose parents had any graduate or professional school, the enrollment rate was 70.8%. These numbers likely reflect three things: parents with higher educational levels are more likely to continue working after becoming parents, they are better able to pay for these programs, and they value the educational benefits of preprimary programs for their children.

HEAD START. The Head Start program, which was established as part of the Economic Opportunity Act of 1964, is one of the most durable and successful federal programs for low-income and at-risk children. Directed by the Administration for Children and Families (ACF), Head Start is designed to help improve the social competence, learning skills, health, and nutrition of low-income children so they can begin school on a more level footing with children from higher-income families. Regulations require that 90% of children enrolled in Head Start be from low-income households.

The ACF notes in "Head Start Program Fact Sheet Fiscal Year 2008" (2008, http://eclkc.ohs.acf.hhs.gov/hslc/About%20Head%20Start/dHeadStartProgr.htm) that in fiscal year 2007, 908,412 children were served by Head Start programs. Of these children, 39.7% were non-Hispanic

FIGURE 6.2

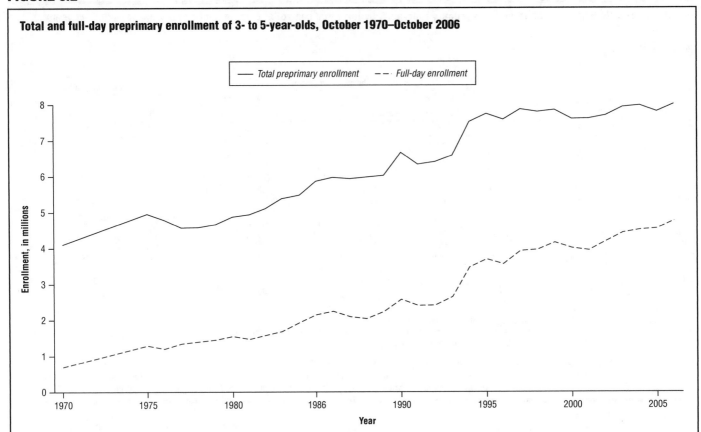

Total and full-day preprimary enrollment of 3- to 5-year-olds, October 1970–October 2006

SOURCE: Thomas D. Snyder, Sally A. Dillow, and Charlene M. Hoffman, "Figure 7. Total and Full-Day Preprimary Enrollment of 3- to 5-year-olds: October 1970 through October 2006," in *Digest of Education Statistics, 2007*, U.S. Department of Education, National Center for Education Statistics, March 2008, http://nces.ed.gov/pubs2008/2008022.pdf (accessed November 7, 2008)

white, 34.7% were Hispanic, 30.1% were African-American, 4% were Native American or Alaskan Native, and 1.7% were Asian-American or Pacific Islander. Most participating children were three and four years old (36% and 51%, respectively). A significant portion (12.2%) of enrolled children had disabilities, including developmental disabilities, health impairments, visual handicaps, hearing impairments, emotional disturbances, speech and language impairments, orthopedic handicaps, and learning disabilities.

According to the ACF, the average cost per child for Head Start in 2007 was $7,326. Between its inception in 1965 and 2007, Head Start provided services to more than 25 million children and their families. The budget for Head Start in fiscal year 2008 was $6.9 billion. The Children's Defense Fund notes in "Head Start Basics" (March 8, 2005, http://www.childrensdefense.org/site/DocServer/headstartbasics2005.pdf?docID=616) that despite these expenditures, Head Start served only about 54% of eligible children because the program continues to be underfunded.

Head Start faced more drastic budget cuts beginning in the middle of the first decade of the 2000s, with its budget declining by more than 10% between 2005 and 2008. As a result of cuts in 2006, the National Head Start Association

explains in *Special Report: Quality of Head Start Programs Imperiled by Steady Erosion of Funding* (February 7, 2007, http://www.saveheadstart.org/backpages/NHSA_January _2007_Budget_Survey_Report.pdf) that 56% of programs reported having cut their services to children—including reducing hours; cutting instructional time, classroom materials, activities, and resources to children; reducing extra services such as mental health, medical and dental, and English as a second language; and decreasing services for children with disabilities. Almost half (47%) had to cut extra services to families, and another 46% of programs had to cut transportation services for children. Over two-thirds (69%) of Head Start programs were forced to cut staff positions and hours and eliminated salary increases and benefits, leading to higher turnover rates.

ELEMENTARY AND SECONDARY SCHOOL

Compulsory Attendance

All U.S. states require students to attend school through at least age 16, and Snyder, Dillow, and Hoffman note that 94.9% of all 14- to 17-year-olds were enrolled in school in 2006. Most industrialized Western nations require children to attend school for about 10 years.

TABLE 6.3

Percentage distribution of the early education and child care arrangements of the 2001 birth cohort at about 4 years old, by type of arrangement and selected child and family characteristics, 2005–06

| | | | Percentage distribution by primary type of care arrangement[b] | | | | | | |
| | | | Home-based care | | Center-based care[c] | | | | |
Child or family characteristic	Percentage distribution of population[a]	No regular nonparental arrangement	Relative care	Nonrelative care	Total	Head Start	Other than Head Start	Multiple arrangements[d]
Total	**100.0**	**20.0**	**13.1**	**7.6**	**57.5**	**12.7**	**44.8**	**1.9**
Sex of child								
Male	51.2	19.3	13.1	7.5	58.0	12.9	45.1	2.1
Female	48.8	20.7	13.1	7.6	56.9	12.4	44.5	1.7
Race/ethnicity of child								
White	53.8	17.9	11.0	9.2	60.1	6.8	53.3	1.9
Black	13.8	16.0	13.9	4.3	62.4	25.4	37.1	3.3
Hispanic	25.1	27.2	15.9	6.2	49.4	18.6	30.9	1.2
Asian	2.6	17.5	16.0	3.4	60.7	5.5	55.3	2.3!
Pacific Islander	0.2	22.3!	45.0!	‡	19.9!	5.0!	14.9!	‡
American Indian/Alaska Native	0.5	20.0	14.0	5.3	59.6	31.1	28.5	1.1!
More than one race	4.0	17.8	17.5	8.9	53.9	12.2	41.7	1.8!
Age of child								
Less than 48 months	16.4	27.3	13.9	8.7	48.0	10.6	37.4	2.2
48.0 to 52.9 months	38.1	19.9	13.0	8.3	56.8	12.0	44.8	2.0
53.0 to 57.9 months	36.5	16.5	13.1	6.7	62.2	14.4	47.8	1.5
58.0 or more months	9.0	20.9	12.0	6.3	58.1	12.0	46.1	2.7
Mother's employment status								
Full-time (35 hours or more)	39.4	8.5	18.5	13.4	57.4	11.4	46.1	2.1
Part-time (less than 35 hours)	19.7	13.4	15.9	8.5	59.3	10.1	49.2	2.9
Looking for work	5.8	28.5	12.6	2.1!	54.7	24.3	30.4	2.0!
Not in labor force	34.3	35.6	4.6	1.5	57.3	13.7	43.7	1.0!
No mother in household	0.8	9.6!	36.0	9.5!	41.1	14.4!	26.7	3.8!
Parents' highest level of education								
Less than high school	10.4	34.0	16.5	4.0	43.4	22.2	21.2	2.1!
High school completion	25.0	22.6	17.1	6.7	51.7	21.4	30.3	2.0
Some college/vocational	31.6	20.6	14.9	7.3	55.5	13.0	42.5	1.7
Bachelor's degree	16.8	16.0	8.4	8.1	65.7	3.3	62.4	1.8
Any graduate/professional school	16.2	9.7	6.2	11.2	70.8	2.0	68.8	2.0
Poverty status[e]								
Below poverty threshold	24.8	27.6	15.0	4.4	51.0	26.3	24.7	2.0
At or above poverty threshold	75.2	17.4	12.5	8.6	59.6	8.2	51.4	1.9
Socioeconomic status[f]								
Lowest 20 percent	20.0	30.5	15.0	5.0	47.1	24.7	22.4	2.3
Middle 60 percent	60.0	19.6	15.0	7.4	56.2	12.5	43.7	1.8
Highest 20 percent	20.0	10.3	5.5	10.7	71.6	1.0	70.6	1.9

!Interpret data with caution (estimates are unstable).
‡ Reporting standards not met (too few cases).
[a]Distribution of weighted Early Childhood Longitudinal Study, Birth Cohort (ECLS-B) survey population between 44 and 65 months of age with data on primary care arrangements.
[b]Primary type of care arrangement is the type of nonparental care in which the child spent the most hours.
[c]Care provided in places such as early learning centers, nursery schools, and preschools, including Head Start.
[d]Children who spent an equal amount of time in each of two or more arrangements.
[e]Poverty status based on Census Bureau guidelines from 2002, which identify a dollar amount determined to meet a household's needs, given its size and composition. In 2002, a family was considered to live below the poverty threshold if its income was less than or equal to $18,392.
[f]Socioeconomic status (SES) was measured by a composite score on parental education and occupations and on family income.
Notes: Estimates weighted by W3R0. Estimates for children at about 4 years old pertain to children assessed between 44 and 65 months.
Race categories exclude persons of Hispanic ethnicity. Detail may not sum to totals because of rounding and suppression of cells that do not meet standards.

SOURCE: Michael Planty et al.,"Table 2–1. Percentage Distribution of the Early Education and Child Care Arrangements of the 2001 Birth Cohort at about 4 Years Old, by Type of Arrangement and Selected Child and Family Characteristics: School Year 2005–06," in *The Condition of Education 2008*, U.S. Department of Education, National Center for Education Statistics, June 2008, http://nces.ed.gov/pubs2008/2008031_App1.pdf (accessed November 7, 2008)

Enrollment

Preprimary, elementary, and secondary school enrollments reflect the number of births over a specified period. Because of the baby boom following World War II (1939–1945), school enrollment grew rapidly during the 1950s and 1960s, when those children reached school age. Elementary enrollment reached a then-record high in 1969, as did high school enrollment in 1971.

In the late 1960s the birthrate began to decline, resulting in a steadily falling school enrollment. An echo effect occurred in the late 1970s and early 1980s, when those born during the baby boom began their own families. This echo effect triggered an increase in school enrollment starting in the mid-1980s. In 1985 public elementary and secondary school enrollment increased for the first time since 1971 and continued to increase, reaching 55.2 million in 2005.

FIGURE 6.3

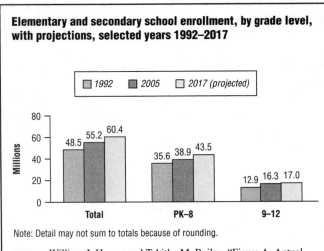

Elementary and secondary school enrollment, by grade level, with projections, selected years 1992–2017

Note: Detail may not sum to totals because of rounding.

SOURCE: William J. Hussar and Tabitha M. Bailey, "Figure A. Actual and Projected Numbers for Elementary and Secondary School Enrollment, Total and by Grade Level: Selected Years, 1992–2017," in *Projections of Education Statistics to 2017*, U.S. Department of Education, National Center for Education Statistics, September 2008, http://nces.ed.gov/pubs2008/2008078.pdf (accessed November 7, 2008)

(See Figure 6.3.) It is projected to reach 60.4 million by 2017. In 2005, 38.9 million students were enrolled in pre-kindergarten through eighth grade and 16.3 million were enrolled in high school.

Private Schools

Enrollment in public schools far surpasses enrollment in private schools. Snyder, Dillow, and Hoffman indicate that in the fall of 2007 only 11% of all primary and secondary school students were enrolled in private schools. Private school enrollment has risen more slowly than school enrollment overall, and as a result the proportion of students enrolled in private schools declined slightly between 1980 and 2007. In 2007, 6.2 million students were enrolled in private schools—4.8 million were in prekindergarten through eighth grade and 1.4 million were in ninth through 12th grades.

CATHOLIC SCHOOLS. According to Stephen P. Broughman, Nancy L. Swaim, and Patrick W. Keaton, in *Characteristics of Private Schools in the United States: Results from the 2005–2006 Private School Universe Survey* (March 2008, http://nces.ed.gov/pubs2008/2008315.pdf), 26.3% of all private schools were Catholic, and 44.4% of private school students attended Catholic schools. Economic and social changes have caused a decline in Catholic school enrollment and in the number of Catholic schools. In *United States Catholic Elementary and Secondary Schools, 2007–2008: The Annual Statistical Report on Schools, Enrollment, and Staffing* (2008, http://www.ncea.org/news/Annual DataReport.asp#full), Dale McDonald and Margaret M. Schultz of the National Catholic Educational Association

find that in 1997–98 there were 8,223 Catholic schools in the United States; by 2007–08 there were only 7,378.

OTHER RELIGIOUS AND NONRELIGIOUS PRIVATE SCHOOLS. The other types of private schools are non-Catholic religious schools and nonreligious (nonsectarian) schools. According to Broughman, Swaim, and Keaton, non-Catholic religious schools made up 49.8% of all private schools in 2005–06 and enrolled 37.3% of all private school students. Nonsectarian schools enrolled only 18.3% of private school students in 23.9% of private schools.

Dropping Out

DROPOUT RATES. Status dropouts are 16- to 24-year-olds who have not finished high school and are not enrolled in school. Snyder, Dillow, and Hoffman report that status dropout rates decreased from 1970, when 15% of young people were status dropouts, through 2006, when 9.3% of young people were status dropouts. (See Table 6.4.) In 2006 the Hispanic status dropout rate was considerably higher, at 22.1%, than that of non-Hispanic African-Americans (10.7%) or non-Hispanic whites (5.8%). (See Table 6.5.)

Dropout rates also fluctuate greatly according to family income. In 2006, 16.5% of people aged 16 to 24 from families who had the lowest incomes (bottom 25%) had dropped out of school, which was more than four times the dropout rate of 16- to 24-year-olds whose families had the highest incomes (3.8%). (See Table 6.4.)

Status dropout rates are consistently lower for women than for men regardless of race or ethnicity. This has been the case since 1977. (See Table 6.5.) In 2006 the status dropout rate for young women aged 16 to 24 was 8.3%. Males of the same age in 2006 had a status dropout rate of 10.3%.

RETURNING TO SCHOOL OR GETTING AN ALTERNATIVE DIPLOMA. The decision to drop out of high school does not necessarily mean the end of a young person's education. Many former students return to school to get their diploma or take the test necessary to obtain an alternative credential or degree, such as a general equivalency diploma (GED). Snyder, Dillow, and Hoffman note that in 2005, 424,000 GEDs were issued. Many young people who earn their GED then go on to get a college education.

Special Populations

STUDENTS WITH DISABILITIES. In 1976 Congress passed the Education of the Handicapped Act, which required schools to develop programs for disabled children. Formerly, parents of many disabled students had few options other than institutionalization or nursing care. The Education of the Handicapped Act required that disabled children be put in the "least restrictive environment," which led to increased efforts to educate them in regular classrooms (known as mainstreaming).

TABLE 6.4

Percent of high school dropouts among persons 16–24 years old (status dropout rate), by income level, and percentage distribution of status dropouts, by labor force status and educational attainment, 1970–2006

Year	Status dropout rate	Status dropout rate, by family income quartile				Percentage distribution of status dropouts, by labor force status				Percentage distribution of status dropouts, by years of school completed				
		Lowest quartile	Middle low quartile	Middle high quartile	Highest quartile	Total	Employed[a]	Unemployed	Not in labor force	Total	Less than 9 years	9 years	10 years	11 or 12 years
1970	15.0	28.0	21.2	11.7	5.2	100.0	49.8	10.3	39.9	100.0	28.5	20.6	26.8	24.0
1971	14.7	28.8	20.7	10.9	5.1	100.0	49.5	10.9	39.6	100.0	27.9	21.7	27.8	22.7
1972	14.6	27.6	20.8	10.2	5.4	100.0	51.2	10.2	38.6	100.0	27.5	20.8	29.0	22.7
1973	14.1	28.0	19.6	9.9	4.9	100.0	53.2	9.2	37.5	100.0	26.5	20.9	27.4	25.3
1974	14.3	—	—	—	—	100.0	51.8	12.3	35.9	100.0	25.4	20.1	28.7	25.8
1975	13.9	28.8	18.0	10.2	5.0	100.0	46.0	15.6	38.4	100.0	23.5	21.1	27.5	27.9
1976	14.1	28.1	19.2	10.1	4.9	100.0	48.8	16.0	35.2	100.0	24.3	20.1	27.8	27.8
1977	14.1	28.5	19.0	10.4	4.5	100.0	52.9	13.6	33.6	100.0	24.3	21.7	27.3	26.6
1978	14.2	28.2	18.9	10.5	5.5	100.0	54.3	12.4	33.3	100.0	22.9	20.2	28.2	28.8
1979	14.6	28.1	18.5	11.5	5.6	100.0	54.0	12.7	33.3	100.0	22.6	21.0	28.6	27.8
1980	14.1	27.0	18.1	10.7	5.7	100.0	50.4	17.0	32.6	100.0	23.6	19.7	29.8	27.0
1981	13.9	26.4	17.8	11.1	5.2	100.0	49.8	18.3	31.9	100.0	24.3	18.6	30.2	26.9
1982	13.9	27.2	18.3	10.2	4.4	100.0	45.2	21.1	33.7	100.0	22.9	20.8	28.8	27.6
1983	13.7	26.5	17.8	10.5	4.1	100.0	48.4	18.2	33.4	100.0	23.0	19.3	28.8	28.8
1984	13.1	25.9	16.5	9.9	3.8	100.0	49.7	17.3	32.9	100.0	23.6	21.4	27.5	27.5
1985	12.6	27.1	14.7	8.3	4.0	100.0	50.1	17.5	32.4	100.0	23.9	21.0	27.9	27.2
1986	12.2	25.4	14.8	8.0	3.4	100.0	51.1	16.4	32.5	100.0	25.4	21.5	25.7	27.4
1987	12.6	25.5	16.6	8.0	3.6	100.0	52.4	13.6	34.0	100.0	25.9	20.7	26.0	27.5
1988	12.9	27.2	15.4	8.2	3.4	100.0	52.9	‡	‡	100.0	28.9	19.3	25.1	26.8
1989	12.6	25.0	16.2	8.7	3.3	100.0	53.2	13.8	33.0	100.0	29.4	20.8	24.9	25.0
1990	12.1	24.3	15.1	8.7	2.9	100.0	52.5	13.3	34.2	100.0	28.6	20.9	24.4	26.1
1991	12.5	25.9	15.5	7.7	3.0	100.0	47.5	15.8	36.7	100.0	28.6	20.5	26.1	24.9
1992[b]	11.0	23.4	12.9	7.3	2.4	100.0	47.6	15.0	37.4	100.0	21.6	17.5	24.4	36.5
1993[b]	11.0	22.9	12.7	6.6	2.9	100.0	48.7	12.8	38.5	100.0	20.5	16.6	24.1	38.8
1994[b]	11.4	20.7	13.7	8.7	4.9	100.0	49.5	13.0	37.5	100.0	23.9	16.2	20.3	39.6
1995[b]	12.0	23.2	13.8	8.3	3.6	100.0	48.9	14.2	37.0	100.0	22.2	17.0	22.5	38.3
1996[b]	11.1	22.0	13.6	7.0	3.2	100.0	47.3	15.0	37.7	100.0	20.3	17.7	22.6	39.4
1997[b]	11.0	21.8	13.5	6.2	3.4	100.0	53.3	13.2	33.5	100.0	19.9	15.7	22.3	42.1
1998[b]	11.8	22.3	14.9	7.7	3.5	100.0	55.1	10.3	34.6	100.0	21.0	14.9	21.4	42.6
1999[b]	11.2	21.0	14.3	7.4	3.9	100.0	55.6	10.0	34.4	100.0	22.2	16.3	22.5	39.0
2000[b]	10.9	20.7	12.8	8.3	3.5	100.0	56.9	12.3	30.8	100.0	21.5	15.3	23.1	40.0
2001[b]	10.7	19.3	13.4	9.0	3.2	100.0	58.3	14.8	26.9	100.0	18.4	16.8	23.8	40.9
2002[b]	10.5	18.8	12.3	8.4	3.8	100.0	57.4	13.3	29.2	100.0	22.8	17.1	21.3	38.9
2003[b]	9.9	19.5	10.8	7.3	3.4	100.0	53.5	13.7	32.9	100.0	21.2	18.2	20.7	40.0
2004[b]	10.3	18.0	12.7	8.2	3.7	100.0	53.0	14.3	32.7	100.0	21.4	15.9	22.5	40.3
2005[b]	9.4	17.9	11.5	7.1	2.7	100.0	56.9	11.9	31.2	100.0	18.9	16.8	21.4	42.9
2006[b]	9.3	16.5	12.1	6.3	3.8	100.0	56.4	11.7	32.0	100.0	22.1	13.4	20.7	43.9

—Not available.

‡Reporting standards not met.

[a]Includes persons employed, but not currently working.

[b]Because of changes in data collection procedures, data may not be comparable with figures for years prior to 1992.

Note: "Status" dropouts are 16- to 24-year-olds who are not enrolled in school and who have not completed a high school program, regardless of when they left school. People who have received GED credentials are counted as high school completers. Data are based on sample surveys of the civilian noninstitutionalized population, which excludes persons in prisons, persons in the military, and other persons not living in households. Some data have been revised from previously published figures. Detail may not sum to totals because of rounding.

SOURCE: Thomas D. Snyder, Sally A. Dillow, and Charlene M. Hoffman, "Table 106. Percentage of High School Dropouts among Persons 16 to 24 Years Old (Status Dropout Rate), by Income Level, and Percentage Distribution of Status Dropouts, by Labor Force Status and Educational Attainment: 1970 through 2006," in *Digest of Education Statistics, 2007*, U.S. Department of Education, National Center for Education Statistics, March 2008, http://nces.ed.gov/pubs 2008/2008022.pdf (accessed November 7, 2008).

The law defined *handicapped children* as those who were mentally retarded, hard of hearing or deaf, orthopedically impaired, speech- and language-impaired, visually impaired, seriously emotionally disturbed, or otherwise health-impaired. It also included children with specific learning disabilities who require special education and related services.

In 1990 the Individuals with Disabilities Education Act was passed. This was a reauthorization and expansion of the earlier Education of the Handicapped Act. It added autism and traumatic brain injury to the list of disabilities covered by the law, and amendments added in 1992 and 1997 increased coverage for infants and toddlers and for children with attention deficit disorder and attention deficit hyperactivity disorder. The law required public school systems to develop an Individualized Education Program for each disabled child, reflecting the needs of individual students. In December 2004 the Individuals with Disabilities Education Improvement Act was signed into law by President Bush, reauthorizing the Individuals with Disabilities Education Act and bringing it in line with the provisions of the NCLB.

As a result of legislation that enforces their rights, increased numbers of disabled children have been served

TABLE 6.5

Percentage of high school dropouts among persons 16–24 years old (status dropout rate), by sex, race and ethnicity, selected years 1960–2006

Year	Total status dropout rate				Male status dropout rate				Female status dropout rate			
	All races[a]	White	Black	Hispanic	All races[a]	White	Black	Hispanic	All races[a]	White	Black	Hispanic
1	2	3	4	5	6	7	8	9	10	11	12	13
1960[b]	27.2 (—)	(†)	—	—	27.8 (—)	(†)	—	(†)	26.7 (—)	(†)	—	(†)
1967[c]	17.0 (—)	15.4 (—)	28.6 (—)	—	16.5 (—)	14.7 (—)	30.6 (—)	(†)	17.3 (—)	16.1 (—)	26.9 (—)	(†)
1968[c]	16.2 (—)	14.7 (—)	27.4 (—)	—	15.8 (—)	14.4 (—)	27.1 (—)	(†)	16.5 (—)	15.0 (—)	27.6 (—)	(†)
1969[c]	15.2 (—)	13.6 (—)	26.7 (—)	—	14.3 (—)	12.6 (—)	26.9 (—)	(†)	16.0 (—)	14.6 (—)	26.7 (—)	(†)
1970[c]	15.0 (0.29)	13.2 (0.30)	27.9 (1.22)	—	14.2 (0.42)	12.2 (0.42)	29.4 (1.82)	(†)	15.7 (0.41)	14.1 (0.42)	26.6 (1.65)	(†)
1971[c]	14.7 (0.28)	13.4 (0.29)	24.0 (1.14)	—	14.2 (0.41)	12.6 (0.41)	25.5 (1.70)	(†)	15.2 (0.40)	14.2 (0.42)	22.6 (1.54)	(†)
1972	14.6 (0.28)	12.3 (0.29)	21.3 (1.07)	34.3 (2.22)	14.1 (0.40)	11.6 (0.40)	22.3 (1.59)	33.7 (3.23)	15.1 (0.39)	12.8 (0.41)	20.5 (1.44)	34.8 (3.05)
1973	14.1 (0.27)	11.6 (0.28)	22.2 (1.06)	33.5 (2.24)	13.7 (0.38)	11.5 (0.39)	21.5 (1.53)	30.4 (3.16)	14.5 (0.38)	11.8 (0.39)	22.8 (1.47)	36.4 (3.16)
1974	14.3 (0.27)	11.9 (0.28)	21.2 (1.05)	33.0 (2.08)	14.2 (0.39)	12.0 (0.40)	20.1 (1.51)	33.8 (2.99)	14.3 (0.38)	11.8 (0.39)	22.1 (1.45)	32.2 (2.90)
1975	13.9 (0.27)	11.4 (0.27)	22.9 (1.06)	29.2 (2.02)	13.3 (0.37)	11.0 (0.38)	23.0 (1.56)	26.7 (2.84)	14.5 (0.38)	11.8 (0.39)	22.9 (1.44)	31.6 (2.86)
1976	14.1 (0.27)	12.0 (0.28)	20.5 (1.00)	31.4 (2.01)	14.1 (0.38)	12.1 (0.39)	21.2 (1.49)	30.3 (2.94)	14.2 (0.37)	11.8 (0.39)	19.9 (1.35)	32.3 (2.76)
1977	14.1 (0.27)	11.9 (0.28)	19.8 (0.99)	33.0 (2.02)	14.5 (0.38)	12.6 (0.40)	19.5 (1.45)	31.6 (2.89)	13.8 (0.37)	11.2 (0.38)	20.0 (1.36)	34.3 (2.83)
1978	14.2 (0.27)	11.9 (0.28)	20.2 (1.00)	33.3 (2.00)	14.6 (0.38)	12.2 (0.40)	22.5 (1.52)	33.6 (2.88)	13.9 (0.37)	11.6 (0.39)	18.3 (1.31)	33.1 (2.78)
1979	14.6 (0.27)	12.0 (0.28)	21.1 (1.01)	33.8 (1.98)	15.0 (0.39)	12.6 (0.40)	22.4 (1.52)	33.0 (2.83)	14.2 (0.37)	11.5 (0.38)	20.0 (1.35)	34.5 (2.77)
1980	14.1 (0.26)	11.4 (0.27)	19.1 (0.97)	35.2 (1.89)	15.1 (0.39)	12.3 (0.40)	20.8 (1.47)	37.2 (2.72)	13.1 (0.36)	10.5 (0.37)	17.7 (1.28)	33.2 (2.61)
1981	13.9 (0.26)	11.3 (0.27)	18.4 (0.93)	33.2 (1.80)	15.1 (0.38)	12.5 (0.40)	19.9 (1.40)	36.0 (2.61)	12.8 (0.35)	10.2 (0.36)	17.1 (1.24)	30.4 (2.48)
1982	13.9 (0.27)	11.4 (0.29)	18.4 (0.97)	31.7 (1.93)	14.5 (0.40)	12.0 (0.42)	21.2 (1.50)	30.5 (2.73)	13.3 (0.38)	10.8 (0.40)	15.9 (1.26)	32.8 (2.71)
1983	13.7 (0.27)	11.1 (0.29)	18.0 (0.97)	31.6 (1.93)	14.9 (0.41)	12.2 (0.43)	19.9 (1.46)	34.3 (2.84)	12.5 (0.37)	10.1 (0.39)	16.2 (1.28)	29.1 (2.61)
1984	13.1 (0.27)	11.0 (0.29)	15.5 (0.91)	29.8 (1.91)	14.0 (0.40)	11.9 (0.43)	16.8 (1.37)	30.6 (2.78)	12.3 (0.37)	10.1 (0.39)	14.3 (1.22)	29.0 (2.63)
1985	12.6 (0.27)	10.4 (0.29)	15.2 (0.92)	27.6 (1.93)	13.4 (0.40)	11.1 (0.42)	16.1 (1.37)	29.9 (2.76)	11.8 (0.37)	9.8 (0.39)	14.3 (1.23)	25.2 (2.68)
1986	12.2 (0.27)	9.7 (0.28)	14.2 (0.90)	30.1 (1.88)	13.1 (0.40)	10.3 (0.42)	15.0 (1.33)	32.8 (2.66)	11.4 (0.37)	9.1 (0.39)	13.5 (1.21)	27.2 (2.63)
1987	12.6 (0.28)	10.4 (0.30)	14.1 (0.90)	28.6 (1.84)	13.2 (0.40)	10.8 (0.43)	15.0 (1.35)	29.1 (2.57)	12.1 (0.38)	10.0 (0.41)	13.3 (1.21)	28.1 (2.64)
1988	12.9 (0.30)	9.6 (0.31)	14.5 (1.00)	35.8 (2.30)	13.5 (0.44)	10.3 (0.46)	15.0 (1.48)	36.0 (3.19)	12.2 (0.42)	8.9 (0.43)	14.0 (1.36)	35.4 (3.31)
1989	12.6 (0.31)	9.4 (0.32)	13.9 (0.98)	33.0 (2.19)	13.6 (0.45)	10.3 (0.47)	14.9 (1.46)	34.4 (3.08)	11.7 (0.42)	8.5 (0.43)	13.0 (1.32)	31.6 (3.11)
1990	12.1 (0.29)	9.0 (0.30)	13.2 (0.94)	32.4 (1.91)	12.3 (0.42)	9.3 (0.44)	11.9 (1.30)	34.3 (2.71)	11.8 (0.41)	8.7 (0.42)	14.4 (1.34)	30.3 (2.70)
1991	12.5 (0.30)	8.9 (0.31)	13.6 (0.95)	35.3 (1.93)	13.0 (0.43)	8.9 (0.44)	13.5 (1.37)	39.2 (2.74)	11.9 (0.41)	8.9 (0.43)	13.7 (1.31)	31.1 (2.70)
1992[d]	11.0 (0.28)	7.7 (0.29)	13.7 (0.95)	29.4 (1.86)	11.3 (0.41)	8.0 (0.42)	12.5 (1.32)	32.1 (2.67)	10.7 (0.39)	7.4 (0.40)	14.8 (1.36)	26.6 (2.56)
1993[d]	11.0 (0.28)	7.9 (0.29)	13.6 (0.94)	27.5 (1.79)	11.2 (0.40)	8.2 (0.42)	12.6 (1.32)	28.1 (2.54)	10.9 (0.40)	7.6 (0.41)	14.4 (1.34)	26.9 (2.52)
1994[d]	11.4 (0.28)	7.7 (0.27)	12.6 (0.75)	30.0 (1.16)	12.3 (0.38)	8.0 (0.38)	14.1 (1.14)	31.6 (1.60)	10.6 (0.36)	7.5 (0.37)	11.3 (0.99)	28.1 (1.66)
1995[d]	12.0 (0.27)	8.6 (0.28)	12.1 (0.74)	30.0 (1.15)	12.2 (0.38)	9.0 (0.40)	11.1 (1.05)	30.0 (1.59)	11.7 (0.37)	8.2 (0.39)	12.9 (1.05)	30.0 (1.66)
1996[d]	11.1 (0.27)	7.3 (0.27)	13.0 (0.80)	29.4 (1.19)	11.4 (0.38)	7.3 (0.38)	13.5 (1.18)	30.3 (1.67)	10.9 (0.38)	7.3 (0.39)	12.5 (1.08)	28.3 (1.69)
1997[d]	11.0 (0.27)	7.6 (0.28)	13.4 (0.80)	25.3 (1.11)	11.9 (0.39)	8.5 (0.41)	13.3 (1.16)	27.0 (1.55)	10.1 (0.36)	6.7 (0.37)	13.5 (1.11)	23.4 (1.59)
1998[d]	11.8 (0.27)	7.7 (0.28)	13.8 (0.81)	29.5 (1.12)	13.3 (0.40)	8.6 (0.41)	15.5 (1.24)	33.5 (1.59)	10.3 (0.36)	6.9 (0.37)	12.2 (1.05)	25.0 (1.56)
1999[d]	11.2 (0.26)	7.3 (0.27)	12.6 (0.77)	28.6 (1.11)	11.9 (0.38)	7.7 (0.39)	12.1 (1.10)	31.0 (1.58)	10.5 (0.36)	6.9 (0.37)	13.0 (1.08)	26.0 (1.54)
2000[d]	10.9 (0.26)	6.9 (0.26)	13.1 (0.78)	27.8 (1.08)	12.0 (0.38)	7.0 (0.37)	15.3 (1.20)	31.8 (1.56)	9.9 (0.35)	6.9 (0.37)	11.1 (1.00)	23.5 (1.48)

TABLE 6.5

Percentage of high school dropouts among persons 16–24 years old (status dropout rate), by sex, race and ethnicity, selected years 1960–2006 [CONTINUED]

Year	Total status dropout rate				Male status dropout rate				Female status dropout rate			
	All races[a]	White	Black	Hispanic	All races[a]	White	Black	Hispanic	All races[a]	White	Black	Hispanic
1	2	3	4	5	6	7	8	9	10	11	12	13
2001[d]	10.7 (0.25)	7.3 (0.26)	10.9 (0.71)	27.0 (1.06)	12.2 (0.38)	7.9 (0.39)	13.0 (1.12)	31.6 (1.55)	9.3 (0.34)	6.7 (0.36)	9.0 (0.90)	22.1 (1.42)
2002[d]	10.5 (0.24)	6.5 (0.24)	11.3 (0.70)	25.7 (0.93)	11.8 (0.35)	6.7 (0.35)	12.8 (1.07)	29.6 (1.32)	9.2 (0.32)	6.3 (0.34)	9.9 (0.91)	21.2 (1.27)
2003[d,e]	9.9 (0.23)	6.3 (0.24)	10.9 (0.69)	23.5 (0.90)	11.3 (0.34)	7.1 (0.35)	12.5 (1.05)	26.7 (1.29)	8.4 (0.30)	5.6 (0.32)	9.5 (0.89)	20.1 (1.23)
2004[d,e]	10.3 (0.23)	6.8 (0.24)	11.8 (0.70)	23.8 (0.89)	11.6 (0.34)	7.1 (0.35)	13.5 (1.08)	28.5 (1.30)	9.0 (0.31)	6.4 (0.34)	10.2 (0.92)	18.5 (1.18)
2005[d,e]	9.4 (0.22)	6.0 (0.23)	10.4 (0.66)	22.4 (0.87)	10.8 (0.33)	6.6 (0.34)	12.0 (1.02)	26.4 (1.26)	8.0 (0.29)	5.3 (0.31)	9.0 (0.86)	18.1 (1.16)
2006[d,e]	9.3 (0.22)	5.8 (0.23)	10.7 (0.66)	22.1 (0.86)	10.3 (0.33)	6.4 (0.33)	9.7 (0.91)	25.7 (1.25)	8.3 (0.30)	5.3 (0.31)	11.7 (0.96)	18.1 (1.15)

—Not available.

†Not applicable.

[a] Includes other racial/ethnic categories not separately shown.

[b] Based on the April 1960 decennial census.

[c] White and black include persons of Hispanic ethnicity.

[d] Because of changes in data collection procedures, data may not be comparable with figures for years prior to 1992.

[e] White and black exclude persons identifying themselves as more than one race.

Note: "Status" dropouts are 16- to 24-year-olds who are not enrolled in school and who have not completed a high school program, regardless of when they left school. People who have received GED credentials are counted as high school completers. All data except for 1960 are based on October counts. Data are based on sample surveys of the civilian noninstitutionalized population, which excludes persons in prisons, persons in the military, and other persons not living in households. Race categories exclude persons of Hispanic ethnicity except where otherwise noted.

SOURCE: Thomas D. Snyder, Sally A. Dillow, and Charlene M. Hoffman, "Table 105. Percentage of High School Dropouts among Persons 16 to 24 Years Old (Status Dropout Rate), by Sex and Race/Ethnicity: Selected Years, 1960 through 2006," in *Digest of Education Statistics, 2007*, U.S. Department of Education, National Center for Education Statistics, March 2008, http://nces.ed.gov/pubs2008/2008022.pdf (accessed November 7, 2008)

in public schools. Between 1976 and 2006 the proportion of all students who participated in federal education programs for children with disabilities increased from 8.3% to 13.8%. (See Table 6.6.) In the 2005–06 school year, the highest proportion of students needed services for specific learning disabilities (5.6%), followed by students who needed help with speech or language impairments (3%) and students who were mentally retarded (1.1%). According to the Office of Special Education Programs, in *28th Annual Report to Congress on the Implementation of the Individuals with Disabilities Education Act, 2006* (January 2009, http://www.ed.gov/about/reports/annual/osep/2006/parts-b-c/28th-vol-1.pdf), 282,733 children from birth through age 2 and 701,949 children aged 3 through 5 received early intervention services in 2004. Another 6.1 million children aged 6 through 21 received special education and related services.

HOMELESS CHILDREN. Homelessness harms children in many ways, including hindering their ability to attend and succeed in school. Homeless children have difficulty with transportation to school, maintaining necessary documents, and attaining privacy needed for homework, sleep, and interaction with parents in a shelter. Experts report that homeless children—compared to children who are poor but housed—miss more days of school, more often repeat a grade, and are more often put into special education classes.

The McKinney-Vento Homeless Assistance Act of 1987 required in Title VII, subtitle B, that each state provide "free, appropriate, public education" to homeless youth. The law further required that all states develop a plan to address the denial of access to education to homeless children.

The McKinney-Vento Homeless Education Assistance Improvements Act of 2001 went further to address inequities that affect homeless children in the public school system. New guidance for states and school systems released by the Department of Education in April 2003 noted the main differences between the old and new programs:

- Homeless children may no longer be segregated in a separate program on the basis of their homeless status

- Schools must immediately enroll homeless students even if they are missing some of the documentation normally required

- Upon parental request, states and school districts must provide transportation for homeless children to the school they attended before they became homeless

- School districts must designate a local liaison for homeless children and youths

HOMESCHOOLED CHILDREN. A number of parents who are unhappy with public schools teach their children at home. According to Daniel Princiotta and Christopher Chapman, in *Homeschooling in the United States: 2003* (February 2006, http://nces.ed.gov/pubs2006/2006042.pdf), approxi-

mately 850,000, or 1.7% of school-age children, were being homeschooled in the spring of 1999. By 2003 that number had risen to 1.1 million students, or 2.2% of school-age children.

Parents choose to homeschool their children for a variety of reasons. The NCES reports in the issue brief "1.1 Million Homeschooled Students in the United States in 2003" (July 2004, http://nces.ed.gov/pubs2004/2004115.pdf) that almost a third (31%) of the home-schooling parents surveyed in the National Household Education Survey said the most important reason they chose to homeschool was concern about the environment of the other schools. Another 30% said they chose to homeschool to provide religious or moral instruction. The third most common reason parents gave for home-schooling was dissatisfaction with the academic instruction available at other schools (16%).

States have differing requirements for parents who teach their children at home. According to the Home School Legal Defense Association, some states, such as Idaho and New Jersey, give parents the right to educate their children as they see fit, and impose only minor controls or none at all. Other states have more strict regulations. Highly regulated states, such as New York, Vermont, Pennsylvania, and a few others, require parents to get curriculum approved, send achievement test scores, or meet qualification requirements. Opponents of homeschooling argue that parents may not be qualified to be teachers, but proponents believe that parents can gain teaching skills through experience, just as other teachers do.

HIGHER EDUCATION—OFF TO COLLEGE

Formal schooling beyond high school increasingly is being viewed as a necessity, not only to a young person's development but also to his or her economic success. Many parents consider helping their children attend college to be an important financial responsibility.

College Entrance Examinations

Most students who want to enter a college or university in the United States must take either the SAT (once known as the Scholastic Aptitude Test, then the Scholastic Assessment Test, now simply the SAT I) or the American College Test (ACT) as part of their admission requirements. The ACT is a curriculum-based achievement test, measuring proficiency in reading, math, English, and science, whereas the SAT is the primary admissions test to measure a student's mathematical and verbal reasoning ability in a way intended to assess readiness for college. Students who take these tests usually plan to continue their education beyond high school; therefore, these tests do not profile all high school students.

MORE ARE TAKING SAT AND ACT EXAMS, WITH MIXED RESULTS. The College Board notes in "SAT Scores Stable as Record Numbers Take Test" (August 26, 2008, http://www.collegeboard.com/press/releases/197846.html) that

TABLE 6.6

Number of children with disabilities who were served by federal programs, as a percentage of total public K–12 enrollment, by type of disability, 1976–77 to 2005–06

Type of disability	1976–77	1980–81	1990–91	1994–95	1995–96	1996–97	1997–98	1998–99	1999–2000	2000–01	2001–02	2002–03	2003–04	2004–05	2005–06
1	2	3	4	5	6	7	8	9	10	11	12	13	14	15	16
							Number served as a percent of total enrollment								
All disabilities	8.3	10.1	11.4	12.2	12.4	12.6	12.8	13.0	13.2	13.3	13.4	13.5	13.7	13.8	13.8
Specific learning disabilities	1.8	3.6	5.2	5.6	5.8	5.8	5.9	6.0	6.0	6.1	6.0	5.9	5.8	5.7	5.6
Speech or language impairments	2.9	2.9	2.4	2.3	2.3	2.3	2.3	2.3	2.3	3.0	2.9	2.9	3.0	3.0	3.0
Mental retardation	2.2	2.0	1.3	1.3	1.3	1.3	1.3	1.3	1.3	3.0	1.3	1.2	1.2	1.2	1.1
Emotional disturbance	0.6	0.8	0.9	1.0	1.0	1.0	10.0	1.0	1.0	1.0	1.0	1.0	1.0	1.0	1.0
Hearing impairments	0.2	0.2	0.1	0.1	0.1	0.1	0.1.	0.2	0.2	0.2	0.2	0.2	0.2	0.2	0.2
Orthopedic impairments	0.2	0.1	0.1	0.1	0.1	0.1	0.1.	0.1	0.2	0.2	0.2	0.2	0.2	0.2	0.1
Other health impairments[a]	0.3	0.2	0.1	0.2	0.3	0.4	0.4	0.5	0.5	0.2	0.7	0.8	1.0	1.1	1.2
Visual impairments	0.1	0.1	0.1	0.1	0.1	0.1	0.1	0.1	0.1	0.1	0.1	0.1	0.1	0.1	0.1
Multiple disabilities	—	0.2	0.2	0.2	0.2	0.2	0.2	0.2	0.2	0.3	0.3	0.3	0.3	0.3	0.3
Deaf-blindness	—	#	#	#	#	#	#	#	#	#	#	#	#	#	#
Autism	—	—	—	#	#	#	#	#	#	0.2	0.2	0.3	0.3	0.4	0.5
Traumatic brain injury	—	—	—	#	#	#	#	#	#	#	#	#	#	#	0.1
Developmental delay[b]	—	—	—	—	—	—	#	#	#	0.4	0.5	0.6	0.6	0.7	0.7
Preschool disabled[b]	†	†	0.9	1.2	1.2	1.2	1.2	1.2	1.2	†	†	†	†	†	†

—Not available.

†Not applicable.

#Rounds to zero.

[a]Other health impairments include having limited strength, vitality, or alertness due to chronic or acute health problems such as a heart condition, tuberculosis, rheumatic fever, nephritis, asthma, sickle cell anemia, hemophilia, epilepsy lead poisoning, leukemia, or diabetes.

[b]Includes preschool children ages 3–5 served under Chapter 1 and IDEA, Part B. Prior to 1987–88, these students were included in the counts by disability condition. Beginning in 1987–88, states were no longer required to report preschool children (ages 0–5) by disability condition. Beginning in 2002–03, preschool children were again identified by disability condition.

[3]Based on the total enrollment in public schools, prekindergarten through 12th grade. Note: Includes students served under Chapter 1 of the Elementary and Secondary Education Act and under the Individuals with Disabilities Education Act (IDEA), formerly the Education of the Handicapped Act. Prior to October 1994, children and youth with disabilities were served under Chapter 1 as well as IDEA, Part B. In October 1994, funding for children and youth with disabilities was consolidated under IDEA, Part B. Data reported in this table for years prior to 1994–95 include children ages 0–21 served under Chapter 1. Counts are based on reports from the 50 states and the District of Columbia only (i.e., table excludes data for other jurisdictions). Increases since 1987–88 are due in part to new legislation enacted in fall 1986, which added a mandate for public school special education services for 3- to 5-year-old disabled children. Some data have been revised from previously published figures. Detail may not sum to totals because of rounding.

SOURCE: Adapted from Thomas D. Snyder, Sally A. Dillow, and Charlene M. Hoffman, "Table 47. Children 3 to 21 Years Old Served in Federally Supported Programs for the Disabled, by Type of Disability: Selected Years, 1976–77 through 2005–06," in *Digest of Education Statistics, 2007,* U.S. Department of Education, National Center for Education Statistics, March 2008, http://nces.ed.gov/pubs2008/2008022.pdf (accessed November 7, 2008). Nongovernmental data from Individuals with Disabilities Education Act (IDEA) database, September 22, 2006.

the number of students who take both the SAT and the ACT has grown steadily. In 2008 more than 1.5 million students took the SAT. This represented an increase of 8% over 2003 and 29.5% over 1998. The article "2008 ACT College Readiness Report News Release" (ACT News, August 13, 2008) states that the number of students taking the ACT increased as well; 1.4 million students took the ACT in 2008, up 9% from 2007. The increased numbers taking the SAT and ACT suggest that more high school graduates are pursuing a college education.

Performance on the SAT is measured on a scale of 200 to 800 for each of three sections, with the established average score being around 500 for each. According to the College Board, in *2008 College-Bound Seniors*, over the period from 1972 to 2008 the average critical reading scores on the SAT declined from 537 to 502. By contrast, the results for the math portion of the SAT dropped and then rebounded over this same period, from 509 in 1972 to 515 in 2008. Writing was tested for the first time in 2006; test takers received an average score of 497 in that year and 494 in each of the two subsequent years. The ACT is scored on a scale of 1 to 36, with 36 being the highest possible score. The ACT notes in *ACT High School Profile Report* (2008, http://www.act.org/news/data/08/pdf/National2008.pdf) that the average ACT scores, after improving for several years, dropped slightly in 2008; in 1970 the average composite ACT score was 19.9, and in 2008 the average composite score was 21.1, down from 21.2 the year before.

CHARACTERISTICS OF TEST TAKERS. More women than men took the tests in 2006—53.6% of those who took the SAT were women. More women than men have taken the SAT since the 1970s as well. In "2008 College Bound Seniors Average SAT Scores" (2008, http://www.fairtest.org/files/2008%20COLLEGE%20BOUND%20SENIORS%20AVERAGE%20SAT%20SCORES.pdf), the College Board states that in 2008, 57% of Hispanic and African-American test takers were women, 51% of Asian-Americans taking the test were women, and 53% of non-Hispanic white test takers were women. Men scored higher on both the critical reading and the math portions of the SAT test in 2008 (average scores of 504 and 533, respectively), compared to women (500 in each section). Women, however, scored higher on the writing section than men did (501 and 488, respectively). The College Board reports that women are continuing to narrow the performance gap with males in the critical reading section of the test.

The College Board explains that despite improvements in the scores of minority students, most lagged behind those of non-Hispanic white students. In 2008 white students scored a mean of 528 on critical reading, 537 on math, and 518 on writing on the SAT. African-Americans scored an average of 430 on critical reading, 426 on math, and 424 on writing, the lowest average scores of any racial or ethnic group. Mexican-Americans scored an average of 454 on

critical reading, 463 on math, and 447 on writing; and Puerto Ricans scored 456 on critical reading, 453 on math, and 445 on writing. Native Americans and Alaskan Natives scored 485 on critical reading, 491 on math, and 470 on writing. Asian-Americans and Pacific Islanders scored an average of 513 on critical reading, 581 on math, and 516 on writing.

According to the ACT, in *ACT High School Profile Report*, the 2008 test results show that Asian-Americans scored an average of 22.9, non-Hispanic whites scored an average of 22.1, Native Americans and Alaskan Natives scored an average of 19, Hispanics scored an average of 18.7, and African-American students scored an average of 16.9. Scores for all groups except African-Americans were up since 2004. In the article "ACT Scores Hold Steady in 2003" (2003, http://www.act.org/activity/autumn2003/scores.html), Richard L. Ferguson notes, "Our research has shown that far too many African-American students are not being adequately prepared for college. They are less likely than others to take rigorous, college-preparatory courses, and they often don't receive the information and guidance they need to properly plan for college." ACT data for 2008 show that fewer minority test takers had taken the core college-preparatory coursework and that groups that had taken more core coursework, such as non-Hispanic whites and Asian-Americans, tended to score higher on the ACT.

Projected Enrollment

Enrollment in institutions of higher education is expected to rise through 2017, due not only to large numbers of children of baby boomers approaching college age but also to the increasing numbers of people of all ages seeking advanced learning. Enrollment in degree-granting postsecondary institutions stood at 17.8 million in 2006 and is expected to reach 20.1 million by 2017. (See Figure 6.4.)

FIGURE 6.4

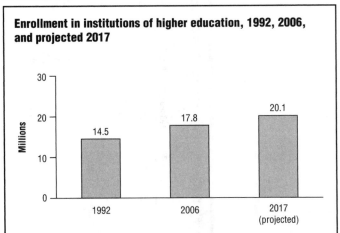

Enrollment in institutions of higher education, 1992, 2006, and projected 2017

SOURCE: William J. Hussar and Tabitha M. Bailey, "Figure C. Actual and Middle Alternative Projected Numbers for Total Enrollment in Degree-Granting Institutions: Selected Years 1992–2017," in *Projections of Education Statistics to 2017*, U.S. Department of Education, National Center for Education Statistics, September 2008, http://nces.ed.gov/pubs2008/2008078.pdf (accessed November 7, 2008)

Community College Enrollment during Economic Downturn

During times of economic distress, in general, more people return to community colleges for job retraining or to learn different skills to pursue new careers. This trend was observed during the global financial crisis, which intensified in late 2008. As described by Caitlin McDevitt, in "Junior College Squeeze: Community Colleges across the Country Are Seeing Enrollment Climb Just as Local Governments Scale Back Funding" (*Newsweek*, December 15, 2008), "the American Association of Community Colleges [AACC] reports that community-college enrollment rose 8 to 10 percent." According to Rachel Streitfeld, in "Unemployed Workers Heading Back to School," (CNN.com, February 14, 2009), AACC president George Boggs "has heard from 75 college presidents reporting double-digit enrollment increases [during the winter 2009] semester." Boggs suggested that "community colleges are a big part of the solution to this economic downturn." However, Boggs explained that even though the community colleges have assisted unemployed workers by decreasing or freezing their tuition, setting up scholarship programs, or using financial assistance to cover the costs of books and transportation, the spike in applications has imposed a heavy financial burden on some schools that have already been struggling to keep tuition costs low. Boggs stated, "Many [community colleges] are reporting that it is the highest-ever enrollment that they have had.... And several are reporting a waiting list of students that they can not accommodate.... It wouldn't surprise me to hear that about a half-million students are being turned away from our community colleges today."

College Costs

Paying for a college education, even at public four-year institutions, now ranks as one of the most costly investments for American families. Snyder, Dillow, and Hoffman indicate that in 2006–07 the average annual in-state cost at a four-year public college, including tuition and room and board, was $12,805. For one year at a private four-year college, the average cost for tuition and room and board was $28,896. Public college tuition varied widely among states, from $2,670 in the District of Columbia to $9,333 in New Jersey. Most states with the highest tuition were in the Northeast and most with the lowest tuition were in the South and West.

FINANCIAL ASSISTANCE FOR STUDENTS. According to Snyder, Dillow, and Hoffman, during the 2003–04 academic year, almost two-thirds (63.2%) of about 19.1 million undergraduates enrolled in postsecondary institutions received some type of financial aid from federal, state, institutional, or other sources to meet their educational expenses. About half (48%) of undergraduates received some form of federal aid. More than half (50.7%) of all students received grants (which do not have to be paid

back), about a third (35.2%) took out loans (which do have to be paid back), and 7.5% were on work-study programs. Federal assistance that goes directly to students includes Pell Grants (the annual maximum was decreased to $4,241 for the 2008–09 award year), the Stafford Student Loan Program (a maximum loan of $19,000 for four years of study for dependent undergraduate students), and Supplemental Education Opportunity Grants (which can range from $100 to $2,000 per year).

Snyder, Dillow, and Hoffman note that during the 2003–04 school year, 62.7% of dependent undergraduate students whose families earned less than $20,000 per year and 77.8% of students whose families earned between $20,000 and $39,999 per year received financial aid. However, due to the high cost of college, students even in high-income brackets received financial aid to help pay for college; 60.5% of dependent undergraduate students whose families earned $100,000 or more received some form of financial aid in 2003–04.

In *A New Era of Responsibility: Renewing America's Promise* (2009, http://www.whitehouse.gov/omb/assets/fy2010_new_era/A_New_Era_of_Responsibility2.pdf), the White House indicates that the Obama administration's proposed 2010 budget included money to increase the Pell Grant maximum award to $5,550 in the 2010–11 school year, as well as to tie future increases in the grant program to inflation. The budget also included a proposal to simplify and standardize the Perkins Student Loan program, which the administration believes can save the government money and allow reinvestment in the program.

PROPOSED TAX CREDIT. According to the White House, in "The Agenda: Education" (2009, http://www.whitehouse.gov/agenda/education/), the Obama administration promised to make college education affordable for everyone by creating an American Opportunity Tax Credit. This credit would refund the first $4,000 of a college education, which the administration estimated would make community college free for most students, and would cover two-thirds of the cost of tuition at a public college. Anyone who claimed the tax credit would be required to volunteer 100 hours in the community in exchange for the credit. A $2,500 tax credit was included in the American Recovery and Reinvestment Act that was signed into law by President Obama on February 17, 2009. The 2010 budget included provisions to make the tax cut permanent.

EDUCATIONAL ATTAINMENT AND EARNINGS

The educational attainment of the U.S. population has risen steadily since the 1940s. In *Educational Attainment in the United States: 2007* (December 27, 2007, http://www.census.gov/population/www/socdemo/education/cps2007.html), the U.S. Census Bureau states that in 2007, 86% of adults older than 25 had graduated from high school—the highest number ever. More than one out of four (29%) had earned a bachelor's degree or more.

The level of educational attainment has traditionally been higher for men than for women. In 2007, however, for the sixth year in a row, the Census Bureau indicates that the high school graduation rate for women aged 25 and over (86.4%) exceeded that of men (85%). In 2007, 29.5% of men and 28% of women had obtained bachelor's degrees or higher. Even though college attainment has increased since 1990 for both men and women, women are narrowing the gap and making faster gains then men.

Educational attainment of the over-25 population also varied by race and ethnic origin. According to the Census Bureau, non-Hispanic whites were the most likely to complete high school (90.6%), followed by Asian-Americans (87.9%), African-Americans (82.4%), and Hispanics (60.3%). Asian-Americans were by far the most likely to be college graduates (51.4%), followed by non-Hispanic whites (31.3%), African-Americans (18.7%), and Hispanics (12.7%).

Education is a good investment, because earning levels rise with increased education. According to the Census Bureau (2008, http://pubdb3.census.gov/macro/032008/perinc/new03_001.htm), for people aged 25 and older who had not finished high school, the average annual income in 2007 was $24,881. High school graduates earned an average income of $33,609 in 2007, and people with an associate's degree earned an average income of $41,447. The incomes of college graduates increased with the level of the degree earned. People with a bachelor's degree had mean earnings of $59,365, whereas holders of professional degrees earned an average of $121,340 in 2007.

CHAPTER 7
JUVENILE CRIME AND VICTIMIZATION

THE UNIFORM CRIME REPORTS AND THE NATIONAL CRIME VICTIMIZATION SURVEY

Two main government sources collect crime statistics. The Federal Bureau of Investigation (FBI) compiles the annual Uniform Crime Reports (UCR). The FBI notes in *Crime in the United States, 2007* (September 2008, http://www.fbi.gov/ucr/cius2007/index.html) that the UCR, which was begun in 1930, now collects data from 17,738 city, county, and state law enforcement agencies.

The second set of crime statistics is the National Crime Victimization Survey (NCVS), which is prepared by the Bureau of Justice Statistics (BJS). Established in 1972, the survey is an annual federal statistical study that measures the levels of victimization resulting from criminal activity in the United States. According to the BJS, in "Crime and Victims Statistics" (August 29, 2008, http://www.ojp.usdoj.gov/bjs/cvict.htm), the survey collects data from a nationally representative sample of approximately 76,000 households each year, containing about 135,300 people, on the "frequency, characteristics and consequences of criminal victimization." The survey was previously known as the National Crime Survey, but it was renamed and redesigned in 1992 to emphasize the measurement of victimization experienced by citizens. The survey was created because of a concern that the UCR did not fully portray the true volume of crime. The UCR provides data on crimes reported to law enforcement authorities, but it does not estimate how many crimes went unreported.

The NCVS is designed to complement the UCR. It measures the levels of criminal victimization of people and households for the crimes of rape, robbery, assault, burglary, motor vehicle theft, and larceny. Murder is not included because the NCVS data are gathered through interviews with victims. Definitions for these crimes are the same as those established by the UCR.

Some observers believe the NCVS is a better indicator of the volume of crime in the United States than the FBI statistics. Nonetheless, like all surveys, it is subject to error. The survey depends on people's memories of incidents that happened up to six months earlier. Many times, a victim is not sure what happened, even moments after the crime occurred. In addition, the NCVS limits the data to victims aged 12 and older, an admittedly arbitrary age selection.

CRIME TRENDS
Violent and Property Crimes

Michael R. Rand of the BJS reports in *Criminal Victimization, 2007* (December 2008, http://www.ojp.usdoj.gov/bjs/pub/pdf/cv07.pdf) that in 2007 U.S. residents experienced 22.9 million violent and property victimizations. Of these crimes, 17.5 million were property crimes (burglary, motor vehicle theft, and theft), 3.7 million were violent crimes (rape or sexual assault, robbery, aggravated assault, and simple assault), and 194,100 were personal thefts (pocket picking and purse snatching). The rate of rape/sexual assault was up from 2005, but the rate for every other type of crime had decreased. (Budget constraints in 2006 changed data collection methods; therefore, 2006 data cannot be compared to previous and current years.)

According to Rand, between 2005 and 2007 the average yearly rate of violent crimes per 1,000 people aged 12 and older was essentially unchanged. In 2005 the violent crime rate was 21.1 per 1,000 people, and in 2007 it was 20.7 per 1,000 people, a decrease of 1.9%. For property crimes, the rate was 154.2 per 1,000 people in 2005 and 146.5 per 1,000 people in 2007, a decline of 5%. The rate for personal theft witnessed an 11.1% decrease, from 0.9 per 1,000 people to 0.8 per 1,000 people. Rand indicates that the 2007 violent and property crime rates were at their lowest levels since 1973, the first year when these data became available.

The UCR reports that most violent crimes—including murder, nonnegligent manslaughter, forcible rape, robbery, and aggravated assault—remained fairly steady between 2006 and 2007, except for forcible rape, which decreased

2.5% between 2006 and 2007. The UCR also recorded decreasing violent crime rates over time. The violent crime rate had decreased from 758.2 per 100,000 people in 1991 to 466.9 per 100,000 in 2007.

According to the UCR, there were an estimated 9.8 million property crimes, including burglary, larceny-theft, and motor vehicle theft, in 2007, down from nearly 10 million in 2006. This decline continued a long-term trend; in 2007, the property crime rate was 3,263.5 per 100,000 people, compared to a rate of 5,140.2 per 100,000 in 1991. This was a decrease of 37% in 16 years.

Trends in Juvenile Crime

According to the FBI, from the mid-1980s through the mid-1990s youth violence and crime grew at rapid rates. In *Juvenile Victims and Offenders: 2006 National Report* (March 2006, http://www.ojjdp.ncjrs.gov/ojstatbb/nr2006/downloads/NR2006.pdf), Howard N. Snyder and Melissa Sickmund of the National Center for Juvenile Justice look at juvenile homicide trends. They find that between 1980 and 2002, murders by juveniles were highest in 1993 and 1994. During this 22-year span, the murders involving juvenile offenders acting alone decreased 68% and murders involving two or more juvenile offenders fell 60%.

The surge in youth crime and violence caused much concern in society. Various groups—public and private—undertook the mission of trying to uncover the reasons juvenile crime was on the rise. Lawmakers responded by toughening existing laws and finding ways to try more juveniles as adults. Courts levied stricter sentences, and parents and educators looked into various programs and methods geared to help their children and students deal with the situation. (See Chapter 10.)

However, the rise in juvenile crime did not last. Snyder and Sickmund note that in the 10-year period between 1994 and 2003, juvenile arrests decreased by 18%, compared to a 1% increase in arrests of adults during the same period. The arrest rate of juveniles for murder in 2003 was the lowest since at least 1980. According to Snyder and Sickmund, "The juvenile violent crime wave predicted by some in the mid-1990s has not occurred."

JUVENILE OFFENDERS

For some young people, their teenage and young adult years are difficult and challenging times. Even though their peers are playing baseball, going to proms, singing in the school choir, heading to college, and making plans for the future, some juveniles and youths are, for whatever reason, committing crimes and having brushes with the law. When dealing with young offenders, each state has its own definition of the term *juvenile*: Most states put the upper age limit at 17 years old, although some states set it as low as 14 years old. When reporting its national crime statistics, the FBI considers those under the age of 18 to be juveniles. The

FBI often breaks its juvenile crime statistics into age-based subcategories, such as age 16 and older and age 15 and younger, to demonstrate how juvenile offenses vary with age. The FBI does the same with youth, who are often defined as 18 to 24. However, some organizations and studies classify youth age ranges differently, citing youths as those aged 18 to 21 or aged 18 to 25.

The U.S. Department of Justice defines crime as all behaviors and acts for which society provides formally approved punishments. Written law, both federal and state, defines which behaviors are criminal and which are not. Some behaviors—murder, robbery, and burglary—have always been considered criminal. Other actions, such as domestic violence or driving under the influence of drugs or alcohol, became classified as criminal actions more recently. Other changes in society have also influenced crime. For example, the widespread use of computers provides new opportunities for white-collar cybercrime, including identity theft and the malicious spread of computer viruses and worms.

Crime can range from actions as simple as taking a candy bar from a store without paying for it, to those as severe and violent as murder. Most people have broken some law, wittingly or unwittingly, at some time in their lives. Therefore, the true extent of criminality is impossible to measure. Researchers can only keep records of what is reported by victims or known to the police.

Risk Factors for Youth Violence

Various government entities, schools, student and parent organizations, and research groups have devoted countless hours to the issue of youth violence. One of their goals is to find ways to recognize the potential for violent behavior in youth before it becomes a serious problem. They work individually and sometimes collectively to outline trends in youth violence and to determine what factors lead to violent behavior.

The Centers for Disease Control and Prevention (CDC) outlines in "Understanding Youth Violence: Fact Sheet" (2008, http://www.cdc.gov/ncipc/pub-res/YVFactSheet.pdf) the risk factors that increase the likelihood that a young person will become violent. These factors include a history of violent victimization or prior violence; drug, alcohol, or tobacco use; association with delinquent peers; a dysfunctional family life; poor grades; and poverty in the family or community. The CDC recommends several approaches to stopping youth violence, including programs to improve family relationships, school-based programs to treat nonviolent social development, role modeling through mentoring programs, and changes to physical and social environments to address the social and economic causes of violence.

In "Warning Signs of Youth Violence" (2004, http://www.apahelpcenter.org/featuredtopics/feature.php?id=38&ch=3), the American Psychological Association lists immediate signs that youth violence is a serious possibility as well as signs over a period that indicate a potential for violence. Signs that violence may be imminent include frequently losing temper, vandalizing, increasing substance use or risk-taking behavior, developing plans to commit violence, enjoying hurting animals, or carrying a weapon. The potential for violence exists when a young person has a history of aggressive behavior or substance abuse, has a strong desire to be in a gang, has a fascination with weapons, begins to withdraw from friends and usual activities, performs poorly in school, fails to respect the feelings or rights of others, or has a history of discipline problems.

In response to the Columbine High School shootings in 1999, the U.S. surgeon general began a comprehensive study of the status of youth and violence in the nation. Issued in 2001, *Youth Violence: A Report of the Surgeon General* (http://www.surgeongeneral.gov/library/youthviolence/) addresses many aspects of crime and violence, including risk factors for violence among youth aged 15 to 18. The report contains detailed information on early onset factors (ages six to 11), which include exposure to violence on television and substance abuse, as well as late onset factors (ages 12 to 14), which include aggression in general, antisocial attitudes, and abusive parents.

Those involved in the study of youth violence are quick to point out, however, that people need to be cautious when reacting to someone exhibiting warning signs. Even though it is important to provide help to a teenager with violent tendencies, harm could be caused by mislabeling him or her as being violent or by overreacting to a set of circumstances.

Homicide

The UCR defines murder and nonnegligent manslaughter as "the willful (nonnegligent) killing of one human being by another." However, it also stipulates that "deaths caused by negligence, suicide, or accident; justifiable homicides; and attempts to murder or assaults to murder,... are scored as aggravated assaults." Approximately 16,929 murders and nonnegligent manslaughters occurred in 2007, down 0.6% from 2006.

In 2007, 17,040 people were identified as murder offenders, including 981 males and 80 females under the age of 18, and 3,574 males and 264 females under the age of 22. (See Table 7.1.) Because the identity of all murder offenders is not known, such figures are lower than they would be if all offenders had been identified. Those under age 18 represented 6.2% of all known murder offenders in that year, whereas those under age 22 represented 22.6% of all known murder offenders. Fewer than one out of 10 of all known murderers were female; 92.3% of all murder offenders under age 18 and 93% of all murder offenders under age 22 were males.

TABLE 7.1

Murder offenders by age, sex, and race, 2007

Age	Total	Sex			Race			
		Male	Female	Unknown	White	Black	Other	Unknown
Total	17,040	10,975	1,206	4,859	5,278	6,463	245	5,054
Percent distribution[a]	100.0	64.4	7.1	28.5	31.0	37.9	1.4	29.7
Under 18[b]	1,063	981	80	2	372	663	21	7
Under 22[b]	3,845	3,574	264	7	1,403	2,321	82	39
18 and over[b]	10,146	9,023	1,098	25	4,766	5,038	218	124
Infant (under 1)	0	0	0	0	0	0	0	0
1 to 4	0	0	0	0	0	0	0	0
5 to 8	0	0	0	0	0	0	0	0
9 to 12	10	8	2	0	4	5	1	0
13 to 16	542	493	47	2	187	344	7	4
17 to 19	1,966	1,843	122	1	699	1,202	48	17
20 to 24	2,772	2,516	250	6	1,104	1,578	59	31
25 to 29	1,891	1,679	201	11	803	1,019	35	34
30 to 34	1,109	982	126	1	550	525	18	16
35 to 39	811	697	114	0	444	341	19	7
40 to 44	680	553	126	1	405	250	19	6
45 to 49	540	453	86	1	328	185	18	9
50 to 54	371	323	46	2	234	125	9	3
55 to 59	231	204	26	1	158	71	0	2
60 to 64	130	112	17	1	98	27	3	2
65 to 69	75	68	7	0	60	13	2	0
70 to 74	26	24	2	0	23	3	0	0
75 and over	55	49	6	0	41	13	1	0
Unknown	5,831	971	28	4,832	140	762	6	4,923

[a]Because of rounding, the percentages may not add to 100.0.
[b]Does not include unknown ages.

SOURCE: "Expanded Homicide Data Table 3. Murder Offenders by Age, Sex, and Race, 2007," in *Crime in the United States, 2007*, U.S. Department of Justice, Federal Bureau of Investigation, September 2008, http://www.fbi.gov/ucr/cius2007/offenses/expanded_information/data/shrtable_03.html (accessed November 11, 2008)

In 2007, 31% of all murderers were known to be white, 37.9% were known to be African-American, and 29.7% were of unknown race. (See Table 7.1.) These proportions were similar for juvenile murderers. Among 1,063 youth under age 18, 663 (62.4%) murder offenders were African-American, 372 (35%) were white, 21 (2%) were "other," and 7 (0.7%) were unknown. Among 3,845 youth under age 22, 2,321 (60.4%) were African-American, 1,403 (36.5%) were white, 82 (2.1%) were "other," and 39 (1%) were unknown.

LAW ENFORCEMENT OFFICERS KILLED. In *Law Enforcement Officers Killed and Assaulted, 2007* (October 2008, http://www.fbi.gov/ucr/killed/2007/), the UCR provides statistics on the number of law enforcement officers feloniously killed between 1998 and 2007. During this 10-year period, 549 officers were killed—the highest number (70) occurred in 2001, not including the 72 deaths resulting from the terrorist attacks on September 11 of that year. In 2007, 57 officers were feloniously killed; six known offenders were juveniles under age 18. Between 1998 and 2007, 6.3% of murder offenders who killed law enforcement officers were under age 18 and 39.4% of offenders were young adults aged 18 to 24.

Rape

The UCR reports that even though there were an estimated 90,427 forcible rapes reported in 2007 (a 2.5% decrease from the previous year), only 17,132 people were arrested for rape in that year. Rape is one of the most underreported crimes, and the low arrest rate demonstrates how few perpetrators are caught. Of those actually arrested, 914 (5.3%) were under age 15 and 2,633 (15.4%) were under age 18.

Aggravated and Simple Assault

The UCR defines aggravated assault as "an unlawful attack by one person upon another for the purpose of inflicting severe or aggravated bodily injury.... This type of assault is usually accompanied by the use of a weapon or by other means likely to produce death or great bodily harm. Attempted aggravated assault that involves the display of—or threat to use—a gun, knife, or other weapon is included in this crime category because serious personal injury would likely result if the assault were completed." In 2007 an estimated 855,856 aggravated assaults were reported. In its arrest reports, the UCR notes that 327,137 people were arrested for aggravated assault in that year. Of that number, 13,662 (4.2%) were under age 15 and 43,459 (13.3%) were under age 18.

By contrast, simple assaults are assaults or attempted assaults not involving a weapon and not resulting in serious injury to the victim. These include acts such as assault and battery, resisting or obstructing the police, and hazing. In its arrest reports, the UCR lists a category called "other assaults" (to differentiate between these types of assaults and aggravated assaults). The UCR notes that 983,964 people were arrested for other assaults in 2007. Of that number, 70,038 (7.1%) were under age 15 and 181,378 (18.4%) were under age 18.

Robbery, Burglary, and Larceny-Theft

Robbery, burglary, and larceny-theft are different crimes under the UCR. Robbery is "the taking or attempting to take anything of value from the care, custody, or control of a person or persons by force or threat of force or violence and/or by putting the victim in fear," and is categorized as a violent crime. Burglary involves "the unlawful entry of a structure to commit a felony or theft," and is classified as a property crime. Larceny-theft, which is also a property crime, is "the unlawful taking, carrying, leading, or riding away of property from the possession or constructive possession of another," and includes crimes such as shoplifting, pocket-picking, purse-snatching, thefts from motor vehicles, thefts of motor vehicle parts and accessories, bicycle thefts, and so on. These offenses, taken together, are disproportionately committed by young people.

The UCR estimates that 445,125 robbery offenses had been committed in 2007, which was a small decrease (0.5%) over the previous year but represented an increase of 7.5% over robberies in 2003. In 2007, 96,720 people were arrested for robbery; those arrested were disproportionately young people. Of that number, 5,601 (5.8%) were under age 15 and 26,324 (27.2%) were under age 18.

In 2007 the UCR recorded 2,179,140 burglary offenses, a decrease of 0.2% from the previous year and a 6.6% decline from 10 years earlier. Burglary has a particularly low arrest rate. The UCR notes that 228,846 people were arrested for burglary in 2007. Of that number, 18,589 (8.1%) of perpetrators were under age 15 and 61,695 (27%) were under age 18.

The UCR recorded 6,568,572 larceny-theft offenses in 2007, a decrease of 0.6% from 2006 and an 11% decline from 10 years earlier. In its arrest reports, the UCR notes that 897,626 people were arrested for larceny-theft in 2007. Of that number, 71,314 (7.9%) of perpetrators were under age 15 and 229,837 (25.6%) were under age 18.

Motor-vehicle theft is also disproportionately perpetrated by young people, usually in urban areas. In 2007 there were 1,095,769 motor vehicle thefts nationwide. More than nine out of 10 (93.1%) motor vehicle thefts occurred in metropolitan areas. In its arrest reports, the UCR notes that 89,022 people were arrested for motor-vehicle theft in 2007. Of those arrested, 4,917 (5.5%) were under age 15 and 22,266 (25%) were under age 18.

Computer Crime

Illegally accessing a computer, known as hacking, is a crime committed frequently by juveniles. When it is followed by manipulation of the information in private, corporate, or government databases and networks, it can be quite costly. Another means of computer hacking involves the creation of what is known as a virus program. A virus program is one that resides inside another program and is activated by some predetermined code to create havoc in the host computer. Virus programs can be spread through the sharing of disks and programs, by downloading executable files on the Internet, or, most commonly, through e-mail attachments.

Cases of juvenile hacking have been reported since the 1980s. In 1998 the U.S. Secret Service filed the first criminal case against a juvenile for a computer crime. The unnamed hacker shut down the Worcester, Massachusetts, airport in 1997 for six hours. The airport was integrated into the Federal Aviation Administration traffic system by telephone lines. The accused gained access to the communication system and disabled it by sending a series of computer commands that changed the data carried on the system. As a result, the airport could not function. (No accidents occurred during that time, however.) According to the Department of Justice, the juvenile pled guilty in return for two years probation, a fine, and community service.

Juveniles are sometimes caught hacking into school computer systems in an effort to change their grades and the grades of other students. At times, as in the case of 23 Fort Bend, Texas, students charged with hacking into the local high school's system, the monetary loss to the school system can be so large as to trigger felony charges. The hackers could have faced second-degree felony charges, carrying a penalty of up to 20 years in prison. However, the students were eventually punished by sending them to an alternative education class within the high school.

Other types of computer crime typically perpetrated by juveniles include trading stolen credit card and Social Security numbers and pirating of computer software that will be sold. Because of computer networks, juveniles and other perpetrators can commit these types of crimes on a large scale. In "It's Not Just Fun and 'War Games'—Juveniles and Computer Crime" (April 26, 2005, http://www.cybercrime.gov/usamay 2001_7.htm), Joseph V. DeMarco, the assistant U.S. attorney in the Southern District of New York, states that "the enormous computing power of today's PCs make it possible for minors to commit offenses which are disproportionately serious to their age." Teens can commit property offenses on a large scale using computers, can portray themselves as adults in an online world, and "appear to have an ethical 'deficit' when it comes to computer crimes." He points out that children and teens who would never commit robbery, burglary, or assault may in fact commit online crimes. For example, in May 2008 a 15-year-old boy was arrested in Downington, Pennsylvania, for hacking into a school computer system and copying files including personal information and Social Security numbers of school employees. Such information could be used to perpetrate identity theft.

Juveniles convicted of computer crimes sometimes face imprisonment in juvenile detention centers. The Department of Justice reports in "Massachusetts Teen Convicted for Hacking into Internet and Telephone Service Providers and Making Bomb Threats to High Schools in Massachusetts and Florida" (September 8, 2005, http://www.usdoj .gov/criminal/cybercrime/juvenileSentboston.htm) that in 2005 a Massachusetts juvenile pled guilty to several hacking incidents and was sentenced to 11 months in a juvenile detention facility and 2 years of supervised release, during which period he was barred from owning or using a computer, cell phone, or any electronic equipment capable of accessing the Internet.

In October 2008, 20-year-old David Kernell, a college student at the University of Tennessee, was indicted for hacking into vice presidential candidate Sarah Palin's (1964–) Yahoo e-mail account the previous month. The article "Details Emerge in Palin E-mail Hacking" (Associated Press, September 18, 2008, http://www.msnbc.msn .com/id/26781334/) notes that the break-in to the personal e-mail account could have ramifications for the government because her administration had encouraged the use of Yahoo accounts rather than government e-mail accounts, "which could possibly be released to the public under Alaska's Open Records Act." In March 2009 Kernell pleaded not guilty to three more charges in the case: fraud, unlawful electronic transmission of material outside Tennessee, and attempts to conceal records to impede an FBI investigation. He faced up to 20 years in prison and a $250,000 fine for the felony charges.

Illegal Drug Use

Various studies show that many violent offenders are substance abusers. For some people, drugs and alcohol may cause violent tendencies to surface. Lloyd D. Johnston et al. of the Institute for Social Research find in *Monitoring the Future: National Results on Adolescent Drug Use, Overview of Key Findings, 2007* (2008, http://www.monitoringthefuture .org/pubs/monographs/overview2007.pdf) that in 2007, 35.9% of 12th graders, 28.1% of 10th graders, and 13.2% of eighth graders had used an illicit drug in the past year. Among 12th graders, marijuana/hashish use was highest (31.7%), followed by narcotics (9.2%), amphetamines (7.5%), barbiturates (6.2%), and tranquilizers (6.2%). Two-thirds (66.4%) had used alcohol in the past 12 months.

Other drugs gaining popularity in recent years included so-called club drugs, such as ecstasy (MDMA), flunitrazepam (known as the date rape drug), GHB, and ketamine. These drugs have been popular among teenagers at dance clubs and raves. Because each of these club drugs is scheduled under the Controlled Substances Act (Title II of the Comprehensive Drug Abuse Prevention and Control Act of 1970), they are illegal and their use constitutes a criminal offense. Johnston et al. note that in 2007, 4.5% of high school seniors had used MDMA, 1.3% had used ketamine, 1% had used flunitrazepam, and 0.9% had used GHB in the previous 12 months.

In its arrest reports, the UCR notes that 1,386,394 people were arrested on drug abuse violations in 2007. Of that number, 21,506 (1.6%) were under age 15 and 147,382 (10.6%) were under age 18.

JUVENILE VICTIMS OF CRIME

Table 7.2 and Figure 7.1 outline the trends in nonfatal violent victimizations and homicides by select age groups

TABLE 7.2

Violent victimization by gender and age, 2006

	Population	Number	Rate*
Gender			
Males	120,513,190	3,187,880	26.5
Females	126,777,010	2,906,850	22.9
Age			
12–15	16,892,570	799,610	47.3
16–19	16,687,150	873,480	52.3
20–24	20,397,690	891,220	43.7
25–34	39,931,470	1,407,710	35.3
35–49	65,886,660	1,320,800	20.0
50–64	51,916,140	677,790	13.1
65 or older	35,578,530	124,120	3.5

*Victimization rates are per 1,000 persons age 12 or older or per 1,000 households.

SOURCE: Michael Rand and Shannan Catalano, "Table 3. Violent Victimization, by Gender and Age, 2006," in *Criminal Victimization, 2006*, U.S. Department of Justice, Office of Justice Programs, Bureau of Justice Statistics, December 2007, http://www.ojp.usdoj.gov/bjs/pub/pdf/cv06.pdf (accessed November 11, 2008)

FIGURE 7.1

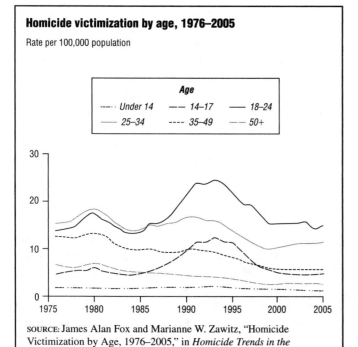

SOURCE: James Alan Fox and Marianne W. Zawitz, "Homicide Victimization by Age, 1976–2005," in *Homicide Trends in the United States*, U.S. Department of Justice, Office of Justice Programs, Bureau of Justice Statistics, July 2007, http://www.ojp.usdoj.gov/bjs/homicide/teens.htm (November 7, 2008)

between 1976 and 2006. During these years the rate of violent victimizations dropped in all age categories, but especially among young people. In "Violent Victimization Rates by Age, 1973–2005" (September 10, 2006, http://www.ojp.usdoj.gov/bjs/glance/tables/vagetab.htm), the BJS indicates that in 1973 the violent victimization rate for those aged 12 to 15 was 81.8 per 1,000 people in that age group. The rate peaked in 1994 at 118.6 per 1,000 people then dropped steadily to 44 per 1,000 people in 2005, its lowest point in the 32 years recorded. For those aged 16 to 19, the rate in 1973 was 81.7. This group also reached its zenith in 1994 at 123.9 and then decreased steadily to 44.3 in 2005. The highest nonfatal violent victimization rate in 1973 was among ages 20 to 24 (87.6). This age group reached its highest point in 1991 with 103.6 and then fluctuated before dropping to 43.2 in 2004; however, it had risen again to 47.1 in 2005. In 2006 the violent victimization rate for 12- to 15-year-olds was 47.3 per 1,000 people, and for 16- to 19-year-olds it was 52.3 per 1,000 people. (See Table 7.2.)

Violent crime rates are highest for young people aged 24 and younger; after age 25 the violent victimization rate declines steadily. According to the BJS, in 1973 16- to 19-year-olds were about twice as likely to be victimized by violent crime as people 35 to 49 years of age in 2005. In 2006 16- to 19-year-olds were about two and a half times as likely as 35- to 49-year-olds to be victimized by violent crime. (See Table 7.2.)

Scott Menard of the University of Colorado notes in *Short- and Long-Term Consequences of Adolescent Victimization* (February 2002, http://www.ncjrs.gov/pdffiles1/ojjdp/191210.pdf) that when someone is victimized as an adolescent, long-term consequences result. When compared to adults who were not victimized as adolescents, adults who were adolescent victims are most likely to have drug problems and more likely to perpetrate violence. They are also more likely to commit acts of domestic violence and become victims of domestic violence than are adults who were not victimized as adolescents. In addition, they are nearly twice as likely to become victims of violent crime and nearly three times as likely to commit property offenses. Their risk of developing posttraumatic stress disorder is also twice as great.

Becoming a victim of crime can have serious consequences—outcomes that the victim neither asks for nor deserves. A victim rarely expects to be victimized and seldom knows where to turn for help. Victims may end up in the hospital to be treated and released, or they may be confined to bed for days, weeks, or longer. Injuries may be temporary, or they may be permanent and forever change the way the victim lives his or her life. Victims may lose money or property, or in the case of homicide their life. In many cases they lose their confidence, self-esteem, and feelings of security.

The effects of crime are not limited to the victim, however. A victim's family is frequently devastated, and the psychological trauma may affect everyone connected to a victim. Victims and their families may experience feelings of fear, anger, shame, self-blame, helplessness, and depression—emotions that can last for years after the event. Those who were attacked in their home or whose home was entered illegally may no longer feel secure anywhere. They often blame themselves, feeling that they could have handled themselves better, or done something differently to prevent being victimized.

In the aftermath of crime, when victims most need support and comfort, there is often no one available who understands. Parents or spouses may be dealing with their own feelings of guilt and anger for not being able to protect their loved ones. Friends may withdraw, not knowing what to say or do. As a result, victims may lose their sense of self-esteem and no longer trust other people. These effects of violent victimization can be particularly devastating when the victim is a young person.

Child Abuse and Neglect

It is impossible to determine how many children suffer abuse. All observers can do is count the number of reported cases—which include only those known to public authorities—or they can survey families, in which case parents may deny or downplay abuse. As a result, estimates of child abuse are generally considered low. The Administration for Children, Youth, and Families (ACYF) is the primary source of national information on abused and neglected children that has been reported to state child protective services agencies.

According to the ACYF, in *Child Maltreatment 2006* (2008, http://www.acf.hhs.gov/programs/cb/pubs/cm06/cm06.pdf), in 2006 an estimated 3.3 million children were alleged to have been abused or neglected and approximately 905,000 children were found to be victims of child maltreatment. Reports most often came from professional sources, such as educators (16.5%), the legal system (15.8%), social service employees (10%), and medical professionals (8.4%), and less often from nonprofessional sources, such as relatives (7.8%), parents (6%), friends and neighbors (5.3%), and a small percentage of the victims themselves (0.6%) and perpetrators (0.1%). (See Figure 7.2.)

In 2006, 64.1% of reported victims suffered neglect, 16% were physically abused, 8.8% were sexually abused,

FIGURE 7.2

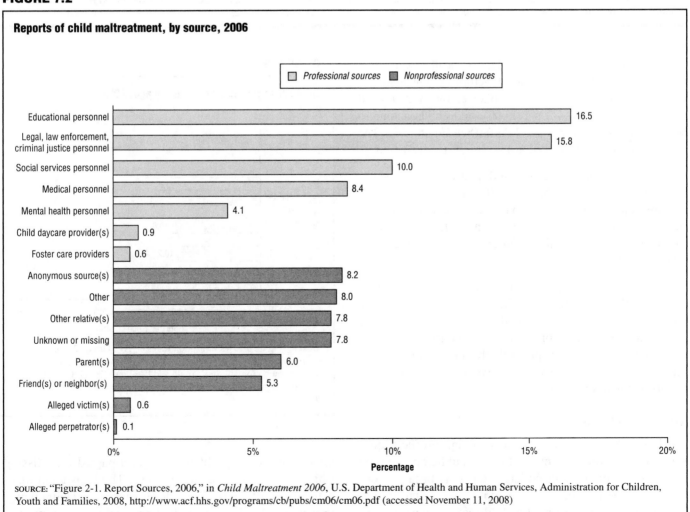

Reports of child maltreatment, by source, 2006

□ Professional sources ■ Nonprofessional sources

Source	Percentage
Educational personnel	16.5
Legal, law enforcement, criminal justice personnel	15.8
Social services personnel	10.0
Medical personnel	8.4
Mental health personnel	4.1
Child daycare provider(s)	0.9
Foster care providers	0.6
Anonymous source(s)	8.2
Other	8.0
Other relative(s)	7.8
Unknown or missing	7.8
Parent(s)	6.0
Friend(s) or neighbor(s)	5.3
Alleged victim(s)	0.6
Alleged perpetrator(s)	0.1

SOURCE: "Figure 2-1. Report Sources, 2006," in *Child Maltreatment 2006*, U.S. Department of Health and Human Services, Administration for Children, Youth and Families, 2008, http://www.acf.hhs.gov/programs/cb/pubs/cm06/cm06.pdf (accessed November 11, 2008)

TABLE 7.3

Child abuse victims by age group and maltreatment type, 2006

Age group	Victims	Neglect Number	%	Physical abuse Number	%	Medical neglect Number	%	Sexual abuse Number	%
Age < 1	100,139	72,314	72.2	14,328	14.3	3,629	3.6	445	0.4
Age 1–3	172,940	125,997	72.9	18,731	10.8	3,948	2.3	4,558	2.6
Age 4–7	213,194	138,886	65.1	32,697	15.3	3,843	1.8	17,539	8.2
Age 8–11	170,944	103,964	60.8	29,312	17.1	3,233	1.9	18,314	10.7
Age 12–15	170,635	94,910	55.6	34,348	20.1	3,447	2.0	28,138	16.5
Age 16 and older	54,564	29,989	55.0	11,998	22.0	1,030	1.9	8,798	16.1
Unknown or missing	2,829	1,727	61.0	627	22.2	50	1.8	328	11.6
Total	**885,245**	**567,787**		**142,041**		**19,180**		**78,120**	
Percent			**64.1**		**16.0**		**2.2**		**8.8**

Age group	Psychological abuse Number	%	Other abuse Number	%	Unknown Number	%	Total maltreatments Number	%
Age <1	3,967	4.0	16,300	16.3	1,097	1.1	112,080	111.9
Age 1–3	10,262	5.9	29,016	16.8	2,114	1.2	194,626	112.5
Age 4–7	14,555	6.8	31,833	14.9	2,570	1.2	241,923	113.5
Age 8–11	13,647	8.0	25,406	14.9	1,947	1.1	195,823	114.6
Age 12–15	12,372	7.3	23,465	13.8	1,950	1.1	198,630	116.4
Age 16 and older	3,524	6.5	7,832	14.4	541	1.0	63,712	116.8
Unknown or missing	250	8.8	126	4.5	2	0.1	3,110	109.9
Total	**58,577**		**133,978**		**10,221**		**1,009,904**	
Percent		**6.6**		**15.1**		**1.2**		**114.1**

Based on data from 51 states.

SOURCE: "Table 3–10. Victims by Age Group and Maltreatment Type, 2006," in *Child Maltreatment 2006*, U.S. Department of Health and Human Services, Administration for Children, Youth and Families, 2008, http://www.acf.hhs.gov/programs/cb/pubs/cm06/cm06.pdf (accessed November 11, 2008)

and 6.6% were emotionally or psychologically maltreated. (See Table 7.3.) The highest rate of victimization was among infants (24.4 per 1,000 children), followed by children aged one to three years (14.2 per 1,000), and children four to seven years of age (13.5 per 1,000). (See Figure 7.3.) The rate of occurrence decreased as the child's age increased.

The most tragic result of child maltreatment is death. The ACYF indicates that in 2006 an estimated 1,530 children died as a result of abuse or neglect. Children in the youngest age groups were the most likely to die of maltreatment; 78% of the children who died were three years old or younger.

The largest group of abusers were mothers acting alone (39.9%) followed by fathers acting alone (17.6%). (See Figure 7.4.) Abuse of children was overwhelmingly perpetrated by parents; only 10% of perpetrators were not parents. Parental abuse is probably the most devastating of all abuse, because child victims have absolutely no place to turn for help or support.

Missing Children

In the 1980s, as a result of several high-profile abductions and tragedies, the media focused public attention on the problem of missing children. Citizens became concerned and demanded action to address what appeared to be a national crisis. Attempting to discover the nature and

FIGURE 7.3

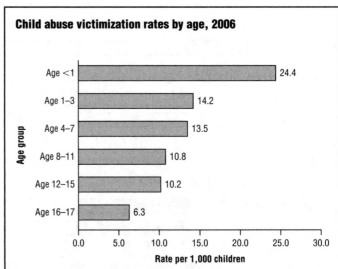

Child abuse victimization rates by age, 2006

SOURCE: "Figure 3-3. Victimization Rates by Age Group, 2006," in *Child Maltreatment 2006*, U.S. Department of Health and Human Services, Administration for Children, Youth and Families, 2008, http://www.acf.hhs.gov/programs/cb/pubs/cm06/cm06.pdf (accessed November 11, 2008)

dimension of the problem, Congress passed the Missing Children's Assistance Act of 1984. The legislation mandated the Office of Juvenile Justice and Delinquency Prevention (OJJDP) to conduct national incidence studies

FIGURE 7.4

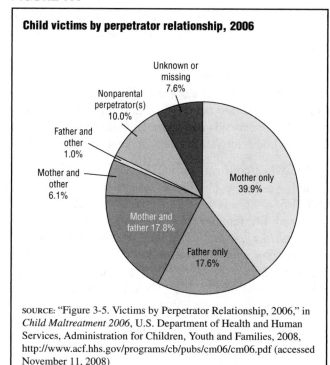

Child victims by perpetrator relationship, 2006

Unknown or missing 7.6%

Nonparental perpetrator(s) 10.0%

Father and other 1.0%

Mother and other 6.1%

Mother only 39.9%

Mother and father 17.8%

Father only 17.6%

SOURCE: "Figure 3-5. Victims by Perpetrator Relationship, 2006," in *Child Maltreatment 2006*, U.S. Department of Health and Human Services, Administration for Children, Youth and Families, 2008, http://www.acf.hhs.gov/programs/cb/pubs/cm06/cm06.pdf (accessed November 11, 2008)

to determine the number of juveniles who were "victims of abduction by strangers" and the number of children who were victims of "parental kidnapping." The result was the National Incidence Studies of Missing, Abducted, Runaway, and Thrownaway Children (NISMART), the first of which was conducted in 1988, with the results published in 1990. The second and more recent NISMART was conducted mainly in 1999, with many of the data published in a series of reports in October 2002.

FAMILY ABDUCTIONS. According to Heather Hammer, David Finkelhor, and Andrea J. Sedlak of the OJJDP, in *Children Abducted by Family Members: National Estimates and Characteristics* (October 2002, http://www.ncjrs.gov/html/ojjdp/nismart/02/index.html), a family abduction is "the taking or keeping of a child by a family member in violation of a custody order, a decree, or other legitimate custodial rights, where the taking or keeping involved some element of concealment, flight, or intent to deprive a lawful custodian indefinitely of custodial privileges." In 1999, 203,900 children were victims of a family abduction. About half (53%) of these were abducted by biological fathers, and 25% by biological mothers. Most family-abducted children were not missing for long— 46% were gone less than a week, and only 21% were away a month or more. Nearly four out of 10 (42%) were abducted from a single-parent family. At the time the survey was done, 91% of the children had been returned, 6% had been located but not returned, and less than 1% had not been located or returned (there was no information on outcomes for 2% of cases).

NONFAMILY ABDUCTIONS. Even though far fewer children are abducted by strangers than by family members, the consequences are often far worse. Violence, the use of force or weapons, sexual assault, and murder are more prevalent in nonfamily abductions. David Finkelhor, Heather Hammer, and Andrea J. Sedlak of the OJJDP state in *Nonfamily Abducted Children: National Estimates and Characteristics* (October 2002, http://www.ncjrs.gov/html/ojjdp/nismart/03/index.html) that 58,200 children were abducted by nonfamily members in 1999. Nearly half (46%) of these were sexually assaulted by their abductors. Only 115 of the abductions were "stereotypical kidnappings," in which a child was abducted by a slight acquaintance or stranger, detained overnight, transported 50 miles or more, held for ransom or with intention to keep permanently, or killed. Most nonfamily abducted children (59%) were 15 to 17 years old and 65% were female. The perpetrators were strangers 37% of the time and were three times as likely to be male as female. Most perpetrators (67%) were aged 13 to 29. Most nonfamily abducted children (91%) were away for 24 hours or less, and 99% returned alive. The remaining 1% were either killed or had not been located at the time of the survey.

RUNAWAYS AND THROWNAWAYS. In *Runaway/Thrownaway Children: National Estimates and Characteristics* (October 2002, http://www.ncjrs.gov/html/ojjdp/nismart/04/), Hammer, Finkelhor, and Sedlak note that runaways are children who meet at least one of the following criteria:

- A child who leaves home without permission and stays away overnight

- A child 14 years old (or older and mentally incompetent) who is away from home, chooses not to come home when expected to, and stays away overnight

- A child 15 years old or older who is away from home, chooses not to come home, and stays away two nights

In the 1970s the term *throwaways* or *thrownaways* was given by researchers to juveniles who were made to leave home or were abandoned. A thrownaway child meets one of the following criteria:

- A child who is asked or told to leave home by a parent or other household adult, with no adequate alternative care arranged for the child by a household adult, and who is out of the household overnight

- A child who is away from home and is prevented from returning home by a parent or other household adult, with no adequate alternative care arranged for by a household adult, and who is out of the household overnight

The OJJDP now combines its estimates of runaways and thrownaways. According to Hammer, Finkelhor, and Sedlak, 1.7 million youths had a runaway/thrownaway episode in 1999. The runaway episode was thought to indicate that 1.2 million of these children were endangered in the following ways:

- The child had been physically or sexually abused at home in the year before the episode or was afraid of abuse upon return (21%)

- The child was substance dependent (19%)

- The child was 13 years old or younger (18%)

- The child was in the company of someone known to be abusing drugs (18%)

- The child was using hard drugs (17%)

Most runaway/thrownaway youth (68%) were 15 years old or older, and half were females. Most runaways (77%) were away less than one week, and more than 99% returned. An estimated 38,600 of the runaways were at risk of sexual endangerment (assault, attempted assault, or prostitution) while away from home.

Murder Victims

According to the BJS, homicide rates for all age groups have been declining since the mid-1990s. (See Figure 7.1.) Even though violent crime has diminished, it still plays a significant role as a cause of death for youth. However, Melonie P. Heron et al. of the CDC indicate in "Deaths: Preliminary Data for 2006" (*National Vital Statistics Report*, vol. 56, no. 16, June 11, 2008) that in 2006 the leading cause of death among both males and females under the age of 24 was accidents. Of the leading causes of death in 2006, homicides and suicides accounted for many abbreviated lives as well, and these deaths increased in number among older youth.

The homicide death rate for infants under age one was quite high at 6.8 per 100,000 in 2006. After that age, the homicide death rate declined to 2.1 per 100,000 among one- to four-year-olds and 1 per 100,000 five- to 14-year-olds. The homicide death rate rose again after age 14.

UCR data confirm that murder victims are disproportionately young people. Out of 14,831 murder victims in 2007, 1,554 victims were under age 18, including 1,070 males and 482 females. (See Table 7.4.) The number of young murder victims more than doubled when looking at all victims aged 21 and under. Of the 3,758 murder victims in this age range, 2,996 were male and 758 were female. One out of 10 (10.5%) murder victims was under age 18, and a quarter (25.3%) was under age 22.

African-Americans are also disproportionately victims of homicide. Nearly equal numbers of whites (6,948) and African-Americans (7,316) were murdered in 2007, even though whites far outnumber African-Americans in the general population, according to the U.S. Census Bureau (April 30, 2008, http://www.census.gov/popest/national/asrh/NC-EST2007-asrh.html). (See Table 7.4.) Of victims under age

TABLE 7.4

Murder victims, by age, sex, and race, 2007

Age	Total	Sex			Race			
		Male	Female	Unknown	White	Black	Other	Unknown
Total	14,831	11,618	3,177	36	6,948	7,316	345	222
Percent distribution[a]	100.0	78.3	21.4	0.2	46.8	49.3	2.3	1.5
Under 18[b]	1,554	1,070	482	2	752	740	40	22
Under 22[b]	3,758	2,996	758	4	1,594	2,035	80	49
18 and over[b]	13,013	10,367	2,641	5	6,089	6,482	301	141
Infant (under 1)	210	116	93	1	139	57	9	5
1 to 4	322	162	159	1	169	142	6	5
5 to 8	88	47	41	0	55	28	4	1
9 to 12	75	39	36	0	39	30	4	2
13 to 16	487	380	107	0	206	265	9	7
17 to 19	1,443	1,272	171	0	538	867	23	15
20 to 24	2,733	2,355	374	4	1,091	1,555	58	29
25 to 29	2,215	1,871	344	0	871	1,284	36	24
30 to 34	1,651	1,366	285	0	735	860	40	16
35 to 39	1,243	949	293	1	575	622	32	14
40 to 44	1,127	787	340	0	596	476	36	19
45 to 49	960	689	271	0	544	381	25	10
50 to 54	698	522	176	0	422	261	11	4
55 to 59	451	338	113	0	268	164	16	3
60 to 64	292	202	90	0	196	80	13	3
65 to 69	181	123	58	0	111	57	11	2
70 to 74	130	84	46	0	96	30	3	1
75 and over	261	135	126	0	190	63	5	3
Unknown	264	181	54	29	107	94	4	59

[a]Because of rounding, the percentages may not add to 100.0.
[b]Does not include unknown ages.

SOURCE: "Expanded Homicide Data Table 2. Murder Victims by Age, Sex, and Race, 2007," in *Crime in the United States, 2007*, U.S. Department of Justice, Federal Bureau of Investigation, September 2008, http://www.fbi.gov/ucr/cius2007/offenses/expanded_information/data/shrtable_02.html (accessed November 11, 2008)

18, 752 were white and 740 were African-American. One out of 10 (10.8%) white victims as well as one out of 10 (10.1%) African-American victims were under age 18; 22.9% of white victims and 27.8% of African-American victims were under age 22. Homicide has been and is the leading cause of death for African-American teenagers, both male and female, although victimization rates for African-American teens declined dramatically between the early 1990s and 2000.

VICTIM-OFFENDER RELATIONSHIP. Snyder and Sickmund state that the most frequent killers of children under age six were their parents, whereas parents were less likely to be involved in the murder of teens aged 15 to 17, although this varied by gender of the child. (See Table 7.5.) Almost two-thirds (61%) of all female juveniles killed were murdered by a parent or stepparent, compared to only 26% of male juveniles. Half (50%) of all male juveniles killed were murdered by an acquaintance, compared to only 29% of female juveniles. Females were also less likely than males to be murdered by a stranger (3% and 18%, respectively).

The risk of being killed by a parent decreased with age—62% of murder victims aged five and younger were killed by a parent or stepparent, compared to 40% of children aged six to 11, 11% of children aged 12 to 14, and 3% of children aged 15 to 17. (See Table 7.5.) The risk of being killed by an acquaintance or a stranger, however, increased with age. About a quarter (28%) of children under age six were killed by an acquaintance, compared to 66% of 15- to 17-year-olds; only 3% of the youngest children were killed by strangers, compared to 25% of 15- to 17-year-olds.

WEAPONS USED IN MURDERS OF JUVENILES. According to Snyder and Sickmund, the number of youths dying as a result of firearms increased 152% between 1985 and 1993 before declining. Even though the number of homicides involving no firearm declined very little between 1993 and 2002, a huge drop in the number of homicides involving a firearm resulted in the overall number of juvenile homicides falling to the lowest level since 1984 in 2002. Nonetheless, almost half (48%) of all juveniles murdered in 2002 were killed with a firearm. Another 22% were beaten/kicked to death or strangled, and 11% were killed with a knife or blunt object. The remaining 19% were killed with another type of weapon, or the type of weapon used was unknown.

The FBI reports that these trends continued in 2007; firearms were used in most murders of juveniles and young adults in that year. Of 1,554 murder victims under the age of 18, 806 (51.9%) were killed with firearms. (See Table 7.6.) Of 3,758 murder victims who were under the age of 22, 2,642 (70.3%) were killed with firearms. A low proportion of the youngest murder victims were killed by firearms, but that proportion rose with age. The most firearms-related murders were in the 20 to 24 age group (2,733 deaths). However, the greatest percentage of firearms-related murders was among those aged 17 to 19 (1,229 of 1,443 murders, or 85.2%). Other weapons most frequently used to kill juveniles included personal weapons—hands, feet, fists, and so on, especially among the youngest children—and knives.

Rape

For several reasons, the statistics on rape are incomplete. The crime often goes unreported. The BJS estimates that only about one-third of the cases of completed or attempted rape are ever reported to police; other organizations estimate that the proportion of reported rapes is even lower. Because its data are collected through interviews, the BJS recognizes an underreporting in its statistics as well. Acquaintance rape is far more common than stranger rape. Most experts conclude that in 80% to 85% of all rape cases, the victim knows the rapist.

TABLE 7.5

Offender relationship to juvenile homicide victims, by age and gender of victims, 1980–2002

Offender relationship to victim	Age of victim					Victim ages 0–17	
	0–17	0–5	6–11	12–14	15–17	Males	Females
Offender known	74%	88%	81%	72%	64%	72%	88%
Total	100%	100%	100%	100%	100%	100%	100%
Parent/stepparent	31	62	40	11	3	26	61
Other family member	7	7	15	11	5	6	7
Acquaintance	47	28	30	58	66	50	29
Stranger	15	3	15	20	25	18	3
Offender unknown	26%	12%	19%	28%	36%	28%	12%

Over the 23-year period, strangers were involved in *at least* 15% of the murders of juveniles. This figure is probably greater than 15% because strangers are likely to account for a disproportionate share of crimes in which the offender is unknown.
Note: Detail may not total 100% because of rounding.

SOURCE: Howard N. Snyder and Melissa Sickmund, "Of the 46,600 Juveniles Murdered between 1980 and 2002, Most Victims under Age 6 Were Killed by a Parent, While Parents Were Rarely Involved in the Killing of Juveniles Ages 15–17," in *Juvenile Offenders and Victims: 2006 National Report*, U.S. Department of Justice, Office of Justice Programs, Office of Juvenile Justice and Delinquency Prevention, March 2006, http://www.ojjdp.ncjrs.gov/ojstatbb/nr2006/downloads/NR2006.pdf (accessed November 11, 2008)

TABLE 7.6

Murder victims by age and weapon, 2007

Age	Total murder victims	Firearms	Knives or cutting instruments	Blunt objects (clubs, hammers, etc.)	Personal weapons (hands, fists, feet, etc.)[a]	Poison	Explosives	Fire	Narcotics	Strangulation	Asphyxiation	Other weapon or weapon not stated[b]
												Weapons
Total	14,831	10,086	1,796	647	854	10	1	130	49	134	108	1,016
Percent distribution[c]	100.0	68.0	12.1	4.4	5.8	0.1	*	0.9	0.3	0.9	0.7	6.9
Under 18[d]	1,554	806	127	61	303	4	0	25	14	22	33	159
Under 22[d]	3,758	2,642	307	98	345	4	0	30	19	36	38	239
18 and over[d]	13,013	9,148	1,655	573	528	6	1	97	35	110	73	787
Infant (under 1)	210	9	4	9	122	0	0	3	3	4	15	41
1 to 4	322	35	9	32	143	0	0	8	6	7	10	72
5 to 8	88	35	9	4	14	1	0	6	1	4	5	9
9 to 12	75	36	11	3	8	2	0	4	1	1	1	8
13 to 16	487	376	62	8	11	1	0	3	1	3	2	20
17 to 19	1,443	1,229	110	24	22	0	0	2	6	8	1	41
20 to 24	2,733	2,234	243	45	59	1	1	8	7	13	10	112
25 to 29	2,215	1,773	206	41	51	0	0	11	2	24	10	97
30 to 34	1,651	1,254	206	35	41	0	0	17	3	10	5	80
35 to 39	1,243	821	199	64	56	1	0	6	4	7	8	77
40 to 44	1,127	697	169	73	60	0	0	17	3	16	8	84
45 to 49	960	547	175	67	61	1	0	9	2	11	9	78
50 to 54	698	360	126	57	66	1	0	6	5	6	9	62
55 to 59	451	202	85	55	39	1	0	9	0	5	0	55
60 to 64	292	129	56	43	25	0	0	2	1	0	4	32
65 to 69	181	83	33	28	11	0	0	3	0	4	0	19
70 to 74	130	62	28	9	12	0	0	3	0	0	2	14
75 and over	261	72	51	37	30	1	0	5	4	9	7	45
Unknown	264	132	14	13	23	0	0	8	0	2	2	70

[a]Pushed is included in personal weapons.
[b]Includes drowning.
[c]Because of rounding, the percentages may not add to 100.0.
[d]Does not include unknown ages.
*Less than one-tenth of 1 percent.

SOURCE: "Expanded Homicide Data Table 8. Murder Victims by Age, by Weapon, 2007," in *Crime in the United States, 2007*, U.S. Department of Justice, Federal Bureau of Investigation, September 2008, http://www.fbi.gov/ucr/cius2007/offenses/expanded_information/data/shrtable_08.html (accessed November 11, 2008)

The UCR defines forcible rape as "the carnal knowledge of a female forcibly and against her will. Assaults and attempts to commit rape by force or threat of force are also included; however, statutory rape (without force) [sex with a consenting minor] and other sex offenses are excluded." Rape is a crime of violence in which the victim may suffer serious physical injury and long-term psychological pain. In 2007 the UCR recorded 90,427 reported rape offenses, a decrease of 2.5% from the year before. The rate of forcible rapes was reported at a rate of 59.1 offenses per 100,000 females.

Rape victims are disproportionately young. According to the BJS, in 2006 females aged 12 to 15 experienced the highest rates (6.4 per 1,000 people), followed by older teens aged 16 to 19 (4.3 per 1,000 people). (See Table 7.7.) Furthermore, the BJS finds that in 2006 only 33.9% of those aged 12 to 19 who acknowledged being victims of rape/sexual assault reported the incident to police. (See Table 7.8.)

Aggravated and Simple Assault

In *Criminal Victimization in the United States, 2006 Statistical Tables* (August 2008, http://www.ojp.usdoj.gov/bjs/pub/pdf/cvus06.pdf), the BJS reports that in 2006 aggravated assault was most common among young people. It occurred at a rate of 8.3 per 1,000 teens aged 12 to 15, 11.6 per 1,000 teens aged 16 to 19, and 11.9 per 1,000 teens aged 20 to 24. After that age the rate began to decline. Among white males, those aged 20 to 24 experienced the highest rate of aggravated assault (12.2 per 1,000 people), whereas among African-American males, 25- to 34-year-olds experienced the highest rate (31 per 1,000 people). (See Table 7.9.) African-American women in the 20 to 24 age group experienced the highest rate (16.1 per 1,000 people) as did white women in the 20 to 24 age group (11.7 per 1,000 people).

The BJS notes that in 2006 simple assault occurred at a rate of 31.3 per 1,000 teens aged 12 to 15, 33.1 per 1,000 teens aged 16 to 19, and 23.2 per 1,000 teens aged 20 to 24, after which the rate began to decline. Younger African-American males had a higher simple assault victimization rate than did white males in the same age group. For example, African-American males aged 16 to 19 had a simple assault rate of 46.8 per 1,000 people, compared to the rate of 26.9 among white males of that age. (See Table 7.9.)

TABLE 7.7

Victimization rates for persons age 12 and over, by gender and age of victims and type of crime, 2006

Gender and age	Total population	Crimes of violence	Completed violence	Attempted/ threatened violence	Rape/Sexual assault[a]	Robbery			Assault			Purse snatching/ pocket picking
						Total	With injury	Without injury	Total	Aggravated	Simple	
Male												
12–15	8,693,790	47.5	17.5	30.0	0.5*	3.6*	0.8*	2.8*	43.4	9.0	34.4	1.2*
16–19	8,495,570	53.7	16.2	37.5	0.7*	8.0	1.7*	6.2	45.0	14.5	30.5	1.2*
20–24	10,247,690	46.8	15.9	30.9	0.0*	9.3	2.4*	6.9	37.5	11.5	25.9	1.0*
25–34	20,079,860	38.2	13.9	24.2	0.3*	6.4	3.1	3.3	31.5	9.4	22.1	0.7*
35–49	32,607,930	19.4	4.1	15.3	0.3*	2.1	0.3*	1.8	17.0	4.7	12.2	1.0*
50–64	25,144,830	15.7	4.1	11.6	0.1*	2.1	1.2*	0.9*	13.5	3.1	10.4	0.3*
65 and over	15,196,130	5.0	1.4*	3.5	0.0*	1.4*	0.5*	0.8*	3.6	1.2*	2.4	0.1*
Female												
12–15	8,208,130	46.3	16.2	30.1	6.4	4.4*	1.7*	2.6*	35.5	7.5	28.0	0.5*
16–19	8,185,810	49.8	17.8	31.9	4.3*	1.1*	0.7*	0.4*	44.3	8.5	35.8	0.9*
20–24	10,123,690	41.6	15.9	25.7	3.6	5.3	2.9*	2.4*	32.7	12.3	20.4	0.7*
25–34	19,836,350	33.8	11.5	22.4	2.5	2.7	1.1*	1.6*	28.7	6.0	22.7	0.5*
35–49	33,263,020	20.0	7.4	12.6	1.0*	1.9	0.7*	1.2	17.1	4.7	12.4	0.8*
50–64	26,769,110	10.9	3.8	7.1	1.0*	0.5*	0.0*	0.5*	9.4	1.9	7.5	0.5*
65 and over	20,381,170	2.1	0.7*	1.4*	0.0*	0.9*	0.1*	0.8*	1.2*	0.3*	0.9*	0.9*

Rate per 1,000 persons in each age group

Note: Due to changes in methodology, the 2006 national crime victimization rates are not comparable to previous years and cannot be used for yearly trend comparisons. However, the overall patterns of victimization at the national level can be examined. Detail may not add to total shown because of rounding.
*Estimate is based on 10 or fewer sample cases.
[a]Includes verbal threats of rape and threats of sexual assault.

SOURCE: "Table 4. Personal Crimes, 2006: Victimization Rates for Persons Age 12 and over, by Gender and Age of Victims and Type of Crime," in *Criminal Victimization in the United States, 2006 Statistical Tables,* U.S. Department of Justice, Office of Justice Programs, Bureau of Justice Statistics, August 2008, http://www.ojp.usdoj.gov/bjs/pub/pdf/cvus06.pdf (accessed November 11, 2008)

TABLE 7.8

Percent of victimizations reported to police by type of crime and age of victims, 2006

	Percent of victimizations reported to the police				
Type of crime	12–19	20–34	35–49	50–64	65 and over
All personal crimes	**34.3 %**	**52.9 %**	**56.0 %**	**54.9 %**	**63.4 %**
Crimes of violence	34.6	52.6	55.8	54.5	64.6
Completed violence	54.7	62.7	74.2	61.3	69.8*
Attempted/threatened violence	24.1	47.0	48.1	51.5	62.3
Rape/sexual assault[a]	33.9*	51.6	46.8*	44.6*	0.0*
Robbery	40.3	58.8	62.6	60.9	74.8*
Completed/property taken	46.9	57.6	68.5	62.9*	81.1*
With injury	58.2*	58.3	75.2*	54.2*	100.0*
Without injury	37.6*	57.1	65.2	74.2*	78.7*
Attempted to take property	31.5*	61.3	43.3*	52.8*	65.8*
With injury	100.0*	54.2*	0.0*	0.0*	100.0*
Without injury	26.2*	64.3	43.3*	52.8*	38.6*
Assault	34.1	51.6	55.3	54.2	59.6
Aggravated	47.3	63.1	63.0	65.8	73.3*
With injury	74.6	79.4	72.5	65.1*	100.0*
Threatened with weapon	32.2	51.9	59.3	66.1	69.3*
Simple	30.1	46.9	52.4	51.0	53.9*
With minor injury	49.7	58.1	83.8	60.6	34.7*
Without injury	22.4	43.3	44.6	48.3	58.0*
Purse snatching/pocket picking	17.1*	72.2*	60.2*	68.8*	56.6*

Note: Many incident characteristics were unaffected or minimally affected by changes in methodology in the 2006 National Crime Victimization Survey. However, caution should be used in comparing 2006 rates of individual variables, particularly those with small sample sizes, to previous years.
*Estimate is based on 10 or fewer sample cases.
[a]Includes verbal threats of rape and threats of sexual assault.

SOURCE: "Table 96. Personal Crimes, 2006: Percent of Victimizations Reported to the Police, by Type of Crime and Age of Victims," in *Criminal Victimization in the United States, 2006 Statistical Tables*, U.S. Department of Justice, Office of Justice Programs, Bureau of Justice Statistics, August 2008, http://www.ojp.usdoj.gov/bjs/pub/pdf/cvus06.pdf (accessed November 11, 2008)

Robbery and Theft

The BJS reports in *Criminal Victimization in the United States, 2006 Statistical Tables* that in 2006 robbery occurred at a rate of 4 per 1,000 teens aged 12 to 15, 4.6 per 1,000 teens aged 16 to 19, and 7.3 per 1,000 teens aged 20 to 24, after which age the rate began to decline. Young males, both white and African-American, had high rates of robbery victimization. (See Table 7.9.)

TABLE 7.9

Violent victimization rates for persons age 12 and over, by race, gender, and age of victims and type of crime, 2006

Race, gender, and age	Total population	Crimes of violence[a]		Robbery		Aggravated assault		Simple assault	
		Number	Rate	Number	Rate	Number	Rate	Number	Rate
White only									
Male									
12–15	6,544,640	306,470	46.8	31,600*	4.8*	53,060	8.1	217,830	33.3
16–19	6,580,880	321,020	48.8	52,750	8.0	85,300	13.0	177,050	26.9
20–24	8,236,420	418,000	50.8	80,380	9.8	100,800	12.2	236,810	28.8
25–34	16,004,580	546,800	34.2	96,530	6.0	83,300	5.2	361,560	22.6
35–49	26,889,110	536,880	20.0	58,220	2.2	119,560	4.4	348,990	13.0
50–64	21,404,540	341,850	16.0	46,180	2.2	69,610	3.3	223,510	10.4
65 and over	13,341,160	72,250	5.4	20,600*	1.5*	17,770*	1.3*	33,880*	2.5*
Female									
12–15	6,258,480	285,930	45.7	29,510*	4.7*	46,790	7.5	173,950	27.8
16–19	6,245,950	302,620	48.5	3,120*	0.5*	40,130	6.4	233,470	37.4
20–24	7,810,160	318,080	40.7	39,900	5.1	91,660	11.7	161,160	20.6
25–34	15,364,100	483,600	31.5	30,460*	2.0*	76,890	5.0	334,710	21.8
35–49	26,640,800	484,440	18.2	46,190	1.7	102,770	3.9	302,160	11.3
50–64	22,337,200	249,060	11.1	10,550*	0.5*	40,930	1.8	175,760	7.9
65 and over	17,689,080	30,490*	1.7*	10,850*	0.6*	5,410*	0.3*	14,230*	0.8*
Black only									
Male									
12–15	1,453,470	69,890	48.1	0*	0.0*	11,960*	8.2*	57,930	39.9
16–19	1,269,160	95,000	74.9	9,420*	7.4*	26,230*	20.7*	59,350	46.8
20–24	1,194,640	48,730	40.8	15,240*	12.8*	4,460*	3.7*	29,030*	24.3*
25–34	2,475,000	150,390	60.8	15,320*	6.2*	76,670	31.0	58,410	23.6
35–49	3,706,580	65,820	17.8	10,240*	2.8*	34,990*	9.4*	20,580*	5.6*
50–64	2,440,920	39,230	16.1	6,510*	2.7*	7,930*	3.3*	24,790*	10.2*
65 and over	1,146,260	3,300*	2.9*	0*	0.0*	0*	0.0*	3,300*	2.9*
Female									
12–15	1,318,550	66,710	50.6	6,270*	4.8*	6,870*	5.2*	36,420*	27.6*
16–19	1,256,840	69,220	55.1	5,970*	4.8*	16,450*	13.1*	37,330	29.7
20–24	1,487,560	69,860	47.0	7,900*	5.3*	23,920*	16.1*	35,360*	23.8*
25–34	2,912,690	130,230	44.7	22,790*	7.8*	36,560	12.6	66,460	22.8
35–49	4,436,600	115,040	25.9	5,430*	1.2*	34,940*	7.9*	74,680	16.8
50–64	3,037,860	30,090*	9.9*	3,530*	1.2*	8,120*	2.7*	18,440*	6.1*
65 and over	1,836,090	8,960*	4.9*	4,250*	2.3*	0*	0.0*	4,700*	2.6*

Note: Due to changes in methodology, the 2006 national crime victimization rates are not comparable to previous years and cannot be used for yearly trend comparisons. However, the overall patterns of victimization at the national level can be examined.
Excludes data on persons of "Other" races and persons indicating two or more races.
*Estimate is based on 10 or fewer sample cases.
[a]Includes data on rape and sexual assault, not shown separately.

SOURCE: "Table 10. Violent Crimes, 2006: Number of Victimizations and Victimization Rates for Persons Age 12 and over, by Race, Gender, and Age of Victims and Type of Crime," in *Criminal Victimization in the United States, 2006 Statistical Tables*, U.S. Department of Justice, Office of Justice Programs, Bureau of Justice Statistics, August 2008, http://www.ojp.usdoj.gov/bjs/pub/pdf/cvus06.pdf (accessed November 11, 2008)

CHAPTER 8

VIOLENCE AND GANGS

THE SCOPE OF THE GANG PROBLEM

Gangs have a long history in the United States, dating back to the 1800s. The United States became a so-called melting pot in the nineteenth century as people of diverse ethnicities and religions entered the country. Some immigrants joined gangs to help them gain a group identity, defend themselves against other groups, and establish a unified presence. Even though people feared street gangs of the nineteenth century, the gangs of the twenty-first century pose a greater threat to public safety than in years past.

Most criminal activities of the street gangs of the early twentieth century involved delinquent acts or petty crimes, such as brawls with rival gangs. As the twentieth century progressed, however, gangs began getting involved with more serious crimes. By the late twentieth century, law enforcement officials had come to regard gang members in general as serious criminals who engaged in the illegal trafficking of drugs or weapons and used intimidation tactics and violence to pursue their goals. Respondents to the National Youth Gang Survey (NYGS) emphasized that a gang was defined by involvement in group criminal activity along with some degree of definition of a group as a separate entity, such as having a name, displaying distinct colors or symbols, or engaging in activities to protect the group's territory. Law enforcement officers note that in the 1980s and 1990s more and more gang members began to support themselves through dealing drugs, such as crack cocaine and heroin. Many were said to have easy access to high-powered weapons. In addition, the proliferation of gangs in the late twentieth century meant that groups moved beyond city boundaries into suburban and rural areas as well. This movement into new territories occurred about the same time that youth violence surged in the 1980s and early 1990s.

Researchers noted various reasons for the growth of gangs during the end of the twentieth century. According to Finn-Aage Esbensen of the University of Nebraska, in

Preventing Adolescent Gang Involvement (September 2000, http://www.ncjrs.gov/pdffiles1/ojjdp/182210.pdf), "American society witnessed a reemergence of youth gang activity and media interest in this phenomenon in the 1980's and 1990's. 'Colors,' 'Boyz n the Hood,' other Hollywood productions, and MTV brought Los Angeles, California, gang life to suburban and rural America." These media portrayals might have further enticed youth to become involved in gangs.

In an effort to track the growth and activities of gangs, the Office of Juvenile Justice and Delinquency Prevention's (OJJDP) National Youth Gang Center (NYGC) began conducting the NYGS in 1996. Arlen Egley Jr. and Christina E. O'Donnell of the NYGC note in *Highlights of the 2006 National Youth Gang Survey* (July 2008, http://www.ncjrs.gov/pdffiles1/ojjdp/fs200805.pdf) that for purposes of the survey, researchers annually query all police and sheriff departments serving cities and counties with populations of 50,000 or more (25,000 or more before 2002), as well as all suburban county police and sheriff's departments. Because gang membership has moved beyond large metropolitan areas, the NYGS also queries a random sample of law enforcement agencies in cities with populations between 2,500 and 25,000 and in rural counties. Not all jurisdictions that receive the survey respond, but a solid majority do. Survey participants are instructed to provide information on youth gangs within their jurisdictions. Motorcycle gangs, prison gangs, adult gangs, and hate or ideology-based groups are not included in the sample.

Statistics about gang membership show that the increased concern about gangs had its basis in the growth of gangs during the 1990s. According to Walter B. Miller of the OJJDP, in *The Growth of Youth Gang Problems in the United States: 1970–1998* (April 2001, http://www.ncjrs.gov/pdffiles1/ojjdp/181868-1.pdf), during the 1970s about 1% of U.S. cities and about 40% of the states reported having problems with youth gangs. By the late 1990s the percentage of U.S. cities with gang problems grew to 7%, and youth gangs were

TABLE 8.1

Percentage of law enforcement agencies reporting gang problems, 2002–06

	Gang problems reported in 2006 (%)	Gang problems ever reported, 2002–2006 (%)
Rural counties	14.9	27.4
Smaller cities	32.6	48.3
Suburban counties	51.0	61.5
Larger cities	86.4	90.5
Overall estimate in study population	33.3	47.3

SOURCE: "Table 1. Percentage of Law Enforcement Agencies Reporting Gang Problems, 2002–2006," in *Highlights of the 2006 National Youth Gang Survey*, U.S. Department of Justice, Office of Justice Programs, Office of Juvenile Justice and Delinquency Prevention, July 2008, http://www.ncjrs.gov/pdffiles1/ojjdp/fs200805.pdf (accessed November 11, 2008)

reported in all 50 states and the District of Columbia. Gang growth in cities soared in the 1980s and 1990s, with the number of gangs reported increasing by 281%. Between 1995 and 1998 gang activity was recorded in 1,100 cities and 450 counties where it had not been reported previously.

At first, gangs tended to be big-city problems—the NYGS indicated that most cities with populations over 100,000 reported that the proliferation of gangs became a problem between 1985 and the early 1990s. After that time, however, gangs spread to smaller areas. It is true that the larger the population, the greater the likelihood of the existence of gangs in that area. Nine out of 10 (90.5%) law enforcement agencies in larger cities reported gang problems between 2002 and 2006. (See Table 8.1.) However, nearly half (48.3%) of all cities with a population of 2,500 to 49,999, nearly two-thirds (61.5%) of all suburban counties, and over a quarter (27.4%) of rural counties reported gang problems in their jurisdictions during this same period.

The huge growth in gangs and gang membership slowed in the late 1990s. Comparing statistics between the 1996 and 2000 surveys, Arlen Egley Jr. of the NYGC finds in the fact sheet "National Youth Gang Survey Trends from 1996 to 2000" (February 2002, http://www.ncjrs.gov/pdffiles1/ojjdp/fs200203.pdf) that "the proportion of respondents that reported youth gangs in their jurisdiction decreased over the survey years, from 53 percent in 1996 to 40 percent in 2000." In 2006, 33.3% of jurisdictions reported gang problems. (See Table 8.1.) In *National Youth Gang Survey, 1999–2001* (July 2006, http://www.ncjrs.gov/pdffiles1/ojjdp/209392.pdf), Arlen Egley Jr., James C. Howell, and Aline K. Major of the NYGC estimate that there were approximately 21,500 gangs present in the United States in 2002. These numbers increased again by 2006. In that year, Egley and O'Donnell indicate that approximately 26,500 gangs with 785,000 gang members were active in the United States.

CHARACTERISTICS OF GANGS

According to the *2005 National Gang Threat Assessment* (2005, http://www.ojp.usdoj.gov/BJA/what/2005_threat_assesment.pdf), by the U.S. Department of Justice, the Bureau of Justice Assistance, and the National Alliance of Gang Investigators Associations, the modern street gang, or youth gang as they are often called, takes many forms. Individual members, gang cliques, or entire gang organizations engage in trafficking in drugs; operating car theft rings; committing homicides, assaults, robberies, and other felonies; and terrorizing neighborhoods. Some of the most ambitious gangs spread out from their home jurisdictions to other cities and states. Yet, some of the movement occurs simply because the gang members' families move to other areas, especially during times of economic growth. However, many gang members come from impoverished, immigrant, or transitional neighborhoods, where children are born into or must contend with second- and third-generation street gangs.

David Starbuck, James C. Howell, and Donna J. Lindquist examine in *Hybrid and Other Modern Gangs* (December 2001, http://www.iir.com/nygc/publications/hybrid_and_other_modern_gangs.pdf) survey data and current research to offer a portrait of the modern youth gang. Various stereotypes exist about gangs. For example, the stereotypical view holds that youth gangs are tightly organized groups made up of African-American or Hispanic inner-city males operating under strict codes of conduct with explicit punishments for infractions of the rules. However, the new hybrid gang can have members from both genders and from different racial groups as well as members having radically opposing viewpoints.

According to Starbuck, Howell, and Lindquist, a modern gang might be made up of African-Americans, white supremacists, and females. The gangs are found in schools and the military and in territories as small as shopping malls. Rules or codes of conduct may be unclear. Hybrid gangs sometimes borrow the symbols, graffiti, and even the names of established organizations, such as those based in Los Angeles or Chicago, Illinois (e.g., Bloods, Crips, or Latin Kings), but are actually locally based and have no connection to those organizations. Rival gangs may cooperate in criminal activities, and mergers of small gangs are common.

Starbuck, Howell, and Lindquist note that in places where gangs are a fairly recent phenomenon, drug sales and distribution are less likely to be major problems. Gang member involvement in drug sales is most prevalent in areas where gangs emerged between 1981 and 1985, at the height of the crack cocaine epidemic. The gangs that emerged in the 1960s and 1970s in Los Angeles and Chicago were highly organized and entrepreneurial and had control of drug distribution across wide areas—and the violent crime that went with it.

Specific Gang Characteristics

Researchers, law enforcement, and community groups devote time to learning more about gangs and the types of characteristics they share. Much study has gone into gang slang, graffiti, hand signs, colors, and initiations, among other characteristics. The goal is to learn more about how gangs communicate and interact, both internally and externally, as well as test themselves and each other. If educators, law enforcement officials, and other concerned adults know how to recognize signs that young people may be involved in gangs, they will be better able to intervene.

Various gang members have created their own slang language. Even though some terms are used in gangs throughout the country, others are only used regionally and within certain gangs. Various terms originated with the infamous Bloods and Crips gangs of Los Angeles, who have been adversaries for many years. Examples include "banging" (involved in gang activities); "colors" (clothing of a particular color, such as jackets, shoes, or bandanas, worn by gang members to identify themselves as part of the gang); "O.G." ("original gangster," meaning a gang member who has killed someone, or a founding member or leader of a gang); "tagging" (marking a territory with graffiti); and "turf" (territory).

Graffiti has been a form of communication since ancient times. Meaning "little scratches" in Italian, graffiti appeared in cave dwellings, on Egyptian temples, and on other natural and human-made objects. In the twenty-first century there are several categories of graffiti; each type is used to get the artists' message out to anyone who can read it. Among the various types are personal musings, tagging, piecing or bombing, and gang graffiti.

The most common type of graffiti is that of personal musings—thoughts written down quickly in public places, such as restrooms and phone booths. Sometimes humorous, this type of graffiti might be of a sexual context or might include memorable quotes. Oftentimes, it concerns race relations. The *2005 National Gang Threat Assessment* notes that both the South and the West have a high level of gang involvement in graffiti.

Tagging is another type of graffiti. A tag is a signature, or moniker, that may incorporate the artist's physical features or symbolize his or her personality. Tags are usually found on exterior building walls in urban areas. They may also appear on mass transit systems (buses and trains), freeway overpasses, and other areas for all to see and wonder how it got there. Tagging first appeared on the East Coast in the late 1960s and made its way to the West Coast by the 1980s. Taggers feel a sense of power and fame as more and more surfaces contain their tags.

Mural-type graffiti is known as piecing or bombing. The piece usually contains elaborate depictions or a montage of images. Oftentimes, slogans appear within the piece. Whereas tags can be done quickly, piecing may take up to several hours and require many cans of spray paint in many colors.

Gang graffiti employs all the aforementioned types. Gangs use graffiti for many purposes. In some instances, it may be a way of communicating messages to other gang members, functioning like a newsletter. Tags or monikers may be used to show a gang's hierarchy. Pieces may memorialize a dead gang member or pay tribute to the crimes committed by gang members. Some pieces may enumerate rules in the gang's society, whereas others may advertise a gang's presence in the neighborhood. Gang graffiti may also serve as a threatening message to rival gangs—as if to say, "Stay away from our turf."

In the twenty-first century, all types of graffiti are perceived as vandalism and a public nuisance and are punishable by law in the United States.

HAND SIGNS. Hand signs are a way of communicating concepts or ideas without using words. However, only those individuals who are familiar with the gesture's meaning are able to understand the message being conveyed. The rise of gang hand signs began in the Los Angeles area during the 1950s. Since that time, many gangs have developed hand signs for use between members of the group. Gang members "throw" or "flash" hand signs as a way of communicating among themselves, such as to send secret messages to other members within the group. For example, placing a clenched fist over the heart means, "I'll die for you."

According to *Recognize the Signs* (November 2005, http://www.nj.gov/oag/gang-signs-bro.pdf), by the New Jersey Office of the Attorney General and the Juvenile Justice Commission, each gang usually has a hand sign that symbolizes affiliation with the gang. For example, the Los Angeles Bloods use the sign B (creating a circle with the thumb and index finger, with the other fingers raised) to signify membership in the gang. Crips use a sign that represents the letter C. Even though this is a good way for gang members to recognize other members or affiliates, it can be used against them as well. A gang might use gestures created by a rival gang in an act called false flagging. When this occurs, a gang member will flash a rival gang's hand sign as a way to infiltrate the opposing gang or to lure an unsuspecting adversary into a bad situation.

Most gangs recognize many universal hand signals. One such ubiquitous sign dates back to World War II (1939–1945)—the sign for "victory," made by raising the index and middle fingers in the shape of a V. Gangs use many universal gestures to intimidate or "dis" (disrespect) rival gangs. A raised fist means "power." Raising the index finger shows that the gang is "number one" and can beat all rivals. Gang hand signs may also appear prominently in gang graffiti.

FLYING THE COLORS. The idea of wearing different colors to identify opposing sides is not new. For example, during wartime opposing armies used different colors to symbolize their cause or protect their territory. Flags, uniforms, and the like were made in the color chosen to represent the nation or army at war. By donning the color of the army, soldiers were easily identified as being on one side or the other, and the enemy could be spotted easily. During the American Revolution (1775–1783), most of the British forces wore red uniforms; thus, they were called the Redcoats. To distinguish themselves from the British, the American colonists chose uniforms of blue.

This is also true of gangs. *Recognize the Signs* notes that for many years they have used color to distinguish themselves from rival gangs, while protecting their territory. Gang members often show support for the gang by wearing "uniforms." Sporting clothes in the gang's colors, such as bandanas, shoes, jackets, jewelry, and other articles of clothing, shows a person's membership in one gang over another. For example, the two largest gangs in the Los Angeles area are the Bloods and the Crips. The Bloods use red, and the Crips use blue. Harold O. Levy notes in "The Great Truancy Cover-Up" (*Yale Review*, vol. 96, no. 3, July 2008) that during lunch time members of rival gangs play poker with red and blue playing cards to signify their gang affiliations. These colors are a way to symbolize the gang's unity, power, and pride.

However, "flying the colors" can be a disadvantage to gangs. The *2005 National Gang Threat Assessment* indicates that even though colors make it easier for other gangs to identify rival members, they also help law enforcement and school officials recognize gang members. Law enforcement officials have been able to crack down on gang-related criminal activities by rounding up juveniles and youths wearing gang colors. In response to this new threat, many gangs have opted to forego their traditional colors and are developing new methods of identification. Like the modern-day army, gang members are beginning to camouflage themselves from their rivals, making their "uniforms" less conspicuous. Wearing a hat tilted to the left may show membership in a gang whose rivals are those who wear their pant legs rolled up. Gang members also use hand signs to identify their affiliation to certain groups.

RECRUITMENT AND INITIATION. People tend to organize themselves into groups of like-minded individuals to meet and participate in group-related activities. Groups offer fellowship—a way to bond with others who share similar interests or goals. This is no different for youth. Scouting, athletics, or debate clubs offer ways for kids to meet new friends and participate in various group activities, such as camping, learning crafts, and so on. The group organizers recruit members by offering experiences that a boy or girl might not have unless he or she is a member of the group.

Even though their activities are often criminal and their recruitment tactics highly aggressive, gangs operate in a similar fashion. Gang recruiters offer prospective members a chance to be a part of something—to gain a sense of belonging that might be lacking in their life. Through the use of graffiti, the wearing of colors or tattoos, or intimidation tactics, the gang recruits new members to increase its power. In turn, some juveniles see this power in the schools or on the sides of buildings and may feel pressured into joining a gang. In some instances, gang members threaten the child or members of his or her family into joining, offering protection from bullies or rival gangs. Others might be eager to join a gang, thinking it is cool and exciting to be part of a clique that engages in criminal activity.

In response to gang recruitment activities, some states and localities have changed their laws to make any kind of gang recruitment, even if it does not involve criminal behavior, illegal. For example, in 2007 Illinois proposed to amend its criminal code by making street gang recruitment on school grounds or public property a felony, even if it did not involve the use or threat of physical force. Gang recruitment of any kind is illegal in Virginia, and recruitment of minors is a felony in New York.

As is common in some social clubs, many prospective gang inductees must undergo an initiation to show the members that they are worthy enough to be accepted into the group. "Jumping in" or "clicking in" to a gang usually involves some type of criminal activity for the inductee to perform. This may include stealing or damaging property, assaulting someone, or carrying and selling drugs. More radical forms of gang initiations may involve drive-by shootings or rape. In some instances, the inductee is "beat-down" by gang members using baseball bats or brass knuckles. In rare instances, a new member may be "blessed in" (not having to prove his or her worth) because a brother or sister is already a member of the gang. Some have difficulty trying to leave a gang. In these cases the youth might be pressured to remain in the clique or might be hesitant to leave because his or her friends and family (including parents) are in the gang.

Studies show that in many cases, the modern adolescent may refuse to join a gang or leave it without fear of reprisal, even though gangs try to maintain the illusion that leaving is impossible. Terence P. Thornberry, David Huizinga, and Rolf Leober report in "The Causes and Correlates Studies: Findings and Policy Implications" (*Juvenile Justice*, vol. 9, no. 1, September 2004) that this was borne out by OJJDP-supported longitudinal studies in Denver, Colorado (1988–1999), and Rochester, New York (1986–1997), as well as the Seattle Social Development Project in Washington (1985–2001), all of which showed that more than half (54% to 69%) of youths who joined gangs in those cities remained for one year or less, whereas only 9% to 21% stayed for three or more years. However, Egley, Howell, and Major find that gang membership appears to be getting older, which indicates that youth living in highly disadvantaged areas, where there is an absence of economic opportunity, may remain in gangs to later ages.

INDICATORS OF GANG INVOLVEMENT. Many groups— such as the California Attorney General's Office, Crime and Violence Prevention Center, in *Gangs: A Community Response* (June 2003, http://safestate.org/shop/files/GYV%20Gangs_Comm_Resp_ADA.pdf); Phelan A. Wyrick and James C. Howell, in "Strategic Risk-Based Response to Youth Gangs" (*Juvenile Justice*, vol. 9, no. 1, September 2004); and the Department of Justice, in "A Parent's Quick Reference Card" (2008, http://www.usdoj.gov/usao/wie/justice_for_all/publications/GangCardforParentsEnglish.pdf) —have compiled lists to aid parents, siblings, educators, and others in looking for signs that a youth has joined a gang. Even though a youth may present several warning signs that might indicate he or she is a gang member, these signs are not foolproof—that is, the youth may actually not be a gang member or even be a "wannabe" or "gonnabe" (at-risk youth). However, the more signs that a youth exhibits increases the likelihood that he or she is headed for gang involvement. The following are some of the warning signs:

- Experiences a sudden drop in school grades
- Lacks interest in school and other activities that were once important
- Becomes truant (skips school)
- Comes home late
- Acts more outwardly aggressive or outright defiant
- Develops a new circle of friends who seem more rough and tough
- Behaves more secretively and is less forthcoming
- Changes clothing style; begins wearing some colors exclusively or wears clothes in a unique way consistently (such as rolling up pant legs)
- Exhibits more antisocial tendencies and becomes withdrawn or uninterested in family activities
- Suddenly acquires costly material possessions (CDs, DVDs, electronics equipment, etc.) or large amounts of cash, and the source of the funds cannot be explained
- Starts using a new nickname (or street name)
- Becomes fascinated with weapons, particularly guns
- Has new cuts and bruises indicating evidence of being in a fight, and is unable to provide a reasonable explanation
- Sports new unusual tattoos
- Writes gang graffiti on notebooks, schoolbooks, and posters
- Develops an increased interest in gangsta rap music
- Hides a stash of spray paint, permanent markers, and other graffiti supplies

- Has encounters with law enforcement
- Shows dependency on drugs or alcohol

Characteristics of Gang Members

GENDER. An overwhelming majority of gang members are reported by law enforcement agencies to be male; this fact changed little over the NYGS survey years. According to Egley, Howell, and Major in *National Youth Gang Survey, 1999–2001*, between 1999 and 2001 an estimated 10% of gang members were female. The larger the population size, the lower the proportion of gang members that are reported to be female; still, in the smallest population areas (fewer than 25,000), only 17% of gang members were female. However, 84% of survey respondents said there were female gang members in their communities. The 2007 *National Youth Gang Survey Analysis* (http://www.iir.com/nygc/nygsa/demographics.htm) estimated that in 2004 in large cities, female gang membership was just over 5%, but in rural communities, it was around 11%. According to the Federal Bureau of Investigation (FBI) in the *National Gang Threat Assessment 2009* (http://www.fbi.gov/publications/ngta2009.pdf), in 2006 the National Youth Gang Center stated that female gang involvement is underreported by law enforcement.

Though the low estimates of females in gangs are typical findings from law enforcement data, these estimates are challenged by other data. For example, Egley, Howell, and Major state that other studies find that 10% to 20% of all female survey participants in gang-problem areas are gang members. Other researchers who survey gang members themselves find higher proportions of female members. According to the 2009 FBI report, a Florida-based study showed that gang members generally reported that females made up less than 15% of gangs, but some respondents stated the numbers ranged from one-quarter to one-half of all gang members. In May 2008 the Office of Juvenile Justice and Delinquency Prevention (OJJDP) found that 29.4% of girls and 32.4% of boys in high-risk, high-crime neighborhoods claimed gang membership. Though the numbers generally remain low, the National Council on Crime and Delinquency stated that female gang members are growing rapidly as a part of the national juvenile justice population. The FBI report also states that though female membership in male gangs continues to increase, the number of all female gangs remains low.

Some differences have been found to exist between female and male gang members. Females involved in gangs are believed to join and leave gangs at an earlier age and at a faster rate than males. Female gang members are also believed to be less involved in serious or violent crimes than male gang members. As a result, this lower rate of serious criminal behavior may not bring female gang members to the attention of law enforcement officials. The FBI states that, "law enforcement officials are less likely to recognize or stop female gang members, and they have experienced difficulty in identifying female involvement in gang-related activity."

AGE. Gang members are not always juveniles; in fact, over time law enforcement agencies have reported that a larger percentage of gang members are adults. Egley, Howell, and Major note that in 1996 half of all gang members were reported to be age 18 and older; by 2001 two-thirds (67%) of all gang members were reported to be adults. However, this proportion varies by the size of the community; in the largest cities adults make up a larger proportion of gang members, compared to the smallest population groups, where juveniles predominate. Still, in 2001, 51% of all reporting law enforcement agencies said that half or more of the gang members active in their communities were juveniles.

Gangs have a particular appeal to some youth. Gangs sometimes serve as families for children whose own families may be dysfunctional. Gang members have said there is often little need to intimidate youngsters to recruit them because they know what youth need and are willing to provide it in return for the child's commitment. Gangs provide emotional support, shelter, and clothing—in essence, just what the child's family may not be providing. However, some children are intimidated into joining gangs either out of fear or for protection from other gangs.

Egley, Howell, and Major also comment on the age ranges of members of youth gangs by area type where gangs operated in 2001. Large cities and suburban counties with populations of 250,000 or more reported the highest proportions of adult gang members; juveniles made up only about 30% of gang membership in these areas. By contrast, small cities and rural counties with populations less than 25,000 reported the highest proportions of juvenile gang members by far (about 70%).

RACE AND ETHNICITY. According to Egley, Howell, and Major, law enforcement agencies reported in 2001 that approximately half of all gang members were Hispanic, 33% were African-American, 10% were non-Hispanic white, and 5% were Asian-American. Minorities are overrepresented among gang members because gangs arise and persist in economically disadvantaged and socially disorganized areas, and minority communities are overrepresented in these communities. The Bureau of Justice Assistance notes in *Addressing Community Gang Problems: A Practical Guide* (May 1998, http://www.ncjrs.gov/pdffiles/164273.pdf) that "it is not necessarily race that explains gang life, for gang members usually come from socially and economically disadvantaged communities." In addition, Egley, Howell, and Major explain that 29% of the 2001 NYGS respondents reported that the racial and ethnic groups other than African-American and/or Hispanic are the majority of gang members in their area; in other words, gang membership tends to reflect the demographics of the disadvantaged community from which it arises.

The *2005 National Gang Threat Assessment* also notes the connection between recent immigrant communities and gangs. New immigrant communities are often isolated by language barriers and difficulties in finding employment. Gangs are attractive to many in Hispanic immigrant communities because they provide support and protection. By contrast, Asian communities are less likely than other communities to report criminal activity to law enforcement agencies. As a result, gangs often victimize these communities.

Gang Types and Activities

THE SPREAD OF GANGS. Several Hispanic gangs originated in California but have since spread throughout the nation. Southern California gang members who moved out of the state united under the name Sureño (or Sur 13). According to the *2005 National Gang Threat Assessment*, in 2001 Sur 13 was present in 35 states across the nation. This group has connections to the Mexican mafia. Norteños are gang members who originated in Northern California; they are believed to have an alliance with an outlaw motorcycle gang that allows them to acquire drugs and aids them in defending against Hispanic gangs from Southern California. Mara Salvatrucha (MS-13) is a El Salvadoran street gang aligned with the Mexican mafia that originated in Los Angeles but spread to Virginia, Maryland, North Carolina, and New York. The Hispanic gang 18th Street, which is open to individuals of any racial background, reportedly has spread across the country and recruits in elementary and middle schools. The Latin Kings is a powerful gang that has split into three factions; its membership is primarily Puerto Rican males, but it does include individuals of other ethnicities. It is particularly active in New York, New Jersey, and Connecticut, where it engages in drug-related crime and bitter territorial wars with other gangs. Law enforcement officials report that they are seeing an increasing effort of some Hispanic gangs to align with one another to organize a criminal network.

A gang subculture has also emerged on Native American reservations. These gangs are primarily composed of youth. They engage in less criminal behavior than other gangs; according to the *2005 National Gang Threat Assessment*, "gang behavior is more about group cohesiveness, predatory activities, and a party atmosphere than it is about organized criminal behavior with a profit motive." Gangs on reservations tend to be small and unaligned with large, national gang networks. Even though violent crime is on the increase, most gang activity on reservations is associated with graffiti, vandalism, and drug sales.

In an effort to learn more about Native American gangs, the NYGC conducted a survey and Aline K. Major et al. reported the findings in *Youth Gangs in Indian Country* (March 2004, http://www.ncjrs.gov/pdffiles1/ojjdp/202714.pdf). The researchers note that the survey included "persons of American Indian, Alaska Native, or Aleut heritage who reside within the limits of Indian reservations, pueblos, rancherias, villages, dependent Indian communities, or Indian allotments, and who together comprise a federally recognized tribe or community." Major et al. report that youth gangs were active in 23% of Native American communities. Fifty-nine percent of communities reporting active gangs estimated the number of gangs between one and five, 19% estimated the number to be between six and 10, and 6% estimated more than 10. Sixteen percent of the communities with gangs believed the gangs consisted of more than 50 people, 12% estimated 26 to 50 people, and 32% reported 25 or fewer. According to the researchers, about 75% of gang members were juveniles. Females made up 20% of Native American gang members. A mix of both males and females existed in 82% of the gangs. About 10% of gangs on reservations were thought to be female-dominated. Nearly four out of five gang members on reservations were of Native American, Alaskan Native, or Aleut descent. The other 22% were of other ethnic or racial backgrounds, most notably Hispanics and non-Hispanic whites.

Some researchers classify gangs not according to their racial and ethnic makeup, but according to what purposes they serve and their organizational structures. In *National Victim Assistance Academy Textbook* (June 2002, http://www.ojp.usdoj.gov/ovc/assist/nvaa2002/toc.html), the Department of Justice's Office for Victims of Crime outlines gang research conducted by the sociologist Carl S. Taylor. Taylor categorized gangs into three types: scavenger gangs, which act spontaneously and lack organization, have frequent changes in leadership, tend to have members who are low achievers, and are regarded unfavorably by other types of gangs; territorial gangs, which are highly organized, prone to fighting to establish territories, use formal initiations, and are formed mainly for social reasons; and corporate gangs, which are highly structured, engage in drug trafficking, require members to live by a strict set of rules with harsh punishments for those who break them, and whose members can be considered actual "gangsters." Members of corporate gangs tend to be more intelligent than members of scavenger and territorial gangs, but they may lack formal schooling.

Reasons for Joining a Gang

Why juveniles, youths, and even adults participate in gangs is the subject of much study in the United States. Studies include those by James C. Howell of the NYGC, in *Youth Gangs: An Overview* (August 1998, http://www.ncjrs.gov/pdffiles/167249.pdf) and in *Youth Gang Programs and Strategies* (August 2000, http://www.ncjrs.gov/pdffiles1/ojjdp/171154.pdf); and Wyrick and Howell. The reasons vary greatly among gang members, but there are a few basic motives. It is important to note, however, that even though these factors may cause some people to join gangs, they do not prompt most people to do so. Some of the most common reasons to join a gang are:

- Feeling marginalized by society and seeking a commonality with others in similar situations
- Wanting power and respect
- Having friends involved in gangs and wanting to be a part of that too
- Desiring a sense of belonging when that is not available through a traditional family setting
- Seeking safety and/or protection from bullies, rival gangs, family members, or others
- Having power in numbers
- Ending poverty and joblessness by turning to criminal activities, such as stealing and drug trafficking
- Needing to feel a sense of purpose
- Having trouble or a disinterest in school
- Living in neighborhoods or communities where other troubled youth roam the streets
- Adding organization and structure to one's life
- Having feelings of low self-esteem that are diminished through encouragement from other gang members

Karl G. Hill, Christina Lui, and J. David Hawkins tracked juveniles in Seattle, Washington, over the course of several years to learn more about their involvement in gang-related activities. They reported their findings in *Early Precursors of Gang Membership: A Study of Seattle Youth* (December 2001, http://www.ncjrs.gov/pdffiles1/ojjdp/190106.pdf). During the multiyear study, the researchers tracked a group of 808 fifth-graders through age 18. They learned that 15.3% (124 students) joined a gang between the ages of 13 and 18. Of those joining gangs, 69% stayed in a gang for less than one year, whereas 0.8% of study participants who joined a gang at age 13 were still in a gang at age 18.

According to Hill, Lui, and Hawkins, those children who stayed in a gang for several years "were the most behaviorally and socially maladjusted," often exhibiting "early signs of violent and externalizing behavior (e.g., aggression, oppositional behavior, and inattentive and hyperactive behaviors)." Children who associated with antisocial peers were more than twice as likely to remain in a gang for more than one year. In *National Victim Assistance Academy Textbook*, the Office for Victims of Crime reports that gangs are starting to recruit younger members, sometimes as young as seven or eight years old.

Hill, Lui, and Hawkins identify various risk factors potentially leading to gang involvement. These factors include having a learning disability, having access to marijuana, experiencing low academic achievement, living near other youth in trouble in the neighborhood, and having a living arrangement that includes one parent along with other unrelated adults.

GANGS IN SCHOOLS

The presence of street gangs is a growing concern in U.S. schools. Various educators and students—urban, suburban, and rural—acknowledge the presence of gangs in their schools. Such gangs are often involved in illegal activities, such as violence, drugs, and weapons trafficking. Gang presence in schools often leads to fear among students who are not affiliated with gangs and may encourage nongang members to join a gang for protection. In schools with significant gang presence, the level of violence is frequently higher than in schools with less gang presence.

Rachel Dinkes et al. address in *Indicators of School Crime and Safety: 2007* (December 2007, http://www.ojp.usdoj.gov/bjs/pub/pdf/iscs07.pdf) the issue of student reports of street gangs in schools. Between 2001 and 2005 urban students were the most likely to acknowledge the presence of street gangs at school during the previous six months. By 2005 over a third (36%) of urban students admitted these gangs were present at their schools. (See Figure 8.1.) Suburban students (21%) and rural students (16%) followed. Even though law enforcement officials surveyed in the NYGS stated that gang membership held steady in the first decade of the twenty-first century, an

increasing number of students reported gang activity at school. In 2001, 20% of students reported gangs at school, and in 2005, 24% of students reported gangs at school.

According to Dinkes et al., the percentages of students reporting gangs in public schools far eclipsed the number in private schools. In 2005, 25% of students in public schools reported gang activities at their schools, whereas only 4% of private school students did. Students at public schools were more likely to report the presence of gangs than were students at private schools, regardless of the school's location.

In terms of race and ethnicity, Hispanics in urban schools (48%) were the most likely group to acknowledge gangs at school in 2005, whereas white rural students (14%) were the least likely. (See Figure 8.2.) In urban and rural schools, Hispanic students were the most likely and African-American students were the second most likely to report the presence of gangs, whereas in suburban schools African-American students (35%) were the most likely to report the presence of gangs, followed by Hispanic students (32%).

Indicators of Gang Presence at School

In *Youth Gangs in Schools* (August 2000, http://www.ncjrs.gov/pdffiles1/ojjdp/183015.pdf), James C. Howell

FIGURE 8.1

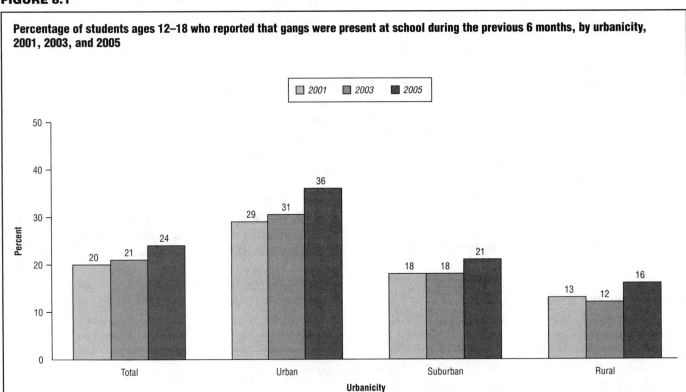

Percentage of students ages 12–18 who reported that gangs were present at school during the previous 6 months, by urbanicity, 2001, 2003, and 2005

Note: All gangs, whether or not they are involved in violent or illegal activity, are included. "At school" includes the school building, on school property, on a school bus, or going to and from school. In 2005, the unit response rate for this survey did not meet National Center for Education Statistics standards; therefore, interpret the data with caution. Population sizes for students ages 12–18 are 24,315,000 in 2001; 25,684,000 in 2003; and 25,811,000 in 2005.

SOURCE: Rachel Dinkes, Emily Forrest Cataldi, and Wendy Lin-Kelly, "Figure 8.1. Percentage of Students Ages 12–18 Who Reported That Gangs Were Present at School during the Previous 6 Months, by Urbanicity: Various Years: 2001–2005," in *Indicators of School Crime and Safety, 2007*, U.S. Department of Education, National Center for Education Statistics, and U.S. Department of Justice, Bureau of Justice Statistics, December 2007, http://www.ojp.usdoj.gov/bjs/pub/pdf/iscs07.pdf (accessed November 12, 2008)

FIGURE 8.2

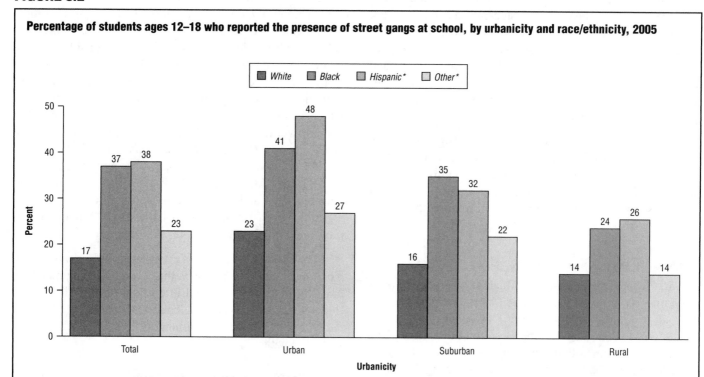

Percentage of students ages 12–18 who reported the presence of street gangs at school, by urbanicity and race/ethnicity, 2005

Legend: ■ White ■ Black □ Hispanic* □ Other*

*Other includes American Indian, Alaska Native, Asian or Pacific Islander, and more than one race. For this report, non-Hispanic students who identified themselves as more than one race were included in the other category. Respondents who identified themselves as being of Hispanic origin are classified as Hispanic, regardless of their race.
Note: All gangs, whether or not they are involved in violent or illegal activity, are included. "At school" includes the school building, on school property, on a school bus, or going to and from school. In 2005, the unit response rate for this survey did not meet National Center for Education Statistics standards; therefore, interpret the data with caution. Population size for students ages 12–18 is 25,811,000 in 2005.

SOURCE: Rachel Dinkes, Emily Forrest Cataldi, and Wendy Lin-Kelly, "Figure 8.2. Percentage of Students Ages 12–18 Who Reported That Gangs Were Present at School during the Previous 6 Months, by Urbanicity and Race/Ethnicity: 2005," in *Indicators of School Crime and Safety, 2007*, U.S. Department of Education, National Center for Education Statistics, and U.S. Department of Justice, Bureau of Justice Statistics, December 2007, http://www.ojp.usdoj.gov/bjs/pub/pdf/iscs07.pdf (accessed November 12, 2008)

and James P. Lynch note that even in elementary and secondary schools, youth gangs can present serious crime problems. They describe various studies that asked surveyed students to explain why they believed gangs were present in their schools. The students' responses included:

- The gang has a recognized name (80%)
- The surveyed student has spent time with gang members (80%)
- The gang members wear clothing or other items identifying their group (71%)
- The gang marks or tags its territory with graffiti (56%)
- The gang commits acts of violence (50%)
- The gang has a recognized territory (47%)
- The gang members have tattoos (37%)
- The gang members have a recognized leader (33%)

Gangs and Drugs at School

Howell and Lynch comment on the connection between drug availability and gang presence at school. They note, "Where none of the drugs was easy to get, only 25 percent of

surveyed students said gangs were present. This percentage increased from 42 percent when only one drug was readily available to 69 percent when seven drugs were readily available, and then dropped slightly when eight or nine drugs were readily available." When eight and nine drugs were available at school, the percentage of students reporting gangs increased to 63% and 62%, respectively. It is unclear whether the availability of drugs was because of the gang activity, or if the presence of gangs was part of an underlying problem that contributed to the availability of drugs. Dinkes et al. note that "the availability of drugs on school property has a disruptive and corrupting influence on the school environment." They also indicate that 25% of high school students reported that drugs were available to them on school property.

Gang Criminality at School

Howell and Lynch include survey respondents' impressions about the presence of gangs in school and its relationship to crime. According to the researchers, "The students reported that most of the gangs they see at school are actively involved in criminal activities. About two-thirds of the students reported that gangs are involved in none or only one of three types of criminal acts: violence, drug sales, or carrying guns. Nevertheless, students said that a small proportion of gangs in schools (8 percent) are involved in all three types of crimes, and these gangs are probably responsible for the most disruption and violent victimization in and around schools." The researchers indicate that other studies include a variety of other criminal activities known to be perpetrated by gang members.

Howell and Lynch also state that gangs contribute substantially to victimizations at school. It is believed that some students join gangs to avoid persecution by gang members. For them, gang membership serves as a form of protection from other students who may have threatened them or wished them harm.

GANG CRIME AND VIOLENCE

In "The Impact of Gang Formation on Local Patterns of Crime" (*Journal of Research in Crime and Delinquency*, vol. 44, no. 2, May 2007), George Tita and Greg Ridgeway acknowledge that gang members commit more crimes and more serious crimes than do nongang members, but they also examine whether the emergence of gangs have an impact on the crime rate. They argue that gangs typically form in areas that have higher crime than other areas, but once gangs form, they attract or generate even higher levels of crime. Tita and Ridgeway state, "The formation of gang set space facilitates drug and shots-fired activity at the neighborhood level, just as gang membership facilitates drug-market activities and gun carrying or usage among active gang members." The following is a discussion of gang involvement in specific criminal activities.

Homicides

Egley, Howell, and Major explain that the impact and severity of gang activity in an area is often measured by the numbers of gang-related homicides. The term *gang-motivated homicides* refers to those murders that further the interests of a gang, whereas *gang-related homicides* generally refers to murders where a gang member is either a perpetrator or the victim. Most localities use the broader gang member–based definition, rather than the motive-based definition, when classifying a homicide as gang related.

According to Egley and O'Donnell, there is a clear relationship between population size and gang-related homicides. Nearly nine out of 10 communities (89%) with populations between 2,500 and 49,999 and 86% of rural counties recorded no gang-related homicides in 2006. However, most law enforcement agencies in communities with a population of over 100,000 people reported at least one gang-related homicide in that year.

Some evidence suggests that even though the number of active gangs and gang membership is holding steady, gang violence is getting worse. According to Arlen Egley Jr. and Christina E. Ritz of the NYGS, in *Highlights of the 2004 National Youth Gang Survey* (April 2006, http://www.iir.com/nygc/publications/fs200601.pdf), two cities, Los Angeles and Chicago, reported in 2004 that more than half of the homicides in those cities were considered gang related, whereas the remaining 171 cities that responded to the survey considered approximately a quarter of all homicides to be gang related. The number of gang homicides in these cities in 2004 was 11% higher than the annual average of gang-related homicides over the past eight years. In *Homicide Trends in the United States* (July 11, 2007, http://www.ojp.usdoj.gov/bjs/homicide/circumst .htm), James Alan Fox and Marianne W. Zawitz state that between 1976 and 2005 gang-related homicides increased eightfold, from 129 in 1976 to 1,119 in 2002, before dropping to 955 in 2005.

The Office for Victims of Crime notes in *National Victim Assistance Academy Textbook* that "youthful gang members have 'no fear of death' and often *how they die* is what is important in gang dynamics. This factor contributes to retaliatory gang violence and criminal acts that are increasingly violent in nature."

Drug Trafficking and Other Crime

Gangs use drug trafficking as a major source of financial gain. According to the *2005 National Gang Threat Assessment*, 31.6% of all law enforcement respondents to the NYGS reported that gangs in their communities were highly involved in selling drugs. Law enforcement agencies believed this was especially true in the distribution of marijuana (64.8%), followed by crack cocaine (47.3%), methamphetamine (39.1%), powdered cocaine (38.2%), heroin (27.9%), and MDMA (23.7%). Gangs in the West and the Northeast are more likely to be involved in selling drugs than are gangs in the South and the Midwest.

Egley and O'Donnell find that gang-related crime had increased in a significant portion of locales across the United States in 2006. Specifically, more than half the law enforcement agencies surveyed reported an increase in gang-related aggravated assault and drug sales, 45% reported an increase in robbery, 39% reported an increase in larceny/theft, 37% reported an increase in burglary, and 30% reported an increase in auto theft. (See Figure 8.3.)

The *2005 National Gang Threat Assessment* also reports that gangs are thought to be increasingly associating themselves with organized crime groups, such as Mexican drug organizations and Asian and Russian organized crime. Imprisoning gang members is thought to do little to curb their activities, and the return of previously imprisoned gang members to communities is believed to intensify criminal activity, drug trafficking, and violence in those communities. In addition, California-style gangs have been found throughout the United States. Furthermore, gang members are becoming increasingly able to use technology and computers to engage in criminal activity.

FIGURE 8.3

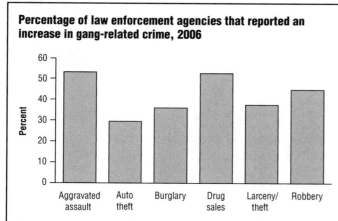

Percentage of law enforcement agencies that reported an increase in gang-related crime, 2006

SOURCE: "Figure 1. Percentage of Agencies with Gang Problems That Reported an Increase in Gang-Related Crime, 2006," in *Highlights of the 2006 National Youth Gang Survey*, U.S. Department of Justice, Office of Justice Programs, Office of Juvenile Justice and Delinquency Prevention, July 2008, http://www.ncjrs.gov/pdffiles1/ojjdp/fs200805.pdf (accessed November 11, 2008)

C. Ronald Huff of Ohio State University conducted a study on gang involvement in crime and reported his findings in *Criminal Behavior of Youth Gangs and At-Risk Youths* (March 1998, http://www.ncjrs.gov/pdffiles/fs000190.pdf). Huff interviewed 50 gang members in four communities: Aurora and Denver, Colorado; Broward County, Florida; and Cleveland, Ohio. As a control, he also interviewed 50 youths from each area who represented the at-risk population but who were not gang members. The results of the interviews indicate that besides being more involved in crime, gang members are also much more likely than nongang members to own guns.

In the study communities, Huff finds that more than 90% of gang members stated that their peers had carried concealed weapons and another 80% admitted that gang members had taken guns to school. About half of the control-group members had friends who had carried a concealed weapon, and one-third acknowledged that friends had taken guns to school. Fox and Zawitz note that the percentage of homicides involving guns was higher among gang-related crimes than in other circumstances, in fact, approaching 100%.

According to the Office for Victims of Crime, in *National Victim Assistance Academy Textbook*, when it comes to crime and punishment, gang members have learned to "work the system": "Experience shows that incapacitation of individual gang members is not sufficient to control gang crime because removing individuals does not diminish the influence of the gang on the street. In addition, gangs have learned the procedural differences between juvenile and adult court and have used these to their advantage. Since gangs consist of both juvenile and adult members, many gangs have come to use juveniles extensively in the commission of crimes. This ensures lenient penalties for adjudicated juvenile offenders."

CONSEQUENCES OF BEING IN A GANG

Being in a gang can be dangerous. Former members can tell many stories about the difficulties one encounters in gang life. Besides living a life with the potential for more violence and crime than the average youth would experience, many other consequences exist. Even though such consequences might vary considerably among individuals, Dana Peterson, Terrance J. Taylor, and Finn-Aage Esbensen, in "Gang Membership and Violent Victimization" (*Justice Quarterly*, vol. 21, no. 4, December 2004), and Thornberry, Huizinga, and Leober address some of the most commonly encountered consequences:

- Becoming a school dropout

- Having little opportunity to secure a good, legal job

- Being unable to hold a steady job

- Becoming antisocial and having difficulty socializing outside the gang

- Having an increased likelihood of being a victim of violent crime

- Entering motherhood or fatherhood at an early age

- Ending up in prison or jail for gang crimes

- Developing a dependency on drugs and/or alcohol

- Experiencing a higher risk of premature death

CHAPTER 9
CRIME AND VIOLENCE IN THE SCHOOLS

School is supposed to be a safe haven where young people can go to learn the basics of mathematics, literature, science, and other subjects, without fearing for their safety, feeling intimidated, or being harassed. Even though school administrators and teachers work toward making the environment safe and secure, crime and violence do find their way into the hallways and classrooms and onto the school grounds. Despite media emphasis on topics such as school shootings, fatal violence at schools is relatively low. Non-fatal crime, however, occurs in far greater numbers, sometimes even more frequently at school than away from school.

Safety is and will continue to be a concern at schools. A rash of school shootings and bomb threats that occurred in the 1990s, and that continue to occur, brought increasing attention to school safety issues and what must be done to protect students; two particularly troubling incidences are the shootings at Colorado's Columbine High School in 1999 and the more recent tragedy at the Virginia Polytechnic Institute and State University in the spring of 2007, in which a student killed 32 people and then himself. Various studies about school violence and crime were issued in the late 1990s and in the first decade of the twenty-first century as researchers examined past trends and tried to predict patterns for the future. Surveys range from how many children bring weapons to school to how many children are injured in fights, are afraid to go to school, or are subjected to disciplinary actions. Educators, school administrators, parents, and students themselves remain vigilant in striving to make schools safe places where youth are able to learn and prepare for the future.

How much crime and violence exist at schools in the twenty-first century? Has it increased or decreased in recent years? What effect did the Columbine High School shootings have on students and public opinion in general? Is there a danger that students, educators, and school officials will underreport school crime and violence to police?

VIOLENT DEATHS AT SCHOOL

During the 2005–06 school year, there were 35 school-associated violent deaths in elementary and secondary schools, including 14 homicides and three suicides. (See Table 9.1.) This number was down from the previous school year, when 50 violent deaths occurred—21 homicides and seven suicides. The most school-associated deaths (including staff, students, and nonstudents) in any year of the study was 57, which occurred during both the 1992–93 and 1997–98 school years.

Rachel Dinkes et al. state in *Indicators of School Crime and Safety, 2007* (December 2007, http://www.ojp.usdoj.gov/bjs/pub/pdf/iscs07.pdf) that between July 1, 1992, and June 30, 2006, 617 school-associated violent deaths occurred across the United States, including 330 homicides of school-age children. Despite the understandable fear generated by the media coverage of events, the possibility of being shot at school is very minimal. Dinkes et al. note, "In each school year, youth were over 50 times more likely to be murdered and were over 150 times more likely to commit suicide when they were away from school than at school." However, Americans were shocked by the rash of school shootings in the 1990s and some were afraid to send their children to school. The shootings at Columbine High School, in particular, weighed heavily on many students' and parents' minds.

Columbine High School

The tragedy began around 11:10 a.m. on April 20, 1999, as senior Eric Harris (1981–1999) arrived at the student parking lot at Columbine High School in Littleton, a suburb of Denver, in Colorado. A short time later, Harris's friend and classmate Dylan Klebold (1982–1999) arrived. Carrying two large duffel bags, they walked together to the school cafeteria. Each of the bags contained a 20-pound (9.1-kg) propane bomb, which was set to detonate at exactly 11:17 a.m. Harris and Klebold looked for an inconspicuous

TABLE 9.1

Number of school-associated violent deaths by location, 1992–2006

Year	Total student, staff, and nonstudent school-associated violent deaths[a]	Homicides of youth ages 5–18		Suicides of youth ages 5–18	
		Homicides at school[b]	Total homicides[c]	Suicides at school[b]	Total suicides[d]
1992–93	57	34	2,689	6	1,680
1993–94	48	29	2,879	7	1,723
1994–95	48	28	2,654	7	1,767
1995–96	53	32	2,512	6	1,725
1996–97	48	28	2,189	1	1,633
1997–98	57	34	2,056	6	1,626
1998–99	47	33	1,762	4	1,597
1999–2000	36	13	1,537	8	1,415
2000–01	30	11	1,466	4	1,493
2001–02	37	14	1,468	6	1,400
2002–03	35	18	1,515	8	1,331
2003–04	36	21	1,437	3	1,285
2004–05	50	21	1,534	7	1,471
2005–06[e]	35	14	—	3	—

—Not available.

[a]School-associated violent deaths include a homicide, suicide, legal intervention (involving a law enforcement officer), or unintentional firearm-related death in which the fatal injury occurred on the campus of a functioning elementary or secondary school in the United States, while the victim was on the way to or from regular sessions at school or while the victim was attending or traveling to or from an official school-sponsored event. Victims include students, staff members, and others who are not students, from July 1, 1992, through June 30, 2006.

[b]Youth ages 5–18 from July 1, 1992, through June 30, 2006.

[c]Youth ages 5–18 from July 1, 1992, through June 30, 2005.

[d]Youth ages 5–18 in the calendar year from 1992 to 2004.

[e]Data are preliminary and subject to change.

SOURCE: Rachel Dinkes, Emily Forrest Cataldi, and Wendy Lin-Kelly, "Table 1.1. Number of School-Associated Violent Deaths, Homicides, and Suicides of Youth Ages 5–18, by Location and Year: 1992–2006," in *Indicators of School Crime and Safety, 2007*, U.S. Department of Education, National Center for Education Statistics, and U.S. Department of Justice, Bureau of Justice Statistics, December 2007, http://www.ojp.usdoj.gov/bjs/pub/pdf/iscs07.pdf (accessed November 12, 2008)

place to leave their bomb-concealing bags among the hundreds of other backpacks and bags there. After choosing a spot, Harris and Klebold returned to the parking lot to wait for the bombs to detonate.

Part of their plan was aimed at diverting the Littleton Fire Department, the Jefferson County Sheriff's Office, and other emergency personnel away from the high school as the pair stormed the school. To achieve this, they had planted pipe bombs 3 miles (4.8 km) southwest of the high school set to explode and start grass fires. As the explosions began, Harris and Klebold prepared to reenter the school, this time via the west exterior steps. That location is the highest point on campus and allows a view of the student parking lots and the cafeteria's entrances and exits. Both Harris and Klebold, dressed in black trench coats, concealed 9mm semiautomatic weapons from view. As they approached, the pair pulled out shotguns from a duffel bag and opened fire toward the west doors of the school, killing 17-year-old Rachel Scott.

After entering the school, they roamed the halls, library, and cafeteria, among other areas, killing 12 other victims, including a teacher, before finally killing themselves. In the process they also injured 23 other students physically and many others emotionally. The details of the event are outlined in *The Columbine High School Shootings: Jefferson County Sheriff Department's Investigation Report* (May 15, 2000) by the Jefferson County Sheriff's Department. Since that time, more documents and videotapes have been made available to the victims' families, the media, and others as well.

Investigations after the Columbine shootings focused on incidents in the boys' past that might have indicated the potential for such violent behavior. Among the people most surprised by the shootings were Klebold's family. Tom Klebold, Dylan's father, told investigators that his son had never showed any interest in guns. The Klebolds told authorities that Dylan had been accepted at the University of Arizona and had planned to study computer science. Klebold's friends and teachers described him as a nice, normal teenager. However, authorities also learned that Klebold and Harris were often subjected to harassment and bullying from other students. Much discussion of this fact was reported by the media, which prompted various research organizations to look into the effects of bullying on juveniles. Some wondered if the ridicule from other students had prompted Harris and Klebold to seek revenge.

The Federal Bureau of Investigation Examines School Shooters

Previous school shooting incidents had prompted the Federal Bureau of Investigation (FBI) to spend two years researching this phenomenon. In *The School Shooter: A Threat Assessment Perspective* (1999, http://www.fbi.gov/publications/school/school2.pdf), Mary Ellen O'Toole of the FBI asserts that the profile of a school shooter cannot be determined, nor is it possible to create a checklist of the warning signs indicating the next juvenile who will bring lethal violence to school. O'Toole's intent, however, is to assist school personnel and others in assessing threats and to keep any planned violence from occurring.

O'Toole uses a four-pronged approach in assessing "the totality of the circumstances" known about a student in four major areas: the student's personality, family dynamics, school dynamics, and social dynamics. O'Toole states, "If an act of violence occurs at a school, the school becomes the scene of the crime. As in any violent crime, it is necessary to understand what it is about the school which might have influenced the student's decision to offend there rather than someplace else."

According to O'Toole, the FBI has established the following factors in making this determination:

- The student's attachment to school—the student appears to be detached from school, including other students, teachers, and school activities.

- Tolerance for disrespectful behavior—the school does little to prevent or punish disrespectful behavior between individual students or groups of students.

- Inequitable discipline—discipline is inequitably applied (or has the perception of being inequitably applied) by students and/or staff.

- Inflexible culture—the school's culture is static, unyielding, and insensitive to changes in society and the changing needs of newer students and staff.

- Pecking order among students—certain groups of students are officially or unofficially given more prestige and respect than others.

- Code of silence—few students feel they can safely tell teachers or administrators if they are concerned about another student's behavior or attitudes. Little trust exists between students and staff.

- Unsupervised computer access—access to computers and the Internet is unsupervised and unmonitored. Students are able to use the school's computers to play violent computer games or to explore inappropriate Web sites, such as those that promote violent hate groups or give instructions for making a bomb.

Despite the factors that might indicate a school will be more likely to be the site of a deadly incident, O'Toole reemphasizes in "School Shootings: What You Should Know" (October 6, 2006, http://www.fbi.gov/page2/oct2006/schoolshootings100606.htm) that there might be nothing that can be done to prevent a violent incident from occurring. However, she states that school personnel should be vigilant by paying attention to students' moods and behaviors and taking all threats seriously.

SECURITY AND DISCIPLINE

After Columbine, as students, teachers, and parents became more worried about school safety, U.S. schools began implementing security measures to try to prevent future violent incidents. According to Dinkes et al., during the 2005–06 school year, 85% of public schools locked some doors and monitored unlocked doors during school hours, 48% required faculty and staff to wear identification, 41% used locked or monitored gates to control school access, 5% used random metal detector checks, and 1% used daily metal detector checks. Nearly all schools (93%) required visitors to sign in.

Security measures differed by school level. Dinkes et al. state that during the 2005–06 school year, buildings or grounds were more likely to be monitored in primary schools than in middle or high schools. Elementary school students were more likely to be required to wear uniforms than older students. Drug tests, security cameras, random sweeps for contraband, and drug-sniffing dogs were much more likely to be used in high schools than in earlier

grades. Critics of increased surveillance in schools contend that bullying, stalking, and harassment present the real risk to students and believe that stronger counseling and early intervention programs are urgently needed.

In fact, efforts to decrease violence in schools have had mixed results. Dinkes et al. find that victimizations declined from 9.5% to 4.2% between 1995 and 2005. However, there was no measurable change in the decline of violent and serious violent victimizations during this period. Violent crimes include rape and attempted rape, sexual assault, physical attack or threat of physical attack with or without a weapon, and robbery. Serious violent crimes are limited to rape and attempted rape, sexual assault, physical attack with a weapon or threat of attack with a weapon, and robbery. In 2005–06, 77.7% of schools experienced at least one violent crime during the year, and 17.1% experienced a serious violent crime.

Disciplinary Problems and Actions

Schools contend with a wide range of disciplinary problems that can affect the safety and positive educational experience of students and staff alike. These include bullying, gang activities, verbal abuse of teachers, disrespectful acts against teachers, widespread disorder in the classroom, cult or extremist group activities, and racial tension. According to Dinkes et al., during the 2005–06 school year, 24% of public schools experienced problems with student bullying. (See Figure 9.1.) A slightly higher proportion of students (28%) reported experiencing bullying at school. Bullying was a particular problem in middle schools; 37% of sixth graders, 28% of ninth graders, and 20% of 12th graders reported that they had been bullied at school.

Other discipline problems at public schools in 2005–06 included undesirable gang activities, student acts of disrespect for teachers, and student verbal abuse of teachers. Whereas 17% of schools overall reported gang activities, over half (51%) of large schools with more than 1,000 students reported gang activities at school. (See Figure 9.1.) Disrespect for teachers was a problem in 18% of schools, whereas 35% of large schools experienced this problem. Verbal abuse of teachers was a problem in 9% of schools overall, but in 20% of large schools.

One of the ways that schools attempt to deal with safety issues is to take serious disciplinary action (suspensions of five days or more, expulsions, and transfers to specialized schools) against students committing crimes and violent acts. Dinkes et al. note that almost half (48%) of public schools took at least one serious disciplinary action against a student during the 2005–06 school year. Three-quarters (74.2%) of these actions involved out-of-school suspensions lasting five days or more, 20.4% involved transfers to specialized schools, and 5.4% were removals with no services for the remainder of the school year.

FIGURE 9.1

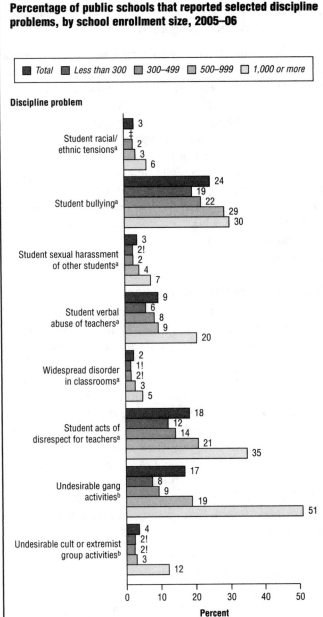

Percentage of public schools that reported selected discipline problems, by school enrollment size, 2005–06

Legend: ■ Total ■ Less than 300 ■ 300–499 ■ 500–999 □ 1,000 or more

Discipline problem

Student racial/ethnic tensions[a]: 3, ‡, 2, 3, 6

Student bullying[a]: 24, 19, 22, 29, 30

Student sexual harassment of other students[a]: 3, 2!, 2, 4, 7

Student verbal abuse of teachers[a]: 9, 6, 8, 9, 20

Widespread disorder in classrooms[a]: 2, 1!, 2!, 3, 5

Student acts of disrespect for teachers[a]: 18, 12, 14, 21, 35

Undesirable gang activities[b]: 17, 8, 9, 19, 51

Undesirable cult or extremist group activities[b]: 4, 2!, 2!, 3, 12

Percent (0 to 50)

! Interpret data with caution.
‡ Reporting standards not met.
[a]Includes schools that reported the activity happens at least once a week or daily.
[b]Includes schools that reported the activity has happened at all at their school during the school year.
Note: Responses were provided by the principal or the person most knowledgeable about crime and safety issues at the school. "At school" was defined for respondents to include activities that happen in school buildings, on school grounds, on school buses, and at places that hold school-sponsored events or activities. Respondents were instructed to respond only for those times that were during normal school hours or when school activities or events were in session, unless the survey specified otherwise. Population size is 83,200 public schools.

SOURCE: Rachel Dinkes, Emily Forrest Cataldi, and Wendy Lin-Kelly, "Figure 7.1. Percentage of Public Schools Reporting Selected Discipline Problems That Occurred at School, by School Enrollment Size: School Year 2005–06," in *Indicators of School Crime and Safety, 2007*, U.S. Department of Education, National Center for Education Statistics, and U.S. Department of Justice, Bureau of Justice Statistics, December 2007, http://www.ojp.usdoj.gov/bjs/pub/pdf/iscs07.pdf (accessed November 12, 2008)

FIGURE 9.2

Percentage of public schools that took a serious disciplinary action for selected offenses, by type of offense, 2005–06

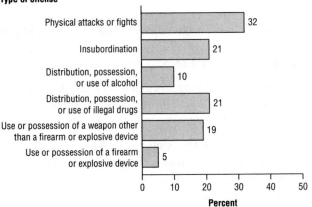

Type of offense

Physical attacks or fights: 32
Insubordination: 21
Distribution, possession, or use of alcohol: 10
Distribution, possession, or use of illegal drugs: 21
Use or possession of a weapon other than a firearm or explosive device: 19
Use or possession of a firearm or explosive device: 5

Percent (0 to 50)

Note: Responses were provided by the principal or the person most knowledgeable about crime and safety issues at the school. Serious disciplinary actions include removals with no continuing services for at least the remainder of the school year, transfers to specialized schools for disciplinary reasons, and out-of-school suspensions lasting 5 or more days, but less than the remainder of the school year. Respondents were instructed to respond only for those times that were during normal school hours or when school activities or events were in session, unless the survey specified otherwise. Population size is 83,200 public schools.

SOURCE: Rachel Dinkes, Emily Forrest Cataldi, and Wendy Lin-Kelly, "Figure 19.1. Percentage of Public Schools That Took a Serious Disciplinary Action for Specific Offenses, by Type of Offense: School Year 2005–06," in *Indicators of School Crime and Safety, 2007*, U.S. Department of Education, National Center for Education Statistics, and U.S. Department of Justice, Bureau of Justice Statistics, December 2007, http://www.ojp.usdoj.gov/bjs/pub/pdf/iscs07.pdf (accessed November 12, 2008)

These serious disciplinary actions were taken for a variety of offenses. About a third (32%) of public schools took serious disciplinary actions in response to physical attacks or fights. (See Figure 9.2.) Twenty-one percent took these actions in response to insubordination; another 21% were taken in response to the distribution, possession, or use of illegal drugs; and 10% were taken in response to the distribution, possession, or use of alcohol. Nineteen percent were taken in response to the use or possession of a weapon other than a firearm, and 5% were taken in response to the use or possession of a firearm or explosive device.

NONFATAL CRIMES

Between 1992 and 2005 the rate of nonfatal crimes against students between the ages of 12 and 18 at school (in the building, on school property, and en route to and from school) generally declined. (See Figure 9.3.) National Crime Victimization Survey (NCVS) data show that even though thefts often occur more frequently at school than they do away from school, the reverse is true of serious violent crimes such as sexual assault, rape, aggravated assault, and robbery. In 2005 nearly 1.5 million crimes

FIGURE 9.3

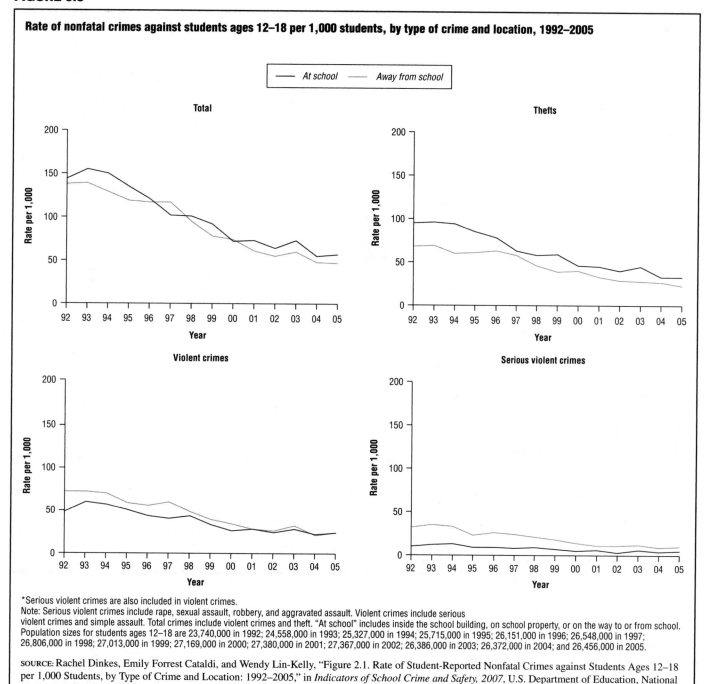

Rate of nonfatal crimes against students ages 12–18 per 1,000 students, by type of crime and location, 1992–2005

*Serious violent crimes are also included in violent crimes.
Note: Serious violent crimes include rape, sexual assault, robbery, and aggravated assault. Violent crimes include serious violent crimes and simple assault. Total crimes include violent crimes and theft. "At school" includes inside the school building, on school property, or on the way to or from school. Population sizes for students ages 12–18 are 23,740,000 in 1992; 24,558,000 in 1993; 25,327,000 in 1994; 25,715,000 in 1995; 26,151,000 in 1996; 26,548,000 in 1997; 26,806,000 in 1998; 27,013,000 in 1999; 27,169,000 in 2000; 27,380,000 in 2001; 27,367,000 in 2002; 26,386,000 in 2003; 26,372,000 in 2004; and 26,456,000 in 2005.

SOURCE: Rachel Dinkes, Emily Forrest Cataldi, and Wendy Lin-Kelly, "Figure 2.1. Rate of Student-Reported Nonfatal Crimes against Students Ages 12–18 per 1,000 Students, by Type of Crime and Location: 1992–2005," in *Indicators of School Crime and Safety, 2007*, U.S. Department of Education, National Center for Education Statistics, and U.S. Department of Justice, Bureau of Justice Statistics, December 2007, http://www.ojp.usdoj. gov/bjs/pub/pdf/iscs07 .pdf (accessed November 12, 2008)

were committed against students at school, including 136,500 serious violent crimes. (See Table 9.2.)

Some students are more likely to be victimized at school than are others. Males experienced a higher rate of crime than females did in general (57 and 56 per 1,000 students, respectively), although females experienced a higher rate of theft (35 per 1,000) than did males (31 per 1,000). (See Table 9.2.) In general, younger students had a higher rate of victimization than did older students. In 2005 65 out of every 1,000 students aged 12 to 14 experienced nonfatal

crimes at school, compared to 49 out of every 1,000 students aged 15 to 18. White students (62 per 1,000) were more likely to experience nonfatal crimes at school than were African-American students (43 per 1,000) or Hispanic students (48 per 1,000).

Physical Fights, Injuries, and Forcible Rape

According to Danice K. Eaton et al. of the Centers for Disease Control and Prevention, in "Youth Risk Behavior Surveillance—United States, 2007" (*Morbidity and Mortality*

TABLE 9.2

Rate of student-reported nonfatal crimes against students ages 12–18 at school and rate of crimes per 1,000 students, by selected characteristics, 2005

Student or school characteristic	Number of crimes				Rate of crimes per 1,000 students			
	Total	Theft	Violent	Serious violent[a]	Total	Theft	Violent	Serious violent[a]
At school								
Total	1,496,300	868,100	628,200	136,500	57	33	24	5
Sex								
Male	776,900	415,300	361,700	77,300	57	31	27	6
Female	719,300	452,800	266,500	59,100	56	35	21	5
Age								
12–14	811,400	436,200	375,300	45,800!	65	35	30	4!
15–18	684,900	431,900	252,900	90,600	49	31	18	6
Race/ethnicity[b]								
White	987,000	604,000	383,000	63,900	62	38	24	4
Black	170,900	88,300	82,600	‡	43	22	21	‡
Hispanic	226,400	128,500	97,900	‡	48	27	21	‡
Other	112,000	47,200	64,800	‡	66	28	38	‡
Urbanicity								
Urban	473,000	222,500	250,500	65,700	64	30	34	9
Suburban	789,200	510,400	278,900	63,300	55	35	19	4
Rural	234,000	135,200	98,800	‡	50	29	21	‡
Household income								
Less than $15,000	88,900	57,000	32,000!	‡	39	25	14!	‡
$15,000–29,999	244,100	94,300	149,800	‡	66	26	41	‡
$30,000–49,999	286,500	128,200	158,300	‡	62	28	34	‡
$50,000–74,999	290,100	168,900	121,200	‡	67	39	28	‡
$75,000 or more	397,200	299,800	97,400	‡	60	46	15	‡

! Interpret data with caution.
‡ Reporting standards not met.
[a]Serious violent crimes are also included in violent crimes.
[b]Other includes Asians, Pacific Islanders, American Indians (including Alaska Natives), and those of more than one race. Respondents who identified themselves as being of Hispanic ethnicity are classified as Hispanic, regardless of their race.
Note: Serious violent crimes include rape, sexual assault, robbery, and aggravated assault. Violent crimes include serious violent crimes and simple assault. Total crimes include violent crimes and theft. "At school" includes inside the school building, on school property, or on the way to or from school. Population size for students ages 12–18 is 26,456,000 in 2005. Detail may not sum to totals because of rounding and missing data on student and school characteristics. Estimates of number of crimes are rounded to the nearest 100.

SOURCE: Rachel Dinkes, Emily Forrest Cataldi, and Wendy Lin-Kelly, "Table 2.2. Number of Student-Reported Nonfatal Crimes against Students Ages 12–18 at School and Rate of Crimes per 1,000 Students, by Selected Student and School Characteristics: 2005," in *Indicators of School Crime and Safety, 2007*, U.S. Department of Education, National Center for Education Statistics, and U.S. Department of Justice, Bureau of Justice Statistics, December 2007, http://www.ojp.usdoj.gov/bjs/pub/pdf/iscs07.pdf (accessed November 12, 2008)

Weekly Report, vol. 57, no. SS-4, June 6, 2008), in 2007, 35.5% of students nationwide reported being in one or more physical fights anywhere (not necessarily at school) during the last 12 months. (See Table 9.3.) Male students (44.4%) were more likely to report this behavior than female students (26.5%). A higher proportion of African-American students (44.7%) and Hispanic students (40.4%) acknowledged fighting than did white students (31.7%). However, the proportions of students fighting decreased as students got older. Ninth grade students (40.9%) fought the most, followed by 10th graders (36.2%), 11th graders (34.8%), and 12th graders (28%).

Dinkes et al. report that even though 35.9% of students acknowledged physically fighting, only 13.6% of students fought on school property in 2005. More male students (18.2%) than female students (8.8%) engaged in fights on school property, and more Hispanic students (18.3%) and African-American students (16.9%) than white students

(11.6%) reported this behavior. The incidence of fighting on school grounds decreased by age in a similar pattern to physical fighting in general.

According to Eaton et al., in 2007 about 4.2% of students noted that they had been injured in a physical fight in the past 12 months, including 5.5% of male students and 2.9% of female students. (See Table 9.3.) African-American students (5.3%) and Hispanic students (6.3%) reported a higher percentage of injuries than did white students (3%).

However, more students reported having experienced dating violence than having been involved in physical fights. In 2007 one out of 10 (9.9%) students said they had been physically hurt by a boyfriend or girlfriend on purpose (hit, slapped, or otherwise physically hurt) one or more times in the last 12 months, including 8.8% of female students and 11% of male students. (See Table 9.3.) African-American students (14.2%) were the most likely to be hurt by a dating partner, followed by Hispanic students (11.1%) and white

TABLE 9.3

Percentage of high school students who engaged in violence and in behaviors resulting from violence, by sex, race/ethnicity, and grade, 2007

	In a physical fight[a]			Injured in a physical fight[a, b]		
	Female	Male	Total	Female	Male	Total
Category	%	%	%	%	%	%
Race/ethnicity						
White[e]	21.5	41.9	31.7	2.0	4.1	3.0
Black[e]	39.4	50.3	44.7	4.2	6.5	5.3
Hispanic	33.5	47.3	40.4	5.1	7.6	6.3
Grade						
9	31.8	49.6	40.9	4.3	6.7	5.6
10	27.2	45.1	36.2	2.1	5.4	3.7
11	23.5	46.3	34.8	2.5	4.6	3.5
12	21.8	34.3	28.0	2.3	4.4	3.3
Total	**26.5**	**44.4**	**35.5**	**2.9**	**5.5**	**4.2**

	Dating violence[c]			Forced to have sexual intercourse[d]		
	Female	Male	Total	Female	Male	Total
Category	%	%	%	%	%	%
Race/ethnicity						
White[e]	7.4	9.3	8.4	11.0	3.2	7.0
Black[e]	13.2	15.2	14.2	13.3	7.8	10.5
Hispanic	10.1	12.0	11.1	11.4	6.2	8.8
Grade						
9	6.3	10.5	8.5	9.2	4.1	6.6
10	8.8	9.1	8.9	13.1	3.4	8.2
11	10.2	10.8	10.6	12.0	5.0	8.5
12	10.1	14.1	12.1	10.9	5.7	8.3
Total	**8.8**	**11.0**	**9.9**	**11.3**	**4.5**	**7.8**

[a]One or more times during the 12 months before the survey.
[b]Injuries had to be treated by a doctor or nurse.
[c]Hit, slapped, or physically hurt on purpose by their boyfriend or girlfriend during the 12 months before the survey.
[d]When they did not want to.
[e]Non-Hispanic.

SOURCE: Adapted from Danice K. Eaton, "Table 9. Percentage of High School Students Who Were in a Physical Fight and Who Were Injured in a Physical Fight, by Sex, Race/Ethnicity, and Grade—United States, Youth Risk Behavior Survey, 2007," and "Table 11. Percentage of High School Students Who Experienced Dating Violence and Who Were Ever Physically Forced to Have Sexual Intercourse, by Sex, Race/Ethnicity, and Grade—United States, Youth Risk Behavior Survey, 2007," in "Youth Risk Behavior Surveillance—United States, 2007," *Morbidity and Mortality Weekly Report*, vol. 57, no. SS-4, June 6, 2008, http://www.cdc.gov/HealthyYouth/yrbs/pdf/yrbss07_mmwr.pdf (accessed November 5, 2008)

students (8.4%). Eaton et al. also find that the higher the grade level, the higher the percentage of students getting hurt by a dating partner—8.5% of ninth graders, 8.9% of 10th graders, 10.6% of 11th graders, and 12.1% of 12th graders reported having been intentionally hurt by a dating partner in the past 12 months.

Eaton et al. also asked students if they had ever been forced to have sexual intercourse, or had been forcibly raped. Overall, 7.8% of students acknowledged being forcibly raped—11.3% of female students and 4.5% of male students. (See Table 9.3.) African-American students (10.5%) were the most likely to report being victimized in

this way, followed by Hispanic students (8.8%) and white students (7%). Ninth graders were less likely than older students to report forced sexual intercourse. These results highlight the high level of sexual and dating violence experienced by high school students.

Bullies and Bullying

Most people can recall certain individuals or a group of children at school being identified as bullies. Such behaviors are not new to schools. Bullies harass certain kids they know will not fight back, including pushing students against lockers and taking their lunch money or other personal possessions; pulling gags in attempts to humiliate others and cause extreme embarrassment; shoving others out of their way; threatening violence or setting up derogatory Web sites about other students; sending threatening or insulting text messages; and disrupting class and making threatening gestures, even toward teachers. Some studies, such as Jill F. DeVoe, Sarah Kaffenberger, and Kathryn Chandler's *Student Reports of Bullying: Results from the 2001 School Crime Supplement to the National Crime Victimization Survey* (July 2005, http://nces.ed.gov/pubs2005/2005310.pdf), divide these bullying behaviors into two categories: direct and indirect. Direct bullying behaviors include physical and verbal attacks and harassment. Indirect bullying behaviors include subtle actions that might be hard for those not directly involved to recognize. These would include psychological activities, such as those listed earlier, as well as obscene gestures, hurtful facial expressions, and turning friends against each other.

During the late 1990s bullying at schools became a major issue of concern for parents, educators, police, lawmakers, and students as increasing numbers of people perceived that bullying had become more aggressive and hurtful. In addition, a rash of school shootings shocked the nation in the 1990s. Many of the school shooters, mainly middle school and high school white males, complained of being bullied, victimized, and harassed frequently. They had grown tired of being picked on and struck back, they said. In fact, DeVoe, Kaffenberger, and Chandler find that students who had been bullied were more likely than other students to carry weapons to school (4% and 1%, respectively). However, most of the victims of school shootings are not the bullies who have harassed the shooters, but average students caught in the cross fire of angry classmates.

DEFINITION AND CHARACTERISTICS OF BULLYING. According to profiles created by various research organizations, such as "Bullying" (May 2008, http://www.aacap.org/cs/root/facts_for_families/bullying) by the American Academy of Child and Adolescent Psychiatry, bullies are most often males, although girls do engage in bullying behaviors as well. Boys are more likely to use physical and verbal abuse, frequently on a one-on-one basis. Girls typically use verbal and psychological tactics. Female bullies often refrain from one-on-one contact, preferring to work in groups. This might include circulating a "slam book" about another person, which is a notebook containing derogatory remarks about the victim written by the bullying group, or e-mailing embarrassing pictures taken by cell phones in locker rooms to a large group of girls. Male victims of bullying are typically bullied by other males, but female victims may be bullied by either male or female students.

Bullies look for situations where they can gain power over someone else through intimidation and threats. Sometimes they work alone; other times they work in groups. Some bullies surround themselves with weaker kids who act as henchmen. Bullies seek out situations to harass others in places such as playgrounds and school hallways that are not being supervised by adults. In this way, there are no adult witnesses to either stop the act or report it to school authorities.

In *Youth Bullying* (May 2002, http://www.ama-assn.org/ama1/pub/upload/mm/39/youthbullying.pdf), Missy Fleming and Kelly J. Towey of the American Medical Association explain that bullies are typically impulsive, have difficulty controlling anger, are easily frustrated, fail to follow rules, and view violence in a positive light. Individual risk factors include a lack of warmth from parents, a lack of parental supervision, and harsh, corporal discipline or child maltreatment. In addition, some schools have higher rates of bullying than do others because there is inadequate adult supervision or because teachers and staff have indifferent or accepting attitudes toward bullying.

In general, Fleming and Towey note that victims of bullies are passive. They are quiet, cautious, sensitive, and insecure people with few friends to step in and help them out of a bullying situation. They have difficulty standing up to people during confrontations, so bullies perceive them to be safe and easy targets. Male victims tend to be physically smaller and weaker than their peers. Any children who have been victims of child maltreatment are also more likely to be victimized by bullies. However, it is important to note that any student can become a victim of bullying, and the fault lies with the bully, not with the victim.

As the prevalence of bullying increases and more parents and educators grow concerned, various studies are being conducted to learn more about bullies, victims, and the frequency of such occurrences. Bullying appears to be on the rise. DeVoe, Kaffenberger, and Chandler report that in 2001 only 14% of 12- to 18-year-olds reported being bullied at school during the previous six months. Dinkes et al. state that four years later, in 2005, 28.1% of 12- to 18-year-olds reported being bullied at school during the previous six months—27.1% of males and 29.2% of females. (See Table 9.4.)

In 2005 white students reported the most problems with bullies (30%). African-American students (28.5%) and Hispanic students (22.3%) reported slightly less trouble. Reports of being bullied diminished with age; 36.6% of sixth graders but only 19.9% of 12th graders reported being victimized by bullies. (See Table 9.4.)

DeVoe, Kaffenberger, and Chandler present survey results of students aged 12 to 18 who reported in 2001 being bullied at school. The researchers find that factors in the school environment affected the incidence of bullying. Students who said there were gangs at school were more likely than other students to report being bullied (21% and 13%, respectively). Likewise, students who reported security guards or police officers in their schools were less likely than other students to report being bullied (13% and 16%, respectively). Hall monitoring by staff was also associated with fewer students being bullied (14% and 18%). Several studies, such as Farah Williams and Dewey G. Cornell's "Student Willingness to Seek Help for Threats of Violence" (*Journal of School Violence*, vol. 5, no. 4, 2006) and Lauren P. Ashbaugh and Dewey G. Cornell's "Sexual Harassment and Bullying Behaviors in Sixth Graders" (*Journal of School Violence*, vol. 7, no. 2, 2008), find that girls are more likely than boys to report and seek help for bullying.

EFFECTS OF BULLYING/BEING BULLIED. DeVoe, Kaffenberger, and Chandler find that bullied students were more likely to engage in a variety of behaviors than students who had not been bullied, including fearing attack, truancy from school or skipping classes, not participating in afterschool activities, carrying weapons, and engaging in physical fights. Students were afraid to attend school and practiced avoidance behaviors such as finding the shortest routes to school or to different places within the school in an attempt to prevent an attack. Being victimized by a bully may also lead to aggressive and/or antisocial behavior. The American Academy of Child and Adolescent Psychiatry notes in "Bullying" that students who are being bullied may even attempt suicide.

In "Relationships between Bullying and Violence among US Youth" (*Archives of Pediatrics and Adolescent Medicine*, vol. 157, no. 4, April 2003), Tonja R. Nansel et al. determine whether bullying is related to other types of violent behavior. The researchers find that boys who acknowledged bullying others at school at least once each week had an increased level of carrying a weapon to school in the last month (43.1%), carrying a weapon in general (52.2%), being involved in frequent physical fighting (38.7%), and being injured in fighting (45.7%). Male bullies who attacked their victims away from school were even more likely to engage in these behaviors. Nansel et al. conclude, "Bullying should not be considered a normative aspect of youth development, but rather a marker for more serious violent behaviors, including weapon carrying, frequent fighting, and fighting-related injury."

TABLE 9.4

Percentage of students ages 12–18 who reported being bullied at school during the previous 6 months, by location, injury, and selected student and school characteristics, 2005

| Student or school characteristic | Total | Location of bullying | | | | Students who were injured[a] |
		Inside school	Outside on school grounds	School bus	Somewhere else	
Total	**28.1**	**79.0**	**27.8**	**8.1**	**4.9**	**24.0**
Sex						
Male	27.1	77.6	28.5	8.7	4.4	30.6
Female	29.2	80.4	27.0	7.5	5.3	17.7
Race/ethnicity[b]						
White	30.0	80.6	27.9	7.6	4.7	24.4
Black	28.5	77.3	25.2	10.8	4.3!	25.9
Hispanic	22.3	74.8	28.7	6.2	4.8	21.7
Other	24.6	76.7	31.2	9.4!	7.9!	20.8
Grade						
6th	36.6	68.2	36.9	7.6	4.7!	32.3
7th	35.0	81.0	30.0	14.2	2.9	31.7
8th	30.4	79.4	24.8	10.4	4.0	27.0
9th	28.1	81.7	28.0	5.1	5.0	21.0
10th	24.9	80.1	23.3	5.4	4.4!	21.2
11th	23.0	80.3	26.9	4.5!	7.2	14.5
12th	19.9	80.0	24.9	4.4!	8.5	12.7
Urbanicity						
Urban	26.0	76.9	28.4	6.5	5.4	23.0
Suburban	28.9	78.5	28.2	8.9	5.2	24.6
Rural	29.0	83.6	25.7	7.6	3.0!	23.8
Sector						
Public	28.6	79.4	27.5	8.3	4.9	24.4
Private	22.7	73.9	31.5	‡	4.2!	18.0

!Interpret data with caution.
‡Reporting standards not met.
[a]Injury includes bruises or swelling; cuts, scratches, or scrapes; black eye or bloody nose; teeth chipped or knocked out; broken bones or internal injuries; knocked unconscious; or other injuries. Only students who reported that their bullying incident constituted being pushed, shoved, tripped, or spit on were asked if they suffered injuries as a result of the incident.
[b]Other includes American Indian, Alaska Native, Asian or Pacific Islander, and more than one race. For this report, non-Hispanic students who identified themselves as more than one race were included in the other category. Respondents who identified themselves as being of Hispanic origin are classified as Hispanic, regardless of their race.
Notes: "At school" includes the school building, on school property, on a school bus, or going to and from school. In 2005, the unit response rate for this survey did not meet National Center Education Statistics standards; therefore, interpret the data with caution. Population size for students ages 12–18 is 25,811,000 in 2005. Location totals may sum to more than 100 because students could have been bullied in more than one location.

SOURCE: Rachel Dinkes, Emily Forrest Cataldi, and Wendy Lin-Kelly, "Table 11.2. Percentage of Students Ages 12–18 Who Reported Being Bullied at School during the Previous 6 Months, by Location of Bullying, Injury, and Selected Student and School Characteristics: 2005," in *Indicators of School Crime and Safety, 2007*, U.S. Department of Education, National Center for Education Statistics, and U.S. Department of Justice, Bureau of Justice Statistics, December 2007, http://www.ojp.usdoj.gov/bjs/pub/pdf/iscs07.pdf (accessed November 12, 2008)

CYBERBULLIES. Justin W. Patchin and Sameer Hinduja report in "Bullies Move beyond the Schoolyard" (*Youth Violence and Juvenile Justice*, vol. 4, no. 2, 2006) that with the advent of the Internet and the increased use of cell phones among students, bullies have found a new way to taunt their victims: cyberbullying, which is also called digital bullying or Internet bullying. Instead of abusing their victims at school, on the playground, or en route to and from school, bullies are now able to taunt their victims day and night via current technology. Victims report receiving hateful and hurtful instant messages, e-mails, and text messages on their cell phones. Use of such technologies allows the perpetrators to be anonymous, if they so choose.

Some students have become the victims of hate-filled Web sites that discuss why the bullies and his or her friends do not like that certain individual. Visitors to such sites are allowed to add their insults and gossip as well. In some instances, visitors have rallied to the defense of the victim

and slammed the bully. Through the use of camera phones, bullies have even taken sensitive photos of students in locker rooms, in restrooms, or while being intimidated. Then the bullies pass them around, either via e-mail or on Web sites. Researchers point out that electronic bullying can be done anywhere and does not involve the bully having any personal contact, especially eye contact, with the victim.

Parents have experienced difficulty in getting the Web sites removed by service providers, who suggest that they are not in the business of censorship and that the content is protected under the First Amendment, which guarantees freedom of speech. Some parents have decided to file lawsuits to get the content taken down. Due to their age and lack of understanding of the law, bullies often do not realize that they are legally responsible for what they put in print.

In "Research Summary: Cyberbullying Victimization" (2005, http://www.cyberbullying.us/cyberbullying_victimization.pdf), Sameer Hinduja and Justin W. Patchin find that in 2005, 34.4% of adolescent respondents had experienced cyberbullying. More than one out of 10 (12.6%) reported they had been physically threatened, and 4.8% were frightened for their safety as a result. The researchers explain that most cyberbullying occurs in chat rooms (55.6%) or through text messaging (48.9%). Victims of cyberbullying reported feeling frustrated (34%), angry (30.6%), and sad (21.8%); only a third (35%) were not bothered by the experience. According to Janis Wolak, Kimberly Mitchell, and David Findelhor of the National Center for Missing and Exploited Children at the University of New Hampshire, in *Online Victimization of Youth: Five Years Later* (2006, http://www.unh.edu/ccrc/pdf/CV138.pdf), the percentage of youth who admitted making "rude or nasty comments to someone on the Internet" had doubled from 14% in 2000 to 28% in 2005.

In one highly publicized case, 13-year-old Megan Meier committed suicide after she was cyberbullied through the social networking Web site MySpace. She befriended a stranger, a boy named Josh Evans, through the site. However, the Josh Evans MySpace account had been created by a group of people headed by Lori Drew, the mother of a former friend of Meier's. "Josh Evans" began sending Meier increasingly hurtful messages and posted bulletins about her. In October 2006 Meier hanged herself in her bedroom. In May 2008 a federal grand jury indicted Drew on one count of conspiracy and three counts of accessing protected computers without authorization to obtain information to inflict emotional distress. Drew was convicted in November 2008 of three misdemeanors but acquitted of felony conspiracy charges.

PREVENTION PROGRAMS. Schools throughout the country have implemented antibullying programs aimed at bringing the subject out in the open. Antibullying efforts are not only geared toward bullies but also at the students and teachers who do not do enough to stop such aggression from occurring. Some victims claim there are teachers who allow bullying to occur, even encourage it. Others say they are afraid to tell teachers because the educators just ignore it and tell the victims to toughen up. Still other victims are ashamed that they cannot stop the bullies so they retreat into themselves and internalize it.

One successful antibullying program, the Olweus Bullying Prevention Program (October 21, 2008, http://www.clemson.edu/olweus/), teaches students, parents, and school staff to work together to address the issue. By discussing bullying and its effects, people learn the consequences of bullying on individuals and on the school environment. Rules and plans are developed and enforced. The Office of Juvenile Justice and Delinquency Prevention (OJJDP) notes that the Olweus program is successful in elementary and junior high schools. According to the article "New Approach to Combating Bullies" (CBS News, December 10, 2003),

the European schools that use the program have cut bullying by 30% to 70%.

Crimes against Teachers

Teachers sometimes fall victim to crimes at school. According to Dinkes et al., the percentage of teachers threatened with injury or physically attacked declined between the 1993–94 and 2003–04 school years. In 2003–04, 7% of teachers were threatened with injury by a student in their school. (See Figure 9.4.) Teachers in city schools were more likely than teachers in other schools to be threatened with injury. Twelve percent of teachers in city schools were threatened in 2003–04, compared to 6% of suburban teachers and 5% of rural teachers. Dinkes et al. report that 4% of public school teachers and 2% of private school teachers said they were actually physically attacked by students from school during the 12 months preceding the survey.

Weapons in School

Violence at school makes students feel vulnerable and intimidated. Sometimes it makes them want to carry weapons to school for self-protection. The Gun-Free Schools Act of 1994 required states to pass laws forcing school districts to expel any student who brings a firearm to school. Dinkes et al. indicate that in 2005, 6.5% of high school students reported they had carried a weapon (a gun, knife, or club) on school property in the last 30 days, down from 11.8% of students in 1993 but higher than in 2003. (See Table 9.5.) A much higher percentage of males (10.2%) than females (2.6%) reported carrying a weapon on school property. The percentage of students who reported carrying a weapon anywhere decreased from 22.1% in 1993 to 17.1% in 2003 before rising again to 18.5% in 2005. Eaton et al. state that in 2007, 18% of students had carried a weapon during the past 30 days, and 5.2% had carried a gun.

According to Dinkes et al., males were more likely than females to carry weapons on school property in all years reported, moving from a high of 17.9% in 1993 to a low of 8.9% in 2003. They were also more likely to carry weapons anywhere, although this dropped from 34.3% in 1993 to 26.9% in 2003 before rising again to 29.8% in 2005. Females were far less likely than their male peers to carry weapons on school property (5.1% in 1993 and 2.6% in 2005) or anywhere else (9.2% in 1993 and 7.1% in 2005). (See Table 9.5.)

Various reasons could explain why students are carrying fewer weapons to school. Enhanced security measures at school, such as metal detectors and locker searches, added in the wake of the highly publicized school shootings in the 1990s, could be partially responsible. Another reason could be the stricter punishment given to those found with guns in school. Many schools have adopted zero-tolerance

FIGURE 9.4

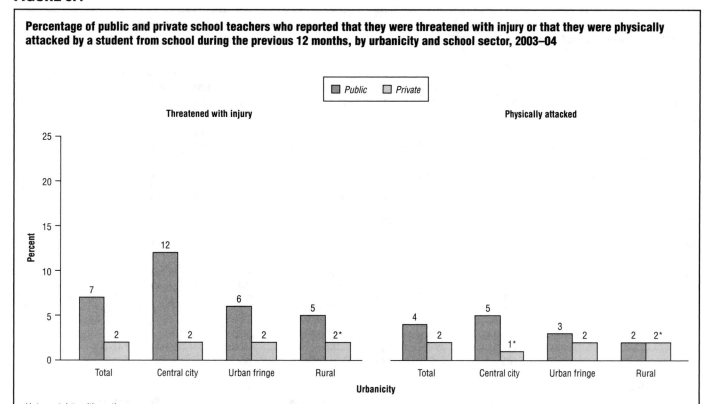

Percentage of public and private school teachers who reported that they were threatened with injury or that they were physically attacked by a student from school during the previous 12 months, by urbanicity and school sector, 2003–04

*Interpret data with caution.

Notes: Teachers who taught only prekindergarten students are excluded. The public sector includes public, public charter, and Bureau of Indian Affairs school teachers. Population size for teachers is 3,704,000 in 2003–04.

SOURCE: Rachel Dinkes, Emily Forrest Cataldi, and Wendy Lin-Kelly, "Figure 5.2. Percentage of Public and Private School Teachers Who Reported That They Were Threatened with Injury or That They Were Physically Attacked by a Student from School during the Previous 12 Months, by Urbanicity and School Sector: 2003–04," in *Indicators of School Crime and Safety, 2007*, U.S. Department of Education, National Center for Education Statistics, and U.S. Department of Justice, Bureau of Justice Statistics, December 2007, http://www.ojp.usdoj.gov/bjs/pub/pdf/iscs07.pdf (accessed November 12, 2008)

rules, resulting in the immediate expulsion of someone who is found breaking those guidelines.

For some students, obtaining guns is fairly easy. The OJJDP notes that young people attempt various methods to secure guns, including stealing them from cars, houses, apartments, stores and pawnshops, and family members. They also buy guns from family members, drug dealers or addicts, stores, gang members, family friends, and others.

WEAPON USE ON SCHOOL PROPERTY. The percentage of students who report being threatened with or injured by a weapon while at school remained fairly steady between 1993 and 2005. Approximately 7.9% of students in grades nine through 12 reported being threatened or injured with a weapon on school property within the past 12 months in 2005. (See Table 9.6.) This figure was a slight increase from 1993, when 7.3% of students reported being threatened or injured by a weapon. Between 1993 and 2005 the percentage remained in the 7% to 9% range—no clear pattern of improvement or worsening can be seen.

Male students received considerably more weapons threats and injuries in all years surveyed between 1993 and 2005 than did female students. Among students from different ethnic and racial backgrounds, the victimization rate was highest among Pacific Islanders in 2005 (14.5%), down from a high of 24.8% in 2001. (See Table 9.6.) Native American students (9.8%) and Hispanic students (9.8%) also had fairly high victimization rates. Asian-American students were the least likely to be threatened by or injured with a weapon in 2005 (4.6%).

The youngest students were the most likely to report being threatened by or injured with a weapon. More than one out of 10 (10.5%) ninth graders reported being threatened or injured with a weapon in 2005, compared to 8.8% of 10th graders, 5.5% of 11th graders, and 5.8% of 12th graders. (See Table 9.6.) Similar patterns were observed in the other years of the survey as well. It may be that younger students are viewed as more vulnerable to intimidation and therefore are more likely to be targets of students carrying weapons.

HAZING

Like bullying, hazing involves humiliating someone into doing something that he or she would not do normally. In some instances, the hazing act is silly and harmless. However,

TABLE 9.5

Percentage of students in grades 9–12 who reported carrying a weapon at least 1 day during the previous 30 days, by selected student characteristics, selected years 1993–2005

Student or school characteristic	Anywhere							On school property						
	1993	1995	1997	1999	2001	2003	2005	1993	1995	1997	1999	2001	2003	2005
Total	22.1	20.0	18.3	17.3	17.4	17.1	18.5	11.8	9.8	8.5	6.9	6.4	6.1	6.5
Sex														
Male	34.3	31.1	27.7	28.6	29.3	26.9	29.8	17.9	14.3	12.5	11.0	10.2	8.9	10.2
Female	9.2	8.3	7.0	6.0	6.2	6.7	7.1	5.1	4.9	3.7	2.8	2.9	3.1	2.6
Race/ethnicity[a]														
White	20.6	18.9	17.0	16.4	17.9	16.7	18.7	10.9	9.0	7.8	6.4	6.1	5.5	6.1
Black	28.5	21.8	21.7	17.2	15.2	17.3	16.4	15.0	10.3	9.2	5.0	6.3	6.9	5.1
Hispanic	24.4	24.7	23.3	18.7	16.5	16.5	19.0	13.3	14.1	10.4	7.9	6.4	6.0	8.2
Asian	b	b	b	13.0	10.6	11.6	7.0	b	b	b	6.5	7.2	6.6!	2.8!
American Indian	34.2	32.0	26.2	21.8	31.2	29.3	25.6	17.6!	13.0!	15.9	11.6!	16.4	12.9	7.2
Pacific Islander	b	b	b	25.3	17.4	16.3!	20.0!	b	b	b	9.3	10.0!	4.9!	15.4!
More than one race	b	b	b	22.2	25.2	29.8	26.7	b	b	b	11.4	13.2	13.3!	11.9
Grade														
9th	25.5	22.6	22.6	17.6	19.8	18.0	19.9	12.6	10.7	10.2	7.2	6.7	5.3	6.4
10th	21.4	21.1	17.4	18.7	16.7	15.9	19.4	11.5	10.4	7.7	6.6	6.7	6.0	6.9
11th	21.5	20.3	18.2	16.1	16.8	18.2	17.1	11.9	10.2	9.4	7.0	6.1	6.6	5.9
12th	19.9	16.1	15.4	15.9	15.1	15.5	16.9	10.8	7.6	7.0	6.2	6.1	6.4	6.7
Urbanicity														
Urban	—	—	18.7	15.8	15.3	17.0	—	—	—	7.0	7.2	6.0	5.6	—
Suburban	—	—	16.8	17.0	17.4	16.5	—	—	—	8.7	6.2	6.3	6.4	—
Rural	—	—	22.3	22.3	23.0	18.9	—	—	—	11.2	9.6	8.3	6.3	—

— Not available.

!Interpret data with caution.

[a]American Indian includes Alaska Native, black includes African American, Pacific Islander includes Native Hawaiian, and Hispanic includes Latino. Respondents who identified themselves as being of Hispanic origin are classified as Hispanic, regardless of their race.

[b]The response categories for race/ethnicity changed in 1999 making comparisons of some categories with earlier years problematic. In 1993, 1995, and 1997, Asian students and Pacific Islander students were not categorized separately and students were not given the option of choosing more than one race.

Notes: "On school property" was not defined for survey respondents. The term "anywhere" is not used in the Youth Risk Behavior Survey questionnaire; students are simply asked how many days they carried a weapon during the past 30 days. Population sizes from the Digest of Education Statistics, 2005 and 2002 for students in grades 9–12 are 13,093,000 students in 1993; 13,697,000 in 1995; 14,272,000 in 1997; 14,623,000 in 1999; 15,061,000 in 2001; 15,723,000 in 2003; and 16,286,000 (projected) in 2005.

SOURCE: Rachel Dinkes, Emily Forrest Cataldi, and Wendy Lin-Kelly, "Table 14.1. Percentage of Students in Grades 9–12 Who Reported Carrying a Weapon at Least 1 Day during the Previous 30 Days, by Location and Selected Student and School Characteristics: Various Years 1993–2005," in *Indicators of School Crime and Safety, 2007*, U.S. Department of Education, National Center for Education Statistics, and U.S. Department of Justice, Bureau of Justice Statistics, December 2007, http://www.ojp.usdoj.gov/bjs/pub/pdf/iscs07.pdf (accessed November 12, 2008)

in the early twenty-first century, parents and educators have become concerned that hazings are getting more and more aggressive and violent. Such hazings, which often occur as initiations to a school or social club, are considered a "rite of passage" to some, just "horseplay" to others, and degrading and devastating to various victims. Some athletic teams claim that hazing is done to toughen up younger players—to help them bond with the team. However, unlike bullying, hazing is often done with the consent of its victims. For example, by succumbing to peer pressure and wanting to be part of the group or clique, many students allow themselves to be subjected to humiliating acts that they do not report.

Hazings, however, can go too far and the victims can be seriously harmed. Some victims have even died. Hazings usually involve older students (veterans) initiating young classmates (newcomers) into the club. The situation can quickly turn violent when the older students gang up on the younger students, who have no idea what has been planned or what they should expect. Researchers note that students will do things in a mob situation that they would never do on their own.

Several cases of brutal hazings received significant news coverage in 2003, one involving a high school football team and the other concerning senior and junior high school girls. The football incident took place at a training camp over the summer. At camp, several players were allegedly sexually abused with pine cones, golf balls, and broomsticks. Three players were charged in the incident and appeared before a judge, who was to decide if they should stand trial as juveniles or adults. The judge ordered the decision sealed.

The incident involving the teenage school girls occurred in what was supposed to be a "powder puff" football game at a local park. Instead, the younger girls were allegedly beaten, kicked, shoved, and pelted with a variety of objects and liquids, including garbage, mud, paint, animal intestines, feces, and urine. Five girls were taken to the hospital as a result. Fifteen students, who were charged with misdemeanors, were identified through witnesses and a videotape that someone made of the melee. Thirty-two were suspended from school. Even though the girls were underage, alcohol was present. Police considered charging some of the girls' parents for providing the alcohol.

TABLE 9.6

Percentage of students in grades 9–12 who reported being threatened or injured with a weapon on school property during the previous 12 months, by selected student characteristics, selected years 1993–2005

Student or school characteristic	1993	1995	1997	1999	2001	2003	2005
Total	7.3	8.4	7.4	7.7	8.9	9.2	7.9
Sex							
Male	9.2	10.9	10.2	9.5	11.5	11.6	9.7
Female	5.4	5.8	4.0	5.8	6.5	6.5	6.1
Race/ethnicity[a]							
White	6.3	7.0	6.2	6.6	8.5	7.8	7.2
Black	11.2	11.0	9.9	7.6	9.3	10.9	8.1
Hispanic	8.6	12.4	9.0	9.8	8.9	9.4	9.8
Asian	[b]	[b]	[b]	7.7	11.3	11.5	4.6
American Indian	11.7	11.4!	12.5!	13.2!	15.2!	22.1	9.8
Pacific Islander	[b]	[b]	[b]	15.6	24.8	16.3	14.5!
More than one race	[b]	[b]	[b]	9.3	10.3	18.7	10.7
Grade							
9th	9.4	9.6	10.1	10.5	12.7	12.1	10.5
10th	7.3	9.6	7.9	8.2	9.1	9.2	8.8
11th	7.3	7.7	5.9	6.1	6.9	7.3	5.5
12th	5.5	6.7	5.8	5.1	5.3	6.3	5.8
Urbanicity							
Urban	—	—	8.7	8.0	9.2	10.6	—
Suburban	—	—	7.0	7.4	9.0	8.8	—
Rural	—	—	5.6!	8.3	8.1	8.2	—

— Not available.
!Interpret data with caution.
[a]American Indian includes Alaska Native, black includes African American, Pacific Islander includes Native Hawaiian, and Hispanic includes Latino. Respondents who identified themselves as being of Hispanic origin are classified as Hispanic, regardless of their race.
[b]The response categories for race/ethnicity changed in 1999 making comparisons of some categories with earlier years problematic. In 1993, 1995, and 1997, Asian students and Pacific Islander students were not categorized separately and students were not given the option of choosing more than one race.
Notes: "On school property" was not defined for survey respondents. Population sizes from the Digest of Education Statistics, 2005 and 2002 for students in grades 9–12 are 13,093,000 students in 1993; 13,697,000 in 1995; 14,272,000 in 1997; 14,623,000 in 1999; 15,061,000 in 2001; 15,723,000 in 2003; and 16,286,000 (projected) in 2005.

SOURCE: Rachel Dinkes, Emily Forrest Cataldi, and Wendy Lin-Kelly, "Table 4.1. Percentage of Students in Grades 9–12 Who Reported Being Threatened or Injured with a Weapon on School Property during the Previous 12 Months, by Selected Student and School Characteristics: Various Years, 1993–2005," in *Indicators of School Crime and Safety, 2007,* U.S. Department of Education, National Center for Education Statistics, and U.S. Department of Justice, Bureau of Justice Statistics, December 2007, http://www.ojp.usdoj.gov/bjs/pub/pdf/iscs07.pdf (accessed November 12, 2008)

More recent incidences of hazing capturing media attention were on college campuses. According to Elaine Korry, in "A Fraternity Hazing Gone Wrong" (November 14, 2005, http://www.npr.org/templates/story/story.php?storyId=5012154), in February 2005 a young man attending Chico State University died in a fraternity hazing ritual, where fraternity pledges were forced to do calisthenics in raw sewage while drinking massive quantities of water. The young man died of water intoxication. Felony criminal charges were filed against the fraternity brothers involved in the incident. Other incidences, as reported by StopHazing.org (http://www.stophazing.org/news/index.htm), include a young male student beaten in late 2006 by seven University of South Carolina students who were later arrested, and a 2007 case at Rochester Institute of Technology (RIT), where six students were hospitalized after being forced to drink dangerously high levels of alcohol to join the school's rugby team. Eight RIT rugby players faced misdemeanor charges following the incident.

Various researchers contend that hazing incidents are underreported. This occurs for several reasons:

- The victim believes hazing is an unpleasant, but a necessary part of joining an organization

- The victim is threatened into remaining silent

- The victim is ashamed and wants to forget that the incident occurred

- The victim assumes everyone has to endure such acts

- The victim does not want to involve parents, school officials, or police because that would bring more trouble from the hazers

Some school administrators, coaches, and parents also play a role in encouraging students to refrain from reporting the incidents by saying that they, too, had to endure such rituals. However, many schools are developing antihazing programs. Besides criminal charges being filed in courts, parents of students victimized by hazings have brought lawsuits against schools and the perpetrators of such events.

AVOIDANCE AND FEAR

Edward Gaughan, Jay D. Cerio, and Robert A. Myers of Alfred University find in *Lethal Violence in Schools:*

TABLE 9.7

Percentage of high school students who did not go to school because of safety concerns, by sex, race/ethnicity, and grade, 2007

Category	Female %	Male %	Total %
Race/ethnicity			
White*	4.2	3.7	4.0
Black*	6.3	6.8	6.6
Hispanic	9.7	9.6	9.6
Grade			
9	7.4	5.8	6.6
10	6.0	4.8	5.4
11	3.9	5.5	4.7
12	4.3	5.3	4.8
Total	**5.6**	**5.4**	**5.5**

Note: Respondents felt unsafe on at least 1 day during the 30 days before the survey.
*Non-Hispanic.

SOURCE: Danice K. Eaton,"Table 17. Percentage of High School Students Who Did Not Go to School Because They Felt Unsafe at School or on Their Way to or from School, by Sex, Race/Ethnicity, and Grade—United States, Youth Risk Behavior Survey, 2007," in "Youth Risk Behavior Surveillance—United States, 2007," *Morbidity and Mortality Weekly Report*, vol. 57, no. SS-4, June 6, 2008, http://www.cdc.gov/HealthyYouth/yrbs/pdf/yrbss07_mmwr.pdf (accessed November 5, 2008)

A National Study (August 2001, http://www.alfred.edu/teenviolence/docs/lethal_violence_in_schools.pdf) that concern about violence is prevalent in school. Thirty-seven percent of those surveyed believed there are "kids at my school who I think might shoot someone." According to the researchers, "20 percent of respondents have heard rumors that another student plans to shoot someone, and 20 percent have also overheard another student actually talking about shooting someone at school." Another 8% acknowledged wanting to shoot someone at school themselves. Finally, only about half of the survey participants said they would inform an adult if they overheard someone's plans to shoot another person.

Some students continue to worry about their safety at school. In 2007, 5.5% of students reported missing one or more days of school in the last 30 days because they believed it was too unsafe at school or going to and from school. (See Table 9.7.) Approximately equal percentages of female students (5.6%) and male students (5.4%) reported this experience. This response to their fear was much higher among Hispanic students (9.6%) and African-American students (6.6%) than it was among white students (4%). Younger children reported not going to school because of safety concerns more than did older children; 6.6% of ninth graders, 5.4% of 10th graders, 4.7% of 11th graders, and 4.8% of 12th graders reported skipping school because of safety concerns in the previous month.

Dinkes et al. also address the issue of fear of attack or harm at school or en route to and from school. The researchers report that in 2005, 6.2% of students aged 12 to 18 reported being afraid of attack or harm at school during the previous six months; this was down dramatically from 11.8% of students in 1995. (See Table 9.8.) In 2005 females (6.6%) were slightly more likely to be afraid of harm than were males (5.9%). Hispanic (10.1%) and African-American (9%) students were more likely than white students (4.5%) to feel afraid of attack at school. Younger students were more likely than older students to fear attack or harm at school. Urban students (10.2%) were far more likely than rural (5.1%) or suburban (4.7%) students to report being afraid of attack or harm. Fewer students were afraid of attack or harm away from school than they were at school (5.1% and 6.2%, respectively).

NO CHILD LEFT BEHIND ACT: PERSISTENTLY DANGEROUS SCHOOLS

The No Child Left Behind Act (NCLB) was passed by Congress in 2001 and signed into law by President George W. Bush (1946–) in January 2002. As a reauthorization of the Elementary and Secondary Education Act of 1965, the NCLB mandated sweeping changes to the law defining and regulating the federal government's role in kindergarten through 12th-grade education. According to the U.S. Department of Education, in "Four Pillars of NCLB" (July 1, 2004, http://www.ed.gov/nclb/overview/intro/4pillars.html), the four principles are:

- Stronger accountability for results

- Increased flexibility and local control

- Expanded options for parents

- An emphasis on teaching methods that have been proven to work

Under the NCLB, schools are required to demonstrate "adequate yearly progress" toward statewide proficiency goals. Those that do not make progress face corrective action and restructuring measures. Reporting of progress is public, so parents can stay informed about their school and school district. Schools that make or exceed adequate yearly progress are eligible for awards. The ultimate goal is that all children will have a quality education by the 2013–14 school year.

Unsafe School Choice Option

Among the various changes that the NCLB required was a provision mandating that states work on making schools safer. The Department of Education explains in "Questions and Answers on No Child Left Behind" (November 17, 2004, http://www.ed.gov/nclb/freedom/safety/creating.html):

Under Title IV of ESEA as reauthorized by the No Child Left Behind Act, states are required to establish a uniform management and reporting system to collect information on school safety and drug use among young people. The states must include incident reports by school officials

TABLE 9.8

Percentage of students ages 12–18 who reported being afraid of attack or harm during the previous 6 months, by location and selected student characteristics, selected years 1995–2005

Student or school characteristic	At school					Away from school				
	1995	1999	2001	2003	2005	1995	1999	2001	2003	2005
Total	11.8	7.3	6.4	6.1	6.2	—	5.7	4.6	5.4	5.1
Sex										
Male	10.8	6.5	6.4	5.3	5.9	—	4.1	3.7	4.0	4.5
Female	12.8	8.2	6.4	6.9	6.6	—	7.4	5.6	6.8	5.7
Race/ethnicity*										
White	8.1	5.0	4.9	4.1	4.5	—	4.3	3.7	3.8	4.2
Black	20.3	13.5	8.9	10.7	9.0	—	8.7	6.3	10.0	7.2
Hispanic	20.9	11.7	10.6	9.5	10.1	—	8.9	6.5	7.4	6.1
Other	13.5	6.7	6.4	5.0	6.3	—	5.4	6.6	3.9	5.9!
Grade										
6th	14.3	10.9	10.6	10.0	9.5	—	7.8	6.3	6.8	5.7
7th	15.3	9.5	9.2	8.2	9.1	—	6.1	5.5	6.7	7.5
8th	13.0	8.1	7.6	6.3	6.9	—	5.5	4.4	5.3	4.9
9th	11.6	7.1	5.5	6.3	5.7	—	4.6	4.5	4.3	3.8
10th	11.0	7.1	5.0	4.4	5.3	—	4.8	4.2	5.3	4.6
11th	8.9	4.8	4.8	4.7	4.5	—	5.9	4.7	4.7	4.1
12th	7.8	4.8	2.9	3.7	3.3	—	6.1	3.3	4.9	5.3
Urbanicity										
Urban	18.4	11.6	9.7	9.5	10.2	—	9.1	7.4	8.1	6.6
Suburban	9.8	6.2	4.8	4.8	4.7	—	5.0	3.8	4.4	4.5
Rural	8.6	4.8	6.0	4.7	5.1	—	3.0	3.0	4.0	4.6
Sector										
Public	12.2	7.7	6.6	6.4	6.5	—	5.8	4.6	5.4	5.1
Private	7.3	3.6	4.6	3.0	3.8	—	5.0	5.1	4.7	4.7

— Not available.
!Interpret data with caution.
*Other includes American Indian, Alaska Native, Asian or Pacific Islander, and, from 2003 onward, more than one race. For this report, non-Hispanic students who identified themselves as more than one race were included in the other category. Respondents who identified themselves as being of Hispanic origin are classified as Hispanic, regardless of their race. Due to changes in racial/ethnic categories, comparisons of race/ethnicity across years should be made with caution.
Note: "At school" includes the school building, on school property, on a school bus, and, from 2001 onward, going to and from school. For the 2001 survey, the wording was changed from "attack or harm" to "attack or threat of attack." Includes students who reported that they sometimes or most of the time feared being victimized in this way. Fear of attack away from school was not collected in 1995. In 2005, the unit response rate for this survey did not meet NCES statistical standards; therefore, interpret the data with caution. Population sizes for students ages 12–18 are 23,325,000 in 1995; 24,614,000 in 1999; 24,315,000 in 2001; 25,684,000 in 2003; and 25,811,000 in 2005.

SOURCE: Rachel Dinkes, Emily Forrest Cataldi, and Wendy Lin-Kelly, "Table 17.1. Percentage of Students Ages 12–18 Who Reported Being Afraid of Attack or Harm during the Previous 6 Months, by Location and Selected Student and School Characteristics: Various Years, 1995–2005," in *Indicators of School Crime and Safety, 2007*, U.S. Department of Education, National Center for Education Statistics, and U.S. Department of Justice, Bureau of Justice Statistics, December 2007, http://www.ojp.usdoj.gov/bjs/pub/pdf/iscs07.pdf (accessed November 12, 2008)

and anonymous student and teacher surveys in the data they collect. This information is to be publicly reported so that parents, school officials and others who are interested have information about any violence and drug use at their schools. They can then assess the problems at their schools and work toward finding solutions. Continual monitoring and reports will track progress over time.

To hold schools accountable for ensuring student safety, the NCLB requires states to create a definition of persistently dangerous schools. States must permit students to have public school choice if their school consistently falls into this category. In addition, student victims of violent crime are also allowed public school choice even if the school is not considered persistently dangerous.

PERSISTENTLY DANGEROUS SCHOOLS: GEORGIA'S EXAMPLE. To illustrate what some states have done to fulfill the NCLB requirements pertaining to persistently dangerous schools, this section focuses on the Georgia Department of Education's (GDOE) efforts. According to the GDOE, in

"Unsafe School Choice Option (USCO)" (2008, http://public .doe.k12.ga.us/aypnclb.aspx?PageReq=AboutUSCO), Georgia defines persistently dangerous schools as:

Any school in which for three consecutive years:

At least 1 student is found by official tribunal action to have violated a school rule related to a violent criminal offense (including aggravated battery, aggravated child molestation, aggravated sexual battery, aggravated sodomy, armed robbery, arson, kidnapping, murder, rape, & voluntary manslaughter) either on campus or at a school-sanctioned event;

At least 2% of the student body or 10 students, whichever is greater, have been found to have violated school rules related to other identified criminal offenses, including non-felony drugs, felony drugs, felony weapons, terroristic threats;

Any combination of [the above].

The GDOE further outlines what happens as a consequence of a school being labeled persistently dangerous:

When a school meets the criteria for three consecutive years, local education agencies (local school districts, herein referred to as LEAs) must within ten school days notify parents of each student attending the school that the state has identified the school as persistently dangerous.

Within 20 school days from the time that the LEA learns that the school has been identified as persistently dangerous, the LEA must give students the opportunity to transfer to a safe public school, including a safe public charter school, within the LEA.

LEAs must adopt a policy that facilitates the transfer of students who are victims of violent criminal offenses. This policy shall provide that the transfer shall occur within ten school days of the commission of the violent criminal offense, and to the extent possible, shall allow victims to transfer to a school that is making adequate yearly progress and has not been identified as being in school improvement, corrective action, or restructuring.

If deemed persistently dangerous, a school will need to show significant improvements to regain its place on the safe school list. Georgia has specific requirements that such schools must follow, which include taking corrective measures. After a year of showing that it is no longer dangerous, a school can reapply to the GDOE. When it filed its report in 2003, the GDOE indicated that no Georgia schools were deemed persistently dangerous.

Reporting Violence and Crime at School

The National School Safety and Security Services notes in "School Crime Reporting and School Crime Underreporting" (February 10, 2008, http://www.school security.org/trends/school_crime_reporting.html) that the unsafe school requirement of the NCLB concerns educators, parents, and police. Some believe schools will be even more hesitant to report crimes so that they will not be labeled as persistently dangerous. They suggest that by falling into this designation, these schools will undoubt-

edly lose enrollment and school funds. As such, schools may begin to underreport such crimes so that they maintain a clean rating.

The National Association of School Resource Officers asked its members in 2004 what effects the NCLB would have on school administrators reporting school-based crimes, and Kenneth S. Trump reported the findings in *School Safety Left Behind? School Safety Threats Grow as Preparedness Stalls and Funding Decreases* (February 2005, http://www .schoolsecurity.org/resources/2004%20NASRO%20Survey %20Final%20Report%20NSSSS.pdf). Most (54%) of those surveyed believed it would result in decreased reporting of crimes at schools. The vast majority (86%) said the number of crimes on school property were underreported to law enforcement.

Dinkes et al. indicate that many crimes, even violent crimes, committed at school are not reported to the police. During the 2005–06 school year, 77.7% of public schools experienced one or more violent crimes but just 37.7% reported violent crimes to the police. (See Table 9.9.) Violent incidents included physical attacks, fights with or without weapons, threats of physical violence with or without weapons, rape, sexual battery (other than rape), and robbery with or without weapons. Low-reporting trends also occurred with thefts. Even though 46% of public schools experienced one or more thefts, just 27.9% reported them to the police.

Proportionally, schools were more likely to report seriously violent incidents to the police, presumably due to the gravity of such offenses. However, even some serious violent crimes were not reported. In 2005–06, 17.1% of public schools experienced one or more serious violent crimes and only 12.6% reported any serious violent crimes to the police. (See Table 9.9.)

TABLE 9.9

Percentage of public schools experiencing and reporting incidents of crime that occurred at school, number of incidents, and the rate per 1,000 students, by type of crime, 1999–2000, 2003–04, and 2005–06

Type of crime	Experienced various types of crime					Reported to police				
	1999–2000 Percent of schools	2003–04 Percent of schools	2005–06 Percent of schools	2005–06 Number of incidents	2005–06 Rate per 1,000 students	1999–2000 Percent of schools	2003–04 Percent of schools	2005–06 Percent of schools	2005–06 Number of incidents	2005–06 Rate per 1,000 students
Total	86.4	88.5	85.7	2,191,000	45.8	62.5	65.2	60.9	763,000	16.0
Violent incidents	71.4	81.4	77.7	1,489,400	31.2	36.0	43.6	37.7	353,600	7.4
Physical attack or fight without a weapon	63.7	76.7	74.3	897,700	18.8	25.8	35.6	29.2	205,400	4.3
Threat of physical attack without a weapon	52.2	53.0	52.2	532,600	11.1	18.9	21	19.7	116,500	2.4
Serious violent incidents	19.7	18.3	17.1	59,100	1.2	14.8	13.3	12.6	31,700	0.7
Rape or attempted rape	0.7	0.8	0.3	300	#	0.6	0.8	0.3	300	#
Sexual battery other than rape	2.5	3.0	2.8	4,200	0.1	2.3	2.6	2.6	3,800	0.1
Physical attack or fight with a weapon	5.2	4.0	3.0	7,000	0.1	3.9	2.8	2.2	3,600	0.1
Threat of physical attack with a weapon	11.1	8.6	8.8	24,800	0.5	8.5	6.0	5.9	9,800	0.2
Robbery with a weapon	0.5!	0.6	0.4	600 !	#	0.3!	0.6	0.4	600!	#
Robbery without a weapon	5.3	6.3	6.4	22,100	0.5	3.4	4.2	4.9	13,600	0.3
Theft[a]	45.6	46.0	46.0	242,700	5.1	28.5	30.5	27.9	119,400	2.5
Other incidents	72.7	64.0	68.2	458,900	9.6	52.0	50.0	50.6	290,000	6.1
Possess firearm/explosive device	5.5	6.1	7.2	12,300	0.3	4.5	4.9	5.5	10,100	0.2
Possess knife or sharp object[b]	42.6	15.9	42.8	90,000	1.9	23.0	12.1	25.0	54,500	1.1
Distribution of illegal drugs	12.3	12.9	—	—	—	11.4	12.4	—	—	—
Possession or use of alcohol or illegal drugs	26.6	29.3	—	—	—	22.2	26	—	—	—
Distribution, possession, or use of illegal drugs	—	—	25.9	117,000	2.4	—	—	22.8	100,500	2.1
Distribution, possession, or use of alcohol	—	—	16.2	46,800	1.0	—	—	11.6	33,600	0.7
Sexual harassment	36.3	—	—	—	—	14.7	—	—	—	—
Vandalism	51.4	51.4	50.5	192,800	4.0	32.7	34.3	31.9	91,400	1.9

— Not available.

Rounds to zero.

! Interpret data with caution.

[a]Theft/larceny (taking things worth over $10 without personal confrontation) was defined for respondents as "the unlawful taking of another person's property without personal confrontation, threat, violence, or bodily harm. Included are pocket picking, stealing a purse or backpack (if left unattended or no force was used to take it from owner), theft from a building, theft from a motor vehicle or of motor vehicle parts or accessories, theft of bicycles, theft from vending machines, and all other types of thefts."

[b]The questionnaire wording for possession of a knife or sharp object differed between survey administrations. In 1999–2000 and 2005–06, the question asked about possession of a knife or sharp object. In 2003–04, the question was changed to refer to possession of a knife or sharp object with intent to harm.

Note: Responses were provided by the principal or the person most knowledgeable about crime and safety issues at the school. "At school" was defined for respondents to include activities that happen in school buildings, on school grounds, on school buses, and at places that hold school-sponsored events or activities. Respondents were instructed to respond only for those times that were during normal school hours or when school activities or events were in session, unless the survey specified otherwise. Population size of public schools is 82,000 in 1999–2000, 80,500 in 2003–04, and 83,200 in 2005–06. Detail may not sum to totals because of rounding. Estimates of number of incidents and schools are rounded to the nearest 100.

SOURCE: Rachel Dinkes, Emily Forrest Cataldi, and Wendy Lin-Kelly, "Table 6.1. Percentage of Public Schools Experiencing and Reporting Incidents of Crime That Occurred at School, Number of Incidents, and the Rate per 1,000 Students, by Type of Crime: Various School Years, 1999–2000, 2003–2004, and 2005–2006," in Indicators of School Crime and Safety, 2007, U.S. Department of Education, National Center for Education Statistics, and U.S. Department of Justice, Bureau of Justice Statistics, December 2007, http://www.ojp.usdoj.gov/bjs/pub/pdf/iscs07.pdf (accessed November 12, 2008)

CHAPTER 10

CRIME PREVENTION AND PUNISHMENT

CRIME PREVENTION

Over the years, politicians, law enforcement officials, teachers, parents, and other concerned citizens have examined countless ideas in an effort to decrease youth violence and crime, from holding parents responsible for their children's crimes to having after-school violence prevention programs. The continuing problem of youth crime has many people devoting significant time and resources to end the cycle of violence. A variety of programs have been implemented in the area of prevention, intervention, and suppression. Efforts are ongoing to determine the effectiveness of such programs. The following sections discuss laws that have been enacted as well as a variety of prevention programs, including community prevention programs, law enforcement prevention strategies, and school-based prevention programs, to try to prevent juvenile crime.

Laws Enacted to Prevent Juvenile Crime

HOLDING PARENTS RESPONSIBLE. Civil liability laws have held parents at least partly responsible for damages caused by their children for many decades. In addition, child welfare laws included actions against those who contributed to the delinquency of a minor. By the 1990s, in response to rising juvenile crime rates, communities and states passed tougher laws about parental responsibility. In "Parent Liability Child's Act" (2008, http://www.enotes.com/everyday-law-encyclopedia/parent-liability-child-s-act), the Encyclopedia of Everyday Law notes that some states now hold parents of delinquent youth criminally liable. However, other less stringent parental responsibility laws are more common. Alabama, Kansas, Kentucky, and West Virginia require parents to pay court costs for their children adjudicated delinquent. Florida, Idaho, Indiana, North Carolina, and Virginia require parents to pay the costs of caring for, treating, or detaining delinquent children. Idaho, Maryland, Missouri, and Oklahoma require parents to pay restitution to the victims of their children's crimes. Nine states hold parents criminally

responsible for storing a loaded firearm in a place that allows minors access to it, and other states hold parents liable if they know their child possesses a firearm and do not confiscate it. The article "Parental Civil Liability for Acts of Minor Children" (August 4, 2008, http://www.lawserver.com/articles/parental-civil-liability-for-acts-of-minor-children) indicates that in about half the states, the "family car doctrine" holds parents responsible for any damage caused by a child driving the family car. These laws are meant to prevent or reduce delinquent behavior among juveniles.

Critics of parental liability state that victims are just looking for someone to blame. They assert that U.S. law usually holds people responsible for crimes only if they actively participate in the transmission of such acts. They believe that if standard rules of law are practiced, the prosecutor of a case should have to prove that the parents intended to participate in a crime to be found guilty. Samantha Harvell, Belen Rodas, and Leah Hendey of Georgetown University explain in *Parental Involvement in Juvenile Justice: Prospects and Possibilities* (November 8, 2004, http://www.crocus.georgetown.edu/reports/parental.involvement.pdf) that judges and probation officers believe parents should be more involved in legal proceedings against minors because they feel the relationship between the parent and child often contributes to delinquency. However, judges and probation officers remain somewhat reluctant to use parental sanctions. In fact, Cathy Keen notes in "UF Study: Americans Give Mixed Reviews to Parental Responsibility Laws" (*University of Florida News*, March 14, 2005) that a 2005 survey found that public support for parental responsibility laws was relatively low, and Eve M. Brank and Jodi Lane of the University of Florida find in "Punishing My Parents" (*Criminal Justice Policy Review*, vol. 19, no. 3, September 2008) that delinquent juveniles did not believe their parents should be held responsible for their crimes.

CURFEWS. To "break the cycle" of youth violence and crime, lawmakers in more than 1,000 jurisdictions have enacted curfews in various cities, towns, and rural areas across the country. According to Arlen Egley Jr. and Aline K. Major of the National Youth Gang Center, in *Highlights of the 2001 National Youth Gang Survey* (April 2003, http://www.ncjrs.gov/pdffiles1/ojjdp/fs200301.pdf), 62% of jurisdictions reporting gang problems used curfews or other ordinances aimed at keeping youth from congregating at night. Of those jurisdictions, 86% argued that such laws "demonstrated at least some degree of effectiveness."

Most curfew laws work essentially the same way. They are aimed at restricting juveniles to their homes or property between the hours of 11 p.m. and 6 a.m. weekdays. Such laws usually allow juveniles to stay out a little later on weekends. Exceptions are made for youth who need to travel to and from school, attend church events, or go to work at different times. Other exceptions include family emergencies or situations when juveniles are accompanied by their parents.

Even though many people believe curfews are important in the fight against youth crime, critics of curfew ordinances argue that such laws violate the constitutional rights of children and their parents. They contend that the First, Fourth, Ninth, and Fourteenth Amendment rights of people are endangered by curfew laws, especially the rights of free speech and association, privacy, and equal protection. Opponents also assert that no studies have proven curfew laws to be effective. In fact, most studies show that curfews have little effect on youth crime, such as Angie Schwartz and Lucy Wang's "Proliferating Curfew Laws Keep Kids at Home, but Fail to Curb Juvenile Crime" (*National Center for Youth Law*, vol. 26, no. 1, January–March 2005), Caterina Grovis Roman and Gretchen Moore's "Evaluation of the Youth Curfew in Prince George's County, Maryland" (March 11, 2003, http://www.ncjrs.gov/pdffiles1/nij/grants/200520.pdf), and Kenneth Adams's "The Effectiveness of Juvenile Curfews at Crime Prevention" (*Annals of the American Academy of Political and Social Science*, vol. 587, 2003).

Community Prevention and Intervention Programs

Prevention measures are programs aimed at keeping youth, particularly at-risk youth, from beginning a life of crime, joining gangs, or otherwise ending up in prison or jail. Intervention programs are designed to remove youth from gangs, criminal activities, and patterns of reckless behavior that would ultimately put the youth in prison or jail. Such programs typically include helping the individual build self-esteem, confidence, and socialization skills while offering education, recreation, and job skills assistance.

Even though this chapter examines a few of the types of programs available, hundreds of such programs exist throughout the United States, some at the national or state levels, but many at the local/community level. Many involve mentoring—having adults and sometimes other students spend time with at-risk youth to help them explore alternatives to violence and crime. Mentoring programs take on a variety of activities, including sports, recreation, and education. Mentors help their subjects gain self-esteem, conflict resolution abilities, peer pressure resistance skills, and confidence.

Many prevention and intervention programs have seen some success with delinquent and at-risk youth, as noted by individuals who credit such groups with turning their lives around or keeping them from heading into a life filled with crime and violence. Other programs have proven to be ineffective. Those that succeed provide alternatives to youth and often a safe place to hang out, make new friends, and learn life skills.

THE CHICAGO AREA PROJECT. Chicago, Illinois, like Los Angeles, California, has been home to many gangs throughout the twentieth century. In an effort to deal with the gang situation on the city's streets, the Chicago Area Project (CAP) was founded in 1934—the nation's first community-based delinquency prevention program. The program, designed by the sociologist Clifford R. Shaw (1895–1957), aimed to work with delinquent youth in poverty-stricken areas of Chicago. Project staff sought to prevent youth from joining gangs and ultimately committing crimes.

To achieve this, CAP advocates believed that improvements needed to be made to neighborhoods and communities. According to CAP (June 5, 2008, http://www.chicagoareaproject.org/about.html), "The agency believes that residents must be empowered through the development of community organizations so that they can act together to improve neighborhood conditions, hold institutions serving the community accountable, reduce anti-social behavior by young people, protect them from inappropriate institutionalization, and provide them with positive models for personal development." The organization emphasizes that juvenile delinquency in low-income areas is a product of social disadvantages—not a flaw of the individual child or of individuals from certain ethnic or racial backgrounds. As of 2008, CAP had grown to include more than 40 affiliates and special projects.

BOYS AND GIRLS CLUBS OF AMERICA. Offering a variety of programs to help youth, the Boys and Girls Clubs of America (BGCA; 2009, http://www.bgca.org/whoweare/) has worked with about 4.8 million children throughout the United States, Puerto Rico, the Virgin Islands, and U.S. military bases in the United States and abroad. In about 4,300 club locations, the group uses 50,000 trained, full-time staff "to enable all young people, especially those who need us most, to reach their full potential as productive, caring, responsible citizens."

Law Enforcement Strategies

OFFICE OF JUVENILE JUSTICE AND DELINQUENCY PREVENTION'S COMPREHENSIVE GANG MODEL. The Office of Juvenile Justice and Delinquency Prevention (OJJDP) advocates the use of a comprehensive gang model developed by Irving A. Spergel to combat gangs. According to the National

Youth Gang Center, in *Best Practices to Address Community Gang Problems: OJJDP's Comprehensive Gang Model, National Youth Gang Center* (2007, http://www.iir.com/nygc/publications/gang-problems.pdf), the model includes five steps to help gang members and their communities. Steps include mobilizing the larger community to create opportunities or service organizations for gang-involved and at-risk youth; mobilizing outreach workers to connect with youth involved in gangs; creating academic, economic, and social opportunities for at-risk and gang-involved youth; using gang suppression activities and holding youth involved in gangs accountable for their actions; and helping community agencies problem-solve at a grassroots level to address gang problems. The model assumes that gang violence is a product of a breakdown in the larger community. According to the OJJDP, in "OJJDP Model Programs Guide" (2005, http://www.dsgonline.com/mpg2.5/mpg_index.htm), evaluations of programs based on the OJJDP model show mixed results, although negative results generally result from poor program implementation.

GANG RESISTANCE EDUCATION AND TRAINING. Hoping to reach students before they become involved in gangs and crime, uniformed police officers throughout the country visit middle schools to discuss the life consequences associated with such activities. The 13-part curriculum, which is offered through the Gang Resistance Education and Training (GREAT) program, was initially created by the Phoenix (Arizona) Police Department and the Bureau of Alcohol, Tobacco, and Firearms in 1991. Because that pilot program met with success, GREAT has expanded to all 50 states and the District of Columbia. Among the topics presented are personal, resiliency, resistance, and social skills. The stated goals of the program are to help youth resist peer pressure, have positive attitudes toward law enforcement, learn ways to avoid violence, develop basic life skills, and set positive goals for the future. According to the article "G.R.E.A.T. Middle School Component" (2009, http://www.great-online.org/corecurriculum.htm), the GREAT curriculum for seventh graders educates students about gangs, violence, drug abuse, and crime; helps students recognize their responsibilities and learn how to make good decisions; fosters communication skills; and teaches anger management skills.

The effectiveness of GREAT training became the basis for a study conducted by Finn-Aage Esbensen and D. Wayne Osgood, who published their findings in "Gang Resistance Education and Training (GREAT): Results from the National Evaluation" (*Journal of Research in Crime and Delinquency*, vol. 36, no. 2, May 1999). Program participants were said to have developed more negative opinions about gangs and more positive attitudes about police. They also reported experiencing lower rates of victimizations, among other things.

SUPPRESSION PROGRAMS. Another method intended to reduce youth crime and violence is called suppression.

This tactic is used by law enforcement agencies throughout the country. Suppression usually involves a show of force, such as saturating an area with many uniformed police officers. The idea is meant to demonstrate to criminals that they are being watched and that criminal activities will not be tolerated. Suppression techniques also include sweeps, where officers sweep through an area rounding up youth and adult offenders. Some suppression programs have proven to be somewhat effective, whereas others have not.

In some areas with high gang activity and violent youth crime, law enforcement personnel have tried suppression techniques. Suppression programs have been tested out in various cities, including Los Angeles, Chicago, and Houston, Texas, among others.

The Houston Police Department Gang Task Force is just one example of the many units of this type operating throughout the United States. Working in conjunction with the Mayor's Anti-Gang Office (2009, http://www.houstontx.gov/publicsafety/antigang/index.html), the task force focuses on areas with high gang activity by providing a highly visible presence in an effort to lessen gang violence and crime. Initiatives aim to target, arrest, and incarcerate gang members involved in criminal activities. At the same time, the Anti-Gang Office works with communities, neighborhoods, service organizations, and schools to provide supportive services to at-risk youth, including counseling, job leads, conflict resolution, and recreation programs. The Mayor's Anti-Gang Office has also provided gang awareness training to individuals, including educators, law enforcement personnel, probation officers, and members of the public since 1994. The group makes use of high-tech devices, such as geomapping and tracking systems. These programs help staff keep track of gang locations as well as youth program assistance sites.

Bill White (1954–), the mayor of Houston, reports in "Houston Mayor White Oversees Gang Free Schools and Communities Project" (April 10, 2006, http://www.usmayors.org/uscm/best_practices/usmayor06/HoustonBP.asp) that suppression is generally not successful alone. Houston provides an example of how suppression can be combined with other program elements, in that the Mayor's Anti-Gang Office uses suppression techniques as one element of the OJJDP's comprehensive gang model, "a paradigm that utilizes five core strategies (community mobilization, provision of opportunities, social intervention, suppression, organizational change and development) to address gang issues within a targeted community."

SCHOOL RESOURCE OFFICERS. The School Resource Officers (SROs) program is intended to improve relations between youth and police. The project, designed to prevent and intercept the commission of youth crime and violence, also gives students and police officers the chance to get to know one another. In some areas, children grow up with contempt for or fear of police. The SRO program works to eliminate these concerns as well as to educate students about the law and provide one-on-one mentoring.

Under the program, a police officer is dispatched to a school as an SRO. The officer works to prevent crime, violence, and substance abuse; makes arrests if necessary during the commission of crimes; counsels students; and conducts classes about law enforcement and school safety. The program calls this the TRIAD concept (police officer, educator, and counselor). To participate as an SRO, candidates must complete a specialized training program. The SRO program is credited with helping reduce youth crime in schools and in the community.

Founded in 1990, the National Association of School Resource Officers (NASRO; 2008, http://www.nasro.org/membership.asp) has a national membership of over 9,000 officers. NASRO holds annual conferences and provides workshops for the SROs about various procedures, techniques, and prevention measures. The association also surveys its members to learn more about current issues affecting the SROs and schools. For example, Kenneth S. Trump of the National School Safety and Security Services notes in *School Safety Left Behind? School Safety Threats Grow as Preparedness Stalls and Funding Decreases: NASRO 2004 National School-Based Law Enforcement Survey* (February 2005, http://www.schoolsecurity.org/resources/2004%20NASRO%20Survey%20Final%20Report%20NSSSS.pdf) that over a third (37.4%) of the SROs believed that gang activity in their schools had increased, another third (38%) believed gang activity had remained the same, and only 8.4% believed gang activity had decreased.

School-Based Prevention Programs

STUDENTS AGAINST VIOLENCE EVERYWHERE. After Alex Orange was shot and killed in Charlotte, North Carolina, while trying to stop a fight in 1989, his classmates at West Charlotte High School decided to organize the group Students against Violence Everywhere (SAVE). SAVE (2007, http://www.nationalsave.org/main/statistics.php) has grown far beyond Orange's high school; in 2007 it had 1,664 chapters with nearly 190,000 student members. The group is active in elementary, middle, and high schools across the United States. Members have their own "colors": orange for Alex Orange and purple for peace and nonviolence.

The group focuses on violence prevention and on helping kids gain life skills, knowledge, and an understanding of the consequences of violence and crime. SAVE helps members overcome negative peer pressure situations through the development of positive peer interactions. It also plans safe activities, including cosponsorship of the National Youth Violence Prevention Campaign (2009, http://www.violencepreventionweek.org/). During the weeklong campaign participants spend each day focused on one aspect of violence prevention. For example, the first day seeks to "promote respect and tolerance," and other days focus on anger

management, conflict resolution, school and community safety, and unity.

BIG BROTHERS BIG SISTERS IN SCHOOL. The Big Brothers Big Sisters program has been serving children for over 100 years. The organization provides one-on-one mentoring services to young people (aged five to 18) throughout the United States. Big Brothers Big Sisters seeks to help youth perform better at school, stay clear of drugs and alcohol, improve their relationships with others, and avoid lives of crime and violence. Under the main program, a child is paired with an adult who spends time with him or her several times each month on outings, which can include sports, recreation, visits to museums or parks, and so on. Through the experience, the "Bigs" help the "Littles" develop life skills, confidence, and self-esteem.

Big Brothers Big Sisters has also developed programs for school children. Through the group's outreach program, volunteers visit schools weekly to provide one-on-one mentoring to students needing help. In addition, high school students also gain experience mentoring elementary school children through the High School Bigs program. While helping older students develop skills working with children, the project helps younger children bond with teens closer to their own age and see that they, too, can grow up to lead a productive life. In *Making a Difference in Schools: The Big Brothers Big Sisters School-Based Mentoring Impact Study* (June 2007, http://www.ppv.org/ppv/publications/assets/220_publication.pdf), Carla Herrera et al. find that children in the program demonstrate eight positive academic outcomes in their first year of being matched with a mentor, including improved overall academic performance. With longer matches, children improved their expectation to attend college.

PUNISHMENT
Juvenile Justice

In *Juvenile Offenders and Victims: 2006 National Report* (March 2006, http://www.ojjdp.ncjrs.gov/ojstatbb/nr2006/downloads/NR2006.pdf), Howard N. Snyder and Melissa Sickmund of the National Center for Juvenile Justice (NCJJ) indicate that juvenile court generally has original jurisdiction in cases involving youth who are under the age of 18 when the crime was committed, when the youth is arrested, or when the offender is referred to the court. In 2004 37 states and the District of Columbia considered the oldest age for juveniles to be 17. Ten states (Georgia, Illinois, Louisiana, Massachusetts, Michigan, Missouri, New Hampshire, South Carolina, Texas, and Wisconsin) used 16—meaning that youth aged 17 are under the jurisdiction of criminal courts. In Connecticut, New York, and North Carolina, the age was set at 15—in other words, 16- and 17-year-olds are tried in criminal court.

When youth crime surged in the 1980s, many citizens called for changes in the juvenile justice system. According to Snyder and Sickmund, 45 states made it easier to transfer juveniles from the juvenile justice system to the criminal justice system, 31 states made a wider variety of sentencing options for juveniles available, 47 states either changed or removed confidentiality provisions of the juvenile justice system, 22 states passed laws that enhanced the rights of victims of juvenile crime, and new programs for juveniles were developed in most states. As a result of these changes, more juveniles were tried as adults in the criminal justice system. Codes regulating state juvenile justice systems now tend to strike a balance between prevention/treatment goals and punishment rather than focusing mainly on rehabilitation.

If the court deems that it is in the interests of the juvenile and the public, juvenile courts in some states may retain jurisdiction over juvenile offenders past the ages discussed earlier. Thus, such courts can handle juvenile offenders until they turn 20 in 33 states and the District of Columbia. Snyder and Sickmund note that Florida uses age 21, Kansas uses age 22, and California, Montana, Oregon, and Wisconsin use age 24 as the cutoff. Extended jurisdiction, however, may be limited by legislation to specific crimes or certain juveniles. Hence, the question of "who is considered a juvenile" does not have one consistent, standard answer. In various states exceptions can be made to the age criteria. This is done so that juveniles can be tried as adults or to provide for procedures under which a prosecutor can decide to handle an offender as a juvenile or an adult.

DOES IT WORK? The Federal Bureau of Investigation (FBI) notes in *Crime in the United States, 2007* (September 2008, http://www.fbi.gov/ucr/cius2007/index.html) that from 1998 to 2007 the number of juveniles arrested for murder and nonnegligent manslaughter dropped 23.4%, and juvenile arrests for most other violent crimes had also fallen. In 2007 only 753 juveniles were arrested for murder and nonnegligent manslaughter, compared to 983 in 1996. As such, some public officials believe that efforts to reduce crime through adult sentencing are working. However, many experts attribute the murder rate decline to expanded after-school crime prevention programs, the decline of crack cocaine and violent gangs, and big-city police efforts to crack down on illegal guns.

Youth on Trial: A Developmental Perspective on Juvenile Justice (Thomas Grisso and Robert G. Schwartz, eds., 2000) discusses some of the problems in transferring juveniles to adult court. The authors note that juveniles have a harder time than adults when making "knowing and intelligent" decisions at many junctures in the criminal justice process. In particular, problems occur when waiving Miranda rights, which allow the juvenile to remain silent and talk to a lawyer before responding to questions posed by police. When a juvenile waives such rights, this can lead to much more serious consequences in adult court than in juvenile proceedings. The authors assert that "questions must be raised regarding the juvenile's judgment, decision-making capacity, and impulse control as they relate to criminal culpability" in adult proceedings. Researchers and experts in child development

explain that before deciding if a youth can be held accountable as an adult for a particular offense, it is important to understand an adolescent's intellectual, social, and emotional development.

Juvenile Arrests

According to statistics maintained by the FBI, the property and violent crime arrest rate for juveniles aged 10 to 17 began to rise during the 1980s. As recorded in the FBI's Property Crime Index and its Violent Crime Index, arrests per 100,000 juveniles in that age bracket decreased for both property and violent crime from around 1980 to 1983. At that point, property crime arrests began a gradual increase, whereas violent crime started to surge in the late 1980s. Around 1995 arrest rates for both property crime and violent crime began to decrease, with violent crimes seeing the greatest reductions.

Between 1998 and 2007 the number of juveniles arrested for all crimes dropped 20.4%; during this same period arrests of adults increased by 0.5%. (See Table 10.1.) Arrests of juveniles for some offenses declined even more drastically. For example, arrests of juveniles for murder and nonnegligent manslaughter dropped 23.4%; for drunkenness, dropped 27.9%; for burglary, dropped 30.3%; for forcible rape, dropped 31.6%; and for motor vehicle theft, dropped 48.8%. Other offenses dropped much less. For example, arrests for drug abuse violations dropped by only 5.9%; for carrying or possessing weapons, by 7.8%; and for sex offenses other than rape and prostitution, by 15%. Arrests of juveniles for prostitution actually increased by 5.7% during this period and arrests for robbery increased by 6%.

In *Crime in the United States, 2007*, the FBI reports that 8.1 million arrests were made nationwide in 2007, a decrease of 3.3% from 1998. In 2007, 15% of all people arrested were juveniles and 85% were adults. Adults were most often arrested for drug abuse violations (923,759 arrests), whereas juveniles were most often arrested for larceny-theft (175,561 arrests). Adults were proportionally more likely to be arrested for violent crime than were juveniles, whereas juveniles were more likely to be arrested for property crime. In 2007, 84% of arrests for violent crime were arrests of adults; however, only 74% of arrests for property crime were of adults.

ARRESTS AMONG SPECIFIC AGE GROUPS. The FBI also records in *Crime in the United States, 2007* arrest rate statistics for specific age groups: under age 15, under age 18, under age 21, and under age 25. Even though 15.4% of all people arrested were juveniles in 2007, almost half (44.4%) of all people arrested were under the age of 25, highlighting that crime is often perpetrated by young adults, rather than juveniles.(See Table 10.2.) These statistics also show what crimes are more likely to be committed by juveniles as opposed to young adults. The table compares the number of arrests for these four age groups against the total number of arrests for all ages in 2007. For each

TABLE 10.1

Ten-year arrest trends, 1998–2007

[7,946 agencies; 2007 estimated population 171,876,948; 1998 estimated population 154,013,711]

	Number of persons arrested								
	Total all ages			Under 18 years of age			18 years of age and over		
Offense charged	1998	2007	Percent change	1998	2007	Percent change	1998	2007	Percent change
Total[a]	8,397,065	8,118,197	−3.3	1,527,681	1,215,839	−20.4	6,869,384	6,902,358	+0.5
Murder and nonnegligent manslaughter	8,232	7,301	−11.3	983	753	−23.4	7,249	6,548	−9.7
Forcible rape	17,148	13,212	−23.0	2,975	2,034	−31.6	14,173	11,178	−21.1
Robbery	68,353	72,355	+5.9	18,439	19,550	+6.0	49,914	52,805	+5.8
Aggravated assault	290,851	257,464	−11.5	42,358	33,314	−21.4	248,493	224,150	−9.8
Burglary	195,696	182,552	−6.7	70,171	48,903	−30.3	125,525	133,649	+6.5
Larceny-theft	791,085	689,037	−12.9	258,540	175,561	−32.1	532,545	513,476	−3.6
Motor vehicle theft	80,925	62,766	−22.4	29,882	15,289	−48.8	51,043	47,477	−7.0
Arson	10,055	9,094	−9.6	5,407	4,391	−18.8	4,648	4,703	+1.2
Violent crime[b]	384,584	350,332	−8.9	64,755	55,651	−14.1	319,829	294,681	−7.9
Property crime[b]	1,077,761	943,449	−12.5	364,000	244,144	−32.9	713,761	699,305	−2.0
Other assaults	768,038	754,280	−1.8	138,780	138,795	*	629,258	615,485	−2.2
Forgery and counterfeiting	67,870	58,832	−13.3	4,250	1,699	−60.0	63,620	57,133	−10.2
Fraud	213,800	147,985	−30.8	6,066	4,480	−26.1	207,734	143,505	−30.9
Embezzlement	11,115	14,065	+26.5	1,018	1,072	+5.3	10,097	12,993	+28.7
Stolen property; buying, receiving, possession	78,371	72,904	−7.0	19,869	13,230	−33.4	58,502	59,674	+2.0
Vandalism	173,617	168,815	−2.8	75,418	64,927	−13.9	98,199	103,888	+5.8
Weapons; carrying, possessing, etc.	109,533	106,080	−3.2	26,395	24,328	−7.8	83,138	81,752	−1.7
Prostitution and commercialized vice	50,082	39,081	−22.0	743	785	+5.7	49,339	38,296	−22.4
Sex offenses (except forcible rape and prostitution)	52,527	45,871	−12.7	9,531	8,106	−15.0	42,996	37,765	−12.2
Drug abuse violations	878,355	1,033,203	+17.6	116,352	109,444	−5.9	762,003	923,759	+21.2
Gambling	5,067	3,289	−35.1	495	360	−27.3	4,572	2,929	−35.9
Offenses against the family and children	85,823	71,305	−16.9	5,765	3,095	−46.3	80,058	68,210	−14.8
Driving under the influence	803,030	788,864	−1.8	11,917	9,867	−17.2	791,113	778,997	−1.5
Liquor laws	375,009	332,231	−11.4	94,257	74,948	−20.5	280,752	257,283	−8.4
Drunkenness	468,796	410,583	−12.4	15,964	11,518	−27.9	452,832	399,065	−11.9
Disorderly conduct	387,534	358,428	−7.5	101,767	104,380	+2.6	285,767	254,048	−11.1
Vagrancy	17,994	16,388	−8.9	1,805	2,719	+50.6	16,189	13,669	−15.6
All other offenses (except traffic)	2,185,863	2,267,145	+3.7	266,238	207,224	−22.2	1,919,625	2,059,921	+7.3
Suspicion	3,463	1,299	−62.5	903	255	−71.8	2,560	1,044	−59.2
Curfew and loitering law violations	104,976	73,217	−30.3	104,976	73,217	−30.3	—	—	—
Runaways	97,320	61,850	−36.4	97,320	61,850	−36.4	—	—	—

[a]Does not include suspicion.
[b]Violent crimes are offenses of murder and nonnegligent manslaughter, forcible rape, robbery, and aggravated assault. Property crimes are offenses of burglary, larceny-theft, motor vehicle theft, and arson.
*Less than one-tenth of 1 percent.

SOURCE: "Table 32. Ten-Year Arrest Trends: Totals, 1998–2007," in *Crime in the United States, 2007*, U.S. Department of Justice, Federal Bureau of Investigation, September 2008, http://www.fbi.gov/ucr/cius2007/data/table_32.html (accessed November 11, 2008)

offense, it presents the number of actual arrests for each age group as well as what percentage of total arrests falls within each age group.

A high percentage does not necessarily indicate a high number of arrests in a category. Instead, it means that age group was responsible for a high percentage of arrests within that category. For example, 147,382 individuals under the age of 18 were arrested on drug abuse violations, which was 10.6% of the total arrests in that category. For comparison, 16,889 people under the age of 18 were arrested for buying, receiving, and possessing stolen property. Even though the number of stolen property offenses is far less than that of drug abuse violations for those under the age of 18, it represented 18.3% of the total arrests for stolen property. Such percentages help law enforcement personnel identify trends and patterns in juvenile crime.

Two categories that consistently had high arrest percentages among each of the four age groups presented in Table 10.2 were arson and vandalism. Two-thirds of arrests for each of these crimes (66.5% and 67%, respectively) were of young adults under the age of 25. Of the 11,451 arrests for arson in 2007, 28% were of youth under age 15, 47.4% were of juveniles under age 18, and 58.3% were of people under age 21. Vandalism was less associated with the youngest juveniles. Of the 221,040 people arrested for vandalism in 2007, 15.5% were under age 15, 38.3% were under age 18, and 54% were under age 21.

Other categories with the highest arrest percentages for those under the age of 15 include disorderly conduct (10.7%), larceny-theft (7.9%), sex offenses, except forcible rape and prostitution (8.9%), and burglary (8.1%). (See Table 10.2.) The under-age-15 group also scored high in two other

TABLE 10.2

Arrests of persons under 15, 18, 21, and 25 years of age, 2007

[11,936 agencies; 2007 estimated population 225,518,634]

Offense charged	Total all ages	Number of persons arrested				Percent of total all ages			
		Under 15	Under 18	Under 21	Under 25	Under 15	Under 18	Under 21	Under 25
Total	10,698,310	461,937	1,649,977	3,159,716	4,753,345	4.3	15.4	29.5	44.4
Murder and nonnegligent manslaughter	10,082	103	1,011	3,027	5,084	1.0	10.0	30.0	50.4
Forcible rape	17,132	914	2,633	4,988	7,433	5.3	15.4	29.1	43.4
Robbery	96,720	5,601	26,324	47,770	62,542	5.8	27.2	49.4	64.7
Aggravated assault	327,137	13,662	43,459	80,724	129,264	4.2	13.3	24.7	39.5
Burglary	228,846	18,589	61,695	103,648	134,198	8.1	27.0	45.3	58.6
Larceny-theft	897,626	71,314	229,837	370,731	478,160	7.9	25.6	41.3	53.3
Motor vehicle theft	89,022	4,917	22,266	37,083	50,174	5.5	25.0	41.7	56.4
Arson	11,451	3,204	5,427	6,676	7,614	28.0	47.4	58.3	66.5
Violent crime[a]	451,071	20,280	73,427	136,509	204,323	4.5	16.3	30.3	45.3
Property crime[a]	1,226,945	98,024	319,225	518,138	670,146	8.0	26.0	42.2	54.6
Other assaults	983,964	70,038	181,378	278,521	413,165	7.1	18.4	28.3	42.0
Forgery and counterfeiting	78,005	294	2,353	11,760	24,739	0.4	3.0	15.1	31.7
Fraud	185,229	886	5,690	22,358	47,593	0.5	3.1	12.1	25.7
Embezzlement	17,015	49	1,288	4,745	7,871	0.3	7.6	27.9	46.3
Stolen property; buying, receiving, possessing	92,215	4,136	16,889	32,394	46,285	4.5	18.3	35.1	50.2
Vandalism	221,040	34,342	84,744	119,283	148,140	15.5	38.3	54.0	67.0
Weapons; carrying, possessing, etc.	142,745	10,577	33,187	58,664	83,152	7.4	23.2	41.1	58.3
Prostitution and commercialized vice	59,390	147	1,160	7,615	16,180	0.2	2.0	12.8	27.2
Sex offenses (except forcible rape and prostitution)	62,756	5,574	11,575	18,399	25,403	8.9	18.4	29.3	40.5
Drug abuse violations	1,386,394	21,506	147,382	392,486	636,465	1.6	10.6	28.3	45.9
Gambling	9,152	226	1,584	3,510	5,013	2.5	17.3	38.4	54.8
Offenses against the family and children	88,887	1,237	4,205	10,005	20,422	1.4	4.7	11.3	23.0
Driving under the influence	1,055,981	398	13,497	107,733	311,920	[b]	1.3	10.2	29.5
Liquor laws	478,671	9,592	106,537	340,122	373,174	2.0	22.3	71.1	78.0
Drunkenness	451,055	1,400	12,966	54,066	128,759	0.3	2.9	12.0	28.5
Disorderly conduct	540,270	57,602	153,293	219,327	300,984	10.7	28.4	40.6	55.7
Vagrancy	25,631	904	2,924	5,775	8,296	3.5	11.4	22.5	32.4
All other offenses (except traffic)	2,948,031	69,448	284,096	625,448	1,088,202	2.4	9.6	21.2	36.9
Suspicion	1,589	78	303	584	839	4.9	19.1	36.8	52.8
Curfew and loitering law violations	109,815	28,949	109,815	109,815	109,815	26.4	100.0	100.0	100.0
Runaways	82,459	26,250	82,459	82,459	82,459	31.8	100.0	100.0	100.0

[a] Violent crimes are offenses of murder and nonnegligent manslaughter, forcible rape, robbery, and aggravated assault. Property crimes are offenses of burglary, larceny-theft, motor vehicle theft, and arson.
[b] Less than one-tenth of 1 percent.

SOURCE: "Table 41. Arrests of Persons under 15, 18, 21, and 25 Years of Age, 2007," in *Crime in the United States, 2007*, U.S. Department of Justice, Federal Bureau of Investigation, September 2008, http://www.fbi.gov/ucr/cius2007/data/table_41.html (accessed November 11, 2008)

categories that are not applicable to those over age 18: curfew and loitering law violations and runaway arrests. A little more than a quarter (26.4%) of all arrests for curfew violations were of people under the age of 15, whereas 31.8% of arrests of runaways were of people under the age of 15. Arrests for murder (1%), fraud (0.5%), forgery and counterfeiting (0.4%), embezzlement (0.3%), drunkenness (0.3%), and prostitution (0.2%) were the least likely to be of children under the age of 15.

All arrests for curfew violations and of runaways were of youth under the age of 18. Besides arson and vandalism, arrests for disorderly conduct (28.4%), burglary (27%), larceny-theft (25.6%), motor vehicle theft (25%), and carrying and possessing weapons (23.2%) were particularly likely to be of youth under the age of 18. (See Table 10.2.) Arrests for driving under the influence of alcohol (1.3%), prostitution (2%), drunkenness (2.9%), forgery and counterfeiting (3%), fraud (3.1%), and offenses against the family and children (4.7%) were the least likely to be of youth under the age of 18.

Despite the overall decrease in arrests of juveniles, delinquency cases handled by juvenile courts nationwide increased by 46% between 1985 and 2005. (See Figure 10.1.) Between 1997 and 2005 the number of public order offense cases increased by 16%, drug law violation cases increased by 3%, and person offense cases increased by 4%. After big jumps between 1985 and 1997, property offense cases decreased 30% between 1997 and 2005.

ARRESTS BY GENDER. Young males were arrested in far greater numbers than young females between 1998 and 2007. However, juvenile female arrest rates grew proportionately in relation to arrests of young males, particularly in violent crime. In 1998 females represented 27% (412,694 out of a total of 1,527,681 juvenile arrests) of the juveniles arrested. (See Table 10.3.) By 2007 the percentage of juvenile arrests who were female had reached 29% (357,093 out of a total of 1,215,839 juvenile arrests). Even though arrests of both young males and young females decreased between 1998 and 2007, arrests of females decreased less. Arrests of males

FIGURE 10.1

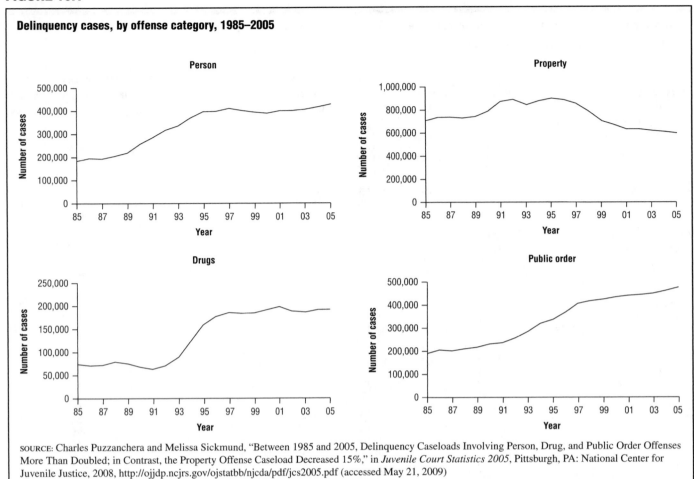

Delinquency cases, by offense category, 1985–2005

SOURCE: Charles Puzzanchera and Melissa Sickmund, "Between 1985 and 2005, Delinquency Caseloads Involving Person, Drug, and Public Order Offenses More Than Doubled; in Contrast, the Property Offense Caseload Decreased 15%," in *Juvenile Court Statistics 2005*, Pittsburgh, PA: National Center for Juvenile Justice, 2008, http://ojjdp.ncjrs.gov/ojstatbb/njcda/pdf/jcs2005.pdf (accessed May 21, 2009)

under the age of 18 decreased by 23% over the decade, whereas arrests of females under the age of 18 decreased by only 13.5%. In some categories, female arrests increased while male arrests decreased.

For example, between 1998 and 2007 juvenile male arrests for aggravated assault dropped by 22.5%, whereas juvenile female arrests dropped by only 17.3%. (See Table 10.3.) Juvenile male arrests for other assaults dropped by 4.4%, whereas juvenile female arrests increased by 10.1%. Arrests of juvenile males for drug abuse violations dropped by 7.9%, whereas arrests of juvenile females for the same offenses increased by 5.9%. Arrests of juvenile males for driving while intoxicated decreased by 23.7%, but for juvenile females increased by 13.8%.

These male and female arrest trends among juveniles reflect to some degree changes in arrest trends among male and female adults. In *Crime in the United States, 2007*, the FBI reports that in 2007, 75.8% (6,150,145 out of a total of 8,118,197 arrests) of all arrests in the United States were of males (all ages). (See Table 10.3.) In that year, 81.7% (286,190 out of a total of 350,332 arrests) of people arrested for violent crime were male, whereas 66.4% (626,799 out of a total of 943,449 arrests) of those arrested for property crime

were male. Between 1998 and 2007 the number of arrests of males dropped by 6.1%, whereas the number of arrests of females increased 6.6%.

According to the FBI's 10-year arrest trends, juvenile males and females engage in many of the same types of crimes. For example, the crime most frequently committed by both males and females was larceny-theft. Even though the numbers of arrests were down for both males and females in this category in 2007, males were arrested 100,043 times and females were arrested 75,519 times for larceny-theft. (See Table 10.3.) As such, juvenile males were responsible for 14.5% (100,042 out of a total of 689,037 arrests) of arrests for larceny-theft and juvenile females for 11% (75,519 out of 689,037). Together, juvenile offenders represented almost 25.5% (175,561 out of 689,037) of all larceny-theft arrests.

Other areas with high arrest rates of both juvenile males and females include other assaults, disorderly conduct, and drug abuse violations. Young males were arrested 91,986 times on other assault charges, whereas young females were arrested 46,809 times for that offense in 2007. (See Table 10.3.) Disorderly conduct resulted in 69,051 young males and 35,329 young females under the age of 18 being arrested, and drug abuse violations accounted for the arrests of 91,800 young males and 17,644 young females.

TABLE 10.3

Ten-year arrest trends by sex, 1998–2007

[7,946 agencies; 2007 estimated population 171,876,948; 1998 estimated population 154,013,711]

	Male						Female					
	Total			Under 18			Total			Under 18		
Offense charged	1998	2007	Percent change	1998	2007	Percent change	1998	2007	Percent change	1998	2007	Percent change
Total[a]	**6,550,864**	**6,150,145**	**−6.1**	**1,114,987**	**858,746**	**−23.0**	**1,846,201**	**1,968,052**	**+6.6**	**412,694**	**357,093**	**−13.5**
Murder and nonnegligent manslaughter	7,342	6,519	−11.2	898	702	−21.8	890	782	−12.1	85	51	−40.0
Forcible rape	16,942	13,079	−22.8	2,914	2,005	−31.2	206	133	−35.4	61	29	−52.5
Robbery	61,410	64,004	+4.2	16,813	17,654	+5.0	6,943	8,351	+20.3	1,626	1,896	+16.6
Aggravated assault	234,040	202,588	−13.4	33,029	25,602	−22.5	56,811	54,876	−3.4	9,329	7,712	−17.3
Burglary	170,504	154,607	−9.3	62,217	42,872	−31.1	25,192	27,945	+10.9	7,954	6,031	−24.2
Larceny-theft	514,574	413,125	−19.7	169,452	100,042	−41.0	276,511	275,912	−0.2	89,088	75,519	−15.2
Motor vehicle theft	68,494	51,382	−25.0	24,689	12,701	−48.6	12,431	11,384	−8.4	5,193	2,588	−50.2
Arson	8,606	7,685	−10.7	4,832	3,880	−19.7	1,449	1,409	−2.8	575	511	−11.1
Violent crime[b]	319,734	286,190	−10.5	53,654	45,963	−14.3	64,850	64,142	−1.1	11,101	9,688	−12.7
Property crime[b]	762,178	626,799	−17.8	261,190	159,495	−38.9	315,583	316,650	+0.3	102,810	84,649	−17.7
Other assaults	593,042	560,655	−5.5	96,249	91,986	−4.4	174,996	193,625	+10.6	42,531	46,809	+10.1
Forgery and counterfeiting	41,508	36,217	−12.7	2,754	1,146	−58.4	26,362	22,615	−14.2	1,496	553	−63.0
Fraud	114,751	82,340	−28.2	3,969	2,849	−28.2	99,049	65,645	−33.7	2,097	1,631	−22.2
Embezzlement	5,584	6,849	+22.7	575	618	+7.5	5,531	7,216	+30.5	443	454	+2.5
Stolen property; buying, receiving, possessing	66,132	57,865	−12.5	17,289	10,809	−37.5	12,239	15,039	+22.9	2,580	2,421	−6.2
Vandalism	147,331	139,748	−5.1	66,314	56,177	−15.3	26,286	29,067	+10.6	9,104	8,750	−3.9
Weapons; carrying, possessing, etc.	100,973	97,822	−3.1	24,048	21,999	−8.5	8,560	8,258	−3.5	2,347	2,329	−0.8
Prostitution and commercialized vice	20,745	11,485	−44.6	349	170	−51.3	29,337	27,596	−5.9	394	615	+56.1
Sex offenses (except forcible rape and prostitution)	48,658	42,369	−12.9	8,870	7,450	−16.0	3,869	3,502	−9.5	661	656	−0.8
Drug abuse violations	723,435	833,941	+15.3	99,691	91,800	−7.9	154,920	199,262	+28.6	16,661	17,644	+5.9
Gambling	4,568	2,769	−39.4	479	347	−27.6	499	520	+4.2	16	13	−18.8
Offenses against the family and children	67,843	53,754	−20.8	3,648	1,885	−48.3	17,980	17,551	−2.4	2,117	1,210	−42.8
Driving under the influence	676,911	626,371	−7.5	9,849	7,513	−23.7	126,119	162,493	+28.8	2,068	2,354	+13.8
Liquor laws	294,553	242,820	−17.6	66,251	47,505	−28.3	80,456	89,411	+11.1	28,006	27,443	−2.0
Drunkenness	409,100	345,502	−15.5	13,056	8,697	−33.4	59,696	65,081	+9.0	2,908	2,821	−3.0
Disorderly conduct	293,691	261,327	−11.0	72,357	69,051	−4.6	93,843	97,101	+3.5	29,410	35,329	+20.1
Vagrancy	14,281	12,761	−10.6	1,505	1,917	+27.4	3,713	3,627	−2.3	300	802	+167.3
All other offenses (except traffic)	1,732,271	1,744,417	+0.7	199,315	153,225	−23.1	453,592	522,728	+15.2	66,923	53,999	−19.3
Suspicion	2,766	1,031	−62.7	686	189	−72.4	697	268	−61.5	217	66	−69.6
Curfew and loitering law violations	73,163	51,116	−30.1	73,163	51,116	−30.1	31,813	22,101	−30.5	31,813	22,101	−30.5
Runaways	40,412	27,028	−33.1	40,412	27,028	−33.1	56,908	34,822	−38.8	56,908	34,822	−38.8

[a]Does not include suspicion.

[b]Violent crimes are offenses of murder and nonnegligent manslaughter, forcible rape, robbery, and aggravated assault. Property crimes are offenses of burglary, larceny-theft, motor vehicle theft, and arson.

SOURCE: "Table 33. Ten-Year Arrest Trends by Sex, 1998–2007," in *Crime in the United States, 2007*, U.S. Department of Justice, Federal Bureau of Investigation, September 2008, http://www.fbi.gov/ucr/cius2007/data/table_33.html (accessed November 11, 2008)

Other crimes most frequently committed by young males and females in 2007 included liquor law violations (47,505 arrests for males and 27,443 arrests for females) and curfew and loitering law violations (51,116 arrests for males and 22,101 arrests for females). (See Table 10.3.) Males also saw high numbers of arrests for vandalism (56,177 arrests), whereas young females were arrested 34,822 times as runaways.

Despite the high number of juvenile crimes, arrest rates for youth under the age of 18 were down in many categories between 1998 and 2007. Young males experienced the greatest decline in the number of arrests for forgery and counterfeiting (down 58.4%), prostitution and commercialized vice (down 51.3%), motor vehicle theft (down 48.6%), and larceny-theft (down 41%). (See Table 10.3.) During this same period young female arrest rates dropped most for forgery and counterfeiting (down 63%), forcible rape (down 52.5%), and motor vehicle theft (down 50.2%). Arrests based on suspicion were down for both young males (down 72.4%) and young females (down 69.6%).

Over the decade juvenile arrests of males increased in only two categories: vagrancy (up 27.4%) and embezzlement (up 7.5%). (See Table 10.3.) By contrast, arrests of young females were up for vagrancy (up 167.3%), prostitution and commercialized vice (up 56.1%), disorderly conduct (up 20.1%), robbery (up 16.6%), other assaults (up 10.1%), drug abuse violations (up 5.9%), and embezzlement (up 2.5%).

ARRESTS BY RACE. African-Americans are disproportionately arrested in the United States. The U.S. Census Bureau (April 30, 2008, http://www.census.gov/popest/natio nal/asrh/NC-EST2007-asrh.html) estimates that in 2007, the U.S. population was 66.3% non-Hispanic white, 12.9% African-American, 4.5% Asian-American, and 1% Native American or Alaskan Native. Hispanics, who can be of any race, represented 15.2% of the total population. In *Crime in the United States, 2007*, the FBI notes that two-thirds (69.7%) of all arrested individuals in 2007 were white, 28.2% were African-American, 1.3% were Native American or Alaskan Native, and 0.8% were Asian or Pacific Islander.

Arrested juveniles exhibited a similar racial distribution; 67% were white, 30.8% were African-American, 1.2% were Native American or Alaskan Native, and 1% were Asian or Pacific Islander 2007. (See Table 10.4.) Among juveniles, a particularly high proportion of those arrested for driving under the influence (93.1%), violation of liquor laws (91%), drunkenness (89.3%), vandalism (78.8%), vagrancy (77.6%), arson (76.4%), and offenses against the family and children (72.8%) were white. A particularly high proportion of those arrested for gambling (95.4%), robbery (67.8%), prostitution and commercialized vice (58%), and murder and nonnegligent manslaughter (57.4%) were African-American. The FBI data on arrests by race did not identify arrest rates by Hispanic origin.

DISPOSITION OF JUVENILES ARRESTED. Ann L. Pastore and Kathleen Maguire report in *Sourcebook of Criminal Justice Statistics* (2003, http://www.albany.edu/sourcebook/ pdf/t4262004.pdf) that in the 1970s a change occurred in the disposition of arrested juveniles. Statistics for 1972 show that 50.8% of arrested minors were referred to juvenile court, 45% were handled within the police department and then released, and 1.3% were referred to criminal or adult court. In other words, almost half of all arrested juveniles were not formally charged with offenses in either juvenile or criminal court. From 1972 to 2000, however, those referred to juvenile court increased to 70.8%, whereas those handled internally and then released dropped to 20.3%. The percentage of juvenile cases referred to criminal or adult court rose to 7%. By 2007 only 19.5% of juveniles arrested were released after being handled internally within the department, 69.6% were referred to juvenile court jurisdiction, and 9.4% were referred to criminal or adult court. (See Table 10.5.) Also included in this table are statistics for the percentage of juveniles referred to a welfare agency (0.4%) and those referred to another police agency (1.2%).

Juveniles in Custody

The OJJDP classifies juveniles in residential placement into three categories: committed, detained, and under a diversion agreement. According to the OJJDP (2009, http://ojjdp .ncjrs.org/ojstatbb/glossary.html), committed juveniles include those placed in the facility as part of a court-ordered disposition; detained juveniles include those held awaiting a court hearing, adjudication, disposition, or placement elsewhere; and voluntarily admitted juveniles include those in the facility as part of a diversion agreement.

Snyder and Sickmund note that of the 109,225 juvenile offenders in residential placement overall in 2003, 74% were committed, 25% were detained, and less than 1% were under diversion agreements. The largest group, committed, was sent to residential placement by juvenile courts. Those being detained were part of a transitory population—those awaiting hearings, awaiting the disposition of their cases, or awaiting transfer to a different type of facility. It is likely that some of the detained individuals were later sent to prison or jail. People in confinement under diversion agreements have entered detention voluntarily. In other words, the juvenile may have volunteered to go to a detention center to avoid going to juvenile court.

DETENTION. About one out of five juveniles are put in detention as their cases are processed in juvenile court. Detention may be used if the youth is judged to be a threat to the community, will be at risk if returned to the community, or may not appear at an upcoming hearing if released. Snyder and Sickmund report that the number of delinquency cases involving detention increased 42% between 1985 and 2002, from 234,600 to 329,800. The largest increase was for drug cases (140%), followed by crimes against people (122%), and public order cases (72%). The number of juveniles detained in

TABLE 10.4

Arrests of juveniles by race, 2007

[11,929 agencies; 2007 estimated population 225,477,173]

Offense charged	Arrests under 18					Percent distribution[a]				
	Total	White	Black	American Indian or Alaskan Native	Asian or Pacific Islander	Total	White	Black	American Indian or Alaskan Native	Asian or Pacific Islander
Total	**1,642,530**	**1,100,427**	**505,464**	**20,504**	**16,135**	**100.0**	**67.0**	**30.8**	**1.2**	**1.0**
Murder and nonnegligent manslaughter	1,011	407	580	15	9	100.0	40.3	57.4	1.5	0.9
Forcible rape	2,617	1,610	966	24	17	100.0	61.5	36.9	0.9	0.6
Robbery	26,291	8,119	17,832	122	218	100.0	30.9	67.8	0.5	0.8
Aggravated assault	43,322	24,674	17,773	470	405	100.0	57.0	41.0	1.1	0.9
Burglary	61,523	40,236	20,176	605	506	100.0	65.4	32.8	1.0	0.8
Larceny-theft	228,699	152,143	70,212	2,966	3,378	100.0	66.5	30.7	1.3	1.5
Motor vehicle theft	22,227	12,191	9,426	339	271	100.0	54.8	42.4	1.5	1.2
Arson	5,397	4,123	1,148	49	77	100.0	76.4	21.3	0.9	1.4
Violent crime[b]	73,241	34,810	37,151	631	649	100.0	47.5	50.7	0.9	0.9
Property crime[b]	317,846	208,693	100,962	3,959	4,232	100.0	65.7	31.8	1.2	1.3
Other assaults	180,615	106,119	71,409	1,857	1,230	100.0	58.8	39.5	1.0	0.7
Forgery and counterfeiting	2,341	1,699	596	21	25	100.0	72.6	25.5	0.9	1.1
Fraud	5,649	3,601	1,916	77	55	100.0	63.7	33.9	1.4	1.0
Embezzlement	1,287	753	498	10	26	100.0	58.5	38.7	0.8	2.0
Stolen property; buying, receiving, possession	16,809	9,203	7,302	127	177	100.0	54.8	43.4	0.8	1.1
Vandalism	84,298	66,406	16,058	1,062	772	100.0	78.8	19.0	1.3	0.9
Weapons; carrying, possessing, etc.	33,040	19,992	12,412	250	386	100.0	60.5	37.6	0.8	1.2
Prostitution and commercialized vice	1,156	473	670	9	4	100.0	40.9	58.0	0.8	0.3
Sex offenses (except forcible rape and prostitution)	11,526	8,139	3,239	77	71	100.0	70.6	28.1	0.7	0.6
Drug abuse violations	146,785	101,152	43,343	1,295	995	100.0	68.9	29.5	0.9	0.7
Gambling	1,584	67	1,511	1	5	100.0	4.2	95.4	0.1	0.3
Offenses against the family and children	4,161	3,029	1,047	60	25	100.0	72.8	25.2	1.4	0.6
Driving under the influence	13,420	12,498	589	238	95	100.0	93.1	4.4	1.8	0.7
Liquor laws	105,799	96,286	5,466	2,965	1,082	100.0	91.0	5.2	2.8	1.0
Drunkenness	12,909	11,532	997	277	103	100.0	89.3	7.7	2.1	0.8
Disorderly conduct	152,817	87,683	62,490	1,602	1,042	100.0	57.4	40.9	1.0	0.7
Vagrancy	2,923	2,267	625	19	12	100.0	77.6	21.4	0.7	0.4
All other offenses (except traffic)	282,244	198,916	77,153	3,313	2,862	100.0	70.5	27.3	1.2	1.0
Suspicion	287	184	100	3	0	100.0	64.1	34.8	1.0	0.0
Curfew and loitering law violations	109,575	69,950	37,532	964	1,129	100.0	63.8	34.3	0.9	1.0
Runaways	82,218	56,975	22,398	1,687	1,158	100.0	69.3	27.2	2.1	1.4

[a]Because of rounding, the percentages may not add to 100.0.
[b]Violent crimes are offenses of murder and nonnegligent manslaughter, forcible rape, robbery, and aggravated assault. Property crimes are offenses of burglary, larceny-theft, motor vehicle theft, and arson.

SOURCE: Adapted from "Table 43. Arrests by Race, 2007," in *Crime in the United States, 2007*, U.S. Department of Justice, Federal Bureau of Investigation, September 2008, http://www.fbi.gov/ucr/cius2007/data/table_43.html (accessed November 11, 2008).

property cases declined by 12% during this period. Figure 10.2 shows that the percent of juveniles who were detained for these cases fluctuated between 1985 and 2002, but did not experience much change overall.

Snyder and Sickmund find that the use of detention increased more for females than for males between 1985 and 2002 (87% and 34%, respectively). However, males continued to be more likely than females to be detained, despite the increase in the use of detention for female juvenile offenders. Likewise, the use of detention increased more for African-American youth between 1985 and 2002 (64%) than it did for white youth (32%). Even though a larger number of white youth than African-American youth were detained, African-American youth were proportionately more likely than white youth to be detained. This disparity was greatest in drug cases—African-American youth were more than two times more likely than white youth to be detained for these offenses.

RESIDENTIAL PLACEMENT. Youths sentenced under the jurisdiction of juvenile courts could be generally confined in residential placement facilities. In 2006, 92,854 juvenile offenders were confined in public and private juvenile correctional, detention, and shelter facilities. (See Table 10.6.) Excluded from this category are juveniles in prisons and jails. Sarah Livsey, Melissa Sickmund, and Anthony Sladky of the NCJJ find in *Juvenile Residential Facility Census, 2004: Selected Findings* (January 2009, http://www.ncjrs.gov/pdffiles1/ojjdp/222721.pdf) that the number of juvenile offenders in custody decreased 7% between 2002 and 2004, probably because of the substantial decline in the number of juvenile arrests since the mid-1990s.

The OJJDP divides juvenile crimes into delinquency offenses and status offenses. Delinquency offenses are acts that are illegal regardless of the age of the perpetrator. Status offenses are acts that are illegal only for minors, such as

TABLE 10.5

Police disposition of juvenile offenders taken into custody, 2007

[2007 estimated population]

Population group		Total[a]	Handled within department and released	Referred to juvenile court jurisdiction	Referred to welfare agency	Referred other to police agency	Referred to criminal or adult court	Number of agencies	2007 estimated population
Total agencies:	Number	663,991	129,404	461,909	2,430	8,141	62,107	5,242	120,286,534
	Percent[b]	100.0	19.5	69.6	0.4	1.2	9.4		
Total cities	Number	560,393	117,588	387,512	1,775	7,098	46,420	3,937	87,798,925
	Percent[b]	100.0	21.0	69.2	0.3	1.3	8.3		
Group I (250,000 and over)	Number	138,954	41,670	94,226	20	604	2,434	37	25,796,709
	Percent[b]	100.0	30.0	67.8	*	0.4	1.8		
Group II (100,000 to 249,999)	Number	82,959	18,009	58,590	378	2,274	3,708	80	12,018,629
	Percent[b]	100.0	21.7	70.6	0.5	2.7	4.5		
Group III (50,000 to 99,999)	Number	105,992	19,497	76,429	414	1,295	8,357	234	15,972,903
	Percent[b]	100.0	18.4	72.1	0.4	1.2	7.9		
Group IV (25,000 to 49,999)	Number	75,606	12,211	53,794	254	1,671	7,676	360	12,405,704
	Percent[b]	100.0	16.2	71.2	0.3	2.2	10.2		
Group V (10,000 to 24,999)	Number	85,504	13,001	59,213	461	688	12,141	793	12,642,471
	Percent[b]	100.0	15.2	69.3	0.5	0.8	14.2		
Group VI (under 10,000)	Number	71,378	13,200	45,260	248	566	12,104	2,433	8,962,509
	Percent[b]	100.0	18.5	63.4	0.3	0.8	17.0		
Metropolitan counties	Number	81,552	8,543	59,834	493	879	11,803	636	24,275,366
	Percent[b]	100.0	10.5	73.4	0.6	1.1	14.5		
Nonmetropolitan counties	Number	22,046	3,273	14,563	162	164	3,884	669	8,212,243
	Percent[b]	100.0	14.8	66.1	0.7	0.7	17.6		
Suburban area[c]	Number	288,762	47,148	198,657	1,429	2,557	38,971	3,278	58,405,783
	Percent[b]	100.0	16.3	68.8	0.5	0.9	13.5		

[a]Includes all offenses except traffic and neglect cases.
[b]Because of rounding, the percentages may not add to 100.0.
[c]Suburban area includes law enforcement agencies in cities with less than 50,000 inhabitants and county law enforcement agencies that are within a metropolitan statistical area. Suburban area excludes all metropolitan agencies associated with a principal city. The agencies associated with suburban areas also appear in other groups within this table.
*Less than one-tenth of 1 percent.

SOURCE: "Table 68. Police Disposition of Juvenile Offenders Taken into Custody, 2007," in *Crime in the United States, 2007*, U.S. Department of Justice, Federal Bureau of Investigation, September 2008, http://www.fbi.gov/ucr/cius2007/data/table_68.html (accessed November 11, 2008).

truancy and running away. Ninety-five percent (88,137 out of a total of 92,854) of juveniles in residential placement in 2006 were delinquents. (See Table 10.6.) The other 5% were status offenders (truants from school, noncriminal ordinances and rules violators, out-of-control youths, curfew violators, and runaways). Approximately 31,704 (34%) juveniles in residential placement were held for offenses against people (homicide, sexual assault, robbery, and aggravated or simple assault); 23,177 (25%) were held for offenses against property (burglary, theft, auto theft, arson, or other property offenses); 15,316 (16%) were held for technical violations; 9,944 (10%) were held for public order offenses; and 7,996 (9%) were held for drug offenses.

According to Melissa Sickmund, T. J. Sladky, and Wei Kang of the NCJJ, in *Census of Juveniles in Residential Placement Databook* (2008, http://www.ojjdp.ncjrs.gov/ojstatbb/cjrp/), the states with the largest number of youth under the age of 21 in residential facilities in 2006 included California (15,240), Texas (8,247), Florida (7,302), Pennsylvania (4,323), New York (4,197), and Ohio (4,149). These six states housed 47% of all juveniles in residential detention. States with the smallest number included Vermont (54), Hawaii (123), and New Hampshire (189).

DEMOGRAPHICS OF THOSE IN RESIDENTIAL PLACEMENT. Sickmund, Sladky, and Kang state that in 2006 juvenile detention facilities were home to a disproportionately larger number of males (85%) than females (15%). Of the males in confinement, 35% had committed offenses against people and 26% had committed property offenses. Females were less likely to commit person offenses (29%) and property offenses (20%) than males were. Proportionally, females in detention were more likely to have committed simple assault than males were (13% and 7%, respectively), but far less likely to have committed sexual assault (1% and 9%, respectively). A larger proportion of males were being held for burglary (11%) than were females (4%). Females were substantially more likely to be held for status offenses (14%) than were males (4%), including incorrigibility (5% of females and 2% of males), running away (4% of females and 1% of males), and truancy (3% of females and 1% of males).

Sickmund, Sladky, and Kang also report that in 2006, 65% of juveniles in residential placement nationwide were members of minority groups. Forty percent of juvenile offenders in residential placement were African-American, 20% were Hispanic, 2% were Native American, and 1% were Asian-American. About one-third (35%) of juveniles

FIGURE 10.2

Number of juvenile delinquency cases involving detention, 1985–2005

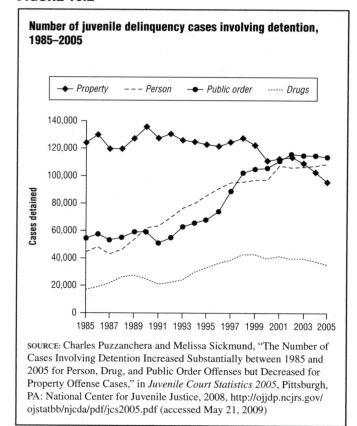

SOURCE: Charles Puzzanchera and Melissa Sickmund, "The Number of Cases Involving Detention Increased Substantially between 1985 and 2005 for Person, Drug, and Public Order Offenses but Decreased for Property Offense Cases," in *Juvenile Court Statistics 2005*, Pittsburgh, PA: National Center for Juvenile Justice, 2008, http://ojjdp.ncjrs.gov/ojstatbb/njcda/pdf/jcs2005.pdf (accessed May 21, 2009)

TABLE 10.6

Juveniles in residential placement, by offense, 2006

Most serious offense	Total
Total	**92,854**
Delinquency	88,137
Person	**31,704**
Criminal homicide	988
Sexual assault	6,792
Robbery	6,707
Aggravated assault	7,289
Simple assault	7,308
Other person	2,620
Property	**23,177**
Burglary	9,037
Theft	4,648
Auto theft	4,650
Arson	651
Other property	4,191
Drug	**7,996**
Trafficking	1,758
Other drug	6,238
Public order	**9,944**
Weapons	3,669
Alcohol	317
Other public order	5,958
Technical violation	**15,316**
Violent Crime Index[a]	**21,776**
Property Crime Index[b]	**18,986**
Status offense	**4,717**
Running away	894
Truancy	863
Incorrigibility	1,917
Curfew violation	96
Underage drinking	524
Other status offense	423

[a]Includes criminal homicide, violent sexual assault, robbery, and aggravated assault.
[b]Includes burglary, theft, auto theft, and arson.
Note: U.S. total includes 1,466 juvenile offenders in private facilities for whom state of offense was not reported and 124 juvenile offenders in tribal facilities.

SOURCE: Melissa Sickmund, T.J. Sladky, and Wei Kang, "Detailed Offense Profile for United States, 2006," in *Census of Juveniles in Residential Placement Databook*, U.S. Department of Justice, Office of Justice Programs, Office of Juvenile Justice and Delinquency Prevention, 2008, http://www.ojjdp.ncjrs.gov/ojstatbb/cjrp/asp/State_Offense.asp (accessed November 14, 2008)

in custody were non-Hispanic whites. Minority groups were overrepresented in residential placements.

Incarcerated Juveniles

In *Prison and Jail Inmates at Midyear 2006* (June 2007, http://www.ojp.usdoj.gov/bjs/pub/pdf/pjim06.pdf), William J. Sabol, Todd D. Minton, and Paige M. Harrison of the Bureau of Justice Statistics indicate that 6,104 juveniles were in prison or jail in 2006. That same year 2,364 juveniles were held in state prisons, down significantly from 3,896 in 2000. (See Table 10.7.) Of the 2,364 juveniles in state prisons as of midyear 2006, 2,259 (96%) were male.

Christopher Harney of the National Council on Crime and Delinquency reports in "Youth under Age 18 in the Adult Criminal Justice System" (June 2006, http://www.nccd-crc.org/nccd/pubs/2006may_factsheet_youthadult.pdf) that both the number of juveniles being admitted to state prisons and the proportion of people under the age of 18 in prisons have been dropping since the mid-1990s. Nearly two-thirds (62%) of these youth have been convicted of a violent offense. However, Harney points out that "the practice of sentencing youth as adults most seriously impacts African-American, Latino, and Native American youth" and that juveniles convicted in the adult system receive little or no rehabilitative assistance and are more likely to recidivate (go back to criminal behavior) than youth convicted of similar offenses in the juvenile system.

Recent breakdowns of juveniles in state and federal prisons by race are not available. However, among 22,100 (20,200 male and 1,900 female) imprisoned young adults aged 18 to 19 in 2006, 9,300 (9,000 male and 300 female) were African-American (42%), 6,700 (6,300 male and 400 female) were non-Hispanic white (30%), and 5,100 (4,900 male and 200 female) were Hispanic (23%). (See Table 10.8.) Of those who were 18 to 19 years old in 2006, the rate of incarceration for African-American males was 1,454 per 100,000; for Hispanic males, 670 per 100,000; and for non-Hispanic white males, 236 per 100,000. (See Table 10.9.) African-American and Hispanic females also had higher rates of incarceration than non-Hispanic white females. African-American young adults have a much higher rate of incarceration than do white juveniles and young adults.

JUVENILES IN JAIL. Between 2000 and 2006 the number of juveniles in local jails fell from 7,615 to 6,104, for a decrease of 20%. (See Table 10.10.) In 2006, 4,836 (79%) juveniles in local jails were being held as adults—meaning they were either being held for trial in adult criminal court or they had been convicted as adults—and 1,268 were being held as juveniles (21%).

IMPRISONING ADULTS AND JUVENILES TOGETHER. Beginning in the 1990s American society experienced a "moral panic" about juvenile crime that Laurence Steinberg argues in "Introducing the Issue" (*Future of Children*, vol. 18, no. 2, Fall 2008) fueled "get tough" on crime policies that treated many juvenile offenders as adults. A number of human rights organizations and juvenile justice groups point out the risks associated with incarcerating juveniles with adults. Among the chief concerns is that being held with

hardened adult prisoners will likely cause youth offenders to become more violent, more tough, and repeat offenders. Instead of rehabilitation and education, such juveniles are subjected to more physical and sexual abuse and violence, increasing their likelihood of showing violent tendencies when returning to society one day.

Youth in adult prisons and jails are more vulnerable to violence than they would be in juvenile-only facilities. The Campaign for Youth Justice notes in *Jailing Juveniles: The Dangers of Incarcerating Youth in Adult Jails in America* (November 2007, http://www.campaign4youthjustice.org/Downloads/NationalReportsArticles/CFYJ-Jailing_Juveniles_Report_2007-11-15.pdf) that youth are at a high risk of sexual assault while imprisoned in adult facilities. In 2005, 21% of all victims of sexual assault were juveniles, while only 1% of inmates were juveniles. The organization Act 4 Juvenile Justice notes in "Youth in Adult Prisons" (2005, http://www.act4jj.org/media/factsheets/factsheet_26.pdf) that juveniles are particularly vulnerable to physical and sexual assault at the hands of both prison staff and adult inmates because of their young age, emotional immaturity, and smaller size. In comparison to juveniles in juvenile-only facilities, those in adult facilities were twice as likely to suffer beatings by prison staff and 50% more likely to be attacked with a weapon. However, the Campaign for Youth Justice argues that merely isolating youth from adult offenders within adult prisons is not a viable answer, because such isolation puts youth at risk for mental illness. The organization notes that "even limited exposure to such an environment can cause anxiety, paranoia, exacerbate existing mental disorders, and increase the risk of suicide." In fact, youth in adult prisons are 19 times more likely than youth in the general population to commit suicide; youth imprisoned in adult facilities are 36 times more likely than youth in juvenile detention centers to commit suicide.

TABLE 10.7

Number of inmates under age 18 held in state prisons, by gender, 2000–06

Year	Total number in prison	Male	Female
2000	3,896	3,721	175
2001	3,147	3,010	137
2002	3,038	2,927	111
2003	2,741	2,627	114
2004	2,485	2,375	110
2005	2,208	2,118	90
2006	2,364	2,259	105

SOURCE: William J. Sabol, Todd D. Minton, and Paige M. Harrison, "Table 7. Number of Inmates under Age 18 Held in State Prisons, June 30, 2000–2006," in *Prison and Jail Inmates at Midyear 2006*, U.S. Department of Justice, Bureau of Justice Statistics, June 2007, http://www.ojp.usdoj.gov/bjs/pub/pdf/pjim06.pdf (accessed November 14, 2008)

TABLE 10.8

Number of sentenced prisoners under State or Federal jurisdiction, by gender, race, Hispanic origin, and age, 2006

Age group	Male[a] Total[b]	White[c]	Black[c]	Hispanic	Female[a] Total[b]	White[c]	Black[c]	Hispanic
Total	**1,399,100**	**478,000**	**534,200**	**290,500**	**103,100**	**49,100**	**28,600**	**17,500**
18–19	22,100	6,300	9,000	4,900	1,000	400	300	200
20–24	197,500	58,500	77,500	46,600	11,500	5,400	2,900	2,400
25–29	245,000	68,300	99,200	60,000	16,100	7,500	4,300	3,300
30–34	227,700	68,200	90,900	53,200	17,200	8,200	4,700	3,000
35–39	213,800	72,800	82,600	44,100	19,300	9,100	5,500	3,200
40–44	197,600	75,100	74,100	35,000	17,900	8,700	5,200	2,500
45–54	216,700	88,300	78,900	34,800	16,200	7,700	4,700	2,300
55 or older	76,500	40,100	21,100	11,500	3,700	2,200	800	500

Note: State sentenced prisoner counts are based on estimates by gender, race, Hispanic origin, and age from the 2004 Survey of Inmates in State Correctional Facilities and updated from jurisdiction counts by gender at yearend 2006. Federal sentenced prisoner counts are based on data from the BJS Federal Justice Statistics Program for September 30, 2006 and updated from jurisdiction counts at yearend 2006.
[a]Sentenced prisoners are limited to those sentenced to more than 1 year.
[b]Total includes American Indians, Alaskan Natives, Asians, Native Hawaiians, other Pacific Islanders, and persons identifying two or more races.
[c]Excludes Hispanics and persons identifying two or more races.

SOURCE: William J. Sabol, Heather Couture, and Paige M. Harrison, "Appendix Table 7. Estimated Number of Sentenced Prisoners under State or Federal Jurisdiction, by Gender, Race, Hispanic Origin, and Age, Yearend 2006," in *Prisoners in 2006*, U.S. Department of Justice, Office of Justice Programs, Bureau of Justice Statistics, December 2007, http://www.ojp.usdoj.gov/bjs/pub/pdf/p06.pdf (accessed November 11, 2008)

TABLE 10.9

Number of sentenced prisoners under State or Federal jurisdiction per 100,000 residents, by gender, race, Hispanic origin, and age, 2006

Age group	Male[a]				Female[a]			
	All males[b]	White[c]	Black[c]	Hispanic	All females[b]	White[c]	Black[c]	Hispanic
Total	943	487	3,042	1,261	68	48	148	81
18–19	515	236	1,454	670	23	15	44	31
20–24	1,800	877	5,153	2,277	113	85	200	142
25–29	2,302	1,103	7,384	2,573	159	122	304	179
30–34	2,270	1,159	7,657	2,480	177	142	360	165
35–39	1,997	1,071	6,685	2,326	183	135	399	194
40–44	1,755	989	5,705	2,120	158	114	352	168
45–54	1,012	566	3,436	1,515	73	49	177	103
55 or older	248	162	820	510	10	7	23	18

Note: Based on estimates of the U.S. resident population on January 1, 2007, by gender, race, Hispanic origin, and age. Detailed categories exclude persons identifying two or more races.
[a]Sentenced prisoners are limited to those serving sentences of more than 1 year.
[b]Includes American Indians, Alaska Natives, Asians, Native Hawaiians, other Pacific Islanders, and persons identifying two or more races.
[c]Excludes Hispanics and persons identifying two or more races.

SOURCE: William J. Sabol, Heather Couture, and Paige M. Harrison, "Appendix Table 8. Estimated Number of Sentenced Prisoners under State or Federal Jurisdiction per 100,000 Residents, by Gender, Race, Hispanic Origin, and Age, Yearend 2006," in *Prisoners in 2006*, U.S. Department of Justice, Office of Justice Programs, Bureau of Justice Statistics, December 2007, http://www.ojp.usdoj.gov/bjs/pub/pdf/p06.pdf (accessed November 11, 2008)

TABLE 10.10

Average daily population and the number of men, women, and juveniles in local jails on June 30, 2000, 2005, and 2006

	2000	2005	2006
Average daily population[a]	618,319	733,442	755,896
Number of inmates, June 30	621,149	747,529	766,010
Adults	613,534	740,770	759,906
Male	543,120	646,807	661,329
Female	70,414	93,963	98,577
Juveniles[b]	7,615	6,759	6,104
Held as adults[c]	6,129	5,750	4,836
Held as juveniles	1,489	1,009	1,268

[a]Average daily population is the sum of the number of inmates in jail on each day for a year divided by the total number of days in a year.
[b]Juveniles are persons under age 18 on June 30.
[c]Includes juveniles who were tried or awaiting trial as adults.

SOURCE: William J. Sabol, Todd D. Minton, and Paige M. Harrison, "Table 9. Number of Inmates in Local Jails on June 30, 2000, 2005, and 2006," in *Prison and Jail Inmates at Midyear 2006*, U.S. Department of Justice, Bureau of Justice Statistics, June 2007, http://www.ojp.usdoj.gov/bjs/pub/pdf/pjim06.pdf (accessed November 14, 2008)

Steinberg argues that at the end of the first decade of the new millennium, get-tough policies were softening "as politicians and the public come to regret the high economic costs and ineffectiveness of the punitive reforms and the harshness of the sanctions." Elizabeth Scott and Laurence Steinberg find in "Adolescent Development and the Regulation of Youth Crime" (*Future of Children*, vol. 18, no. 2, fall 2008) that by 2008 the justice system was once again recognizing that age and maturity level needed to be taken into account when calculating punishment for crimes. They suggest that most juveniles who commit crimes are "adolescence-limited" offenders who will mature out of their criminal tendencies; however, contact with a harsh, adult corrections system can push juveniles into adult criminality. Instead, the authors state,

successful programs "seek to provide young offenders with supportive social contexts and authoritative adult figures and to help them acquire the skills necessary to change problem behavior and attain psychosocial maturity."

Other surveys support the idea that get-tough attitudes appear to be changing. The survey "New NCCD Poll Shows Public Strongly Favors Youth Rehabilitation and Treatment" (February 7, 2007, http://www.nccd-crc.org/nccd/pubs/zog byPR0207.pdf), which was conducted by Zogby International for the National Council on Crime and Delinquency, finds that the American public supports rehabilitation and treatment for young people, not prosecution in adult criminal courts or incarceration in adult jails or prisons. Nine out of 10 people surveyed believed this approach might help prevent crime in the future, and seven out of 10 believed imprisoning juveniles in adult facilities would increase the likelihood that they would commit future crimes. Most people believed that youth should not be automatically transferred to adult court, but that such transfers should be handled on an individual basis.

Children and the Death Penalty

Until 2005 convicted criminals could be executed for crimes they committed as juveniles. Victor L. Streib of Ohio Northern University reports in *The Juvenile Death Penalty Today: Death Sentences and Executions for Juvenile Crimes, January 1, 1973–February 28, 2005* (October 7, 2005, http://www.law.onu.edu/faculty_staff/faculty_profiles/coursematerials/streib/juvdeath.pdf) that between 1973 and 2005, 22 offenders were executed for crimes they committed when they were younger than 18. The U.S. Supreme Court has considered many cases concerning the practice of executing offenders for crimes they committed as children. In *Eddings v. Oklahoma* (455 U.S. 104 [1982]), the Court found that a juvenile's mental and emotional development should be considered as a mitigating factor when deciding whether to apply the death penalty, noting that adolescents are less mature and responsible than adults and not as able to consider long-range consequences of their actions. In this case, the court reversed the death sentence of a 16-year-old who had been tried as an adult.

Subsequent Supreme Court rulings have further limited the application of the death penalty in cases involving juveniles. In *Thompson v. Oklahoma* (487 U.S. 815 [1988]), the court found that applying the death sentence to an offender who had been 15 years old at the time of the murder was cruel and unusual punishment, concluding that the death penalty could not be applied to offenders who were younger than 16. However, the following year the court found in *Stanford v. Kentucky* (492 U.S. 361) that applying the death penalty to offenders who were age 16 or 17 at the time of the crime was not cruel and unusual punishment.

The court was asked to reconsider this decision in 2005. In *Roper v. Simmons* (543 U.S. 551), the court set aside the death sentence of Christopher Simmons by a vote of five to four, concluding that the "Eighth and Fourteenth Amendments forbid imposition of the death penalty on offenders who were under the age of 18 when their crimes were committed." Snyder and Sickmund note that few states applied death penalty provisions to juveniles at the time of the *Roper* decision, even though 20 states allowed juveniles to be sentenced to death under the law.

IMPORTANT NAMES
AND ADDRESSES

Child Trends
4301 Connecticut Ave. NW, Ste. 350
Washington, DC 20008
(202) 572-6000
FAX: (202) 362-8420
URL: http://www.childtrends.org/

Children's Defense Fund
25 E St. NW
Washington, DC 20001
(202) 628-8787
1-800-233-1200
E-mail: cdfinfo@childrensdefense.org
URL: http://www.childrensdefense.org/

**Federal Interagency Forum on Child
and Family Statistics**
URL: http://www.childstats.gov/

Feeding America
35 E. Wacker Dr., Ste. 2000
Chicago, IL 60601
1-800-771-2303
FAX: (312) 263-5626
URL: http://www.secondharvest.org/

Guttmacher Institute
1301 Connecticut Ave. NW, Ste. 700
Washington, DC 20036
(202) 296-4012
1-877-823-0262
FAX: (202) 223-5756
URL: http://www.guttmacher.org/

National Center for Children in Poverty
215 W. 125th St., Third Floor
New York, NY 10027
(646) 284-9600
FAX: (646) 284-9623
E-mail: info@nccp.org
URL: http://www.nccp.org/

National Center for Education Statistics
1990 K St. NW
Washington, DC 20006
(202) 502-7300
URL: http://www.nces.ed.gov/

**National Center for Missing
and Exploited Children**
Charles B. Wang International Children's
Building
699 Prince St.
Alexandria, VA 22314-3175
1-800-843-5678
FAX: (703) 274-2200
URL: http://www.missingkids.com/

National Center for Victims of Crime
2000 M St. NW, Ste. 480
Washington, DC 20036
(202) 467-8700
FAX: (202) 467-8701
URL: http://www.ncvc.org/

National Crime Prevention Council
2345 Crystal Drive, Ste. 500
Arlington, VA 22202
(202) 466-6272
FAX: (202) 296-1356
URL: http://www.ncpc.org/

**National Institute on Drug Abuse
National Institutes of Health**
6001 Executive Blvd., Rm. 5213
Bethesda, MD 20892-9561
(301) 443-1124
E-mail: information@nida.nih.gov
URL: http://www.nida.nih.gov/

**National Youth Gang Center
Institute for Intergovernmental Research**
PO Box 12729
Tallahassee, FL 32317-2729

(850) 385-0600
FAX: (850) 422-3529
E-mail: nygc@iir.com
URL: http://www.iir.com/nygc/

**National Youth Violence Prevention
Resource Center**
PO Box 10809
Rockville, MD 20849-0809
1-866-723-3968
FAX: (301) 562-1001
E-mail: NYVP@safeyouth.org
URL: http://www.safeyouth.org/

**Office of Juvenile Justice and
Delinquency Prevention**
810 Seventh St. NW
Washington, DC 20531
(202) 307-5911
URL: http://www.ojjdp.ncjrs.org/

**Office of National Drug Control Policy
Drug Policy Information Clearinghouse**
PO Box 6000
Rockville, MD 20849-6000
1-800-666-3332
FAX: (301) 519-5212
URL: http://
www.whitehousedrugpolicy.gov/

Office of the U.S. Surgeon General
5600 Fishers Lane., Rm. 18-66
Rockville, MD 20857
(301) 443-4000
FAX: (301) 443-3574
URL: http://www.surgeongeneral.gov/

Urban Institute
2100 M St. NW
Washington, DC 20037
(202) 833-7200
URL: http://www.urban.org/

RESOURCES

Many government agencies in Washington, D.C., publish timely information on their programs and the U.S. population. The U.S. Census Bureau publishes statistics on American life in its *Current Population Reports*, including *Income, Poverty, and Health Insurance Coverage in the United States: 2007* (Carmen DeNavas-Walt, Bernadette D. Proctor, and Jessica C. Smith, August 2008), *America's Families and Living Arrangements: 2007* (July 2008), *Educational Attainment in the United States: 2007* (December 2007), *Custodial Mothers and Fathers and Their Child Support: 2005* (Timothy S. Grall, August 2007), *Fertility of American Women: June 2004* (Jane Lawler Dye, December 2005), *Who's Minding the Kids? Child Care Arrangements: Winter 2002* (Julia Overturf Johnson, October 2005), *Children's Living Arrangements and Characteristics: March 2002* (Jason Fields, June 2003), *Married-Couple and Unmarried-Partner Households: 2000* (Tavia Simmons and Martin O'Connell, February 2003), *Demographic Trends in the 20th Century* (Frank Hobbs and Nicole Stoops, November 2002), *Age: 2000* (Julie Meyer, October 2001), and *Maternity Leave and Employment Patterns, 1961–1995* (Kirsten Smith, Barbara Downs, and Martin O'Connell, November 2001).

The Federal Interagency Forum on Child and Family Statistics, in *America's Children in Brief: Key National Indicators of Well-Being, 2008* (2008), provided invaluable data on many aspects of children's health and well-being. The U.S. Department of Health and Human Services provided a wide assortment of statistical data concerning health issues. Its Centers for Disease Control and Prevention (CDC) issues the *Morbidity and Mortality Weekly Report*, which focuses on various aspects of death and disease. The CDC's "Youth Risk Behavior Surveillance—United States, 2007" (Danice K. Eaton et al., June 2008) was the source of survey information on risk behaviors among U.S. high school students. The CDC is also a leading source of AIDS statistics with its quarterly *HIV/AIDS Surveillance Report*.

Child Health USA 2007 (2008), published by the Maternal and Child Health Bureau, reports the health status and needs of American children. *Child Maltreatment 2006* (2008) counts cases of child abuse reported to state child protective agencies. The Administration for Children and Families provided data on child support collections, and *The AFCARS Report* (September 2006) by the Adoption and Foster Care Analysis and Reporting System provided data on the number of children in the foster care system.

The Social Security Administration, Office of Policy, offered helpful statistics on children receiving Supplemental Security Income. The Bureau of Labor Statistics, which is part of the U.S. Department of Labor, provided data on employment and unemployment.

The *National Vital Statistics Reports*, published by the National Center for Health Statistics (NCHS), provided statistics on births and infant mortality. The NCHS also published *Health, United States, 2007* (2007), which gives invaluable data on many health conditions, birthrates, fertility rates, and life expectancy.

The U.S. Department of Agriculture provided estimates of expenditures on children from birth through age seventeen. Its Center for Nutrition Policy and Promotion calculates how much it costs to raise a child in *Expenditures on Children by Families, 2007* (Mark Lino, March 2008).

The National Center for Education Statistics, which is part of the U.S. Department of Education, published the *Digest of Education Statistics, 2007* (Thomas D. Snyder, Sally A. Dillow, and Charlene M. Hoffman, March 2008) and the *Condition of Education 2008* (June 2008), which provided important statistics on education in the United States.

The Bureau of Justice Statistics provided important information on juvenile crime and victimization in *Key Crime and Justice Facts at a Glance* (January 2009), *Criminal Victimization, 2007* (Michael R. Rand, December 2008), and *Homicide Trends in the United States* (James Alan Fox and Marianne W. Zawitz, July 2007). The Federal Bureau of

Investigation's *Crime in the United States, 2007* (September 2008) covers crime and victimization.

The Office of Juvenile Justice and Delinquency Prevention (OJJDP) of the U.S. Department of Justice was a valuable resource of information about youth violence, crime, and gangs in the United States. Various sources of the OJJDP provided important data that helped in the compilation of this book. These included *Highlights of the 2006 National Youth Gang Survey* (Arlen Egley Jr. and Christina E. O'Donnell, July 2008), *National Youth Gang Survey Analysis* (2006), *Juvenile Offenders and Victims: 2006 National Report* (Howard N. Snyder and Melissa Sickmund, March 2006), *National Youth Gang Survey, 1999–2001* (Arlen Egley Jr., James C. Howell, and Aline K. Major, July 2006), *2005 National Gang Threat Assessment* (2005), "Youth Gangs in Indian Country" (Aline K. Major et al., March 2004), *Highlights of the 2001 National Youth Gang Survey* (Arlen Egley Jr. and Aline K. Major, April 2003), "National Youth Gang Survey Trends from 1996 to 2000" (Arlen Egley Jr., February 2002), and *The Growth of Youth Gang Problems in the United States: 1970–1998* (Walter B. Miller, April 2001). The annual reports of the National Youth Gang Survey, which is prepared by the OJJDP, were also helpful.

The National Center for Children in Poverty provided information on children in low-income households. Child Trends provided research on adolescent sexual activity. The Guttmacher Institute provided information on abortion rates among teenagers in the journal *Perspectives on Sexual and Reproductive Health.*

INDEX

Page references in italics refer to photographs. References with the letter t *following them indicate the presence of a table. The letter* f *indicates a figure. If more than one table or figure appears on a particular page, the exact item number for the table or figure being referenced is provided.*

Mott, Frank L., 72
MS-13 (Mara Salvatrucha), 114
Mulder, Tammany J., 1–3, 5
Murder. *See* Homicide
Myers, Robert A., 133–134
MySpace, 130

N

NACCRRA (National Association of Child Care Resource and Referral Agencies), 39
Names/addresses, 155
Nansel, Tonja R., 128
Narcotics, 97
NASRO (National Association of School Resource Officers), 136, 142
National Adolescent Health Information Center, 61
National Alliance of Gang Investigators Associations, 110
National Association for Regulatory Administration, 38
National Association of Child Care Resource and Referral Agencies (NACCRRA), 39
National Association of School Resource Officers (NASRO), 136, 142
National Center for Children in Poverty, 155
National Center for Education Statistics (NCES)
    contact information, 155
    on homeschooling, 88
    on preprimary school, 81
    on test results, 78
National Center for Health Statistics (NCHS)
    on health insurance, 43
    on infant mortality, 58–59
    on physician visits, 42–43
National Center for Juvenile Justice (NCJJ)
    on juvenile crime trends, 94
    on juvenile justice, 142–143
    on juveniles in residential placement, 149, 150
National Center for Missing and Exploited Children, 155
National Center for Social Statistics, 10–11
National Center for Victims of Crime, 155
National Council on Crime and Delinquency (NCCD), 113, 153
National Crime Prevention Council, 155
National Crime Victimization Survey (NCVS)
    description of, 93
    on nonfatal crimes at school, 124–125
National Education Association (NEA), 79
National Education Goals Panel, 77
National Gang Threat Assessment 2009 (FBI), 113
National Head Start Association, 82

National Highway Traffic Safety Administration, 61
National Household Education Survey, 88
National Incidence Studies of Missing, Abducted, Runaway, and Thrownaway Children (NISMART), 101
National Institute of Child Health and Human Development (NICHD), 38
National Institute on Drug Abuse, 155
National Institutes of Health
    on abstinence pledge, 74
    on SIDS, 61
National School Lunch Program
    expenditures, participation in, 23
    total participation, 27t
National School Safety and Security Services, 136
National Survey of Family Growth, 67
National Victim Assistance Academy Textbook (Office for Victims of Crime), 115, 119
National Youth Gang Center (NYGC)
    on comprehensive gang model, 140–141
    contact information, 155
    on curfew laws, 140
    on gang member characteristics, 113
    NYGS of, 109–110
    on reasons for joining a gang, 115
    Youth Gangs in Indian Country, 114–115
National Youth Gang Survey (NYGS)
    on gang crime, 118
    on gang problem, 109–110
    law enforcement agencies reporting gang problems, 110t
National Youth Gang Survey, 1999–2001 (Egley, Howell, & Major), 113
National Youth Gang Survey and Analysis (National Youth Gang Center), 113
"National Youth Gang Survey Trends from 1996 to 2000" (Egley, Howell, & Major), 110
National Youth Violence Prevention Campaign, 142
National Youth Violence Prevention Resource Center, 155
Native Americans
    arrests by race, 148
    childbearing by teens, 71
    children living in foster care, 12
    children with HIV/AIDS, 53
    college entrance exams scores, 90
    fertility rate for, 2
    gangs, 114–115
    Head Start children, 82
    infant mortality rate of, 59
    juveniles in residential placement, 150
    weapons at school and, 131
NCCD (National Council on Crime and Delinquency), 113, 153

NCES. *See* National Center for Education Statistics
NCHS. *See* National Center for Health Statistics
NCJJ. *See* National Center for Juvenile Justice
NCLB. *See* No Child Left Behind Act
NCVS. *See* National Crime Victimization Survey
NEA (National Education Association), 79
Neural tube defects, 41
Nevada, cost of child care in, 39
A New Era of Responsibility: Renewing America's Promise (White House report), 75, 91
New Hampshire
    oldest age for juveniles in, 142
    teen birthrates in, 71
    youth in residential facilities in, 150
New Jersey
    homeschool requirements in, 88
    Latin Kings in, 114
New Jersey Office of the Attorney General, 111, 112
New Mexico, 71
"New NCCD Poll Shows Public Strongly Favors Youth Rehabilitation and Treatment" (NCCD), 153
New York
    cost of child care in, 39
    gang recruitment in, 112
    homeschool requirements of, 88
    juvenile justice, age of juveniles, 142
    Latin Kings in, 114
    youth in residential facilities in, 150
"Next Round Begins for No Child Left Behind" (Paulson), 77–78
NICHD (National Institute of Child Health and Human Development), 38
The NICHD Study of Early Child Care and Youth Development: Findings for Children up to Age 4 1/2 Years (NICHD), 38
NISMART (National Incidence Studies of Missing, Abducted, Runaway, and Thrownaway Children), 101
No Child Left Behind Act (NCLB)
    accountability, 77–78
    charter schools, 79–80
    flexibility, 78
    future of, 80
    parental options, 79
    persistently dangerous schools, 134–136
    principles of, 77
    proficiency testing, 78
    proven educational methods, 79
    school crime/violence and, 134–136
    Twenty-First-Century Community Learning Centers, 33
    voucher controversy, 79